G000117477

Alternative M
Making Choices

Gert Keunen

Contents

Alternative Mainstream
Making Choices in Pop Music

Gert Keunen

Antennae
Valiz, Amsterdam

Introduction

Music is a vital part of my existence. I listen to music, play music, and compose music. I think about music, write about music, and teach about music. After having read an article by Rudi Laermans about a book written by rock sociologist Simon Frith, I decided to study sociology. After college, I entered the professional world of music, where I took up various roles: freelance music journalist, music programmer at an arts center, and label manager with a record company. I became a lecturer at schools of higher education offering programs of study in pop music, taught courses on the history of music and the music industry, and published books about the history of pop. I was even a member of a governmental committee that gives advice on the public funding of pop artists. All these years I remained a musician, a composer, and the driving force behind a band of my own.

Although the creation of music remained the highest attainable good, as a sociologist I kept a keen interest in the world of music, curious about how it was built and was structured, how it developed and changed. Admittedly, the field of view seemed limited. Flanders and the Netherlands are very small regions. Yet I quickly learned that the world of pop music is also very small. It is a world of like knows like, where everybody has each other's number. To work as a professional in this world means to 'stumble' into it, to bump into the same people repeatedly, and to enter a small and intimate circle of insiders, whatever their radius of action. Almost as a rule, the people in this world talk about the same bands, those that make the crossover to the outside world — the 'hypes.' My sole wish as a music lover has always been to discover as many forms of music as possible. I found it natural to seek *difference*. These years inside the music circuit, however, forced me to think about *sameness*, and to start asking questions about the origins of the hypes. How is it possible that everybody talks about the same bands? What makes people talk about *some*, yet the *same* bands, while remaining silent about *other* bands? Moreover, why is it that only a small percentage of the legion of bands that stands at the gates gets ample airplay, concerts, press and, consequently, is able to reach a sufficiently large public?

In the world of professional musicians performing live on stage, the distinction between front stage and back stage is real, practical and essential. It seems oddly appropriate that this distinction is also central to one of the most venerable paradigms in sociology, famously presented by Erving Goffman: the dramaturgical perspective. One way or another, all musical artists exist on stage. Front stage is the space where artists communicate with an audience, where there is no mediation or selection, and where the connection happens in real time. Back stage is the place where the mediation never ends and the selection process runs nonstop. It is a space where music industry professionals often build and destroy artists, or their reputations. The questions that haunted me were daunting. Who are the 'players' involved in the selection process? Which criteria do they put into play for selecting this or that music? What exactly is the impact of their selections?

Not all players have the same influence on artists' chances of breaking through, and the world in which these dynamic players exert their influence is anything but static. In addition, there is the 'crisis.' It has kept the industry, or at least its discourse, in a tight grip. The story, as told by the industry and organizations that represent its interests, is familiar. Many of the traditional consumers of music share and exchange music through digital carriers that escape the control of the industry. These sharing communities, leeching and seeding immense collections of music, do so illegally. They harm the artists, as well as those that surround them. They have sent the sales of CDs into a dramatic free fall. Sponsors backed out, and traditional recipes failed to provide.

Today, it is clear that the problem itself offers the solution. Former leading players attempt to reposition themselves, while new and legal digital channels try to conquer a niche of their own. The complex of actions and events, causes and effects, problems and questions that the music industry has come to represent, became the subject of my doctoral research project. The results of this study are presented in this book.

About the Book

This book examines the mechanisms and logics of decisions, choices and selections made by people working on the pop music circuit. When confronted with new music, these people decide to select or *choose to choose* the music they wish to offer a stage, airplay or press coverage. Or which music they choose to put aside and deny the light of day. In other words, what they allow to sign to their label, are willing to put on the market, or simply reject.

To study this selection practice, and the general frames of thought and valuation at its basis, sufficient depth was needed. The inquiry had to offer adequate justification for the method it would employ and needed to draw a deliberate and sharp defining line around its object. As a result, this book does not examine the pop music circuit in its totality.[1] Pop charts, hit parades and entertainment music (the so-called 'mainstream') are outside its scope, as are subcultures and niches (the so-called 'underground'). The book focuses exclusively on the music segment that lies between the 'mainstream' and the 'underground.' This segment is introduced as 'the alternative mainstream,' and it refers to a *cultural construct*. Rather than a musical style, alternative mainstream is primarily music that the leading national music actors *select,* or, at a certain moment, *choose* to pick up and work on. As far as a background check could tell, this particular segment of the pop music circuit has never been identified or 'worded' in this way. The segment is populated by those active players in the professional music world who direct themselves to the so-called 'music lovers.' The alternative mainstream is a formidable buffer zone, which serves as a repository of music. At the same time, it commands a dominant presence in the national market of concerts, media and CD releases. It is the segment where economic and cultural logics meet in a most prominent manner.

This study of pop music – or 'popular music' – does not discuss anything on the receiving side, the consumer. It is not concerned with preferences, or the ways in which audiences make use of them. It is solely occupied with the areas of production and distribution, and, in particular, with those various actors in the music industry that surround the artists.

Finally, the inquiry is also geographically delineated. Its radius is mainly limited to the Flemish music circuit. There are positive indications that the discussed mechanisms can be transposed to an international context or easily converted to other regions. Nonetheless, the examples and the actors that make up the raw material of the study are all situated in Flanders. Even when the inquiry covers a broader social and economic context, Flanders is the case study. This specific focus proved to be the best way to bring out the networks of interaction, and it provided the best way for studying them. Consequently, the inquiry is situated in the middle of micro and macro levels, focusing on the music that circulates within. It is not about international careers, but concerns itself with the question of how music is able to spawn isolated national attention, regardless of its place of origin, and how it is able to reproduce this attention across all borders, from nation to nation.

Selections or selection mechanisms in the pop music circuit can be studied in several ways. The basis here lies in the different criteria of selection employed by the actors who operate in the music circuit's alternative mainstream. These criteria are used to legitimize their actions, implicitly in everyday practice, explicitly when they justify actions in moments of crisis, in the face of criticisms raised by peers, or when they are expected to withstand tests of loyalty and trust. Central to the study are not the facts brought up by the respondents, but their judgments and opinions, and the way they construe their arguments. The study concentrates on the relation between symbolic (artistic, cultural and social) and economic logics. The central question thus becomes the following: are the actors guided by individual preferences or do they allow the market to dictate their thoughts, and thus, their actions? The focus is on how the consecutive selections unfold and why they proceed the way they do. The book takes a close look at the criteria that underpin these selections and seeks a way of classifying different criteria in terms of different logics. The inquiry also discusses the context in which choices are made, the social factors that influence the decisions and the networks of interaction in which the logics operate. The gaze of the book then turns on the players that are active in the pop music circuit. The focus shifts to how the gatekeepers guard access to the alternative mainstream and how the actors interrelate: is there a pattern of cooperation and collaboration, or do the players work against one another, and is a model of conflict more suitable? Processes of selection (may) have an effect on artistic careers, on how these are built or blocked, and hence on the dynamics of the music field. The book will also address this aspect, but marginally. Finally, it will zoom in on the impact digital alternatives may have on the selection mechanisms.

In the end, the aim of this study is simply to gain a deeper insight in the pop music circuit. It attempts to uncover some of the conventions that are active in the music world and to flesh out the rules of the game. Through the analysis of the alternative mainstream, a synthetic and descriptive model will emerge that is flexible enough to interpret and explain the dynamics and diversity of practices in the world of music.

Research Method

Every serious academic study requires a discussion of the existing body of research or theory on the subject, a complex whole of concepts and conceptions, of problems and solutions, of issues and views that form the status quo of thought and inquiry. This author's doctoral dissertation extensively discussed and interacted with such a theoretical body. The book by contrast deliberately leaves out the literature study, the systematic review of sociological theories. At the same time, it does not shy away from referring to highly illuminating theoretical views.[2] It is, and will always be, a study in the sociology of culture, never discussing the music itself, but the ways in which actors in the music field deal with it. It observes a specific social network, the alternative mainstream, and zooms in on one particular alternative mainstream, the Flemish variant. The analysis concentrates on the selections made in this network, explores what sort of beliefs, values and norms are at the heart of these selections, and in what ways they are institutionalized. It makes observations of how people enter in interaction with one another, and how they are continuously engaged in a process of symbolic attribution. They interpret the world, constantly ascribe 'meaning' to the world (and consequently also to music). In the same way, they interpret their own actions and those of others.[3]

The study aims to provide insight into the motives of people who are active in the music circuit. Indeed, following Actor Network Theory (ANT), the most logical step to take was to start from the actor (the singular), make the actor the basis of the inquiry, and detect and retrace the network — that is, 'the social' - through this actor. The intention is not to determine criteria of selection with the goal of empirically testing or verifying a theoretical framework or a hypothetical model. Open categories with rather vague descriptions were key to allowing the actors to determine the course. This would in turn allow determining the logics of selection in a rather inductive way.[4] ANTs favored and well-known mottos really do say it all: 'to follow the actors,' 'to allow the actors to do the job for us' (Latour 2005: 12 and 36).

This is a study in qualitative research. The central data were supplied by a series of open in-depth-interviews conducted with selected players in the alternative mainstream segment of Flanders' music industry. In total, the set of data includes 28 interviews with a mean running time of almost two hours. The core of the study is limited to 24 interviews, which took place between 2009 and 2011. The other four followed later (in 2012), and served as a tool for control and feedback. The majority of interviewed actors were selected in the course of the inquiry. Essential to the project was to find enough, and enough relevant, actors for every type of player in the pop music circuit: actors from the concert circuit (music club programmers, festival organizers, booking agencies), from the record circuit (majors as well as independents), artist managers and people from the media (radio producers, journalists, from newspapers and magazines). Because of the mixed professional practices and career movements, some are able to discuss, and comment on, more than one function or role.[5] The appendix contains a complete list of the interviewed respondents, as well as a brief résumé of each. It should be mentioned that elements from informal conversations with others have also found a way into the argument.

The larger part of this book (from Chapter 3 onwards) relies on the judgments and valuations of the interviewed actors, the respondents. The research process involved constant structuring and ordering, synthetizing and analyzing of data retrieved from these interviews. The process consisted in carefully stripping these data from their hidden properties, and gradually revealing the story. During the analysis, all data were made anonymous. There were two reasons for doing so. The first is that this study is concerned with the thought processes of the respondents and those logics of interpretation adopted by them, not with the facts they bring up. Anonymous quotes render the story more general and are more productive when the processes of symbolic attribution need highlighting. Secondly, the primary goal was to map out implicit conventions, often hidden in affirmations of explicit conventions. Anonymity thus became a working principle for the whole analysis. Information acquired off the record was obviously treated as anonymous. There are some passages where the identity of the respondents can be easily discovered. These cases almost certainly never involve information of a sensitive nature. Sometimes it was necessary to mention explicitly the

particular organization to which a respondent belonged, thereby implicitly opening the door to identification. Wherever the text inappropriately reveals the identity of the cited respondent, readers should always view this as an unavoidable or undesired, and never intentional, side effect.[6]

Besides the interviews and the consulted literature, this book also shows traces of participatory observation. This author's years of professional experience, networking, interaction and dialogue with friends confer an important benefit on both the theoretical study and the field research. The experience proved very helpful in interpreting and analyzing the interview material. It allowed for better assessments of the references made by the respondents, as well as the context of their statements. In addition, active participation in the field provided a stronger relationship of trust with the respondents. This, in turn, made them more inclined to tell just that little bit extra (off the record), more than they would have done if they had been dealing with somebody they did not know personally.

The book consists of two parts. Chapter 1 and Chapter 2 provide the (theoretical) background for the study. Chapter 1 defines 'alternative mainstream' by way of a popular, die-hard opposition that marks the pop music discourse: 'underground' and 'mainstream.' Chapter 2 scrolls through the academic literature on the subject. It examines the aesthetics and ideology that exist in the segment, and explains why the alternative mainstream is also a cultural construction. In Chapters 3 to 7, the field research occupies center stage. Chapter 3 serves as a bridge, looking at the social-economic context ('the digital revolution') which ranks as a marginal condition for the decisions made on the medium level. Chapters 4, 5, 6 and 7 study the selection mechanisms from the different logics that can be distinguished in the field of practice, and identify individual, organizational, positional and second-order selections. Here the *respondents* assume their leading role. The chapters analyze observations of the observations made by the interviewed actors, the lead actors in the story. It is an empirically grounded story about the functioning of the music industry, a zoom-in on its façade and a peek behind it, a Janus-faced close-up of front stage and back stage.[7]

Notes

1 In the Anglo-Saxon world, people use the terms 'popular music,' 'pop music' and 'rock & roll' in a way that differs from the use in Belgium and the Netherlands. Adopting theBelgian/Dutch perspective, the equivalents of 'popular music,' 'pop music' and 'rock' should be 'pop music,' 'pop' and 'rock.' In this study, 'pop music' is used as a collective name for allpossible forms of music that arose from the hybridization of entertainment music (and music entertainment), of folk, jazz and blues (ranging from rockabilly to punk, from gospel to house, from delta blues to death metal, from ska to dubstep, etc.). 'Rock & roll' is a specific type of music from the 1950s that was popularized by Elvis Presley (see Keunen 2002).

2 This study does not start from one specific author, school or theoretical approach, but employs various authors and approaches as one toolbox, applying them to a *world* (Becker, Bourdieu, Actor-Network Theory, Heinich, Boltanski & Thévenot, various *popular music studies*...). Bourdieu is the most frequent point of reference, but his theory is significantly 'corrected' in a pragmatist manner.

3 In sociology, there are roughly two long-standing approaches to the concept of culture.The first is the 'mentalist' approach (the tradition of Durkheim, which defines culture as an ensemble of values, norms and beliefs). The second is the 'interpretive' or 'interpretationist' approach (the tradition of Max Weber, which seeks to understand culture through relations of meaning) (see Laermans 2010: 171). I usually subscribe to the latter. Similar to Nathalie Heinich's sociology of art (2003) this inquiry seeks to understand the considerations and motives that form the starting point of actors when they confer value on works of art in the world of art and thus evaluate them.

4 A related theory is the so-called *grounded theory*. The method proposed by Glaser and Strauss proposes to rebuild a theory from the ground up, starting from a general problem, the existing literature, empirical data and/or comparative field research (Maso & Smaling 2004: 28-30).

5 Two organizers are also radio producers. One person who worked for a record firm is also an artist manager, and used to be a journalist, as well as a record shop owner. One head of a record label is a manager and a person in charge of promotion with another firm. One artist manager is also a festival organizer and the owner of a music café. One music club programmer and one booker are also festival organizers, etc. On top of that, some respondents are active in the mainstream segment (for instance, the heads of labels that belong to majors), while others are closer to the underground (as is the case with one indie label, one organizer and one magazine journalist). These highly crosscutting professional profiles made it possible to compare the alternative mainstream with the other segments.

6 Researchers who carry out studies in their own biotope evidently run the risk of *going native*, of experiencing and *living* the world in the exact same ways as the objects of study that inhabit it (Maso & Smaling 2004: 104). This author is fully aware of the risk, and of the possible limitations incurred by certain deliberate choices. Nevertheless, the (high)degree of involvement in the circuit actually permitted a nuanced approach. It is because of the personal music career that the connection with the research object in general has become less stifling. It enabled the study to keep a critical distance, which should provebeneficial to the study.

7 Gender fairness or neutrality in academic writing is an obvious concern, but poses difficulties. The systematic use of 'he or she' and 'his or her,' or strange variants like 's/he,' is a tiresome, distracting solution. Substituting 'they' as a singular person is still considered as ungrammatical and therefore not acceptable in formal academic English, although Merriam-Webster's Collegiate Dictionary writes: 'The use of they, their, them, and themselves as pronouns of indefinite gender and indefinite number is well established in speech and writing, even in literary

and formal contexts.'. I have taken the trouble of omitting pronouns and using indefinite articles, substituting neutral pronouns and applying passive forms, and generally chose phrasings with plural use of 'they' and 'their,' often specifying the implicit subjects, such as 'actors' or 'those who.' Other than that, it is perhaps important to note that the majority of the respondents (the interviewed music industryprofessionals)were male. Sometimes a general observation derived from a statement of a male interviewee simply allowed for 'masculine' phrasing. Any unintentionally neglectful uses of 'he' or 'his' that have escaped the bias-free eye, are to be blamed on the author of this book [translator's note].

1. Mainstream versus Underground

Once upon a time, a long time ago, artists had direct, unmediated contact with their public. The troubadour shared his daily chanted reports directly with the people in the marketplace. By way of overstatement, one could say that the music industry established itself as soon as people had the idea of lodging themselves between artists and their public. The nineteenth century saw the rise of publishers, who commissioned particular individuals to write songs for them, which they then sold to the public via performing artists. Since then, an entire industry has grown around music, including managers and management agencies, record companies and labels, bookers and booking agencies, concert organizers or promoters, (copy)rights organizations, and so on. More and more artists wish to put (their) art on the right road and if possible better themselves financially along the way. To the artists of today these intermediary players are not simply a necessary condition for making contact with the public of their dreams. In fact, the system built around music also generates the necessary artistic and financial career opportunities.

Nevertheless, the idea of direct communication is central to the world of musical experience. It is during a live concert that artists are able to 'feel' their audience, to look a (limited) portion of the audience straight in the eye, especially if the concert is followed by a public appearance and the artists sell merchandise to the interested fans. The army of loyal music lovers never bothers with the regiment of go-betweens that separates them from their leader. As soon as fans have entered the concert venue, their eyes are solely on the performing artist. When they put on a CD, they 'feel' the artist's close presence. Online, they may able to make personal contact with them.

This distinction between front stage and back stage is typical of life in the professional universe of music. Back stage, music is a branch of industry like any other, yet front stage it is as if every intervention by music industry players disappears into thin air. To some, music itself is (merely) a product that is put on the market. To others, music is the carrier of cultural meaning. Both, however, relate to the same music, and the former attitude need not exclude the latter: the fact that the music lover can be front stage is explained by the fact that there is a backstage. The music industry is an imbroglio of interaction networks, which bestows a very particular value on the music. It provides the music with a reason for existence. It does this for all actors involved, ranging from the creator via all sorts of in-between positions to the public. This first chapter aims to render these networks intelligible. It will examine on a macro-level how the pop music circuit is constructed. It seeks to identify its structural components. The investigation will serve as a basis for the introduction of a new typology, which will divide the pop music circuit into three segments.

Analyzing the Pop Music Circuit

‖ Production Circuits and Music Industry Actors

The first question the analysis requires is evident: what exactly is the pop music circuit? A *circuit* may be described as a durable network of actors (people, organizations) that are interconnected and are active within one identical context where a common product is circulating. In this sense, a circuit is the same as what Becker called an *art world* (1982) or what Bourdieu has famously called a *field* (1989). Thus the pop music circuit is one, separate circuit among many other circuits, such as jazz, classical music or world music. In turn, the pop music circuit is composed of several genre circuits. Built around a specific genre, each with its own players, the genre circuits operate in a relatively autonomous way. Within the circuit, various directions and scenes of styles can be distinguished. The view of pop music in this study takes the word in its broadest sense (see Keunen 2002): all styles and genres that, for about a century, have grown out of blues, jazz, folk and entertainment music: from rock & roll to soul, from crooners to rappers, from death metal to dubstep. Anyone who observes the pop music circuit and its various genre circuits through the looking glass of economics will focus on the industrial branch that has risen around the production and exploitation of music. Using a simple model of communication – a transmitter sends a message to a receiver via a medium, one could say that the music industry (as a medium) mediates between the artist (the transmitter) and the public (the receiver) in order to allow the artist to bring out his music (the message). In the music industry, the cultural transfer mainly occurs in two ways: by way of a sound carrier or by way of concerts. Around each of these, a branch of industry has developed which obeys a purely economic market principle. In academic studies (such as *popular music studies*, the field of academic researchers who write about pop music), the music industry is often wrongly identified with the record business or industry. Following De Meyer and Trappeniers (2007: 7-12), this study will view the industry as an independent economic circuit. In this circuit, music is exploited in three separate, yet mutually dependent sub-circuits: the circuit of live performances (the concert circuit), the circuit of phonographic production (the sound carrier circuit), and the circuit of music publishing (the rights circuit). Within each of these, three different flows can be distinguished: a musical message flow, a money flow and an information flow.

In the sound carrier circuit, music is put on the market and distributed via sounds carriers. These are usually a physical CD or a digital download (see Keunen 2009). In most cases, record companies are responsible for the manufacturing and production. These can be big, international firms, often quoted on the stock exchange, and invariably, they are part of an even bigger (entertainment or communication) concern. The big players are called 'majors.' The companies can also be smaller, independent firms that are exclusively concerned with music: the 'independents' or 'indies.' Artists can close an artist's or license deal with such a firm, but they can also release a recording on their own record (which, by the way, is more and more the case). The sound carriers are then distributed by distribution companies (as far as physical carriers are concerned) and by *music service providers* or *aggregators* (when it involves downloads). Through the *retail* (the retail business, the wholesalers, store chains, web shops, etc.), they end up with the public.

In the concert circuit, artists perform before a live audience. A bookie or booking agency presents the artist to the concert promoters or organizers (of music clubs, festivals or other halls and platforms) and receives a fixed booking fee from the promoters, or independently takes charge of organizing concerts and festivals (for which in each case the appropriate location is rented). Such bookies or booking agencies not only sell the (domestic) artists with whom they have an agreement, but also handle the (foreign) artists that are offered to them through an international agent. In each country, this agent seeks out the best-suited bookie or booking agency in accordance with the profile of the international artist.

For both sound carriers and live performances, rights are put into force. Because copyrights and royalties arrange the public presentation of protected musical works, the rights circuit is marked by money flows (via publishers, rights associations and management firms for proxy rights).[1] Then, the different media present a selection of their offer to the target audience. These media comprise the written or printed press (newspapers, magazines), broadcast radio, television (both private and public), and the online media (musiczines, blogs and other web sites). The legal framework is controlled by the government (VAT, social security, standards for noise nuisance, etc.), who can intervene if necessary by correcting the market by way of subsidies. Finally, artists often make use of talent or artist managers or management firms to represent them in the communication between all these actors. Artists' managers take charge of the music's business side, the artists' career developments and the production coordination. For this, they receive a percentage (usually 15%) of all the musician's revenues. In this way, the artists can fully focus on the artistic process, even though they can choose to work without managers and remain or become *self-managed artists*.

The various actors are situated either at the input pole of the music industry or at the output pole. The manager, record firm or bookie introduces artists to the industry (input), while the media, retail and concert promoters present the artist to a public (output). A schematic – and considerably simplified – representation of these production and exploitation circuits may look like this:

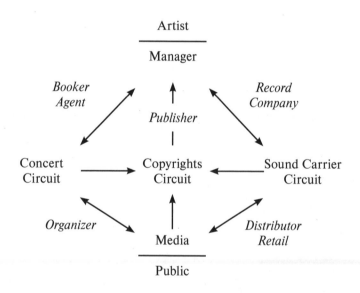

Schema 1 *A simplified representation of the music industry's exploitation circuits.*

The rise of the internet has put new pressure on the model above. As was widely publicized, the digital transformation of society, and especially the digitization of audiovisual objects, has had a significant impact on the music industry's modus operandi. Newly surfaced online players have pushed a reluctant, traditional record industry into the Digital Age. Consequently, music in cyberspace is sometimes viewed as a fourth circuit (see, for example, De Meyer & Trappeniers 2007). In these adapted models, a virtual environment is created for each of the three previously identified circuits. Things may change, yet for the industry things largely remain the same, or, rather, it is business as usual. Record companies adapt, and they adopt new strategies, such as closing deals with social networks, web shops and streaming platforms. Therefore, the idea of a new fourth circuit is a step too far. Instead, digital musical communication needs to be acknowledged as an increasingly important and essential component of the traditional circuits, which pushes the latter into a process of continuous updating.

Within the production and exploitation circuits, actors occupy different positions. Depending on their function in the whole, actors engage in forms of interaction with other actors. The fact that different players in the pop music circuit enter in forms of cooperation is also explained by the degree of fragmentation in the distribution and consumption of music. As Jason Toynbee has pointed out (2000: 17-19), it is this state of fragmentation that prevents actors from gaining singular, individual control over the whole. In cinema, the Hollywood studio system uniquely, yet briefly, represented a way of organizational monopoly and control, from private idea to public venue, from abstract input to concrete output. All large studios had their own producers, writers, directors, actors, songwriters, composers, conductors and symphonic orchestras. In addition, they owned publishing houses and theater chains, thus closing the circle from start to finish. The sequential functions of releasing and distributing music, exploiting the rights, handling press and publicity, providing radio airplay, broadcasting music videos, organizing live performances, and selling records cannot be contained in, or controlled by, one single organization.

The division or classification of Schema 1 can explain the economic logic at work in pop music as a branch of industry, as well as the consequences of the occupied position on the actors' behavior or actions (see below). At the same time, though, such a division is merely a generalization: it ignores the diversity and heterogeneous nature of the pop practice. It remains silent about the different types of pop music that are produced in this practice, and about the cultural value of music. To find out how the pop music circuit is structured, a starting point is found in a dichotomy that repeatedly pops up in the pop discourse: mainstream versus underground.

‖ Large-Scale versus Small-Scale Production

In circles of music lovers, journalists, music industry professionals, sociologists or *popular music studies* academics, there is a general inclination to think in terms of dichotomies such as underground/mainstream, alternative/commercial, pop/rock (see, amongst others, Toynbee 2000, Frith 1984, Shuker 2008). These opposing categories implicitly or explicitly derive from the traditional opposition between 'high-brow' and 'low-brow' culture (see p. 62).

In sociology, Pierre Bourdieu and his—now classic—view of the cultural field best framed the dichotomy. The French sociologist distinguishes two different modes of artistic production, each with a different attitude towards the economy and the public: large-scale production and limited or small-scale production. The first has a short production cycle, addresses the broad public and conforms to already existing wants. Small-scale production, by contrast, has a longer production cycle, addresses the limited audience of co-producers and 'connoisseurs,' and takes risks. Each mode results in a different type of art. Avant-garde art, for instance, is small-scale and heterodox, wants to shatter conventions and professes the principle of *l'art pour l'art* — art for art's sake. Contrasted with the avant-garde, Bourdieu situates 'bourgeois art,' that is, the dominant art form that purports to preserve the status quo (the orthodox mode of thought). When the ruling art institutions consecrate it, avant-garde can, however, all the same become part of large-scale art. In this way, Bourdieu says, the opposition between 'commercial' and 'non-commercial' is translated to the practice of artistic discourse, and art is distinguished from non-art. Bourdieu's analysis, in other words, does not start from aesthetic criteria.

Instead, his angle is that of the sociology of culture, which reveals an embededness that engenders the dualist opposition.

On the face of it, Bourdieu's distinction can easily be transposed to the pop music practice. It would be possible to distinguish two types of pop music, or — better — to divide the pop music circuit into two segments. Music for a large audience is mainstream, and the subcultural genre circuits (built around specific genres, functioning in a relatively autonomous manner) are active in the underground. Such a classification can be found in numerous academic publications (e.g., Hibbett 2005, Bannister 2006 and Toynbee 2000). Toynbee's analysis (2000: 25) is based on the distinction between centralized, global and industrialized production (with broad distribution and a relatively slow pace of innovation), on the one hand, and decentralized, local and innovating networks, on the other hand. In between, as Toynbee points out, there is a continuum, which, for that matter, is also what Bourdieu thinks: the large-scale or small-scale modes of production are two extremes (total submission to demand versus absolute independence from the market). In practice, these are never factually attained. Producers of culture move between the commercial and the cultural poles, and are to a greater or smaller extent guided by either the former or the latter (Bourdieu 1989: 258-259 and 1993b: 174). Indeed, pop music has an infinite number of nuances between the music that reaches only a very small audience and so-called 'commercial' music. Grossberg (1997), too, makes this observation: pop culture unfolds itself as a complex gamut of possibilities where neither the mainstream nor the marginal are homogeneous.

That being said, any literal conversion of a theoretical construction in the vein of Bourdieu's system is bound to fall short. Bourdieu neglected to look at the changes caused by pop culture in the cultural field, and consequently he has had very little to say about pop culture (see also Hesmondhalgh 2006). Furthermore, in Bourdieu's view only bourgeois art and (consecrated) avantgarde make up legitimate culture and the professional cultural field. Pop culture (and therefore pop music) is dismissed as illegitimate low- or middlebrow culture. The traditional division between highbrow (higher) culture and lowbrow (lower) culture is indeed also inherent to Bourdieu's view. In a literal sense, his schema only applies to cultural forms, hence his intensive studies of traditional art forms such as literature or visual arts, and in particular the small-scale production of these arts. In the pop music circuit, large-scale production cannot be exclusively linked to the preservation of the status quo and neither can small-scale production be merely associated to shattering conventions. For Bourdieu's schema and terminology to be useful in the case of pop music, they need some modifications.

For this reason, this study proposes a different typology. The starting point remains the initial dichotomy between mainstream and underground. Limiting the classification of music circuits to an underground and a mainstream segment, however, is too great a simplification of the music practice. In order to gain better insight in the dynamics that are active between the different segments of the pop music circuit, a third segment needs to be added. It strikes a bridge between the two segments and is central to the conducted research: alternative mainstream.

The Three Segments of the Pop Music Circuit

It may be true that there is no consensus about what is commercial, alternative or mainstream. Nevertheless, it is exactly because of the frequent use of these terms that they provide a solid basis for distinguishing different segments within pop music. To define the concept of 'alternative mainstream,' a clear delineation of the concepts of 'mainstream' and 'underground' is needed. In the practice of pop, as well as in *popular music studies*, these terms are mostly left undefined. They are used in a vague sense, and apply to the most diverging phenomena. That which is often designated with the term 'underground' (or 'indie'), is in the perspective of this study a form of 'mainstream.' What is usually considered 'mainstream' is again just a tiny bit different from the typical hit parade music. In most cases, when the term 'alternative' is on somebody's lips, it is believed to be synonymous with 'underground' (see, for example, Kärjä 2006, Bannister 2006, Kruse 1993, Straw 1991, Hesmondhalgh 1999 and Toynbee 2000). This is the reason for introducing the term 'alternative mainstream,' which is almost never used in this sense, even though a lot has been written indirectly about it in popular music studies.[2]

The division of the pop music circuit in three segments is not based on any aesthetic value judgment, but on four other factors. The first is the attention music can expect to receive from the gatekeepers of the pop music circuit (indirectly, this also covers the popularity on the consumption side: the size of the target group and the degree of financial success). The second is the infrastructural context and the supply, on the production side(this component includes the players that emerge in one single segment, as well as those who are specialized in it). The third determining factor is the relation vis-à-vis the economic (understood in the way Bourdieu defines the production circuits). The fourth and final factor is the cultural meaning the actors attribute to the segment (it involves cultural values, which form the subject of the next chapter). At the same time, this classification or division is also a cross-section that runs through genres and actors. A specific genre circuit can be active in three segments. The same labels, media and platforms can be present everywhere and music lovers can be fond of both mainstream and of underground. Apart from this, artistic success is possible in every segment, while the chance of financial success, by contrast, becomes greater according to the extent to which players find themselves closer to or deeper in the mainstream. In any case, this division makes it possible to deal with the crisscross of styles, genres and groups and to reveal some of the basic mechanisms of the pop music circuit.

The typology proposed here is an ideal type, in the way Max Weber intended the term: a theoretical construction which as such is never found in the real world, yet helps us to examine empirically and to understand this reality. Furthermore, a schema like this can never fully grasp the dynamics of the music field or show how artists' careers can unfold within this field. The inquiry will demonstrate that such a segmentation is indeed very much alive in the pop music circuit.

‖ Mainstream

When somebody talks about 'poppy' music, everybody usually thinks of accessible, hit-prone and often melodic music for a large audience. These characteristics certainly apply to the mainstream. Mainstream music is primarily created for a broad audience. The majority of those who make up such an audience do not necessarily view themselves as music lovers, nor are they occupied with music in a particularly driven way. If the hit parade is the barometer for mainstream success (at least it used to be so, see p. 51), it is clear why there are smash hits. Hits only occur when great numbers of people that are not in the habit of buying any sound carriers suddenly start to buy music.

Typical of mainstream is the fact that it is — like it or not — easy to access. Because mainstream acts are omnipresent in the media, any well-socialized citizen is familiar with them. The mainstream act on TV is the musical act 'of the hour' that performs on a talk show or entertainment program, or is featured in showbiz news; it is the act that dominates music shows or *The Voice*-style TV talent hunt shows, where mainstream songs are performed by debutants. Mainstream music occupies the national hit radios, the family radios, or it is widely covered in popular dailies and weekly magazines.[3] Stubborn opponents may very well be able to avoid these media; they cannot however escape mainstream music itself. Mainstream is forced upon the masses in supermarkets, waiting rooms and train stations without anyone communicating anything, let alone asking for permission.

Not surprisingly, mainstream music covers all aspects of the music industry. It is produced by the national and international music industries (first and foremost, the major record companies, but it may very well be specific independents). It is distributed by local record shops and store chains, but in supermarkets, gas stations, newspaper stores, and so on. Whoever wants to reach a large audience needs to be everywhere that audience maybe.

Mainstream can also be synonymous with *middle of the road* (MOR), the music of the happy medium or the common denominator (De Meyer & Trappeniers 2007: 108). As Toynbee (2000: 122-123) puts it: each conjuncture in the mainstream is a temporary, hegemonic union which binds together different social groups and subsumes their distinct political and aesthetic values. The result of all this is the creation of a meta-community and a mass market. Despite its omnipresence, both outside in the world, and inside in the music business, mainstream does not need to be or become a specific style. Music of the most widely divergent genres, from very different corners, can achieve mainstream success. From a stylistic point of view, the hit parade or top charts constitute a motley crew, even if each era has its dominant features. Think , for example, of Chuck Berry and Elvis in the fifties, The Beatles and The Supremes in the sixties, Stevie Wonder and Abba in the seventies, Madonna and Michael Jackson in the eighties, The Backstreet Boys and Britney Spears in the nineties, Robbie Williams and Kanye West in the past decade, or One Direction today. Yet Bing Crosby, Frank Sinatra, The Sound of Music and countless disco acts, equally represent mainstream. The mainstream may contain schmaltz and vaudeville or cabaret artists, but also rock artists who made it from the alternative mainstream to the mainstream (see p. 51). In each segment, artists may indeed occupy different positions.

Great musical innovations are never a necessity for the mainstream. Occasionally it provides adjusted versions of hypes spilling over from the alternative mainstream (an example is Britney Spears dressed up in dubstep style). For artists to be able to reach a large audience, they must take care not to deviate too much from the norm. The music they make must be intentionally conformist. It is no coincidence then, as Frith (2001: 96) puts it, that popular tunes usually express commonplace, readily recognizable feelings: love, loss, and jealousy. For the

consumer, in any case, the emphasis is often more on entertainment than anything else is. This is why mainstream music — beautiful, catchy and well-made though it may be — does not require much to achieve the desired effect. Hence, this study wants to make a clear distinction between mainstream and alternative mainstream. Seeing that many like to use the label 'pop' to refer to mainstream music, the term 'mainstream' could be swapped for 'entertainment mainstream,' 'showbiz mainstream,' 'variety mainstream' or even 'pop mainstream' (see also p. 62).

Large-Scale Production and the Culture Industry

Pop music's mainstream comes close to what Bourdieu (1989) calls the large-scale mode of production, where a broad audience and a short production cycle are the essential elements. By taking a minimum of risks and through safe investments, the goal is to make a profit (economic capital) in the short run (although this can never be guaranteed, and even if it is not the only underlying motive). When the most popular forms of music are involved, production can be modified and tailored to the existing wants. It can thus be cast into the established, known forms. In Bourdieu's view, these are defensive strategies aiming to preserve the status quo. It explains the great emphasis on bestsellers (nine days' wonders) and classics (bestsellers in the long run). Yet in actual practice, the high number of loss-making records that are released (see also Hesmondhalgh 2006: 225) contradicts this. Bourdieu has a point when he says that success is heavily dependent on the attention paid or publicity made via the media. Sustaining the fire, or maintaining, nurturing and mobilizing the contact with the media is of central importance (Bourdieu 1989: 267). Adorno's analysis (1972) of the commodification in the cultural industry also fits in this — but perhaps without taking over the negative connotation the German added to his theory. Production, according to Adorno, is standardized and rationalized. Standardization refers to the fixed standard recipes and formulas that are worked into the ground. Here, every innovation is nothing more than old wines new bottles: 'the eternally same dressed up as the newly different' (Adorno 1972: 180). Because culture is industrialized, it is also rationalized. Commercial techniques of diffusion originating in the economic sector are applied to culture as if it were washing powder. The greater the commercialization of the standardized 'art,' the greater the emphasis put on the individuality of the 'stars' — Adorno speaks of 'pseudo-individualization.' Yet in his view, which puts him on the same level of Clement Greenberg (1986) in his essay *Avant-Garde and Kitsch* from 1939, the culture industry merely sells ready-made effects. The response that needs to be provoked is prescribed.

Similar mechanisms can be identified in the music industry. For instance, when some of the mega hits are created, especially when a strong team produces them that does the product development behind the scenes (e.g., Motown, Stock Aitken & Waterman and the many boy bands; see Keunen 2002). Then, as Adorno points out, the illusion is created that individual stars are involved. The fan believes that the artist is telling a highly personal story. Whether this study should endorse Adorno's claim that this a form of mass fraud (because, in his view, the culture industry leaves no room anymore for individuals that judge autonomously and critically), and that quantity always supersedes quality, remains to be seen. Frith (1987: 136-137), for example, is right to claim that pop is equally able to voice authentic feelings. Gust De Meyer, too, has a legitimate point when he wonders why the desire to reach a larger segment would be easier than to settle in a smaller segment (1995: 31), or why the experience of 'inferior' music would not be as meaningful as that of 'superior' music (1994: 125). Both Adorno and Bourdieu implicitly assume that the large-scale culture industry is indeed inferior, while this does not have to be the case by definition. The fact that music is the outcome of grandiose marketing actions, does not necessarily subtract from its value. Putting aside the machine behind mainstream acts, and contrary to what Adorno may think, the truth is that some mainstream acts do write their own songs and that they do this as sincerely as all other musicians. The challenge is to address an audience that is as broad as possible, both from economic and artistic perspectives. Most mainstream acts genuinely want to be mainstream, a truth that is acknowledged by proponents as well as opponents of this music. Regi, front man of the Flemish dance act Milk Inc., once said in an interview:

> We have always been more than a dance group. We are a pop group that brings music for a large audience. The thing is that the audience didn't realize this in the beginning.
> (JIM 19.11.2008)

Cross Marketing

The fact that Regi made this statement in a reality TV program created around him, is itself an example of cross media marketing or cross marketing, a form of cross promotion. Its basic method consists of making sure that an artist receives as much attention as possible on as many different platforms as possible. This leads to the next element needed to delineate the mainstream: the relation with economics and with the market value of the music. Here, Adorno's notion of rationalization is indeed applicable. The (positive or negative) cultural evaluation of music is, after all, something different from its economic embeddedness. The sacred importance attached to marketing is an illustration of the latter. Creating stars and forcing a mainstream breakthrough is simply not possible without marketing. In addition, standard modes of publicizing or advertising involve setting up adequate actions aimed at the most suitable product/market-combinations with the media, the retail trade or on the internet. These cannot always sufficiently achieve the basic goal of establishing success among a vast and wide audience. Because of the interconnection of major corporations — as components of multi-national entertainment concerns — with other sub-branches of the entertainment branch, marketing increasingly becomes massive, varied and cross-media-oriented. The foundations of this development were laid a long time ago. They go back to Bing Crosby's era, for instance. In many ways, Crosby was the first megastar in pop history. His solo career took shape from the 1930s on, and it was developed on all fronts at the time. It included record recordings or concerts, but also radio and television broadcasts, parts in films and musicals, and accompanying motion picture sound tracks. The effect was a circular movement: thanks to his name recognition and brand awareness, Crosby received more attention from the media and the entertainment industry, which in turn increased his reputation (see also Toynbee 2000: 21). The success of this interaction became a standard in the mainstream.

In addition, name recognition or brand awareness pushes merchandising upwards. Dutchman Colonel Parker, Elvis' manager, gained a world-wide reputation thanks to his clever, sophisticated activities in this area. Never before had a name and a picture of a singer been associated with so many products. A comparable, striking phenomenon in the Low Countries, Belgium and the Netherlands, is the commodification and exploitation of the children's act K3 (the name refers to the three identical initials of the girls' names). What else can one say of an act that appears on toothbrushes, writing materials, perfume, dolls, jigsaw puzzles, clothing, cookies, ice cream, fried snacks and more of the same tasty and toothsome products (Petitjean 28.03.2009)? The effect of such an economic logic becomes even more lucrative when the boundaries of the entertainment circuit are crossed and the brand awareness built inside the circuit is capitalized by strategic deals with the business world: sponsor deals, endorsement and product placement. Sponsor deals are of all time. In the sixties, for instance, Coca-Cola used music by The Supremes and Aretha Franklin in radio commercials, a practice that became ever more frequent. Today, such a sponsor deal is preferably not a one-time action. Now it fits in with long-term collaborations and a comprehensive marketing plan, a sophisticated road map that pairs the artists with the right products for the right target group at the right time. Campaigns therefore need to be planned to coincide with new releases. Destiny's Child, as trade magazine Billboard wrote (Paoletta 14.01.2006), provided a fine example of this. The girls group (and, following the break-up, the individual members during their solo careers) had deals with McDonald's, Walmart, Pepsi, Tommy Hilfiger and L'Oréal. In addition, their music was used in a motion picture (*Charlie's Angels*), the women started their own movie careers, started a clothing line, launched bathing and cosmetic products, and there were Mattel dolls (Barbie) made of them. The deal artists strike with Pepsi is not just a sponsor deal, but comprises a three-year-partnership during which the beverages manufacturer supports the album and the tour. It is indeed a fine example of cross marketing, where there is a full awareness of the synergy that can be created and that exists between *band* and *brand*. As Mathew Knowles (manager and father of Beyoncé) says: 'Destiny's Child was the textbook example of how the cooperation between management, artist, record label and entertainment lawyers should be.' (Paoletta 14.01.2006). In such practices one action can build on the other, which will result in both reinforcing and boosting each other. Whoever appears in ads, will receive more media attention exactly because of that. In 2005, Joss Stone advertised for GAP. The jeans brand's sales went up, but Stone's own record sales equally soared, increasing by 15%. What's more, the commercial won her an appearance on Oprah Winfrey's television show. It made her single break through to number 18 in the Billboard 200 (Paoletta 17.09.2005). In other words, campaigns of this sort can considerably augment the name recognition of an artist. Today, consumers want their music and media to be available at any time in any place on every conceivable device (notebook or tablet, mp3 player or smartphone, through streaming and in the *cloud*). The potential for brand marketing has grown sizably. When an artist is present on numerous platforms, and the deals are multi-channel and strategically planned, there will be greater attention for concerts, on the internet and in the media. 'Record labels and brands are growing towards each other because their understanding of each other's needs is getting better and better,' says Jeff Straughn of Island Def Jam, who secured deals with Nike, Clinique and LG mobile phones for Rihanna (Paoletta 30.09.2006). In every case, the artists link up with a hip product, thereby presenting themselves in the way they personally prefer. The audience eagerly consumes the publicity and feels as *cool* as the artist does. The same holds for the so-called 'product placements': brand names that pop up in song lyrics (Paoletta 18.02.2006). 50 Cent, Kanye West and Black Eyed Peas love to sing about luxury products as Mercedes-Benz, Cadillac, Nike or Louis Vuitton. Whatever deal may be behind it, product placement presumably always occurs in a spontaneous fashion. Fans regard stars as cultural tastemakers and consequently they buy the same products. Especially when it concerns hits: Adidas' sales, for example, went up notably when Run-DMC had a hit with 'My Adidas' in 1986. When rappers 8Ball and MJG rapped about Grey Goose vodka in 2004, the drink's sales exploded by 600% (Chipps 21.08.2004). Add to this that rappers have always been great businesspersons, and perhaps this capacity enabled them to climb up the social ladder (Hoefkens 11.09.2012). Apart from making music, they occupy themselves with production or selling of — among other things - liquor (Puff Daddy, 50 Cent, Ludacris), clothing (Jay Z, Run-DMC) and earphones (Dr. Dre). Snoop Dogg admits: 'By linking up with hip products, I can be close to the people, even if I don't have a CD out.' (Mitchell et al. 20.05.2006).

‖ Underground

While nobody can avoid running into the mainstream, it is not possible to make contact with the underground without putting some personal effort into it. The underground does not concern itself with the trends and hypes of the (alternative) mainstream and does not have a direct line with the national or international players in the (alternative) mainstream industry. Yet now and again actors in the latter segment do signal tendencies from the underground (the specialized evening programming by radio channels such as BBC Radio 1, Studio Brussels in Flanders or 3FM in the Netherlands). Underground also appears on the smaller stages of the big festivals (Glastonbury, Pukkelpop, Lowlands etc.). Occasionally, one can even read about it in the music pages of quality newspapers. This media attention can be the beginning of more general media attention that can gradually lead to a breakthrough in the alternative mainstream, provided attention is continuous during a certain period.

The underground, however, is a separate circuit that is hard to describe in clear-cut fashion. Like the alternative mainstream, it is a segment in the pop music circuit that is composed of several and mutually differing underground environments or niches. Its heart beats in divergent genre circuits and music scenes (see Keunen 1996 and 2002). A genre circuit grows around a specific musical genre, operates in a given stylistic idiom and co-shapes this idiom (such as techno, blues, hip-hop, hardcore guitar rock, metal, reggae or, in more distant past, the psychedelic counterculture). In turn, it can contain various subcultures, each built around a subgenre or style, operating nationally or internationally. Typical of a music scene is its local embedment: a local variant and thus a specific approach of a genre or style, with its own local color. A music scene can be a breeding ground for new genres — the original setting from which a new genre emerges. It can also be a place for actors to experience an already established genre in complete independence, detached from the (alternative) mainstream. Finally, it can be a remnant of an already long forgotten genre. Other than that, the same scene can harbor several genres. In this case, the local connection takes precedence, allowing variegating groups to run into each other in the same pubs or play areas.[4]

The underground further defines itself by a more limited hybridization of actors. In the (alternative) mainstream the same record companies, concert halls and media exist for a diversity of musical genres and styles. In the underground, this infrastructural framework is more pronounced, varying from genre to genre. Musical characteristics of style are only one aspect of a music genre, and the social and cultural context constitutes the actual condition for its existence. Every underground environment — and most notably the genre circuits — have built their own independent (and often international) infrastructural framework which has dissociated itself from the developments in the majors industry, boasting their own record labels, shops, concert venues, magazines, etc. This is the reasons why Toynbee (2000: 27) also calls these underground environments *proto-markets*: cultural free zones that have not been marketed yet, which 'the music industry' — however vaguely he may define it — has difficulty capturing, and where innovation actually occurs. By definition, new genres and styles originate in underground environments.

Conformism and Progress

Nonetheless, underground is certainly not a type of music. The segment is as multifaceted as the musical styles that inhabit in it. Neither is it forcibly 'special' or 'difficult' music, solely destined for 'freaks.' On the contrary, conformist and progressive tendencies are everywhere, also in the underground. This, of course, is an ideal-typical distinction. In practice, musicians are situated somewhere in-between, combining both repetition and difference. The former provides a surname, the latter a first name. It is probably even not exaggerated to state that most underground environments are conservative (as is the case in certain subcultures of hardcore circuits: the hardcore of guitar rock or of techno, the blues purists, etc.). Because of the strong cultural embeddedness, the fulfillment of expectation prevails. Movements that push innovation to the extremes expose themselves to stern reprimands or even exile. Typical of a conformist attitude is that a musician attempts to get as close as possible to a genre in the most faithful way, and that he or she gives the task a highly personal interpretation without ever endangering its recognizable features. Death metal groups wants to be seen as strong death metal groups by their fellow genre members, rappers want to put their best raps to the beat of the moment, and house deejays will build personal sets that match the club's vibe of the hour. Yet even then, both orthodox and heterodox signals can be discerned. The extent to which musicians try to push the genre in a new direction and open doors using terms like 'originality' and 'creativity' as their buzzwords, is telling of their progressive attitude.[5] When several equally minded people embrace an obstinate musical course, a new scene can be born (see also Becker 1982). The scene becomes a warm nest to which its members can retire, where they can withdraw, far from any of the known actors in the music industry. Scenes work as bohemian environments, as marginal circuits outside of the established and existing institutions which never attempt to find acceptance in the music industry. In *Die Boheme* (1968), Kreuzer defines bohemians as a social group, as a subculture of intellectuals at the fringes of 'official,' dominant or legitimate culture. They adopt a negative anti-bourgeois attitude towards this culture, represent a leisure ethic against the ruling work ethic, and they never 'produce' something simply because others can 'consume' it. In fact, to be a bohemian is to make a deliberate escape from the mass-market system (Frith & Horne 1987: 33).

> Their art was not made for popular consumption; popular tastes were both ignored and despised. Bohemian art was essentially elitist; the bohemian community was confined to the chosen, to other artists. [...] They are cultural radicals not just as the source of the formalist avant-garde, but also in institutional terms—they don't work (and thus outraged bourgeois moralists have always denounced successful bohemians...) (Frith 1981: 98 and 266)[6]

In the scene, music is made for fellow musicians and a small group of fans, and there are alternative channels for concerts and distribution. An example of a bohemian environment is the New York Downtown scene of the late 1980s and the 1990s (with John Zorn and the music club/record label Knitting Factory; see Keunen & Keunen 1996). Another example is the so-called Recommended scene of the 1970s, when European bands (such as Henry Cow, Universe Zero and Art Zoyd) grouped together, had their own record label (Recommended Records), a magazine (*RéR Quarterly*) and concert areas. In *File under Popular* (1985: 133), Chris Cutler of Henry Cow writes that many of them evolved from 'not being able to play along in the market' to 'not wanting anymore.' Characteristic elements were:

> Firstly, their independence, their implacable opposition to the 'business' of rock; secondly, a determination to pursue their

own work in spite of the disinterest of the big commercial rock circuits (Cutler 1985: 133).

At the heart of a scene are two elements that accord with the rules of small-scale production described by Bourdieu. The first is a stubborn refusal of economic profit, the second the acquisition and accumulation of symbolic capital. Conventions only exist to be shattered. Players mainly make investments that are risky and long-term. Everyone, finally, wholly endorses the doctrine of *l'art pour l'art*. The limited mode of production is, for that matter, typical of all underground circuits or music scenes. In underground environments, recognition and prestige are more important than economic profit or the fulfillment of a large audience's expectations. Artists never intentionally create music for a broad and anonymous audience of non-producers. The music primarily confines itself to their own peer group, the limited audience of co-producers and 'symbolic value producing individuals' (critics, connoisseurs, music freaks). Contrary to what Bourdieu says, however, the underground does not only demonstrate avant-garde (or progressive) tendencies. It also has conservative (or conformist) tendencies.

From Underground to Alternative Mainstream?

Because underground artists operate in the margins of the pop world, financial success can never be more than a dream. The money flows are too small for artists to make a living with their music. Record sales remain small, fees for concerts are low, and royalties provide only modest sums of money or nothing at all (not all underground artists are members of a copyright association). Either artists are underground prophets (out of sheer necessity) or they toil away at a career while hoping that the alternative mainstream will pick them up. If the latter does occur, there is no discernible stylistic difference between underground and alternative mainstream groups. The fact remains that not everybody is able to win the lottery. The majority of those who fail to pass the selection are still able to ascribe the reason for their lack of success to their consistent loyalty to non-commercial principles (Toynbee 2000: 26-27). Yet even those who would rather have it differently will gladly spend the rest of their time in the underground environment with only a small amount of money. This is primarily because they love to play music and long to do this as much as possible. Another reason is that they are able to be part of 'the scene' and win fame in a subculture. Thornton (1990), therefore, speaks of 'subcultural capital' (see p. 75).

Underground music usually remains stuck in the context in which it originated. This may be both the local scene and the very narrow international community that often makes up the underground circuit, setting the limits within which a group is able to tour. Success and opportunities of playing live may considerably increase, however, when the underground artists make music that conforms to the view of the genre held by the opinion-making leaders of the alternative mainstream. In short, they can augment their chances when their music is in accordance with the trends and hypes of the hour. Readers may think, for example, of how electronic dance music broke through in the middle of the 1990s as soon bands started adding the elements of vocals, guitars, song structures and a live performing band to the style or genre. Well-known examples are The Prodigy and Faithless. The success of the Def Jam label (Run DMC, Beastie Boys), which introduced rock guitars into hip-hop, is in the same class. Going back even further, the 1960s witnessed The Byrds bringing Dylan covers, which catapulted a folk group into the charts and hit parades for the first time in pop history. Similarly, in the 1950s, black R&B became white mainstream as soon as Bill Haley and Elvis appropriated the music (see Keunen 2002).

Provided the music industry picks it up and pitchforks it into the (alternative) mainstream, niche music too can turn a profit. In Bourdieu's terminology, it would sound like this: underground music becomes consecrated avant-garde when the established institutions adopt it, when it turns into classics, and when its refusal and denial of economics loses its sharp edges. When it happens, a large chunk of the genre circuit may receive attention. This can be either an entire music scene (for example, Seattle's grunge) or a handful of groups from the scene (this was the case in the 1960s when The Rolling Stones emerged from the London circuit of Blues clubs). From all this, it is clear that schema 2, as it is proposed here, must be interpreted as a dynamic schema (see p. 51). In this way, for instance, the spheres that represent the underground can change position, first remaining far from the (alternative) mainstream, then nearly overlapping with it.

Alternative Mainstream

To divide the pop music circuit into two segments, underground and mainstream, is to simplify the practice of music considerably. The argument here would be jumping to conclusions if it labeled artists who lack mainstream success or ambition as underground acts, or conversely filed successful underground artists straightaway under mainstream. A dynamic aspect of the pop music circuit lies in between the mainstream and the underground. It is therefore necessary to introduce a third category that strikes a bridge between the two segments: the alternative mainstream. The term echoes that of 'alternative rock' that popped up in the music press at the start of 1990s to refer to various, somewhat harder playing rock groups that had become successful since the grunge hype. The term is partially also a reference to the then existing MTV show *Alternative Nation* (even though the alternative mainstream is broader than rock alone and is not limited to a specific musical style).

To advance 'alternative mainstream' as a central term of research is not without its dangers. On the one hand, the term's first part ('alternative') is a commonly used and ideologically charged word from the discourse of pop. On the other hand, the term's second part ('mainstream') seems to debunk this ideology (see p. 90). Whatever connotations the term may elicit, this study employs normative or value-charged terms that have a particular usage in the field as generally descriptive terms.

Even though it is a form of mainstream, the alternative mainstream in the model presented here is different from the mainstream described earlier. The category also does not coincide with the underground. At any given time, this sort of music does not so much enjoy the undivided attention of the *entertainment* circuit, but rather of the most influential actors of the *professional* music circuit, that is, the music press, the record labels, managers, bookers, promoters and media. Because these actors are confined to one particular country, each country has its very own alternative mainstream.[7] To a great extent, therefore, alternative mainstream is a variable construction that is continuously made and remade by specific professional actors. A striking element is that these music professionals may emerge from the established music industry as well as from small, independent organizations.

Compared to the more delineated structure of an underground environment, the alternative mainstream is characterized by hybridization on the level of organizations and audience. Here, musical omnivores often take the place of genre purists. The genres and structures that are built around them are closely, if not inextricably interwoven. The same media, record companies and concert promoters are active within widely diverging genres. In each particular time frame, they select the most suitable genre out of a vast supply of genres, and present it to the larger public (because it is the public of the mass media). This public, in turn, consists of musical omnivores. They listen to greatly differing styles and, in the same way of the decision makers, they may think that they are picking the best items from the supply. The alternative mainstream is the turf of *the* music lovers, those who follow the press, are open to new trends, go to concerts, listen to new releases via streaming and purposefully buy sound carriers. For actors who want to be well up on the pop music circuit, or — better — want to be part of it, must be familiar with the alternative mainstream's agenda.

At this point, it is perhaps useful to give a brief presentation of the main players, since the conceptual analysis in the next chapters will proceed from the case study of Flanders.[8] In the Flemish alternative mainstream, music can break through when it can count on the attention of certain players. The first group consists of public radio stations Studio Brussels and Radio 1. StuBru is an 'alternative' pop music station for young people and partially also a current affairs news station. Especially shows in daytime and weekend programming, such as *De Afrekening* and *De Hotlist*, have great influence. The second group comprises weekly magazines *Humo* and *Focus Knack*, and daily papers *De Morgen* and *De Standaard*. *Humo* is a 'general' independent magazine that started off as a radio and television guide, but developed into a critical, also rather 'alternative' magazine that discussed current affairs, but also contained a solid section about pop music. *Focus Knack* is a weekly entertainment magazine that mainly focuses on film, television and pop music. It is published as a supplement of the leading current affairs and politics magazine *Knack*. Both *De Morgen* and *De Standaard* are so-called 'quality papers,' the leading dailies that sport a solid supplement of culture. The main players in the live circuit are the following: major venues such as AB, short for Ancienne Belgique, or smaller music clubs such as Democrazy, Nijdrop, Het Depot, Trix or MOD; festivals such as Rock Werchter and Pukkelpop, but also Leffingeleuren, Boomtown, Feest in het Park, Lokerse Feesten etc.; and finally *Humo's* competition for fledgling bands *Humo's* Rock Rally. Artists may associate themelves with alternative management agencies, such as Rockoco, Gentlemanagement and Keremos, independent record firms or booking agents such as Peter Verstraelen Bookings, Quiet Concerts and Toutpartout, or are housed by majors and ruling booker and promoter Live Nation.[9]

Public Attention and Financial Success

Underground music and local success acts can cross over to the alternative mainstream and receive (inter)national praise or gain a transnational following. The alternative mainstream, indeed, creates the hypes and trends of the hour. The media and the music industry pluck acts from the underground, bring them into circulation and give them full attention. This explains why at regular intervals every possible daily paper or weekly magazine will publish an interview with the same artists. It explains why their music gets constant airplay (it is put in the playlist) and why the same bands appear on the concert agendas. Thanks to this concerted action, groups and styles can be dominantly present in the segment for prolonged periods. Sometimes hard rock plays first fiddle, sometimes techno. Sometimes it is a fleeting hype (trip hop), sometimes a universally celebrated scene (such as the Brooklyn scene with Yeasayer, Grizzly Bear and TV on the Radio, or the dubstep of Kode9, Skream and Burial), sometimes a longer-lasting trend (punk, grunge, nu-folk) or the nth revival (Woodstock and The Beatles are up for another jubilee every so many years). The dominant music often pushes other bands or styles further in the background, causing them to disappear or end up back in the underground. It even looks like groups or genres only exist for as long as the media and the industry pay attention to them and continue to label them as objects of great public interest. The alternative mainstream is a succession of momentary snapshots, often fueled by evolutions in the genre circuits. It is a mirror image or even watered-down version of the sound and fury produced by the underground. The music industry and the media never cease to follow the comings, goings and doings of the different genre worlds and the latter are highly sensitive to trends. Exactly because the industry and the media constantly seize the music from obscurity and procure vast attention, the alternative mainstream turns into a form of mainstream. It is an observation fans would probably hate to acknowledge, but the music might just as well take position in the industry of the mainstream, as an equal potential object of carpet-bombing attention provided by the mainstream media.

Thanks to the public attention and the name recognition artists may possess in the alternative mainstream, they often enjoy a financially attractive career. In the practice of music the various money flows are interrelated (which this study will confirm, see further), because those who have plenty of media attention, will get more and better paid concerts, and will sell more sound carriers and merchandising. An artist who is well-liked by the alternative mainstream will receive more royalties, collect bigger fees and earn more from copyrights (performing or performance rights for playing the music in public, for concerts and radio airplay, mechanical reproduction rights for CDs *and* rights by proxy). Because the revenues from these money flows are directly proportional to the extent to which the artistic activities are in the public eye, solid publicity is of key importance. This includes publicity gained from the primary actions of record companies, booking agents or managers. It also covers the side effects of the subsequent media attention (interviews in national media, participation in entertainment and talk shows on TV, or charity and benefit actions). The days when marketing and sponsoring were dirty words to the alternative mainstream's in-crowd have long gone. In the 1960s Jim Morrison could still be furious when the other members of The Doors allowed 'Light My Fire' to be used for an automobile ad. Some decades later, Bob Dylan had no trouble making publicity for Cadillac, iPod and Starbucks, and neither did The White Stripes for Coca-Cola, Arno for Lancia or Keith Richards for Vuitton (Hirschberg 30.09.2006 and De Meyer 2010: 298). Bono (U2) may be a do-gooder; he is also a highly creative evader when it comes to taxes and being shareholder of Facebook and Live Nation on the other hand (De Meyer 2010: 10-11). What has been standard practice in hip-hop for a longer time, has slowly but steadily penetrated as far as the 'respected' rock environment. The idealism and mistrust of bourgeois capitalism that characterized the heydays of punk has never been so far away as now. What artists once considered 'selling out' has now become a way of 'buying in.' A song that ends up in the right ad or game, wins synchronization rights for the artist, but may also have a larger impact on an artist's career than a record contract may have. As Frank Zappa would sing, being ironical: *'We're only in it for the money.'*

When the Economic and the Cultural Join Hands

Financial success, too, is related to artistic success. Plenty of attention, interest and favorable reviews in the media or enjoyed among the actors of the music industry illustrate the respect, and consequently also the reputation, which an actor is able to acquire. As Toynbee (2000: 7) succinctly puts it: 'The intense desire for money is also a desire to be adored.' This is the reason why the cultural and the economic logic meet each other in the alternative mainstream. One thing is that, contrary to what Bourdieu claims, financial success is perfectly able to yield symbolic capital (see further). Another is that it is exactly here that a significant portion of pop music is situated which Bourdieu's schematic view has nothing to tell about. Granted, Bourdieu admitted that the art trade is characterized by a certain ambiguity: an artist's goal may very well be the pursuit of symbolic recognition, the refusal of economics is never an absolute denial of economic interests. It is also true that, as Bourdieu claims, 'the accumulation of symbolic capital (...) is quite capable of producing "economic" profit, under particular circumstances and within a certain period of time' (Bourdieu 1989: 247). In the world of pop music, these 'double practices' take things a step further. Typical of this world is precisely the interwoven nature of large-scale and small-scale modes of production, or the application of small-scale mechanisms of distinction in the area of large-scale production. Large-scale production can also emit an idiosyncratic view of the world. Artists as diverse as David Bowie, Radiohead or Prince produce music with a 'double code': innovative music for a large audience. They are creative within the walls of the mass market. A typical expression of this is the reply David Byrne (Talking Heads) gave to the question whether his music was a form of art or a product:

> I feel I'm successful when I combine both, when people have forgotten the distinction between the two. If I can do a video that can be artistically successful and still get shown on TV, then I've reached the best of both worlds. (Byrne, cited in Frith & Horne 1987: 175)

This shows that the aim to preserve the status quo or the desire to shatter conventions is not related to the scale of the mode of production. More, in order to maintain a status in any music scene, an actor needs to gather both cultural and economic capital. Some form of cultural entrepreneurship is a more than welcome asset: a strong artistic story cannot ignore the need for solid promotion.

David Hesmondhalgh (2006: 221-223) agrees. In his view too, large-scale production is infinitely more differentiated than Bourdieu suggests. On top of that he asserts that also the 'production for co-producers' can be consumed by millions who are not producers or connoisseurs. A large audience enjoys quality TV series (type HBO), and the artists that gained the highest degree of canonization in rock music eventually proved to be popular (The Beatles, Bob Dylan, Radiohead). Symbolic goods can be produced for internal, artistic or intellectual motives, but just as well respond to an external demand. A possible way of putting it is that artists in the alternative mainstream want to hold on to their personal autonomy and for this purpose make use of the mass media, without themselves being used by the media. Full participation or immersion in the music industry does not necessarily entail an artist having to give up a portion of his or her creativity. Only, it is then that musicians stand a better chance at getting a more favorable distribution. This was shown following the major deal Sonic Youth closed with Geffen in 1988. At first the deal was perceived as a sell-out (and initially the band's music *did* become more accessible). Then it became clear that it *did not* impede the band's urge for experimentation. The group simply had more options to do what they wanted to do. With respect to this, Walker says the following about Laurie Anderson (at the time of her hit 'O Superman') in his book *Pop into Art — Art into Pop*:

> Laurie Anderson has demonstrated that avant-garde artists can reach mass audiences without loss of artistic integrity, if they are prepared to embrace modern means of communication and mass production.
> (Walker 1987: 134)

According to Frith and Horne, Pink Floyd is the group that gave best evidence of the fact that personal autonomy and the use of mass media do not need to exclude each other.

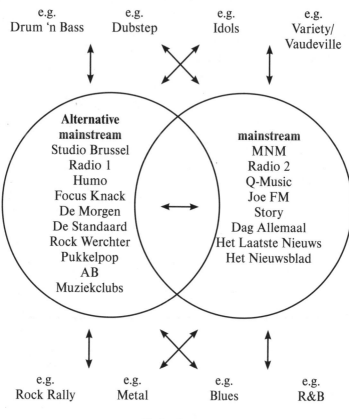

UnderGround

e.g. Drum 'n Bass   e.g. Dubstep   e.g. Idols   e.g. Variety/ Vaudeville

Alternative mainstream
Studio Brussel
Radio 1
Humo
Focus Knack
De Morgen
De Standaard
Rock Werchter
Pukkelpop
AB
Muziekclubs

mainstream
MNM
Radio 2
Q-Music
Joe FM
Story
Dag Allemaal
Het Laatste Nieuws
Het Nieuwsblad

e.g. Rock Rally   e.g. Metal   e.g. Blues   e.g. R&B

UnderGround

Schema 2 *The segments model, containing the three segments of the pop music circuit*

Alternative Mainstream

50

> The group had resolved the tension they'd originally
> felt between artistic and commercial logic by asserting
> complete artistic control and becoming astonishingly
> rich anyway!
> (Frith & Horne 1987: 98)

It is understood that not all alternative mainstream artists have similar success. The attention paid by the industry and the media occurs in stages of intensity and fluctuates. Nonetheless, the intertwined functioning of a cultural and an economic logic is a constant in the alternative mainstream. Whether Pink Floyd or Sonic Youth are involved, or artists of the hour such as Sufjan Stevens, Vampire Weekend or Burial, does not make one iota of a difference.

The Segments Model – Dynamics, Positions and Economic Logic

Schema 2 below can shed more light on dividing the pop music circuit in three segments. As was said before, the model is an ideal-type. What matters is the dynamics between the segments. For example, artists can be selected and move up from the underground to the alternative mainstream, become a steady member or retire afterwards to the niche where it all started. The attention groups enjoy in the alternative mainstream can also undergo a scaling-up, which causes them to end up in the mainstream. This success can be either temporary or lasting. The model, therefore, is a great tool for mapping out artist careers or certain genre evolutions. Via the alternative mainstream, certain styles (such as dubstep) can get a foot in the door in mainstream and 'hang out' there for some time. Others, by contrast, are immediately embraced by a certain section of the mainstream without them having to demand respect in the alternative mainstream (such as hard style, trance and the former gabber, or particular forms of hip-hop and R&B in The Netherlands). Indeed, this is far being the case.

The proposed segments nevertheless resist precise delineation. Some types of music are easier to categorize than others. One band specifically focuses on one segment, while another band almost stumbles into it by chance. A run-of-the-mill black metal band or techno artist chooses the Underground, while

schmaltz, variety, and other showbiz artists, pop divas and *boy bands* clearly aim at the mainstream (regardless of them having success or not). In addition, practical reality always harbors a twilight zone, or it manifests a gradual overlapping. It explains why certain artists become idols for the alternative mainstream and still manage to score mainstream hits, or conversely, why mainstream artists can (still) count on respect from the corner of the alternative mainstream. This is most frequent in the case of the big names, the classics or the canonized alternative mainstream (such as U2, Prince or The Beatles). In music circles, people tend to rave about their music, and their big hits have become part of the collective memory. In many cases only the hits will be part of the mainstream, while the larger number of (old) releases of the same group are confined to circles of connoisseurs (obvious examples are Pink Floyd, Bob Dylan, Nick Cave, Tom Waits, Metallica or Frank Zappa). The segments, indeed, are not so much artist-related as they are music-linked: the same artist may reside in the alternative mainstream for the duration of one project, and descend into the underground for another (a good example is Flemish guitarist Mauro Pawlowski, who combines being a member of dEUS with solo projects).

Hit Success and Economic Profit

This three-way distinction of 'underground/alternative mainstream/mainstream' is primarily a cultural construct, as the next chapter will clearly show. Because of this, the dividing lines between the three segments still exist. Nevertheless, the question remains whether this cultural division is also based on an economic division. Is the position occupied by an artist in the pop music circuit also determined by the entry and ranks in the charts and by financial success? The inquiry will lead for a while along this track, by way of exploration, and without any immediate need for empirical content analysis. As far as the hit parade and charts are concerned, and limiting the scope to the example of Flanders, the study relied on the annual charts and other 'special' lists of the *Ultratop*, the official hit list (Jaspers 2006 and www.ultratop. be), as well as data from studies by De Meyer (2010). In the *Ultratop*, there is a notable distinction between singles and albums. Among the 100 best-selling singles of a given year, the artists from the alternative mainstream can be counted on the fingers of one hand. Among the album lists, their presence climbs up to one third and even half of the artists. This can be an indication that hit success is a significant parameter in determining the mainstream. To give an idea: the artists who scored the highest numbers of hits in Flanders in the period 1995-2005 are: Céline Dion, K3, Helmut Lotti, Get Ready!, Britney Spears, Clouseau, Madonna, Backstreet Boys, Marco Borsato, Milk Inc., Will Tura, Robbie Williams and X-Session (Jaspers 2006: 499). In the list of #1-rankings for singles and albums together, these artists are also accompanied by U2, Eminem, Metallica and Red Hot Chili Peppers (Jaspers 2006: 499). An album hit list is therefore a combination of mainstream and alternative mainstream. Rather, a fraction of the alternative mainstream also enjoys mainstream success. However, in the list of 'longest #1-ranking albums' exclusively mainstream artists such as Borsato, Lotti and Clouseau are running the show (Jaspers 2006: 500). From a different angle, De Meyer also arrives at this conclusion (2010: 98-103). He drew up a meta-list of all singles that appeared in the hit parades from 1956 until 1996 (by weighting the #1s with the number of weeks they remained in the charts). In doing so, he wanted to prove that at least in Flanders there is no case of rock supremacy. His method was a bull's eye, because a look at the list reveals that the 'typical' alternative mainstream groups are extremely rare and that exclusively mainstream artists occupy the top positions.

When it comes to singles, however, these last few years have seen a remarkable change. From the moment when the hit parade calculus started to include digital downloads, the presence of 'alternative' artists remarkably became more frequent (a fact that is also evidenced by the field study for this book). In Flanders the difference between the standard hit parade and the special 'alternative album' list merely signifies that in the latter the Dutch-speaking artists and showbiz artists are absent. The result is that for the time being the hit parade is less suitable as a barometer. In the past, public success invariably led to high record sales. Today it has become far from clear how many sold copies a hit ranking actually represents. To what extent it remains an indicator, is not something with which this book must concern itself. Still, a study commissioned by the European Music Office (Legrand 2012), which gathered market data on airplay and legal downloads from all over Europe between September 2010 and August 2011, revealed two important things. The first is that there is a strong correlation between airplay and downloads (in the top 50, 74% constitutes identical numbers). The second is that mainstream artists (Bruno Mars, Adele, and Rihanna) hold the top positions, without exception. Even in their top 200 rock is only very modestly present.

Another way of distinguishing mainstream from alternative mainstream could be the artists' financial success and the economic profit. At the international level, *Billboard* published an overview of the best-earning pop artists of 2010 (Waddell et al., 06.03.2010, De Meyer 2010: 111). In this overview, the top of the mainstream and of the alternative mainstream mingle amicably (Madonna, Pink, Beyoncé, Michael Jackson and Céline Dion on one side, and U2, Bruce Springsteen, Coldplay, Metallica, Kings of Leon and Bob Dylan on the other). Financial success, indeed, is at all times the privilege of the artist with name and fame is. The difference between the two segments is clearer on the Flemish market. This is demonstrated by two studies that investigated the wealth of the artists' companies or firms (Debels 2011 and Verduyn 2003). Their official data reveal the same line that is discernible in the hit lists: the highest regions of the top of the richest Flemish artists are only populated by mainstream names.

Financial success and an entry in the charts or hit parades indicate the economic logic in the pop music circuit, but are only partially successful in substantiating the distinction 'mainstream/ alternative mainstream.' What is of great importance is the fact that the alternative mainstream includes the sort of music that actors in the music circuit (professionals and public) think is 'alternative.' In addition, this obviously involves the cultural value added to it, and the way in which a process of symbolic attribution may take place in it. Precisely these matters are addressed in the next chapter.

Recap 1

This chapter puts forward the concept of the alternative mainstream as a separate segment in the pop music circuit. Usually, when someone wants to gain an understanding of the pop music circuit, and of the way in which it is structured, two other classifications or categorizations are promptly suggested. The pop music circuit is viewed as a combination of three production circuits: the circuit of sound carriers, of concerts and of rights. This division tells us a lot about pop music as an economic branch of industry, but does not map out the dynamics in the field. To cover this dynamics, the pop discourse is marked by the distinctions underground/mainstream, alternative/commercial, and pop/rock. The sociology of culture can contextualize the distinctions by means of Bourdieu's ideal-type of small-scale versus large-scale mode of production. A classification based on the practice of the traditional arts, however, proves to be far from readily transferable to the practice of pop. Now and again, strictly small-scale and strictly large-scale modes of production do turn up in pop music, but an interesting segment of this falls right between those stools. The mechanisms of distinction of small-scale production are mobilized in the large-scale mode of production. This conjunction of cultural and economic arguments was determined as the typical feature of the alternative mainstream.

The introduction of this third segment allows for a clearer demarcation of the other two. In the terminology of this study, 'underground' represents separate little worlds of genre and music scenes, with their own infrastructural apparatus, cultural values and beliefs, and a rather limited social aura or effect (wanting to get to know it better requires personal effort and commitment). 'Mainstream,' then, is the music that aims at a large consumer market, at an audience that does not necessarily concern itself with music in an enthused manner, but finds music important as a form of entertainment. People encounter mainstream music everywhere, whether they like it or not. The music this study calls 'alternative mainstream,' is music that is equally directed at a mass market, but whose primary target group is 'music lovers' and which circulates among certain national actors in the music industry and the media. Between these segments, a dynamical exchange exists: groups can move up from one segment to another, and gatekeepers guard the access roads.

Notes

1 The process of selection described in this book is of a different nature than the actions and procedures in the copyrights circuit. For this reason, copyright falls outside the scope of study. An artist (such as a composer or lyricist) usually subscribes to membership of a copyright management firm or institution, which protects clients' copyrights, serves as financial go-between to collect royalties in their name whenever their works are used publicly. This includes works if transmitted on a sound carrier, used via the media, at concerts, during parties, in public buildings, office spaces, waiting rooms, shops, etc.. However, authors can also sign a release contract with a publisher. The latter will exploit the works to the maximum of time and space, enablingthem to generate more royalties—a service for which the publisher receives one third (the Netherlands) or half (Belgium) of all of the composer's royalties. Whenever sound recordings are used publicly, the user also needs to pay proxy rights (fair fee). These are intended for performing musicians and producers.

2 Regev (2002) distinguishes between 'pop' en 'pop/rock': the latter seems to resemble my characterization of the alternative mainstream. Apart from this, I only found two instances in the literature where the term 'alternative mainstream' is used, although not in the sense it is employed in this study. Kärjä (2006) wrote an article on three different canons (a *prescribed*, *alterna-tive* and *mainstream* canon, interpreting 'alternative' as 'underground') which was entitled 'A prescribed alte-native mainstream.' Bannister (2006) is the only one who casually mentions the term *alternative mainstream*, yet purely as synonymous with the stylistic denotation *alternative rock* used primarily in journalism for Britpop, grunge and garage rock.

3 It is rather easy to identify the players in each country. Here are some examples from Flanders and the Netherlands. The Ultratop 50 is the official hit parade in Flanders, while

the Netherlands has its own Top 40. The most popular TV show with showbiz news in Flanders used to be *De Rode Loper*; equivalent shows in the Netherlands are *Shownieuws* and *RTL Boulevard*. For Flemish popular music the TV program *Tien Om Te Zien* (Ten to Watch!) was iconic, while mainstream pop in the Netherlands reached the small screen via *Toppop3* (in the solid British tradition of *Top of the Pops*). Talent hunts are the same in all countries: *Idols*, *The Voice* and *X-Factor*. National hit radios in Flanders are MNM, JOE FM and Q-music, in the Netherlands 538, Sky Radio and Q-music (BBC Radio One in Great Britain). Many national regions name their family radio station Radio 2 (in the Netherlands, Flanders and the UK). Finally, there are popular dailies (in Flanders *Het Laatste Nieuws* and *Het Nieuwsblad*, in the Netherlands *De Telegraaf*, *AD* and the free papers *Metro* and *Sp!ts*) as well as popular weekly magazines (*Story* and *Dag Allemaal* in Flanders, *Privé* and *Weekend* as Dutch counterparts).

4 This could be 'the local scene': groups lacking direct affiliation to a genre circuit start their careers on small, local stages. For many fledgling artists, this is the start on a course on which to remain.

5 Or, as Laermans (2009) argues: in their works, artists invariably exhibit a combination of freedom and dependency, of autonomy and heteronomy. Besides this, radically progressive musicians can deviate from the basic genre to such an extent that they cease to part of it. Still, progressive innovations in style can equally develop into new basic properties to which others will start to conform (see Keunen 1996 and 2002).

6 Frith, Simon (1981). *Sound effects: Youth, Leisure, and the Politics of Rock'n'roll*. New York: Pantheon Books.

7 The situation closely resembles what happens in the mainstream, since everything revolves around record labels: because there are local divisions of international firms, a largely similar alternative mainstream can arise in largely different countries, as largely similar groups are involved in largely similar cases.

Apart from this, each country obviously also possesses its own local color.

8   The field research offered confirmation of the enumerative description that follows. Furthermore, the actors constantly referred to one another in the interviews, which made it easier to delineate the segment.

9   By way of comparison with the Flemish situation, and for information purposes, this note gives an overview of the pop music circuit in the Netherlands. The alternative mainstream is found on radio stations 3FM (among those is *3voor12 Radio*, part of the extended multimedia platform *3voor12*, including news, video and the *listening pole*) and at the time also Kink FM. On TV, talk show *De Wereld Draait Door* programs one minute of live music on a daily basis. In the printed press, music magazine *OOR*, daily papers *de Volkskrant* and *NRC Handelsblad* form the triumvirate. As far as live performances are concerned, the alternative mainstream groups aspire to perform at the main venues Paradiso, Melkweg, 013, Vera or Tivoli, and at festivals such as Pinkpop, Lowlands, Eurosonic Noorderslag or Into The Great Wide Open. The Dutch also have their national contests, such as De Grote Prijs van Nederland and De Beste Singer-Songwriter van Nederland. Online-specialized web radios like KX Radio and Pinguin Radio carry the torch.

2. Alternative Mainstream as a Cultural Construct

> Artists write rock music for themselves, not with the
> initial intention of making money, but to make music —
> and, possibly, to stretch its limits and boundaries a little
> further. This is music that may last forever, becoming
> 'classic' in the process. On the other hand, POP music
> is written with the sole intention (normally) of making a
> quick buck, either for the artist(s) or (more than likely)
> their record label.
> (Martin C. Strong, cited in Shuker 2008: 125)

Pop music discourse — formed and performed by journalists and people from the music industry, academics and rock theorists, music lovers and musicians — often makes a distinction between pop music that is labeled as commercial and pop music that is more than merely a commercial product. 'Pop' and 'rock' are the terms that make this distinction. Rock is the 'better pop,' seeking to distinguish itself from 'commercial pop.' One category symbolizes authentic expression (underground). The other does not differ from mass culture and commodities (mainstream).

More important than the question as to why these are worded in the way they are, is the question why they are formulated as such. By doing so, one ascribes a meaning to music, attributing a value to it. Music thus receives a meaning, a surplus value. Exactly those people who have a predilection for underground or so-called 'alternative' music are the ones who talk about it in this particular manner. They interpret pop music, and at the same time express a normative, qualitative judgment. That is why the difference between pop and rock is more than a journalistic cliché. Rock is also a cultural construct (which, it might be added, is much broader than 'guitar rock' alone).

In the previous chapter, the alternative mainstream was defined as a structurally separate segment in the pop music circuit. A matter of greater importance, however, is to try to understand the way in which in this segment value is ascribed or attributed to cultural products. In this chapter, which keenly concerns itself with theory, the central question is whether it is possible to detect specific, culturally shared beliefs and values in the alternative mainstream. The approach further relies on what diverse *popular music studies* have to say about certain recurrent value judgments about rock music. In the pop music circuit, the typical aesthetics of rock will distinguish between pop and rock, and this reveals itself best in the so-called 'canon of rock.' The question to ask is how this aesthetics and canon (as a mechanism of distinction) facilitate the segmentation of the pop music circuit, and what exactly might be the function of this discourse? To what extent does an ideological dimension characterize the aesthetics of rock, and how does this aesthetics purport to conceal and mask the economic practice of the music industry?

The Aesthetics of Rock

Rock versus Pop

As a cultural construct, the alternative mainstream is defined by the totality of beliefs, values and norms that are the connecting thread running through the rock discourse. One of these important values of rock culture is, for example, that rock should be a 'symbol of self-expression,' or negatively formulated, that 'rock must never be commercial.' The value can also be interpreted as a sign of distinction, a desire for, and pursuit of, status.[1] Music lovers who choose rock would rather not be associated with the mainstream, which they regard as commercial. They like to distance themselves, and to *distinguish* themselves from the segment. To make music out of commercial objectives and to create or embody music with some degree of artistic integrity are like day and night, two entirely different things. Alternatively, as Iain Chambers (1985: 119) puts it: '"Real" or "authentic" music, opposed to the commercial pap of pop.' It is fairly typical that a university college that calls itself 'Fontys *Rock* Academy' chose to reserve space for 'rock' in its name, making sure that the outside world would never get the impression that the college provides an education for pop stars. Pop, after all, has a negative connotation: surely commerce and entertainment or not a place for respected artists? Radiohead is all right, but Backstreet Boys is definitely not. At best, mainstream music is a reason to smile (by mocking 'dead wrong music'). The music press, too, thinks in this way, De Meyer says. He calls it a form of rock racism:

> The singers of schmaltz, Flemish songs and poppy tunes receive no attention whatsoever from the side of the politically correct pop critics. On the contrary: if it's anything like possible, the popular genres are mercilessly put to the sword.
> (De Meyer 2010: 93)

Thus, the old opposition between 'highbrow' and 'lowbrow' culture gets an encore, but now within the field of pop music. It is strange to see it manifest itself here, because the opposition originated from the battle fought in the field. Dating back to the rise of modernity, but reaching momentum in the post-WW2 era, a constant war has been waged against popular culture by the proponents of the classical arts. All cultural products that were produced and distributed in a mass market and 'consumed' by a non-specialist public, as though they meant nothing more than recreational products, belonging to leisure activities, are assessed by the afore-mentioned proponents as inferior and a menace to 'serious' culture. (De Meyer 1995: 65-74). Proponents of pop music who resent that others label their music as 'light music,' use the same distinction between artistic and commercial (or between art and kitsch). For this reason, they use the same arguments as the proponents of highbrow culture or the opponents of lowbrow culture.

The distinction between highbrow and lowbrow made its entrance in pop history in the late 1960s, when rock music decided that it had been around long enough to declare itself grown up (see Keunen 2002). From then on, the artists' motives for making music had to cease being commercial once and for all, whatever the dependency of the industry on commerce and regardless of their being active in the same industry. Rock musicians had to have a story to tell or a point to make, and they were not (solely) in it for the money or because the music industry prescribed it in that way. Simon Frith aptly describes the opposition between the rock and the pop of the 1970s as follows:

> Rock bands addressed a market of hip, largely male music freaks that bought LPs. (...) Rock music meant long studio sessions, rich and elaborate sound patterns: this was the music that was meant for expensive stereo sets, FM radio and college gigs. This sort of music was marketed without any appeal to the mass teenage taste. It did not meet the demands of a weekend of dancing for the working class youth, it sounded mismatched for a cheap transistor radio, and it had scarcely any idols to decorate the walls of the teenagers' bedrooms. (...) Pop was sold in dance halls and discos, on 'Top of the Pops' and Radio Luxemburg. Pop was bought by a mass market, of dancing, hit-crazy, female fans.
> (Frith 1984: 232-233)

Although the description is more suited to the progressive rock of the 1970s than it is to today's guitar rock, every time the important aspect is respect in '*the* music scene.' Another example: today Jamie Lidell enjoys greater credibility than Justin Bieber, just as in the glam rock of the 1970s David Bowie 'deserved' more respect than Gary Glitter did, whatever the extent of his success. In the words of Street:

> Chart-oriented pop can be distinguished from rock, for
> example, by the emphasis on live performance and by
> the character of its audience. Rock's following tends to
> be male; pop fans tend to be younger and female. (...) In
> rock, there is the ethos of self-expression, which draws an
> intimate tie between the personal and the performance.
> In pop, and in other musical forms like soul, this connec-
> tion does not weigh so heavily. (...) Rock and pop stars
> play to different rules.
> (Street 1986: 5)

Before going on with the argument, two main things should be noted. The first, deliberately repeating what was said in the previous chapter, is that in popular music studies the terms 'mainstream' and 'underground' have widely divergent meanings, which can often be contradictory. Usually, pop is associated with 'mainstream,' rock with 'alternative' or 'underground.' But it is equally possible that rock is considered to be mainstream (Kärjä 2006), that the real underground is never mentioned, or that underground and alternative are merely synonymous. Here lies the first reason why this study needed to introduce the term 'alternative mainstream': to be able to distinguish the rock music discussed in this section from niche music (underground) and popular entertainment (mainstream), and thus follow with greater precision the cultural distinction made in the practice of pop.

Apart from that, the term 'rock' is too limiting. The academic writer quoted in this chapter primarily deals with 'rock' music, while the qualities attributed to 'rock' can just as well be applied to some forms of electronic dance or hip-hop. A similar observation goes for the term 'alternative.' In pop music discourse, the term often refers to guitar rock groups starting from the 1990s (by extension also for singer-songwriters or the forms of electronic Dance that were accepted by the Rock press). Yet the concept of rock covers more than the abovementioned genres and eras. The term 'rock' needs to be stretched and opened up to cover all music to which people attribute similar values. All the more so because this study wishes to use the term 'pop music' as a 'container' or umbrella name that covers the various forms of rock, apart from electronic music and what is commonly considered 'pop.'

The central issue is indeed the symbolic action, the values attributed to the music. Here lies another reason why it is important to talk about 'alternative mainstream.' Alternative mainstream is not a music style. A cultural construct reaches beyond rock alone. The outcome of all this is that readers should convert or mentally translate 'rock' into 'mainstream' for the rest of the argument. The term will continue to pop up, because the current literature remains the point of reference. Readers should simply view the distinction between rock and pop as the alternative mainstream purporting to distinguish itself from the mainstream.

The alternative mainstream's typical values come to the fore in two aspects. On the one hand, they are contained in what the literature calls 'the aesthetics of rock' (at least since Richard Meltzer's book). On the other hand, they are embedded in the social context and the sense of group belonging. The next sections go more deeply into both of these aspects.

The Rock Canon and the Romantic View of Art

To distinguish rock from pop, and to regard certain forms of music as better or superior to other forms, does not merely indicate the beliefs and values that characterize the alternative mainstream. It also points in the direction of a specific aesthetics that is active in the pop music circuit. To find out what this aesthetics looks like, an examination is needed of the music that is believed to be the 'better form of pop music.' This system of normative judgments reveals itself most profoundly through the 'canon,' the rock canon. Pop music discourse perhaps rarely uses it, even though the content that it denotes is tacit knowledge, always assumed (Jones 2008: 119). Briefly put, the canon is formed by the music that all actors think has resisted the ravages of time and thus has earned its rightful place in the collective memory. Drawing up such a canon is not a simple task.

Even so, in the past decade, articles and books about the rock canon have become more frequent in popular music studies

(Jones 2008, Shuker 2008 and a thematic issue of *Popular Music* from 2006). Only the music that is best at meeting the requirements of the aesthetics of rock stands a chance of being admitted to the rock canon. In a way, the canon is the interim outcome of the battle that is continuously fought in the field (see further on). The canon does not contain all music that certain actors would count as the alternative mainstream, but only the timeless classic (the canonized alternative mainstream, as Bourdieu would probably label it). This book is more concerned with the gateways, entrances or accesses to the canon than with such classics. It focuses on the decisions on whether or not to select music at a given time and the actions that follow from them. The aesthetic values that are embedded in such a canon are a good point of departure in determining the aesthetics of the alternative mainstream. Antti-Ville Kärjä (2006: 18) also notes music genres are often defined by way of their canonized chart-toppers or smash hits. Therefore, the next section will list the main characteristics of canonized music.

The Rock Canon

The word 'canon' derives from official religious language. It was used to refer to the list of saints and sacred books.[2] Somewhere along the way, the art world adopted the term. In art canonization, it refers to the process of selection of those things that are deemed worthy of being repeated over and over again and being kept alive in memory (Kärjä 2006: 5). The outcomes of this process are artists and works that have successfully stood up to the ravages of time, and have become more valuable and ever more lasting in time. Examples are Shakespeare in literature, Rembrandt and Picasso in visual arts, or Bach, Beethoven and Mozart in classical music.

> A canon is the collection of works and artists that are widely accepted as the greatest in their field. (...) These works are passed down from one generation to the next, and the artists are celebrated in histories and honored with centennials. (...) Such a reductive account of history and culture masks a complex and contradictory set of values and mechanisms that have been passed down over the years in the form of the canon.
> (Jones 2008: 5)

A traditional canon really only exists in the world of the 'highbrow arts.' People study the canon in schools and universities, perform the canon in concert halls, and exhibit the canon in galleries and museums (Jones 2008: 5). Although it may be altogether less clear-cut and pronounced, the process of canonization can also occur in pop music. This is easily deduced from the lists of 'best albums.' Ralf Von Appen and André Doehring (2006) conducted a comparative study of several album top-100s. They drew up a meta-list of 30 albums, based on 38 lists that were compiled between 1985 and 2004. Of these lists, 14 had been drawn up by critics; the origin of the remaining 24 was the public. The majority of lists, 23 to be exact, originated in the U.S. or the U.K., but the researchers also included Dutch and Flemish lists in the study. The image below shows the albums that made it on the list.

1 **The Beatles** *Revolver,* 1966
2 **The Beatles** *Sgt. Pepper's Lonely Hearts Club Band,* 1967
3 **Nirvana** *Nevermind,* 1991
4 **The Beatles** *White Album,* 1968
5 **The Beach Boys** *Pet Sounds,* 1966
6 **The Beatles** *Abbey Road,* 1969
7 **Pink Floyd** *Dark Side of the Moon,*1973
8 **The Velvet Underground** *The Velvet Underground & Nico,* 1967
9 **Bob Dylan** *Blonde on Blonde,* 1966
10 **Radiohead** *OK Computer,* 1997
11 **Van Morrison** *Astral Weeks,* 1968
12 **The Rolling Stones** *Exile on Main St.,* 1972
13 **Marvin Gaye** *What's Going On,* 1971
14 **The Sex Pistols** *Never Mind the Bollocks,* 1977
15 **Bob Dylan** *Highway 61 Revisited,* 1965
16 **U2** *The Joshua Tree,* 1987
17 **Radiohead** *The Bends,* 1995
18 **The Stone Roses** *The Stone Roses,* 1989
19 **The Clash** *London Calling,* 1979
20 **Bob Dylan** *Blood on the Tracks,* 1975
21 **Jimi Hendrix Experience** A*re You Experienced?,* 1967
22 **The Smiths** *The Queen Is Dead,* 1986
23 **R.E.M.** *Automatic for the People,* 1992
24 **Fleetwood Mac** *Rumours,* 1977

25 **U2** *Achtung Baby,* 1991
26 **Pearl Jam** *Ten,* 1992
27 **Bruce Springsteen** *Born to Run,* 1975
28 **The Beatles** *Rubber Soul,* 1965
29 **The Rolling Stones** *Let It Bleed,* 1969
30 **Oasis** *(What's the Story) Morning Glory?,* 1995
   (*The Mother of All Greatest Albums Top-30s* as revealed by
   Von Appen & Doehring 2006: 23)

Even on the face of it, a list such as the one above displays a number of striking characteristics. Bands with classic, traditional complement produced nearly all of the abovementioned albums. All the albums were major releases. A more obvious point of interest is that they were exclusively made by Anglo-Saxon artists. Add to this that white, male performers mainly populated classic rock, that few or none of the artists were black or female, and anyone can get the general idea. Equally relevant is the fact that the history of music is marked by one period that shows the highest intensity or frequency in canonization: the mid-1960s to the mid-1970s. The oldest album dates from 1964, and the larger part of the list was produced in the sixties and seventies (64%), while the eighties and the nineties each produced a meager 12% (although this could very well shift up with one generation)

The list has a clear-cut delineation, which betrays the presence of aesthetic criteria (Von Appen & Doehring 2006). It is no coincidence, and therefore hardly surprising, that there is no room here for Bill Haley or the Bee Gees, that the 'awkward' 1980s are underrepresented, or even that not *Please Please Me* but *Revolver* by The Beatles is on the list. In the development or formation of a canon certain genres, styles and artists are omitted, deliberately shunned, and particular elements of 'roots' are preferred above others (blues, for instance, is 'more relevant' than Tin Pan Alley's popular song) (Kärjä 2006: 12). This, actually, may function as a general statement about the entire rock discourse. Keith Negus (2002: 512) arrived at the conclusion that the British music industry favors rock artists above pop or soul and that conventional white, male guitar groups are approached from a long-term perspective, while soul and R&B are experienced as ad hoc. Roy Shuker (2008: 121), too, notices a broadly accepted high/low-antithesis within pop music, because critics, fans and artists treated pop genres as disco and dance in a denigrating manner. In the same logic, albums are 'better' than singles: they are accorded higher value in the normative construction.

It is typical of the individual nature of the alternative mainstream and of the concomitant aesthetics, that music considered 'too' underground or 'too' mainstream, or alien to the 'respected' genres, is not admitted to the canon. A list of the best albums is indeed an entirely different thing than a list with the best-selling albums. International bestsellers (such as *Thriller* by Michael Jackson or *Back in Black* by AC/DC) are nowhere to be found on the list.

Carys Wyn Jones (2008) also carried out a far-reaching, thorough analysis of similar lists. She compared the lists with one another and singled out ten albums[3] as the basis for a content analysis of CD reviews. She found the latter in articles and books that featured exactly the kind of lists discussed here. They are of the 'classic rock albums' type, include well-known series such as *The Rough Guide To* as well as special editions of music magazines about certain artists and masterpieces. Jones does not discuss pop music in its totality, but rather as a specific category in the (rock) music defined by albums. The aim of her study was to investigate and analyze the way in which a canon of classic albums is built in the realm of rock music, and to examine to what extent this canon is built and is further developed based on canonical models in literature and classical music. Thus, it appears that rock music's artistic perception and expression of value judgments are still very much the product of a Romantic view of art, developed in the classical arts from the 18th century onwards. As I hope will become clear from the argument, it makes sense to dwell a little longer on this view, and look at the specific effect it had on artistic perception with respect to rock and pop.

The Romantic View of Art

In communication about art, artistic perception is dominated by an individualized view of art. Art is the outcome of the creative expressions of artists and people should judge or evaluate their works as autonomous and isolated objects (the line of reasoning here follows Rudi Laermans' argument in Laermans 2004). The assumption, also pointed out by Howard S. Becker (1982: 14), is that the creation of art requires a special talent, a gift or a knowledge and skill that only few people possess, and that everybody can learn to know and understand this extraordinary talent through the works created by the artist. In the oeuvre developed by the artist the works are felt to refer to each other and the artist is perceived as a genius at work. An oeuvre, therefore, is an isolated, individual and coherent whole that shows the artist's individuality, his or her personal talent and capacity to 'remain true to him- or herself.' The basic assumption, indeed, is that artists do not live off their art, but for their art. Art must always be a vocation and cannot be determined by external factors or social pressure. At most, success is a gift received after the fact. To phrase this with Weber's concepts: the artist acts in a value-rational, and not in a goal-rational manner.

In this sort of discourse, the starting point is a Romantic view of art. The belief in the validity of this view has deep roots, originating in or through modernity (Calinescu 1977). As the 18th century ended, the cultural field evolved as an autonomous space. As a result of the 'functional differentiation process,' art detached itself from other social institutions and was no longer created in active service of the sovereign, the church, the aristocrat, the patron or in paid employment by certain actors (see also Elias 1983, Wolff 1987 and Drijkoningen & Fontijn 1986). Consequently, art ceased to fulfill an instrumental and serving function. Artists stop occupying a subordinate or subservient position and are able to act independently and according to their own insights. They can now retire into their ivory towers, and dedicate themselves and their work to the pursuit of the principle of *l'art pour l'art*, art that produces art for its own sake. It did not take long for the concept of the genius to kick in, reinforcing the idea that a work of art is the outcome of a transcendent personality. (Van den Braembussche 2007: 194). Thus, it should not come as a surprise that art is frequently defined as 'the utmost individual expression of the utmost individual personality.' Romanticism, consequently, takes individuality, originality, as well as virtuosity as its central tenets. The Romantics dismiss the principle of order and rationality pursued by classicism. In their view, creativity overrules any conformism to formal rules (De Meyer 2010: 280, Becker 1982: 15 and Van den Braembussche 2007: 112). The logical outcome of this belief is that artists hold a position above any law of art, and even any law of society. Typical of the Romantic Movement is, after all, the key importance of emotional discharge, of *Sturm und Drang*. Romantics are always in turmoil and unrest, constantly searching. They are sensitive and sentimental creatures, highly tuned in to the senses and dominated by the sentiments (a neutral term, used in the 18th and 19th century to denote 'feelings' or 'emotions'). Their pursuit is that of the irrational, the imaginary, the indomitable, and the realm of emotions (see p. 135).

Rock and Romanticism

A similar aesthetics has also permeated pop music. Jones (2008: 27 and 39) observes that the guiding elements in the discourse about canonized albums are Romantic values. Terms in the style of 'masterpiece, sublime, *classic*, genius, originality, craftsmanship, complexity, honesty, authenticity, genuineness and personal struggle' are the most typical which she found returning in reviews of the albums. Von Appen and Doehring (2006) observe the same network of recurrent values. At first, they detected a cluster about values such as innovation, expression and authenticity. At a later stage, a cluster crystallized around originality, homogeneity, complexity or simplicity and 'beauty.' There is no sign of a generally accepted hierarchical order ruling the use and effect of these values, but there can be no doubt that authenticity is the value that leads the way. In Frith's words:

> The rock aesthetic depends, crucially, on an argument about authenticity. Good music is the authentic expression of something – a person, an idea, a feeling, a shared experience, a Zeitgeist. (...) The suggestion is that pop music becomes more valuable the more independent it is of the social forces that organize the pop process in the first place; pop value is dependent on something outside pop, is rooted in the person, the auteur, the community or the subculture that lies behind it. If good music is authentic music, then critical judgment means measuring the performers' 'truth' to the experiences or feelings, they are describing.
> (Frith 1987: 136)

Artistic motives must always come first and unconditionally be of greater importance than commercial motives. Michèle Ollivier's study (2006: 103-107) also gives evidence of this normative distinction. Authenticity is the leading criterion for prestige. Only when people show courage, emotion, and give proof of their integrity and honesty, are they regarded as talented, creative and credible. In the same sense, Jones (2008: 30 and 66) notes that the reception of a rock album is invariably marked by emphasizing the work's aesthetic power and never by highlighting its commercial success, regardless of the absolute fact that the album is in all possible aspects a commercial product. This explains why the canon only lists works by 'authors' and does not admit music made for functional reasons, such as scores or soundtracks, nor compilation albums produced for visibly exclusive economic motives. As De Meyer sums up the characteristics of the authentic artists:

> They are the artists who speak their mind or talk from the heart, believe in what they sing, and are not afraid of any personal unburdening of the mind. They are credible, but not too confident, and mysterious. They steer clear from pop clichés in arrangements, from bombast and grandiloquence or sentimentality, yet hint at the deeper layers of their work. They avoid coming across as artificial, pretentious or contrived, and will never settle for the so-called commercial sell-out, whatever the consequences. They are the artists who play 'real' instruments (not electronic devices), and who can never be accused of faking, on the contrary, often stress the purity of the genres they perform. (De Meyer 2010: 5)[4]

Jones (2008: 39) adds a legitimate observation. She argues that artists become more credible and authentic proportionate to the degree to which they need to suffer for their art. The result is undiluted myth making. Artists as myths, as Romantic geniuses, are different from the other people who surround them. This difference in status explains the significance of qualitative criteria such as originality and individuality. Geniuses are expected to come up with individual styles, they cannot produce anything that looks or sounds or reads like something by somebody else. Copying is *the* taboo. Breaking the boundaries or rules of genres begets positive evaluation. Take Bob Dylan, for instance, who redefined rock music. Take Marvin Gaye, who pushed the boundaries of soul into uncharted territory (Jones 2008: 30-31). For artists to desire to be autonomous, entails the obligation to write their own work.

Since the 1960s, this has indeed become the standard reality of the music world (Keunen 2002). Songwriters have more prestige than performers, arrangement writers, and session musicians or cover artists. This is the necessary condition. If not met, artists are not creative, original, or authentic.

Typical of the canon is that it includes artists who are able to present and represent a sizeable oeuvre. The oeuvre becomes the framework or touchstone for any evaluation of the individual works. *Exile On Main St.* by The Rolling Stones is not so much praised because of its originality, but because the group had reached a peak in (representing) a particular style (Jones 2008: 34). Albums that are too experimental do not appear in the lists of *greatest albums* (the form of music that is discussed in a magazine such as *The Wire*, for instance, is considered too 'underground' for a canon). This can only be the case when time has shown that the album had a great influence on other artists (as is demonstrated by *Velvet Underground & Nico*). Once certain artists have been admitted to the canon, their work is labeled as good. Possible shortcomings are ignored, any errors are glossed and the veil of approval is cast over the past as a whole. This is true of certain groups that started out as too poppy, but evolved in a different, now worthy direction. Only when they stopped touring and retreated into the studio, far from screaming teenager girls, were The Beatles taken seriously. The occasionally bathetic, banal tunes from the early years ('one inch off throwaway-music,' as producer George Martin describes it; BBC 1996) are considered as a first step to the later 'masterful' records. Groups need to possess a certain amount of maturity, if they want to stand a chance of being admitted to the canon. Apart from this, they need to have withstood the *test of time*: fast hit success or cultural fast food is not appreciated (Ollivier 2006: 103-104). Jones sums up the characteristics of canonized music:

> The ideal work can be conceived of as an album that is a coherent body of work as a whole (not singles with 'filler'), that possesses the canonical criteria of originality, complexity and truth and is associated with an autonomous artist/genius. This idealized 'canonical' album demands repeated listening and can sustain multiple interpretations, has withstood the test of time and influenced subsequent albums, but it is also complete in

itself, forming an object of endless study and value.
Jones 2008: 42

A Self-Willed Aesthetics of Rock

The aesthetics of rock is largely in keeping with the aesthetics that is (or has been?) dominant in the classical arts. Nevertheless, there are differences. This may indicate that a separate aesthetics is active in pop music that only applies to itself. There are parameters that are central to the evaluations made by critics of classical music, but remain absent in pop music: formal features, for instance, concerning harmonics, melody and rhythm, complexity of the composition and instrument virtuosity in performing. In pop music, it is the *sound* that matters, and that is as far as aesthetic qualitative criteria go. The *sound* is the pinnacle of quality control, however vague the explanation of the concept may be. What it seems to indicate, is the elusive physical and emotional make-up or quality that characterizes much of the pop music (Shuker 2008: 97).

This is also obvious inside the studio, where another meaning of the notion of authenticity surfaces. Pop records are often experienced as more authentic when they sound primitive and raw. The use of lo-fi vintage equipment and not too many over-dubs, gives a more credible, uncommercial and uncompromising impression (Bannister 2006: 84). Because a live performance feels superior to music lovers, 'live in the studio' has become the touch-stone for record production (although spontaneity and improv can just as well be a deliberately constructed effect). This *pure sound* is also a criterion to assess musicians. At times they are self-taught non-professionals (Jones 2008: 86-87). Rock is proud of its amateur feeling, a mentality of do-it-yourself and anti-intellectualism.

Other typical rock values are its youthful disposition, hedonism (liquor, cigarettes and drugs), the importance of an image (also in promos and CD inlays), nihilism, a touch of the rebel, social contestation (resistance against the elder generation or against society or the system) and the slowly developed career following long years of hard labor (Jones 2008: 87-92 and Frith 1981). It does not end with the significance of the rock personality. The concept of genius too may acquire a different interpretation in pop music. There is the individual genius (Dylan), but there is also the collective genius (The Beatles), in which the whole has indeed become greater than the sum of its parts (Jones

2008: 80-81). Equally, a criterion such as originality can acquire a different meaning in rock than in the traditional aesthetics. Here it may indicate, among other things, the strange or weird tone of new sounds, the poetic dimension of the lyrics, innovation inside the studio and the role of the producer.

Rock and Community

The values rock (alternative mainstream) uses to legitimize itself before other forms of music, are not exclusively found in (Romantic) aesthetics, but also in a sense of belonging to a group, a social bond or 'in-group feeling.' In rock culture, the idea of the *rock community* is of central importance. It is the belief in a connection or bond between performers and audience (see also Negus 1996: 149, Grossberg 1992 and Frith 1981, 1984 and 1987). According to Frith (1981: 159) this idea came into being in the 1960s when rock received an injection of folk and proceeded to interpret and profile itself by means of folk values. Music was viewed as an authentic reflection of an individual experience or social situation, and rock as an expression of a way of life. Street (1986: 214) is wholly in accord. He believes pop fans are isolated consumers that assemble, unite, and mass because of their essentially individualist wish for consumption. Rock music lovers, by contrast, are brought together by a sense of community, by a common, shared experience.

Indie Rock
A textbook example of this value system, both with respect to the aesthetics and the in-group feeling, is found in the form of guitar rock that was also dubbed *alternative rock* by the press (covering British indie rock and American grunge of the 1990s). Because of its double position, this musical current can also rank as the prototype of alternative mainstream: a music world that is proud of its independence and fights shy of the mainstream yet cannot be called 'underground' any longer. In pop literature and the media, indie rock is considered 'alternative' and even a specific kind of *underground*. As will become clear, it has a hard time asserting a claim to that status when the distinction mechanism becomes active. Again, the fact that the underground label is used in this case provides a reason why this study insists on speaking of 'alternative mainstream.'

The theorists of pop have written much about this type of music. American anthropologist Wendy Fonarow studied the British indie scene for ten whole years. She found that indie is essentially a notion of great vagueness — a usual, even frequent property of cultural categories — and one that bundles many definitions. The term can refer to a music genre, a specific mode of production and distribution or a way of life (Fonarow 2006: 25-78).

First, as a music genre indie is a subcategory of rock (this is a deliberate generalization, not limited to the British variant studied by Fonarow). This music originated from the punk scene and had its breakthrough in the mid-1980s. The music can be either punk-oriented or based on pop and rock of the 1960s (a distinction that also took shape in the 1990s when grunge was differentiated from Britpop, which continues to characterize the sound of rock today; see Keunen 2002). As main stylistic features of indie rock Fonarow (2006: 50) mentions guitar- and song-oriented, melodic, devoid of solos and technological decoration, rudimentary and 'pure' (The White Stripes, Franz Ferdinand, Arcade Fire, Bloc Party etc.). Hesmondhalgh (1999: 38) adds that indie built a canon with references to white underground rock. Well thought-out and/or sensitive lyrics related to the singer-songwriter tradition lead the way, leaving no room for funky rhythms and dance beats that head the charts, and neither for blues-based 1970s rock (*cock rock*) or black dance music. The aesthetics of rock rejects 'pop' and mainstream rock, but also shuns excesses such as metal (Shuker 2008: 125-127). A typical symptom of this exclusion is the fact that the Netherlands-based *OOR's Pop Encyclopedie* first three editions (1982, 1984, 1986) classified all hard rock and metal under the ironic heading 'Zware Jongens,' for lack of a better term.[5]

Secondly, from the music industry's perspective, indie music is a mode of distribution. Independent music is released on independent labels, but is by definition also distributed by an independent distributor. Hesmondhalgh (1999: 35 and 41) points out that never before a music genre derived its name from the industrial organization that operated behind it. The indie scene set up a new, independent infrastructure, detached from the major corporations. It became an underground network with indie record labels, releases on the artists' own account, specialized shops, concert clubs, fanzines and *college radios*. Music lovers without formal training, amateurs that learned the profession along the way, put up this infrastructure.

According to Matthew Bannister (2006), however, this indie scene did not grow organically out of the punk networks, but was a child born from the media. Indie fans view themselves as critics and read magazines such as *NME* (*New Musical Express*) and *Melody Maker*: consequently, they are the determining factors in the formation of the indie story. Others too put their mark on the story: the *college radios*, for instance, which made sure that the bands, could break through or gain a cult status, without any help from a major record company (Kruse 1993: 33). Around these *college radios,* a subculture arose, uniting musicians, fans, label owners, record dealers and radio deejays.

For the most part, these and similar alternative music scenes can be defined geographically, but they also share the community or in-group feeling and are connected with each other by shared interests and tastes. This is the reason why indie is also a way of life, constituting the third element in Fonarow's definition. In her own words, it is an *ethos*, in which autonomy, being independent from and vis-à-vis society is the central point. It is a countercultural resistance against the market, a specific subculture, which allows its members to distinguish themselves from the mainstream culture.

The indie culture is further marked by the fact that indie artists and indie lovers are also record collectors who like to refer to the classics of the genre (Hesmondhalgh 1999: 36 and 47). Getting to know the old records and gaining the status of connoisseurship forms an initiation rite (rite of passage) for younger artists, a condition for their admittance to and acceptance by the scene. In this process, record dealers and small labels fulfill the role of mentors and tastemakers for the musicians. The canon functions as a collective point of reference, a tool to learn to know the history of music and to spread cultural capital, even though this is never said with so many words in the public discourse (Bannister 2006: 82-86 and Straw 1991: 378). For fear of making the wrong the impression, coming across not cool or original enough, musicians keep their cars close to their chest and rather not show that they 'know a lot.' Nevertheless, freedom of the indie culture in the political economy (no major labels) is paired with artistic integrity and aesthetic quality (Hibbett 2005: 58). It is no secret that indie is at the same time an aesthetic value judgment: music is only good when it is honest and genuine, and the outcome of an independent, artistic quest.

The indie scene is also a battleground where — as was pointed out before — the opposing forces of highbrow and lowbrow may get at it again. Indie feels superior, more authentic than mainstream.

> Indie ideology views their music as raw and immediate, while mainstream music is regarded as processed and mediated by 'overproduction'; indie bands can reproduce their music in concert and even improve upon it, while mainstream bands use too many electronic effects to reproduce their music live.
> (Shuker 2008: 21)

Certainly, the indie eyes, and thus the artists, are better served with a second-hand touring van than with a modern, fully equipped touring bus cruising from stadium to stadium. Mainstream is associated with large-scale production, not indie. Indie needs to remain as small-scale as possible. Indie label Beggars Banquet's Martin Mills is right on track when he says:

> The priority for majors is to make quick bucks for their shareholders. (...) When you are trying to ensure you hit the top of the charts, then you tend to be more formulaic. Independents tend to take a long-term view, and see themselves as providing a cultural service rather than running a business.
> (Martin Mills, in: *Billboard* 27.01.2007)

Indie and Underground Logic

Apart from the position occupied by 'alternative' music in the music industry — more about this in 2.3 — it is striking to see how the music scene maintains an underground logic. In an underground environment, the illusion of the audience being able to make personal and direct contact with the artists is still real. Artists personally take charge of merchandising after a concert. In small venues, artists and members of the public can even buy each other a drink. Whereas in the mainstream the moment of production and that of consumption are increasingly separated from each other, it is the underground's desire to restore a sense of intimacy. The community feeling prevails and music is an expression of solidarity. People want to be part of the scene; the crowd wants to become part of the in-crowd. Because the environment has created its own channels, a specific in-group feeling surfaces: this is a group with its own musical values and customs, with a specific view on how music should be made and how it should sound. Those who share the group feeling, have put on the right (sub)cultural glasses or 'genre specs' (a concept which was at the center of a previous publication; see Keunen 1996). The music, indeed, can only be fully appreciated with the right genre glasses. Outsiders, by contrast, will have a hard time to see through or penetrate to the heart. As a result, they will more easily reject it. In her study of British club culture and electronic dance music Sarah Thornton (1995: 11-14) puts forward the notion of subcultural capital, as a complement to Bourdieu's concept. Those who wear the right clothes in the dance scene have the right records; they know the dance steps and master the language without having to put much effort into it; and they possess the hipness of sufficient subcultural capital. This capital is a sign of distinction and is therefore defined and distributed via the subculture's own media (fanzines, flyers, pirate stations, etc.).

Because of this, underground has the likings of a secret society, functioning as an honorary nickname or sobriquet (Heesterbeek 2002). To an underground artist, the only thing that matters is respect in the underground environment itself. Within this environment, conflicts can arise, the stakes being either the preservation of the 'real' group feeling, or — because of the outspoken *we*-nature and in relation to other genres — the ultimate genre itself (*us versus them*). But regardless of family feuds or tribal disputes being fought out or not (see Keunen 1996), what serves as a glue in the underground environment is the sure-thing rejection of something that is the absolute antithesis of underground in the eyes of the underground itself (however ambivalent this feeling may be): the commercial music industry. No wonder then that artists who sign a major deal and manage to break through in the (alternative) mainstream thanks to the contract are often considered traitors by the underground environment, or even accused of selling out. As Thornton (1995: 124) evocatively phrases the matter: '"selling out" means *selling* to *out*siders.' Think to think of the career turn made by Metallica, or the crossover ventured by Sepultura, Sick of It All or Sonic Youth.

Hesmondhalgh (1999) conducted a study of label One Little Indian, put up by musicians formerly belonging to punk group

Crass, and thus obviously rooted in the idea of independence and collective or cooperative participation. He recalls how the punk activists were very unhappy with Björk's first solo record on One Little Indian. The album was too soft. It was not simply *over*produced, but *too* overproduced. It was, in short, at total odds with their lo-fi punk attitude. The fact of the matter is that artistic success, defined in accordance with its own norms, is the underground's mainspring. Other parameters apply, which inevitably differ from those employed by the (alternative) mainstream. Symbolic and aesthetic values must prevail over economic and commercial values. In fact, in underground eyes the latter do not even qualify as values. Exactly this or similar underground logic is used by indie and other 'alternative' rock — or, more generally, the alternative mainstream — to distinguish themselves from the 'pop' mainstream.

Selections and Canonization in Pop Music as a Social Process

The Romantic view of art survives remarkably well in the pop circuit. The view lies at the foundation of the canon and aesthetics of rock, or more generally the alternative mainstream. Sociologists, though, love to debunk this view as a myth. Artists, after all, belong to a social network, a necessary condition for any realization of their wish to be seen and looked at as artists. From the day artists started to offer their work to an anonymous audience on the free art market, an anonymous network came into being that linked up producers with consumers. The fact that other players have taken position right in the middle of this direct communication, and that these guard the access roads, is simply the price artists must pay in exchange for their independence (Elias 1983: 216-217). In Bourdieu's view, the image of the 'creating artist' is therefore a well-founded misrepresentation or deception:

> The ideology of the creating artist (...) conceals the fact
> that the art dealer (...) is not only the one who exploits
> the artist's work by turning the 'sacred' into a business
> thing or deal, but at the same time also the one who con-
> secrates a product (...) by 'discovering' it, putting it on the
> market, exhibiting, publishing or performing it.
> (Bourdieu 1989: 249-250)

Bourdieu calls this mechanism the consecration cycle: 'symbolic bankers' (publishers, gallery owners, academies, critics etc.) attach their reputation to works of art and thereby introduce them into the art world. Thus, art is the result of a social process. The players in the music industry and the media are those who confer a surplus value on certain music in the selection process. In other words, aesthetic classification schemas do not arise organically from the content of music (or other cultural texts), but are the outcome of the collective actions of people who are involved in the artistic process. Aesthetic classification schemas are constructions that are slowly developed and maintained by the interaction between the field participants. This is more or less the consensus. What the social process looks like in detail, is an entirely different matter and cause for great division and discussion among sociologists. Becker (1982) starts from the way in which people cooperate, the conventions that result from this cooperation and the manner in which all this leads to a consensus. Bourdieu (1984), by contrast, departs from a model of conflict. In his now famous view, a cultural field is a battlefield, the ground where a continuous war is waged between 'the powers that be' and 'the newcomers' or challengers. Because the balance between the two sides may constantly change, the value attribution to art may also never cease to be up for change.

The players in the cultural field are usually called *gatekeepers*, as they are in the widely cited and now classic *filter/flow-model* by Hirsch (1972). In the model, Hirsch shows how a new product gradually makes its way through the cultural industry. Every time it passes the different stages in the system (*flow*), it needs to be reselected (*filter*). From the artist, via the producers (record company, music publisher, and studio), distributors, shops and media, to the consumer: each time the right access or entrance (*gate*) needs to be opened. Yet because music selection is not a one-way traffic, the gatekeepers can also be viewed as 'cultural intermediaries.' The fact is that exchange arises between the persons or organizations that mediate between artist and consumers (Hesmondhalgh 2006: 226 and Negus 2002: 62).[6] They are co-determinants of the (surplus) meaning of cultural products, a process that is far from neutral. The intermediaries can exert power and influence on each other, which determines how music is produced.

Canonization in Pop Music

The development and establishment of a canon in the pop music circuit corresponds to Bourdieu's description of the consecration cycle. Here too a symbolic value is bestowed on culture, which is then elevated to the *doxa* or consensus (that is, the aesthetics of rock). Different from Bourdieu's view, however, is that the cultural in the practice of pop is equally influenced by the commercialization and marketing. Pop music disposes of other 'consecrating institutions' than the classical arts. A position resembling that of a gallery owner in the visual arts is hard to find in pop music, or it would have to be an artist manager or the head of a record company. In the latter case, the analysis immediately winds up in the economically oriented positions. Music in the pop music circuit is also 'consecrated' by the industry and the mass media. Music can only withstand the test of time, and it will only be appreciated by different generations, if it is first culturally reproduced. In addition, it must undergo a special treatment, which enables it to differentiate itself from other music. The instances of this cultural reproduction and treatment are various: books and articles are written about the music, and journalists form an opinion about it; recordings are distributed, promo campaigns are launched, and concerts are arranged; the music is heard on the radio, other producers respond to it, industry awards are won by it, etc. (see also Jones 2008: 67 and Hesmondhalgh 2006: 222).

Rock Critics and Aesthetics

Not all players, though, have an equal share in the process of canonization (which is also one of the central items in the research conducted for this book). The gravitational point in canonization turns out to be the media. So much that all researchers agree on this (Kärjä 2006: 17, Frith 1987: 136, Bannister 2006: 79, Regev 2002: 254, Van Venrooij 2009: 318, Jones 2008: 104). The press determines the dominant taste and the way in which history is interpreted and selectively re-interpreted. Canonization in the pop music circuit does proceed along an 'official' track, but passes through the pen and ink of non-professional fans who write about music and become professional journalists. Self-taught enthusiasts (Atton 2009: 56) typically populate rock journalism. Their knowledge of popular forms of culture is distilled from their consumer role. Besides, rock journalists are not simply fans, they also interpret the music they listen to and function as symbolic producers who create meaning or as ideological *gatekeepers*, as Frith calls then (1984: 182). They play a part in enabling the music to sell and they provide it with a cultural meaning.

From the late 1960s on, the music press gradually slipped into the role of *meaning maker.*[7] It was then that pop music was subjected to serious analysis for the first time, and that musicians were described in terms of being *auteurs* (Shuker 2008: 68 and 162-166, McLeese 2010: 439-440). In Great Britain and the United States, this new type of journalism was spread through music magazines such as *Rolling Stone* and *NME*. Articles were published about historical figures, trends and recordings, lists of *greatest albums* often accompanied by special compilations that gave shape to the popular memory. When books about styles and artists, essays, guides, encyclopedias and historical studies followed, it was clear that the formation of a canon had been set in

motion. This also explains why the aesthetics of rock dominated the discourse.

The discourse is not only found in the written or printed press, or by extension in radio broadcasting. Television, too, became a powerful medium in the realization of a canon. Fine examples of targeted, goal-oriented historiography are British music shows such as *The Old Grey Whistle Test*. Especially music documentaries such as *Classic Albums* (the *making of* 'classic albums') and the now 'renowned' BBC-documentaries about the history of rock (*Dancing in the Street, Walk on By, Seven Ages of Rock* etc.) were instrumental in objectifying the historically arbitrary selection. Consecrated players in film brought in the whole weight of prestige: think of Martin Scorsese's documentary films about Dylan, The Stones and *Blues*. They receive worldwide broadcasting on TV and are released and re-released on DVD or Blu-ray, thereby highlighting the historic importance of a particular type of performers. The fact is that the musicians and bands celebrated in this kind of documentaries are invariably the 'authentic' artists and icons of pop history, instead of the commercially most successful. A canon, therefore, is more than a simple operation of cataloguing or recording the past. It shapes and reinterprets this past and determines the way in which the public has to look at it.

It is hardly surprising that the most frequently canonized artists are considered inviolable. No man or woman can criticize The Beatles for no reason in particular other than the wish to express personal taste. In 2010, the famous Abbey Road pedestrian crossing was recognized for its 'cultural and historical importance,' following advice from English Heritage, and listed as a Site of National Importance.[8] In this respect some commentators make mention of 'rockism.' The term was coined by the Anglo-Saxon music press to bring up the biased preference for rock of journalists (Bannister 2006: 88) and since then it also pops up among academics (De Meyer 2010: 5). Wolk gives the following definition:

> Rockism (...) is treating rock as normative. In the rockist view, rock is the standard state of popular music: the kind to which everything else is compared, explicitly or implicitly.
> (Wolk 04.05.2005)

A good example of this 'rockism,' and of the way in which the sort of social process can contribute to mythologizing, is the notion of the *rock era*, as pop history was often described in earlier times (the story is found with Gillett 1983, Wicke 1987, Chambers 1985 and Frith 1988a). The *rock era* tells the story of music history as a narration with clearly demarcated ruptures, with a beginning and an ending, a birth and a death. The origin lies in the mid-1950s (with Elvis), a high point or apex is reached at the end of the 1960s (with *Sgt. Pepper's Lonely Hearts Club Band* by The Beatles), mere advance characterizes the bulk of the 1970s (symphonic rock), and the end comes with punk in the late 1970s (The Sex Pistols). Various publications refuse to have anything of this (Keunen 1996 and 2002, also Negus 1996: 136-139). The fact of the matter is that both the beginning and the end of the *rock era* are relative notions that depend on perspectives. Many classic 'rock' records (for instance, *Sgt. Pepper's*) offer much more than rock alone, and at the time of the 'classic rock albums' *The Sound of Music* was the most popular album of the 1960s. The story of rock can indeed be told in many different ways. Yet the fact itself that many people subscribe to the consensus about *the rock era* is telling of the (success of) canonization process. This is far from a neutral activity, as Negus (1996: 138) is right to point out. History is constructed by selecting particular sounds and by omitting other sounds. This is the reason why it is perfectly possible to keep on thinking of Bob Dylan or Led Zeppelin as the ultimate touchstone and consequently think that the music of the 1980s or electronic dance music is inferior.

Industry and Canon Formation

The press is not the only player in the development of the canon. The music industry's actions also have a great influence on the process. The truth is that only music that is distributed and promoted stands a chance of canonization. Marketing actions serve the purpose of attributing a surplus value to music. One of the strategies, for instance, is the repeated releasing of the back catalogue (*reissues*). This is the industry's way of stimulating further attention for the classics in the collective memory. A great occasion for doing this is the digital remastering of old records or of the complete back catalogue of famous bands. Birthdays or biographical facts also present a reason for the re-release of an album: George Harrison's death, the nth anniversary of

John Lennon's death, the nth birthday of *Sgt. Pepper's* etc.; or 10 and 20 years *Nevermind,* Kurt Cobain's death... The re-edition may get a unique touch if the record company adds previously unreleased material to the package, or publishes the CD with a booklet or a DVD. Reissues do not always come at a lower price: when the price is the same as a new release, the economic value underscores the symbolic value (Von Appen & Doehring 2006: 28).

The record industry is assisted in the process of myth making by the film world. This can be via a solo action or together with the record companies in a joint marketing campaign, since the record companies and film production or distribution companies are often part of the same mother entertainment concern (Shuker 2008: 150 & 155). The world of film brings surplus value when the artists are presented in a film (Elvis, The Beatles and Prince, for instance, had a marketing plan in which film was prominent), when it concerns concert films (*Woodstock, Monterey Pop, The Last Waltz, Gimme Shelter*) or in case of films based on 'real and rocking rock stories' (*The Doors, Last Days*). These films may have a commercial as well as a cultural impact. They capture specific moments in the history of rock and lend a positive surplus value to certain artists and music styles.

The general conclusion, therefore, is that promotional campaigns, marketing strategies and other actions have a powerful influence on the way people perceive artists and consecrate them. These are economic actions with cultural consequences. Ollivier (2006: 105-106) arrived at the conclusion that this sort of actions co-determine whether an artist is regarded as authentic or not. Her findings are in keeping with Peterson (1997) who argues that actors and organizations in the music industry socially construct authenticity through the continuous *authenticity work.*

A final example of the impact of social processes is the practice of award presentations. These may count as a kind of *gathering of the tribes* (similar to the VIP-tents at big festivals, where primarily social capital is exchanged or traded in an informal fashion). The award ceremonies are important moments where consecration is celebrated. As in literature, with the Booker Prize's great symbolic and commercial impact (the press writes about it, the winners get a special spot in the stores etc.), the awards or prizes such as the British Mercury Prize have an effect on the process of canonization. In this respect, Watson and Anand (2006) studied the impact of the Grammy Awards in the US. Because the presentation of these awards is based on a selection made by experts, only artistic merits count. As a result, a ceremony of this kind plays a critical role in the construction of prestige in the field: heroes are praised and symbolic capital is accumulated. In addition, these awards also bring in economic capital. The crowned artists can enjoy larger sales and thanks to the live coverage on MTV (and reports about this in the international press) enjoy greater media attention. The selection made by the experts inevitably has a great influence on the public's choices. Ollivier (2006) arrived at the same conclusion in a study of the Félix Awards in Quebec. The televised presentation allowed artists to reach a larger audience, which resulted in increased sales, access to foreign markets and extra attention at special events organized by the government (Ollivier 2006: 110). In Flanders, the MIA (Music Industry Awards) generates the same effect of massive attention on TV and in the press (in addition, it appears the sales go up dramatically, Post 14.01.2010). In the Netherlands the 3FM Awards and (to a lesser extent) the Edison awards have an identical touch of magic. These awards play their part in the consecration cycle (Bourdieu), but they also demonstrate that organizational processes have an impact on artistic careers and consumer markets (Peterson).

Canon, Distinction and Habitus

The effects of a canonization process are not as innocent as they may appear. A canon is also a strategy of distinction. Exactly by giving attention to *this particular* music and distinctly not to *that other* music, a strategy is activated of differentiating between what counts as 'art' and what does not. By taking a specific aesthetics and a specific sense of belonging to a community, rock (or, more generally, the 'alternative' mainstream) seeks to distinguish itself from pop (the 'real' mainstream). The canon is not only an authoritative, but also an authoritarian list of works and authors, because those who make the list are regarded by the establishment as truly and really great and because the list shows the superiority of one group over the other (Bannister 2006: 80). Similar conceptions of 'class struggle' and the pursuit of distinction in the sense Bourdieu gave to it, are found in many analyses by pop theorists. Take Von Appen and Doehring, for example:

They invest their cultural capital, their knowledge of music, and change it into social capital on the market, which the canon represents to them. (...) From the assumed artistic hierarchy of the records emerges a social hierarchy achieved through distinction from the mainstream. (...) They form a milieu around magazines or radio stations, in which they distinguish themselves quantitatively as well as qualitatively from those who consume mass products and genres of lower social prestige.
(Von Appen & Doehring 2006: 28-29)

Because critics, media and industry actors employ a canon that distinguishes them from others, some authors are led to conclude that they share the same taste and social background: male, white, from western countries, middle class, between 20 and 40 years of age, and having enjoyed a higher education. In Bourdieu's terms, these people share a habitus (interiorized and culturally determined classification schemas that are the result of social circumstances and in turn direct the actions, see Bourdieu 1984: 466-468). They are people with shared dispositions and values, situated in the same environment.

Typically, people from the alternative mainstream think of themselves as omnivores with regard to music. This is only true relatively speaking, because not all genres enjoy an equally high esteem. A study by Negus (2002: 512-513) carried out in the late 1980s and the 1990s about the key decision makers in the British music industry, confirms this. The cultural intermediaries come across as *open-minded* and very much in touch with 'the street,' yet their agendas do not offer the slightest reflection of the diversity of music existing in the UK. Their eyes are not always focused on the available talent or the public demand. Instead, they maintain a series of traditional borders and hierarchies that find their way in the manner of signing artists and going about marketing. The selections have mainly grown historically and have favored the development of a certain type of music industry. Thus, their shared values and joint experiences do not only give shape to the entrance gates of the music industry, they also determine the direction in which the industry is working.

The canon tells something about the frame of reference shared by the actors in the segment of the alternative mainstream. It is what drives the music industry to apply the aesthetics of rock, to choose rock above pop/soul, albums above singles, and songwriters above session musicians. The purpose is to distinguish the actors from the public at large, the common people, which can also be gathered from the music that makes it to the critics' *best of*-lists or that wins a special award. Von Appen & Doehring (2006: 27) register a difference in the lists drawn up by the critics and those put together by the public. Critics, after all, would lose their expertise if their list were to prove identical to that of their public. For the critics to keep the status of opinion leaders and opinion makers, the list needs to contain a few albums that form less obvious choices. At the same time, the list cannot deviate too much, provided they still want to belong to their own target group. At the presentation of the Félix Awards in Quebec, Ollivier (2006: 111) observed a difference between the prizes selected by the professionals and those by the public: the public at large consistently voted for the more popular artists. In the Netherlands, the same distinction with a difference is present: the 3FM Awards crown more popular artists winners of the Prize of the Public than they do with the Pop Prize, which is voted by a jury. The MIA in Belgium, too, give ample evidence of this difference. When the Flemish music prizes were still called Zamu Awards and exclusively chosen by the music professionals, they were the annual high mass of the Flemish alternative mainstream (only artists such as Admiral Freebee and dEUS got to take home the prizes). Since the Zamus were reformed and transformed into the MIAs and since the prizes are determined for the larger part by the public, also Clouseau, Milk Inc., Bart Peeters and Natalia are among the winners, while especially hits are making the difference. It is no accident that the alternative artists thank the bulk of their MIAs to a mainstream hit, witness the prizes won by Selah Sue, Triggerfinger, Absynthe Minded and Daan.

The Ideology of Rock and the Relation with the Music Industry

The important task assumed by the aesthetics of rock and by underground values in the alternative mainstream's discourse may also contain an ideological dimension.[9] Especially the distinction rock (considered 'honest' and 'authentic' music) aims to make with 'standard' pop music constitutes the ideological heart of the alternative mainstream. This is primarily a matter of perception: the segment views itself as an alternative for mainstream, whereas it too is a form of mainstream. Waving the aesthetics of rock, the actors legitimize their positions in the pop music circuit and conceal the mainstream properties that are present. To view alternative mainstream as an ideology is to attribute 'an incorrect or deceitful view of reality' to the actors in the segment (De Jong 1997: 44). It is tempting to debunk the ideology (which is precisely why the term is often heavily burdened in sociology), to unmask the deceit. The chief vector of the debunking approach to social science is found in Marxist sociology (such as that of Adorno, among others). Yet the issue can just as much take form if other perspectives are adopted. A good example is the book De Meyer (2010) wrote to burst the bubble of 'rockism' ideology, exactly by breaking a lance for the popular and the 'commercial.'

> Of key importance is that a part of the pop music universe distances itself from another part: rock versus pop tunes. Most of the myths deconstructed by us have been articulated on the side of rock. It is there that the obvious properties of all pop music, without distinction, either rock or pop tunes, are disaffirmed and negated. It is there that several myths hold dominion. Behold the myths of the rebellious nature of rock music and of the sell-out, of the social impact of rock music and of the opposition between the culture industry and creativity (...). Other myths join them, such as the myth of American pop imperialism and of the authenticity of rock music, of the pop star without an image, the rock & roll lifestyle and the counterculture... Indeed, the open-minded rock lover is itself a myth. (...) Those who settle in a myth are acting 'as if.' They believe their own lies, and conservatively establish themselves in a self-created world in which the so-called paradoxes (such as the co-existence of creativ-

ity and commerce) simply do not exist. (...) It is fair to say that the blind and the pretending populate the rock establishment.
(De Meyer 2010: 380-381)

The ideological bias of the rock discourse is most pronounced when it concerns the relation with the music industry. It is there and then that the aesthetics of rock and values such as authenticity are used to cast a veil over the economic reality of music, to conceal and mask the unquestionable fact that rock is just as much mass culture and commodity than pop. The symbolic process of meaning-making, as it becomes visible and is thrown into relief within the pop music circuit, is indeed related to the context in which the process takes place — to be more precise, to the *negation* of this context. Frith (1981: 160-168) pointed out earlier that this is precisely the reason why rock in the 1960s (and in the next decades) attached so much value and weight to authentic folk values and to the community feeling that went along with it. The latter, however, is in his view nothing but — and has everything of — a myth. As it so happens, it is not the music that is created in a community, but it is the musical community that is created by the music and the musical experience. 'The importance of the myth of rock community is that it *is* a myth,' he says (Frith 1981: 168).

Romanticism versus the Culture Industry

The Music Industry as the Big Bad Wolf
The field of tension between music as a product of mass culture and as a carrier of authentic expression constantly recurs in the pop discourse and therefore enjoys quite some attention among pop theorists. In Frith's groundbreaking sociological studies of pop music of the 1980s, this was already the connecting thread, and it seems that nothing much has changed since then. Just because journalists, fans and musicians emphasize the cultural value of music — and they do this via the aesthetics of rock — they look at the industry as if it were an evil thing, a big bad wolf. As a result, artists are expected to stand above the demands of the record firm — even if they are under (a major) contract — and to pursue nothing else but artistic greatness: rock as resistance against

commerce (Jones 2008: 84-85). The artists, after all, are the *good guys*, the industry are the *bad guys*. The industrialization of music, Frith adds (1988a: 11), leads to passive consumption and corrodes the group feeling as well as the quality of the music. Negus (1996: 36 and 40-42) too says that the social and political potential and the critical effect of the 'better kind of music' is annihilated by a ruthless, commercial corporate machine that wants to control creativity and that leaves the public with little choice. The charge is far from new. Adorno (1972) made a name for himself with this claim. From a neo-Marxist corner, he accused the culture industry of reducing human beings to consumers that are merely appendages of the culture machine. Adorno saw little value in music produced under capitalism. He complains about the loss suffered by art of its aura, its autonomous position vis-à-vis the rest of social life. The culture industry has made sure that qualitative (aesthetic) values are supplanted by quantitative values and that commercialization increasingly takes possession of cultural life. In the culture industry, all products are made and distributed according to planned, rationalized organizational procedures (the conveyor belt or production line). The goal in this is maximal profit (a typical property of Fordism, see below).

Adorno's critique of the culture industry under capitalism may be old and classic, his observations are hardly any different from the contemptuous tone with which people often talk about the industry and the most 'popular mainstream' in certain music circles. Better, however, is to look at the attitude towards the industry from the positions occupied by the organizations in the music field. In a prominent and authoritative article Jon Stratton (1983b: 144-149) describes how pop music is caught in a give-and-take between its status as symbolic good and the reality of it being an economic product. On the one hand, there is the position of the record industry, an economic branch of industry as any other. Musicians may very well wish to establish a profile with a certain the artistic feel; nevertheless, as soon as a record ends up with a record company, the music shifts from the private domain of the artist to the public domain of the marketplace. From being a cultural product, music becomes necessarily an economic product. Because of the free market's economic logic the relation between record companies is marked by competition. Within each company, however, there is also an internal competition, as the different releases that are simultaneously put on the market enter in a relation of rivalry. The survival of a firm is determined, after all, by its performance and achievements on this economic market. That is why the investment put into an artist depends on his or her potential success. Yet on the other hand — still according to Stratton — 'music as commodity' is constantly challenged by 'music as form of culture.' The artist does not want his creation to be regarded as a product. Music is also viewed as a cultural item by the press and the public — where all music must eventually present itself. In the cultural field, the individual and unique character of a work of art measures the artistic value. This focus on the singular seems a mirror image of the capitalist practice, which by definition, as Adorno showed, takes rationalization via standardization of products as its point of departure. The press therefore seeks to find originality and emotional commitment among the listeners, and the latter first discuss the quality of the music.

As I have said earlier, such a Romantic music discourse functions as an ideology that hides social factors and makes everyone involved forget that music is also economic, traded commodity or merchandise. This enables the public to have a bond or be connected with an artist, without the interference of the capitalist processes that bring about this music: by emphasizing and highlighting the cultural, the economic can be concealed. It explains, Stratton (1983b: 148) says, the prominent position taken in the discourse by individualistic terms such as *liking* (taste) and *involvement* (emotional involvement). In another article (1983a: 298) he adds that this is also the way in which the media — organizations which are also economically oriented — acquire their cultural legitimacy and their status as cultural gatekeepers. The same mechanism is active on the production side: even the industry feels the need for the ideology. It may very well be true that its economic logic is at complete odds with the views held by the artists and the public, industry still claims that they too are only in it for the music. The fact, De Meyer says, is that in the end the music industry exists 'by the grace, paradoxically enough, of all those who think that they are anti-commercial and anti-industry' (1994: 118).

Romanticism as a Product of Capitalism
The Romantic ideology is not merely a medicine for the economic nature of the music industry; it is also a typical product of capitalism. This was already a claim made a long time ago

by White and White (1965): the logic of the market requires an emphasis on the unique and the individual. An artist must have his or her own hallmark (of authenticity) if he or she wants to be saleable on the free market (see De Bruyne & Gielen 2011: 4-6). Stratton (1983b: 150-156) says the same: Romanticism does not only surface because the artist wants to react to the economic logic of the record company, but also, and primarily, because the tenet of innovation is shared by Romanticism and capitalism. Because the life span of cultural products is that short, and the music market resists any rationality and statistical prediction, it simply has to be the uniqueness of the music that needs to be emphasized. Big firms opting for rationality and predictability still need to highlight the Romantic ideal of artistry, individuality and originality when they want to do enough business and achieve enough sales, in short, want to survive. This also applies to the concert circuit, where the contact between audience and artist is direct and unique.

In all this, a fundamental critique on Adorno's view of the culture industry lies slumbering. To claim that the cultural industry starts from standardization and rationalization is at the same time to claim that 'the more "alike" a record is, the more popular it should be' (Stratton 1983b: 155). This, however, is not the case in the music industry. Standard records are not by definition more popular. It is exactly the uniqueness of the music that can make the difference (not all music is equally 'good'). Adorno also fails to explain the fact that only a limited number of releases actually make a profit and that some records are more popular than others are.

The Joint Action of Symbolic and Economic Values

Music Industry and Post-Fordism

To claim that music is not simply a cultural product, but also an economic product hardly kicks up any dust today. As De Meyer writes: 'It is a myth that there exists non-commercial rock music. It is a myth that commerce stands in the way of music' (2010: 32). It even seems to be understood that symbolic and economic values go hand in hand. Certainly, the process of post-modernization, and in particular post-Fordism, is believed to have changed the relationship between the cultural and the economic. Thinking in terms of standardization and rationalization, as was described above, used to be typical of Fordism. From WW2 on, capitalism transformed itself into a consumer society in which the role of mass media, advertising industry and production of consumer goods became ever-greater (see also Jameson 1984: 78-80). In the music industry, a hit factory like Motown in the 1960s illustrated in an unparalleled manner how much an intensive division of labor, standardized production and marketing campaign can secure successes (see Keunen 2002). Due to the oil crisis of 1973, among other things, the modernist principles of progress and growth began to lose their credibility. The world also became globalized and digitalized: this was the dawn of the Post-Fordist economy (Hardt & Negri 2002: 283-284). In order to survive in those globalized times, industry was forced to take a flexible stance and purposively seek out new products and market segments (Harvey 1990: 141-197). The music industry, equally faced with a struggle for survival, was forced to resort to drastic mergers, redirection of production from a vague mass market to specialized market niches that are predetermined and defined through market research, and swift responses to changes in a fragmented market. Mass production and consumption dissolved into specialized production and consumption. As a result, marketing continues to gain importance. Today's marketer needs to be creative, keep an eye on the right product/market combination (PMC) and the *unique selling proposition* (USP), based on an analysis of strong and weak points, opportunities and threats (SWOT-analysis).

Frith (1988b: 110-113) proposes the notion of *talent pool*, which came to replace the traditional model of rock success (*the rock*). In former days, an artist needed to start building a fan base with live concerts before there could be any talk of a record deal. A local hero (on an indie label) could then pass on to superstar status (thanks to a major deal). From the 1980s, however, the dynamics would emanate from the center: the music industry changed into a globalized center, fed by a series of markets, genres and institutions, nibbling at the edge. Proceeding from this, a selection is made for worldwide consumption, which is then exhaustively marketed. In the 1980s, many authors in popular music studies therefore started writing about the evolution of pop music. It was then that synth pop became dominant, which, to rock idealists came across as taking the commercial a step further. It would still become a trend: even today in each case managementand record company carefully coordinate marketing well in advance. This was so for Oasis in the 1990s (Hesmondhalgh 1999): selective showcases for key journalists, artificial *white labels* for promotion, journalists being invited to rehearsals, the classic male rock customs, angry young men (or feisty little brothers always brawling). Today this *pool-model* is still fully active, witness the fact of the numerous so-called 'internet hypes.'

Nevertheless, it is better to be careful with general hypotheses about the fragmentation of the market. Hesmondhalgh (1996: 51-57) is right to dismiss the *flexible specialization* described above as a misleading set of assumptions about possible changes in the music industry. Paying attention to niches and reacting with swiftness to changes in a fragmented market are, after all, strategies of all times, having been pursued time and time again. The market has always known specialized firms (indies, but also majors) and the fact is that the music industry has always made an appeal to external professionals as independent specialists (producers, 'pluggers,'[10] and others). In the music industry, Fordism never ceased to go hand in hand with Post-Fordism, and it is hardly any different today. Fordist mass production also had its share of specialized production targeted at niche markets, and today bulk selling is still the center of the industry (see p. 111). All this ties in with an analysis made by Virno (2004: 56-67). In his view, the culture industry is a forerunner of Post-Fordism. Even in Fordist times, the culture industry operated according to principles that only afterwards came to dominate: the emphasis on the individual, the informal, the improvized, and the communicative.

The Relationship Between Indies and Majors

At present both majors and indies are making their way on the market of flexibility, globalization and digitalization. In many studies, however, indies take up a privileged position, as was shown in foregoing account of indie rock. Independent or alternative music is frequently discussed as if it really was *independent*, devoid of and free from commercialization. The basic assumption never changes: indie is the breeding ground for new music, and as soon as it breaks, the majors come in to take over. It is they who exploit the music and in doing so wreck the autonomy of the indies (see Bannister 2006: 77, Negus 1996: 37-42 and Hesmondhalgh 1996: 46-47). Yet the infrastructure built around it just as much provides evidence to the contrary: at times, independent labels have (economic) ties with major labels. They can strike a license deal with majors or agree to allow the major handle their distribution. Majors can acquire a control share in indies or even buy up the label. It often happens that majors start their own 'fake indies' as a sub-label with the purpose of securing an easier entrance in the indie charts (Fonarow 2006: 35). This, indeed, is a general trend in the alleged 'alternative' music scene. In the 1970s, for instance, EMI owned the sub-label Harvest for progressive rock, and two decades later the company set up the electronic dance music label Positiva.

Furthermore, nothing stops major firms from offering contracts to underground artists. It does not matter to them whether it is indie rock (REM), noise rock (Sonic Youth), grunge (Nirvana), metal (Sepultura), punk rock (Green Day), drum 'n bass (Roni Size) or hardcore punk (Helmet). Nirvana is a textbook example of a band that was born in the circuit of *college radios*, alternative record stores and clubs, but made the switchover to a major, MTV, big store chains and hit radio stations. Especially MTV was essential in making it possible for alternative rock to enjoy large-scale publicity. It explains why musically and socially opposite, conflicting, and even incompatible music genres can find their way and even make headway within the same capitalist structures. Holly Kruse (1993: 34) is being more than ironical when she writes: 'Defining yourself in opposition to mainstream music merely means that Warner can sell you the Throwing Muses instead of Madonna.'

In addition to this, independents can also develop strategies for turning a career into a worldwide success. By collaborating with different independent distributors, by going from market to market, and closing separate distribution deals, an indie release can be simultaneously put on diverse markets, and indies can adopt the international marketing techniques of the majors (Billboard 01.04.2006). The success of bands such as Arctic Monkeys, The Prodigy or Franz Ferdinand prove that worldwide releases and ditto success are not the private property – so to speak – of majors. Franz Ferdinand, for instance, was signed to the British Domino label, was distributed in home country Scotland by Vital, in the Benelux, France and Spain by Pias, in Germany by Rough Trade, in Denmark and Finland by Playground, in Austria by Edel and in the US licensed to Epic. This enabled the band to sell a million CDs in the UK, and double this through sales in other countries. The same goes for Arctic Monkeys who thanks to Domino hit the charts in thirteen different countries by way of the same network.

It is therefore undoubtedly a fallacy or misrepresentation to over-romanticize indies. They are just as capable of coveting financial success as any large-scale producer. In the same way that creative autonomy within the walls of a major is perfectly possible, it is also not necessarily so that small firms are exclusively occupied with aesthetics or taking a political stand. Employing the underground logic, one could denounce collaborations with majors as a betrayal of the ideals. Yet this is far from what the labels themselves think or have to say about it. The case studies of the labels One Little Indian and Creation give ample evidence of this (Hesmondhalgh 1999: 52-56). With the former, PolyGram bought in via a control share, the second was sold to Sony. For the labels, all this is merely part of a process of professionalization. In their view, a major deal is nothing but a strategy to be able to earn money without *selling out*, 'to challenge the "mainstream" on its own terrain' (Hesmondhalgh 1999: 52). In Creation's view, it was a way of achieving success on a national and international level and seeing their *classic pop dream* come true. The musical conservatism that the label represented was not just the effect of their closing a major deal. From the start, the label willingly intended to achieve success specifically by highlighting the traditional aesthetics of rock. Having secured a major deal these indies do not only get to keep their indie image, they can also benefit from a financial safety net and are able to put up a shield between the business world on the one side and those who are uncomfortable with the business side on the other.

In short, the indie scene may very well sport an underground ideology; the truth is that they are no longer able to assume that status. The reason for naming this segment in pop music 'alternative mainstream' instead of 'alternative,' 'underground' or 'niche' is precisely the fact that this music is actually a type of mainstream music and is no longer underground. Some rock theorists, however, conclude from the fact that the clearcut distinction between indies and majors has become blurred, that the dichotomy pop/rock has disappeared. Thus Van Venrooij (2009: 317-330), analyzing the content of CD reviews in the *Los Angeles Times*, observes that genre borders are blurring and that critics are slowly dropping the strict or obstinate distinction between (illegitimate) pop and (legitimate) rock because in most cases commercial and artistic values are paired or combined. Yet he is also forced to confirm that there is still evidence of a sort of meta-category of music, which survives and thrives, which has less trouble making it through or to the selections. It is a category that includes rock, but just as much contains hip-hop, techno and some forms of 'pop.' This meta-category, previously identified by Motti Regev (2002) and dubbed *pop-rockization*, is exactly what the term 'alternative mainstream' intends to denote. In this case aesthetic classifications must not be confused with the fact that commerce and creativity need not be in a constant face-off, but are indeed interwoven. This has always been the hypothesis proposed by Frith (1984). In his view, there is less conflict between art and commerce in rock than in any other mass medium. Furthermore, it does not mean that the alternative mainstream's ideological values have lost their significance. Quite the contrary, says Negus (1996: 47), notably rock musicians and their fans are keeping the creed alive. Dowd (2004: 237) too ascertains that, leaving aside the point of possible aspired success, small record firms employ a logic that emphasizes the aesthetic and casts a veil over the commercial. In a case study of label Wax Trax!, Lee (1995) says that the concept of indie still functions as a system of belief with certain modi operandi and values that differ from those subscribed to by the majors. The wish subsists to position oneself in an independent and 'alternative' niche market, even though one is actually not situated outside, but inside the system.

It is therefore clear that 'independent' and 'alternative mainstream' remain ideological concepts. What matters to bands belonging to the segment of the alternative mainstream is that they themselves think or believe that they are making music detached from the 'commercial' industry. An interview with Brett Anderson (Suede) in *Billboard* illustrates this well. While the fact of the matter was that Nude Records had a license deal with Sony, the singer still manages to claim:

> The independent music industry is the only place that allows bands to develop. We don't intend to betray it and run off to some multinational corporation.
> (Hesmondhalgh 1999: 54)

Another example is Sick of It All, who had signed to a major label, but kept singing that

> 'In the underground integrity lies within, in the underground image doesn't mean a thing'.
> ('Step Down' on the CD *Scratch the Surface*, 1994; see Heesterbeek 2002)

The 'alternative' is not found in the production or distribution of the music, but in the fact that players define themselves as 'alternative,' 'unique,' 'authentic.' This has serious consequences for the approach taken to any analysis of the pop music circuit. Instead of choosing the 'debunking' path, this study, following Boltanski and Thévenot (2006), proposes that the important aspect lies in the justifications the actors use when they are facing a test of legitimacy. These are accounts of actions taken by people, which only make sense in a particular world that has a particular value or higher common principle as its central criterion. Any critique addressed from another realm is considered inadmissible, because it is raised by employing a different central value. These conflicts of worlds and principles are situations in which persons and things are constantly interacting and are being mobilized (ANT calls them *actants*, a word that skips the distinction between subjective individual and objective entities) explaining how differentiating processes of meaning-making are set in motion.

Recap 2

The discourse about underground and mainstream often employs the dichotomy or opposition between artistic and commercial. This is clearly shown by a survey of what in popular music studies has been written on the distinction pop/rock. Rock symbolizes the 'better sort of' pop music that seeks to distinguish itself from what, in its own eyes, is commercial pop. At the same time, this a good description of what this study calls 'the alternative mainstream.' Rock is then a cultural construct that ascribes certain values to particular forms of pop music, which are borrowed from the Romantic tradition: good music needs to be authentic, original and non-commercial. The rock canon, as it indirectly surfaces via various end-of-the-year-lists, illustrates this aesthetics of rock. Rock is also believed to be music that is borne by a community. In this special group, the collectively shared pattern of values and the typical in-group feeling need to be differentiated from the 'real' mainstream. It is in this practice of difference and distinction that the rock community reveals to what extent the process of its canonization is a *social* process.

The distinction between pop and rock also has an ideological dimension. The alternative mainstream wishes to view music as a purely cultural product and therefore attempts to conceal that it is also commodity or merchandise. In the discourse, the emphasis is on the Romantic view as a defensive response to the commercial, or on throwing a veil over certain economic principles. Yet in the same way that Romanticism is a product of capitalism, 'alternative' music too is a product of the culture industry. The fact that an economic and a symbolic logic are intertwined is actually typical of the alternative mainstream.

Interlude

The Road to Research and the Pragmatist Turn: A Brief Theoretical Clarification

Now that the concept of 'alternative mainstream' has been defined by way of the area of tension between cultural and economic determinants, it is perhaps time to take a look at how the segment originates and materializes, and to make a start with presenting some findings of research on the subject.

The players in the pop music circuit must first select music. What they consider relevant, desirable, good, useable or *credible* can be admitted to the alternative mainstream, leaving aside the point whether the music comes from the underground or mainstream or is straightaway made for this segment. This study needs to gain insight into how the selections actually happen and exactly what motives are in the running when they actually happen.

As has already been said, the view that consists in looking at selections as a social process dominates the sociology of culture. Yet since the late 1980s and early 1990s, this now classic view, especially Bourdieu's theory of the field, has run into quite some antagonism. On the general level of the philosophy of social science, French sociologists Luc Boltanski (a former collaborator of Bourdieu) and Laurent Thévenot, as well as Bruno Latour and the proponents of the Actor-Network Theory or ANT, have taken the philosophical school of pragmatism as a starting point for 'the pragmatist turn' in sociology. In some preceding contexts 'the anthropological turn' was used for the movement in social studies that wanted to get back to the actual actors in their everyday environments. 'Follow the actors' was the famous motto that was phrased and spread by Latour, who called himself an anthropologist of science. With respect to pop music, the names of Nathalie Heinich and Antoine Hennion need to be mentioned.

Pragmatists reject the general classification matrix of, for example, Bourdieu. They do not subscribe to the rules of the game that are allegedly ingrained in the habitus of people and that direct or guide actions. Instead, they examine how people behave in real-life situations and therefore take the singular actor as the starting point. They turn their gaze to the extraordinary and the manner in which actors act differently according to the situation. In this way they observe that people in passing or formulating judgments make an appeal to different interpretation matrices or value regimes – collective as well as individual – that exist alongside or cross one another, and which can change as a result of the interaction between the actors. In their seminal work *On Justification: The Economies of Worth*, Boltanksi and Thévenot distinguish between six 'worlds' that people inhabit to interpret concrete situations.[11] Each of these worlds has a different central evaluation and valuation principle or *higher common principle*: the world of inspiration (art), the domestic world (tradition), the world of fame (public opinion), the civic world (collectivity), the world of the market (competition) and the world of industry (efficiency).[12]

These basic pragmatist principles were also the starting point for the research that led to this book, although Bourdieu's achievements were never out of its scope. Pascal Gielen (2003) did the same with his study of artistic selections in contemporary dance and visual arts. In order to analyze artistic selections, Gielen notes a double dichotomy: on the one hand, actors operate in either singular or collective regimes of value; on the other hand, they make an appeal to content and context logics. This matter will be discussed later on, but at this point is worth noting the following: either one thinks in terms of the work of art and the artist (the singular regime of value on which the Romantic view of the author is based), or one focuses on artistic or social referents (collective regime of value).

Because of their general nature, these logics are also easy to apply to the pop music circuit. Then again, as is often the case with sociologists studying those traditional arts, there is not always a ready-made solution for a highly hybrid market such as that of pop music. First, this is not an unambiguous and easily understood cultural field, where participants function in the same social context and know the genres and history of the field. Pop music is characterized by a crisscross of genre worlds and geographically differentiated markets (local, national and international), and therefore contains numerous social contexts and cultural patterns, of which, for example, the players of the Flemish alternative mainstream are not always fully aware. In addition, it is the economic context that makes the difference in the case of pop music – perhaps even more than in the traditional arts. It is plain to see that economic factors in the pop music world are often decisive: sales figures, market potential, sponsor deals and so on, are invariably what cut the selection knot. Another thing is that reasoning based on current affairs, popularity or functionality of music, or one that takes the radio potential into account, are equally important in this circuit. Moreover, a radio station that plays a record is quite another thing than a concert promoter who programs a band. Unlike with dance or theatre (one-time stage activities) or visual arts (durable objects of art), music has several options of expression: sound carrier is a durable physical object, a concert is a one-time event. This is what makes music so unique, but at the same time makes it harder to determine the criteria of selection.

One consequence of this is that this study of selection mechanisms in the alternative mainstream will have to discuss some complementary logics and criteria. As was said earlier, there is no need to start from a conceptual model that will be subjected to the empirical test. Instead, following ANT, this study takes the *actors* themselves as first base, and then attempts to arrive at a synthesizing model of analysis based on their accounts, their lines of thought and reasoning, their argumentations and justifications. The anchor and crutch in the performed field study are a few broadly interpreted points of interest that should render the data collection and processing workable. Thus the remainder of the book will look at an individual logic of legitimization (an internal frame of reference where personal taste plays a leading role, the singular), and at a positional logic (selections made from the position occupied by actors in the field, the collective). Besides this, organizational and macro-economic arguments are documented. An attempt will be made to observe the economic, artistic, political, social and other regimes of values in the manner they appear next to, and cross one another, and to study them as separate realities. What follows will examine how the (established) national players in the pop music circuit attribute a specific value to some forms of music and how this selection takes shape throughout the field.

Notes

1. If we proceed from an interpretative concept of culture, meaning making also implies the classification and categorization of things that are thus distinguished from one another. This, of course, is in keeping with Weber and the way in which Lévi-Strauss describes it (Laermans 2010: 180). Choosing rock and not pop is therefore a symbolic classification schema *and* a distinction mechanism.

2. In a religious context, the word refers to an authoritative list of books accepted as Holy Scripture. Hence, it designates certain fixed tenets, precepts, principles and regulations concerning faith or morals proclaimed or decreed by a church. It is synonymous with dogma and related to belief, conviction, credo, creed, ideology — terms that fit in nicely with the rock canon's mode of functioning [translator's note].

3. Bob Dylan (*Highway 61 Revisited*, 1965), The Beach Boys (*Pet Sounds*, 1966), The Beatles (*Revolver*, 1966), The Velvet Underground (*The Velvet Underground & Nico*, 1967), Van Morrison (*Astral Weeks*, 1969), Marvin Gaye (*What's Going On*, 1971), The Rolling Stones (*Exile on Main St.*, 1972), The Sex Pistols (*Never Mind the Bollocks*, 1977) and Nirvana (*Nevermind*, 1991) and the only entry that differentiates her list from that of Von Appen & Doehring: Patti Smith (*Horses*, 1975).

4. This is a translation of the original Dutch text [translator's note].

5. The English equivalent would be something between 'Tough Guys' and 'Heavy Duty' [translator's note].

6. This term is also borrowed from Bourdieu (1984) and is on the rise in popular music studies (Hesmondhalgh 2006, Negus 1996 and 2002, Nixon & du Gay 2002). In Bourdieu's view, the cultural intermediaries form a specific part of what he calls the 'new petty bourgeoisie,' more specifically the media (Bourdieu 1984: 325 and 359). The term is used in a much broader sense by the academics who study pop music. It can also refer to managers and marketers behind themusic, even include technical personnel and accountants.

7. The word 'meaning maker' is used fairly often in philosophical or religious (con)texts. One notable example of 'philosophy versus religion' is found in philosophical anthropologist Daniel Dennett's description of human beings as creatures that have evolved to the stage of meaning making. All humans are meaning makers by (evolutionary) nature, Dennett argues, dismissing the claim of religious believers that atheists are unable to give meaning to life because they have no concept of God, since God is considered to be the ultimate meaning maker. In the sense of a person attributing meaning to something in a particular, even specialized cultural and social process, which leads to it becoming a mechanism of distinction — i.e. in Bourdieu's sense, as a symbolic (co-) producer — the term is confined to academic literature [translator's note].

8. The original zebra crossing, where the photograph was taken, was moved several meters for rather mundane traffic management reasons somewhere around the end of the 1970s or the start of the 1980s. It is significant that no original features or record of the exact location remain. At the time, the cultural consecration was still very much in the making. Roger Bowdler, head of designation at English Heritage, remarked: 'This is obviously an unusual case and, although a modest structure, the crossing has international renown and continues to possess huge cultural pull.' John Penrose, Minister for Tourism and Heritage, said: 'This London zebra crossing is no castle or cathedral but, thanks to The Beatles and a 10-minute photo-shoot one August morning in 1969, it has just as strong a claim as any to be seen as part of our heritage.' [translator's note]

9. Sociology uses the term 'ideology' for the set of ideas that is said to justify the social structure of a group (Dobbelaere 1987), serves to protect the established interests of the group, interprets and often systematically distorts social reality in order to achieve their set objectives in a socially acceptable way (Berger 1963: 42-43 and 118). An ideology can also determine the collective action of

individuals, because it fills the function 'of a social consciousness of the collective condition and of their interests and goals' (De Jong 1997: 44).

10   The word 'plugger' is confined to the Dutch music industry jargon, and has nothing to do with its use in the English language, where it is used with purely derogatory intent and sexual connotation. A 'plugger' is someone 'in service of a record label or hired by artists or music bands to promote their music, usually with radio stations or other actors in the music or entertainment business' [*translator's note*, source: http://nl.wikipedia.org/wiki/Plugger].

11   De la justification: les économies de grandeur was first published in 1989, finally translated in 2006.

12   Boltanski & Chiapello 2006 add a seventh world to the model of cities: the world of projects.

3. Digitization, Selection Pressure and Uncertainty Context Factors in the Decision-Making Process

The rise of the Internet changed everything. It meant the death sentence for the traditional music industry, allowing musicians to break through without the help of the record companies, the newspapers or the radio. Social media and streaming sites, Internet forums and blogs have taken the place of these actors. At least, that is how the story often goes.

Whether it really has come to this, is a (complementary) question this study seeks to address, and attempts to answer. The new online players were never consulted, but the question remained whether these new channels had already gained the same impact as the old players, and especially whether the familiar *gatekeepers* — the object of study — were forced to change their selection methods. Selections, after all, are not made in total isolation, detached from social, cultural and economic determinants. Peterson pointed out that technological changes could lead to other modes of selection (Peterson & Anand 2004). Before taking a look at the actual selection process (the medium level with its individual and social aspects), this chapter will zoom in on the socio-economic context in which the actors of the pop music circuit operate, as well as the marginal conditions that influence and direct the decision (the macro-level).

Digitization, and the entirely new communication of music that arose as a direct result of it, do indeed play a leading role in the decision making process. The Internet revolution has led to an oversupply on the one hand, and alternative modes of operating on the other All this has generated an immense amount of selection pressure and uncertainty among the actors in the pop music circuit. The record circuit, but also the concert circuit (which has less trouble with the music industry's crisis) and the media, are forced to learn to cope with the new situation, and to think about how they are and will be able to reach the public today. In this way, a study of the 'old guard' in these digital times does not have to be an anachronism.

Oversupply and Alternative Channels

Harsher Selection Caused by Oversupply

'We all agree on the fact that there are too much (sic) records being released, only we still have to agree on who should stop.' This is what British artist Mixmaster Morris once told the author of this book in an interview (Keunen 23.09.1998). There is an element of truth in his crack about the situation. On the supply side, there does not seem to be any inhibition on the number of releases. All respondents of this study agree. There is an oversupply of music, even much more than already used to be the case. 'To be able to follow this, you need an extra life,' one radio maker claimed. 'Everybody is making their own music. It almost seems that there are now more artists that there are people who buy music,' a big shot in the record industry added sarcastically. This oversupply is the outcome of the record industry losing a large part of the control over the supply and the consumption of music. In former times, the record industry primarily determined what artists could put a sound recording on the market. The A&R managers of today's record companies — Artist & Repertoire, the persons who are responsible of signing new artists — have ceased to be *gatekeepers*. Technological developments have made it much easier to produce a recording that meets the quality standards of sound technology. Musicians with a modest home studio (and a basic set-up of hardware and software) are able to release single-handedly their own music, without even the slightest input from a record company or a recording studio. Some respondents are happy with this democratization of music caused by the Internet. Yet more music is not always synonymous with more good music. A radio maker says:

> In earlier times, the A&R-manager was someone who managed to sift the wheat from the chaff, which made sure we all got fairly decent products on our desks. With the Internet, because there is no filter anymore, you get a lot of junk on your plate. Now we face a gigantic ocean, and a gigantic amount of fishes are being dropped in it.

Oversupply leads to harsher selections, whether one likes it or not. The supply increases, yet the number of available slots

do not. Consequently, more and more artists fall by the wayside. Some are eliminated, often brutally. Journalists of the written press claim they are simply not able to listen to all the CDs they receive, let alone review them. Radio producers cannot play everything, which causes artists to experience greater difficulties in getting airplay. Promotional collaborators of distribution companies are unable to give publicity on each label they distribute, let alone for every single release on these labels. In addition, because all artists want to perform live, concert promoters increasingly lag behind in listening to the dozens of offers that end up on their desk every week. A surplus of releases cannot be handled by the system, or by the media, the industry or the public. Competition has increased. Artists are blocking one another, and bands that resemble each other are forced to fight it out among one another and in public. Being aware of this is not always an agreeable experience for the respondents. Working in the music industry has become more burdensome, frustrating and tiring. Professionals can no longer see the wood from the trees, follow (up on) the offer and decide which is good and which is not in it.

To produce an oversupply, however, was formerly a deliberate strategy of the music industry, a way of coping with the risks of the free market and of functioning in an uncertain environment. Already in the 1970s, Hirsch (1972) emphasized that record companies were deliberately releasing more, then observing how the market reacted and subsequently got to work on only a few titles. He famously called this strategy '*overproduction and differential promotion of new items*' (Hirsch 1972: 652). Only a handful of the many new ideas receive effective distribution and promotion, and those with the lowest sales are eliminated. Because the a priori assumption is that a series of releases will fail, much investment has to be put into the production of a catalogue that is large enough to ensure the survival of the company thanks to a limited number of lucrative albums (Stratton 1983b: 146). In 2010, a mere 10% of the global supply is said to have generated 90% of the business (Vantyghem 29.01.2011: C10).[1] There is, indeed, an enormous gap between a small number of mega successes and the overwhelming majority of poorly selling records.

The strategy of overproduction is typical of major record companies. Yet it has increasingly become a reality among the smaller labels and distributors. According to the respondents in this study, this is a new phenomenon. The number of promo CDs journalists receive from independents has become incalculable. An indie distributor claims he is working on about a hundred releases a week: 'At present, the great paradox of the record industry is that while record sales are constantly dropping the number of releases is constantly rising.' Another distributor phrases it in this way:

> Following the panic reaction and the opportunistic style of the majors, the indies also think: we'll do ten releases; one out of ten scores; out of the nine we're stuck with, we'll eliminate seven. The line of reasoning is this: it used to be we sold five times two thousand CDs; now that we are unable to get that, we'll go for ten times one thousand.

All this fits in with the thesis of *the long tail*, a concept launched by Chris Anderson (2006): *selling less of more*. De Meyer (2010: 221), however, notes that investing in risky niche products is only possible when there are also mega sales. This perhaps explains why some respondents observe that record firms, as well as management agencies, have become more stringent on the input side and more fastidious in signing artists. Record firms have stopped pushing increasingly more through the bottleneck. Nowadays they would rather be a football team in the premier league with fewer artists, and thus a team that stands out from the rest, than a team from the minor leagues with too many artists. Add to this the fact that bands with a contract also get fewer chances. The head of a record company comments:

> Twenty years ago, when a band did not succeed right away, it would get three chances, three albums. Ten years ago, this was down to two, and now this is exactly one, unless there is a clearly noticeable growth curve. In any case, the trend today is to sign less, think a little longer and stop giving endless chances. I think this is really harmful. Like they say, the first poems are usually not the best, right?

The latter sentence really underscores the small amount of time artists are afforded to grow and develop. Oversupply and the fact that everybody can afford his or her own little spot on the Internet, makes the experience of music a fleeting and fragmented

phenomenon. The alternation of bands has increased at speed, as has time in which hypes come into being and burn up. Thanks to all sorts of blogs, the public is able to pick up music much faster than ever. With some nostalgia, the head of a label reminisces the time when a CD such as *Born to Run* (Bruce Springsteen) would be *top of mind* for as long as four or five months:

> Now it doesn't matter who it is. Even Editors: after two months the record's done. Did I say two months? I meant four weeks! Records rarely get to have the impact that they sometimes deserve as works of art. Everything has become consumerism, and we, the record companies, are nicely going along with it.

The number of bands that manage to hold their chin above water has not become larger than before, people ascertain in the interviews I conducted. More bands can enjoy a small amount of attention (occasional airplay, only to disappear completely afterwards) and only a minority really becomes big. Breaking out of the niche, therefore, is hard. At the same time, however, oversupply forces artists to come up with a new record each time, if they want to get a bit of attention. This causes oversupply to grow even more, while selection pressure never ceases to increase. Some players are resigned to this development, such as this publicist: 'If you would grant everything the same priority, it would drive you mad. You must learn to be happy with anything that succeeds and try to be not too frustrated about whatever does not succeed.'

The Power of the Multitude

Building a Public Outside the Traditional Channels
On the production side, there is an oversupply. On the side of consumption, there is the Web 2.0 (or 3.0 and 4.0, whatever suits the reader) and the 'free story' (not so much the 'open source' ideality as the 'bit torrent' reality). The illegal downloading of music is a 'success.' To give an idea: in the first half of 2012 about three billion songs were estimated to have been downloaded globally, and in Belgium the illegal trafficking of music was estimated to be twice as big as the legal is (Vantyghem 21.09.2012). In addition, the Internet is no longer a one-way-traffic, which

also happens to provide new opportunities for artists and their careers. A point brought up many times by the respondents in this study is the existence of alternative channels for getting music to buyers, which emerged as an effect of digitization. The least revolutionary strategies are those of successful artists (such as Prince or Radiohead) who made it big in the 'traditional' era ('when everything could still be perfectly controlled,' according to one promoter). They are exploiting the fame they previously gained to set up 'ground-breaking' actions on the Internet to get to their audience. Radiohead, for instance, initially sold its album exclusively online in exchange for a free contribution (even though it hit the store shelves afterwards just like any other time). More notable is the fact that young and new artists, even before they do anything else, are able to build a fan base almost single-handedly, both at home and abroad. This makes the traditional players' influence on the market shrink, according to some commentators. One manager says:

> With respect to the ways of picking up, a lot more is happening outside of the industry, of which we have no knowledge whatsoever. The public's share in the decision-making has grown. In earlier times, a demo was only intended for the industry, today it is the start of building an audience. A public can be created without the traditional established channels, by making use of the Internet, a mailing list and concerts.

The point made by this manager is that artists have already built their fan base or some foundation of an audience before they may have a chance of being picked up by the industry or the media. Flemish examples cited by the respondents are The Bony King of Nowhere, Selah Sue and Milow. Because the public support was already present, the industry had no other choice but to follow. According to some, the situation has already moved beyond this point. Artists can allegedly only get a record contract if they have built such an initial audience.

Record companies and artist managers, for their part, are equally bent on using the online platforms as new tools for A&R. Besides a fan base or basic audience, actors can also build a basic business thanks to digitization. One of the managers confirms this: 'We are now able to get to more gatekeepers than before – certainly abroad.' It is true that the process of exchanging music over the Internet may work rather vaguely. Nevertheless, one of the effects is, for instance, that successful performances in the live circuit do not necessarily go hand in hand with traditional media attention. A booking agent testifies:

> I think the younger public listens less to the radio and is more focused on the online story. Even though I mustn't exaggerate this, I do run into more and more concerts selling many tickets for bands that do not necessarily get much airplay on the radio, yet in one way or the other are alive on the Internet. (...) It is possible to have concerts for a band that have no single out on the radio, nor a CD in our country, yet are able to sell two hundred tickets simply because there is an audience that follows the band, a very young public that goes its own way. (...) Even on the level of a concert venue such as the Ancienne Belgique in Brussels, I think there are enough examples that show it can be done without radio airplay. Tokio Hotel, for example. The band may thank its breakthrough to extra airplay; they were launched thanks to the online story. More than that, a number of stations only started to play Tokio Hotel because of the public's pressure. Granted, perhaps these are only a few exceptions. Still, I sense that the online phenomenon is gaining significance and that the influence of the traditional media is becoming a bit smaller.

Others, too, conclude that the key players in the music industry have become less powerful and that unlike in earlier times the public too has acquired decision authority. This is in keeping with a concept from political philosophy called 'the crowd' (or *multitude*) (Virno 2004, Hardt & Negri 2002 and 2004). Unlike the masses that are passive and can be manipulated, the multitude possesses a creative force (Hardt and Negri 2004: 10-11). It consists of unique 'singularities' with lasting differences (in culture, race, sex, sexual inclination, but also in profession, lifestyle, world view or ambition). Yet through cooperation, it is able to form an open and expansive network. This is why the multitude also possesses power and why it is able to revolt (Hardt & Negri 2002: 389-402). This is shown by the illegal behavior in downloading and the success of torrent sites. The social media — transnational communities that have become global thanks to telecommunication — also illustrate the power of the multitude. Today's 'active consumer' individually determines what he or she listens to and shares his or her preferences with 'friends' via network sites.

It does not come as a surprise to the Internet generation that even the interviewed actors from the alternative mainstream note that they have less power and that the initial selection is made by the public. Much has changed in the selection procedure. Still, as will become clear, not *that much* has changed. The main thing, which is central to this study, is that ambiguity is rife. The respondents that bring up the digital changes are also the respondents that claim the importance of the internet should not be overestimated. The diminished impact of the traditional media is largely situated in certain niches and scenes, the undercurrent of music or, using this study's terminology, the underground. A record executive puts it as follows:

> Certainly, the Internet should not be underestimated. At the same time, the whole thing is often informal, no strings attached. Everything can be extremely fleeting. The problem with the Internet is that you may be able to reach an incredible amount of people, yet the impact may be gone just like that. When I look at myself, how many times I watch a video from start to finish I think it's about 1 out of 20 times. (...) And does it even work, via the Internet? For ten years now, the same examples have been cited over and over again: Lilly Allen and Arctic Monkeys. (...) Are there really any other examples? To be sure, there are bands who have made it by way of the Internet, (...) but there must be at least a billion bands on the Internet. So it seems it doesn't work. Of course, I won't deny the importance of YouTube, Facebook, Spotify, Deezer, MySpace, Soundcloud, etc. These are visiting cards and distribution channels the likes of which we have never seen. But the breakthrough? (...) Internet is an enormous spider web. At which corner of the web do you have to be to reach enough people? And are these people even the right people? (...) As for music, It think nothing much has changed. Take, for example, a band like

Isbells in Flanders: in the end, the radio single on Studio Brussels made the big difference. The same goes for Milow: his candle was very nearly burned up, but thanks to the 50 Cent cover all stations played him.

Several respondents emphatically attempt to put the public's deciding force into perspective. By definition, managers and record firms direct and orchestrate the known internet hypes (including Lana Del Rey). In fact, it is a marketing strategy to create the illusion that these acts were 'discovered' by the public (and the media) (see also Chapter 6). For now, the argument leaves aside the question of the actual impact made by the digital alternatives (in the long run, and with respect to the volume of the public) and runs ahead of the research results revealed and discussed in the next chapters. The interviewed respondents almost unanimously claim that the traditional media's role is far from played out, and that they remain a crucial link in the selection process. There is indeed a consensus among the respondents about the fact that circulation on the Internet is and must be an important and decisive first step, yet that this is not enough for an artist to break through. Things are obviously different for those who deliberately aim at a niche in the underground. Still, to be able to become known to a larger public and make a career in the alternative mainstream (that is, to gain national fame), the traditional media remain a necessary condition (see also pp. 203 and 314).

The Changed Role of Record Companies and Stores in the Selection Process

Crisis in Record Land

If there is one item that keeps coming back in discussions about the effects of the Internet revolution, it is the role played by record companies. In the practice of pop, and in literature, the music industry is often tacitly identified with the record industry (see also Williamson & Cloonan 2007). These record companies have suffered heavily because of 'the crisis in the music industry' (as opposed to the concert circuit). For information purposes, a few statistics are needed. In the period 2004-2010, the value of the global record industry dropped by 31% (IFPI 2011: 5), while business — for physical carriers — even fell by 61.4% in the period 2000-2011 (Maeterlinck 13.02.2012).[2] Not surprisingly, many of the voices heard for this study claimed that the record company now plays a smaller role in the music circuit than it used to. It is less often cited as the music industry's axis. The changed position is evidently connected with the loss of control over the supply that was mentioned earlier. This loss of control has consequences for the relationship between the record company and the media. If the selection process is viewed as a succession or sequence of decisions made by *gatekeepers* – as in Hirsch's *filter/flow-model* (1972) mentioned above – then it is the record company that determines what is released, when it is released and when it becomes available to the media. These days, this is no longer always the case. The record company is robbed of some of the means it once had to manipulate the media by the simple use of records, and to exert influence on the airplay. In the words of a record company executive:

> In former times, for example, for two whole weeks preceding the release, I was the only Belgian who had the album 'O.K. Computer.' I literally was the first of all Belgians to have the album in my hands. I'm not going to brag about this, but such a thing does engender a certain form of feeling privileged, of vanity and satisfaction. If you get this power, you can either use it or abuse it. But the fact is that nobody gets this kind of power anymore. Take, for example, the worldwide release of a Katy Perry single. One minute later, it's all over the Internet, all over the airwaves, and on every single radio. It no longer depends on our plugger.

The radio producers confirm that they are already in possession of half of the records before any of the companies pays them a visit: 'Much is being sent digitally and there is *Radio Ventures* [compilation CDs from abroad produced exclusively for radio stations, GK] which allows us to exert close control and indicate whatever either interests us or not.'

Certainly a digitalization has also changed the relationship between the promoters and record companies. As one programmer points out:

> To be able to book anything, the record companies are no longer needed. When I started working here in 1997,

every single time I needed to request CDs from the
record firms before I was able to book anything. Now you
just listen online and the booking can follow much faster.

Because the Internet now fulfills this task of informing,
the record firm can exert less influence on the selection. For
the promotion of concerts, the live circuit does not necessarily
need the help of record firms. The promoters' own mailing lists
and media contacts are often all it takes. In addition, especially
when it comes to foreign bands, the record company's A&R-
function sometimes shifts to the agent, as one booking agent
says. Because, to an artist, live concerts increasingly appear to
be of greater importance than CD releases, he or she will not
necessarily go to the trouble of getting a (new) record released
before knocking at a booking agent's or publicist's door. One
publicity manager claims that this is why a booking agent may
sooner have knowledge of the exact time of a CD release than
the distributing company may. 'These days, one out of two times
I am forced to say to a booking agent about foreign bands that
are distributed by us: "no, I don't know this CD or band," while
I should already have been working on them: Very frustrating,
indeed.' Yet before the actors in the concert circuit come to the
fore, the artist managers and management agencies take over
certain tasks of the record companies.

Record Companies and Promotion

Still, the record company has not yet played its part — far from
it. One the one hand it experiments with alternative business
models, such as the 360° model in which the company also shares
in revenues from concerts and merchandising, and sometimes
even handles bookings and management, buying up firms for
this purpose, or the model where the firm goes out to seek the
investment capital with the fan/'shareholder.' The company
repositions itself through the exploitation of digital *content*
(downloads, streaming, mobile market etc.). As far as the latter
is concerned: in 2012 digital sales of music reached 34% of total
sales (IFPI 2013: 6).[3] On the other hand — of greater important
to this study — the record company is still very much the crux of
an artist's promotional story, certainly with the bigger names. If
anything, promotion has gained significance in the Internet age.
The reason is that anybody can be present on the Internet, yet

being able to be noticed in the masses, is quite another story. Even though there are increasingly more independent promoters and management agencies, when it comes to promotion, the record firm still possesses a lot of expertise, which is why it remains its core task. In this respect, as far its relationship with the media is concerned, little has changed, as is clearly shown by the interviews. Contrary to what was suggested above, record companies remain the principal, leading input. For daytime programming on the radio, few searches are made by way of the Internet, and the radio is not going to play any records that are not distributed by the known record firms, or that are not found in the record stores or on iTunes. This also applies to the written press: the music still needs to be released and distributed if it wants to make it to the press. Certainly in the case of a foreign band, the contacts are still run via a record company, which will attempt to influence the selection by the media in the same manner as before. This explains why the record firm keeps on making publicity by tradition: taking care of the CD reviews in the written press and of airplay on the radio, arranging interviews and setting up special promotions. It is true that record companies have smaller budgets at their disposal for big competitions and it is said that also the so-called facility trips or junkets (offering exclusive trips for journalists in order to create goodwill and putting the horse to their cart) have become less frequent. All things being equal, though, it is business as usual. Besides, the CD is far from being extinct, as long as it remains necessary for promotional purposes. One publicist emphasizes that journalists would rather receive a CD than a download link, certainly in the case of less known artists. 'They prefer to listen to the pile of CDs on their desk, when they get a download link they think the record is less important.' The only difference with the past is that the record company's promotional campaign was mainly targeted at the media. The media used to be the main way to get to the public. Nowadays, playing the Internet is a new promotional strategy: attempts are made to create a buzz in the hope this is later picked up by the media, and heightened. Then it appears the public is the gatekeeper, although the mechanisms that are active behind the scenes are similar to those of former times.

Since the record firm is still taking charge of promotion, it often runs into a conflict with the concert circuit. It feels like a thorn in the record company's flesh that it puts time and money into the promotion of an artist with ever decreasing CD sales, while concert promoters keep on earning money with live concerts without having to invest a single dime in the artists. Moreover, as a record manager adds to stress the point, whenever ticket sales are not what they should be, and the promoter is the first to ask the label to make extra publicity for the concert. Here, indeed, it is a relation of tension that holds, rather than a relation of cooperation.

Retail Runs into Trouble

Digitization has not only altered the job description of a record company. It also changed the task profile of the record stores. It even seems that the classic form of retail is on the brink of complete disappearance. This is not only because certain artists choose to hand out their music free, on the Internet or as a premium with a paper or magazine. The record store once possessed great power. Only the records that were in the store were allowed to be sold. The selection made by the buying agents of stores, and the either eye-catching or obscure place allocated to the CD in the store, were vital in the process. Especially the retail trader — 'real music freaks that were combing through CDs long after hours,' as a record executive describes them — used to be a confidential advisor to music lovers, who could suggest or recommend CDs to them. These times are gone thanks to digitization. Another label boss puts it as follows:

> It used to be that a retail business could enforce a breakthrough. Now they are ordering such small numbers of titles that labels are even refusing to have them delivered. And because stock costs money, record stores no longer have stock. People start thinking likewise, they won't have it any longer in the store.

This explains why music lovers who still get their physical CDs will sooner get their stuff through online mail order companies (such as Amazon.com, Bol.com, Proxisazur.be or Play.com), or download from a web shop. Thanks to digitization, the customer also has easier access to unknown underground artists only rarely found in the record store.

Because the local record dealer is vanishing, business is also dropping for the wholesale trade. Add to this the fact that nowadays department stores prefer to do their own purchasing of CDs rather than having them done by a wholesale trader (shelf keeper). Because of all this, the part of the wholesale business is largely played out. What are left are the store chains and department stores.[4] They are still active in the selection process, but the supply, which is obviously dependent on the buying agent in service, is often smaller and much more tailored to the bigger names. Consequently, as one record company executive asserts, the record firm only focuses on music 'that is relevant for today' (the priorities of the hour) and on strictly targeted back catalogue actions (*reissues*, compilations), to which the record firm can apply the familiar sales strategy. Earlier, some light was shed on the role of re-releasing old titles in the canonization process (see p. 82). These actions, however, also serve mainly economic purposes. When, for instance, in 2009 the catalogue of The Beatles was remastered, it rocked the international charts. Sales figures also show that this market is growing and that record companies are willing to go very far in the number of times the same material is being released in a slightly different form without the fans starting to complain too much (Christman 11.11.2006). Moreover, as long as there is a demand for these titles, the companies will continue to release them, for every budget and every target group (special editions for the fans, budget series for the public). The costs of such re-editions or compilation CDs are so low that the risk of a badly selling title is not that great, while there is easy profit to be made from a large sale. Two record companies had this to say about the back catalogue:

> This is the leverage we still have in dealing with the dealers. The back catalogue covers more than 50% of our turnover. New releases are for a younger target group. Only, it is a group with a limited budget.

> Because the largest audience is made up of young people and because they are also the biggest downloaders, you simply have to go back to stuff that is a little bit older. Simply because you are forced to do so, because there at least you are still able to sell CDs. In the other segments, by contrast, you tend to take fewer risks.

One of the consequences is also that many small bands fall by wayside of the distribution story and only manage to sell CDs after concerts, via mail order or as downloads. It explains why the power of retail in the selection process continues to diminish, causing the selection to take place elsewhere. The record company describes it as follows:

> The selection isn't made on the floors of the store chains. You can easily fill those floors with one title if you put the money on the table. Only, when these fail to go out, you have to get them back. So you can only do this with stuff of which you can reasonably assume that it's going to be sold. That's not the place where things happen. The first step is always the fight fought in the media.

Handling Uncertainty

The main effect of the current oversupply and the fleeting status with which music tends to come and go, is the uncertainty about what will either work or will not work — both in issuing CDs and in organizing concerts or playing music on the radio. Because the culture market, and especially the market of pop music, are fairly unstable and subject to change, people like their products in great quantity, as diverse as possible and invariably new. Because the public is large and unknown, the investments made by the music industry are always unpredictable. As was also observed by Becker (1982: 122-123), the industry is not always sure about who will consume the works, under what circumstances and to what effect. Uncertainty has become the dominant feeling in the pop music circuit. It leaves a significant mark on selection and is the cause of the ambiguity that surfaced in the interviews. This is why ambiguity is nothing less than the central theme of this study. As will become clear, the basic condition of ambiguity allows for numerous logics of selection to be adopted according to the needs of the situation. Bauman (2011) pointed out that uncertainty and ambivalence are typical of these post-Fordist times. In what he prefers to call 'liquid times,' there are no stable patterns left. Everything is subject to change, and flexibility has become the key word.

Concert promoters, for instance, are unsure because they are having a harder time to assess a crowd's turnout. CD sales figures have ceased to be an indicator, and even media attention is not always a relevant matter, simply because this attention is not (already) present at the time of the booking. What remains is the 'gut feeling.' In the words of one programmer:

> Because you book three or four months well in advance, it is hard to assess how strongly a band is in the public eye, and sometimes you can get too optimistic. At the time of the booking, a band can be very hot, but two months later this may very well be completely gone. Which is why still tend to do many irresponsible things (laughs).

Programmers are constantly confronted with fleeting hypes, making it harder to program. A festival promoter:

Sometimes you act too soon, and sometimes you act too late. The speed with which things change is so great that keeping close control is not evident. The result is that I, representing a small festival, have stopped venturing to do things that are superhot at a given moment of time.

When it is impossible to estimate the size of the public reached, a festival promoter who has several stages at his disposal cannot assess either on what stage he should put what band.

In the past, when you booked something in October, you knew until the next year that it could carry a main stage or a small stage. Now it happens that you are unable to put a band in a small tent, for security reasons only, because there are 5000 people turning up to see this band. Last year we had troubles with Rusko, Magnetic Man and Benga and Skream. In January, they were nothing, small peanuts. But things get spread so fast that on the day of the festival the tent proved to be twice too small. In former times, something could remain underground for a much longer period, which was the case with drum 'n bass. All of this has accelerated because of digitalization.

Uncertainty is rampant, also for the actors in the record industry. This is not only because of the still dropping CD sales. To advertise or offer publicity to a product has also become much harder due to the oversupply. One person responsible for promotion says to be lucky to be able to work for so many fine releases. At the same time, he admits he has trouble telling the press they are all fantastic, because doing so would cost him his credibility, all of which becomes harmful to the releases. After all, his is not the only firm to put out a flow of releases. Other distributors venture upon the same stage. 'And then each of us has to try to make it to one of the quality papers at least once in a week,' he sighs. On the side of a record firm's A&R, the motto has become to avoid 'losing one's shirt' once too often. Tension exists between the supply of artists on the one hand ('everybody' wants to have a CD released) and the actual artists that the industry is picking up (only a small fraction of the artists will have everything going for them).

Some of the interviewed actors consider the digitization process a form of democratizing music. In their opinion, this is in itself a good thing. Others, however, are far less approving and cite the Internet specifically as the main cause of uncertainty, fleetingness or volatility. Because of the much wider diffusion of the experience of music and because people are more inclined to listen to individual tracks instead of to full albums, there is much less control over what seems to be current or what is not. There are much more instances of 'blanks' or 'dummies,' as one radio person in charge phrases it. It also explains why the actors in the music industry often act on the off-chance, hoping for the best. Many respondents compare achieving success in the music industry to a lottery show. One person in charge of promotion with 20 years of professional experience admits he still cannot say which song can or will be picked up by the radio. A concert promoter tells a personal anecdote about a tour manager who once asked what job he did: 'when I replied: "I'm a concert promoter," he in turn replied: "So, you're a gambler."' One journalist says:

> Above all, pop music is arbitrariness. What works? What doesn't work? What becomes a hit? What doesn't? Why is a band at a given time the greatest band in the world only to see its next three albums bomb? You simply can't estimate anything. At the same time, it's what makes pop music such a fantastic thing.

As with any other lottery, you need to have luck. Unfortunately, the impact of selection is always risky. Thus, a label manager recalls having run the same promotional campaign for two bands, but as it turned out, it meant success for one band, and not for the other. '*It is gambling, not an exact business*' or '*you win some, you lose some*' are recurring statements in the interviews. This corresponds to what Laermans (2004) — following Menger — says about the artistic process of the artist: even for those who have a good network, the artistic career never stops being uncertain and risky. Personal decisions are constantly crossed by those of others, and the repercussions are never fully predictable. Apart from the individual choices made by the artists, also those made by others can help or block a career. For this reason, career decisions are always structurally uncertain. It is therefore difficult to plan a career strategically. Any success in undertaking resembles 'a lottery with swaying fortunes' (Laermans 2004: 15).

What is said about an artist's career can easily be extrapolated to other actors in the world of art. In the same way, the selection process in the pop music circuit is accompanied by uncertainty. How actors learn to deal with this, and which strategies they adopt to try to reduce this uncertainty, is an interesting subject for this study.

Recap 3

Decisions made by actors of the pop music circuit are not made in isolation. The truth is that developments at the macro level are determining selection. Thus, digitization creates marginal conditions. Because of the opportunities created by the Internet and because of new technological developments, certain alternatives for the regular modus operandi and the conventions within the music industry were born. Firstly, to produce and release music has become easier. As a result, the oversupply has become even greater. Yet because the number of slots that can be taken has not increased, a more stringent selection has become imperative. Secondly, everybody is able to build a basic audience and every musician can take charge of his or her own career by way of the Internet. Thirdly, the 'active consumer' has become a new player, who is able to indicate on his or her own terms what music either deserves to be picked up or not. All this is said to be able to undermine the traditional music industry.

Leaving aside the issue whether the role of the industry is played out or not (record companies, for instance, remain important in the promotional story), it is a fact that this evolution causes uncertainty in the music circuit. Because of the oversupply and the fleetingness with which music tends to come and go, what is going to work is never known in advance. The pop market is highly volatile and subject to change, sales figures have stopped being an indicator of success, the public has become large and unknown. To work in the music industry is a lottery. Decision-making in the pop music circuit is never free of risk, a condition that engenders selection pressure.

Nevertheless, the actors in service need to select music on a daily basis. The study will keep in mind the marginal conditions that were formulated in this chapter, and can now proceed to the order of the day: what are the logics that can be discerned in the selection process?

Notes

1   According to calculations made by *Billboard* (figures of 2004) 53% of the turn-over in the U.S. was made with only 0.5% of the total number of CDs released (Christman 04.03.2006: 22-23). In the Netherlands, too, the number of titles that are able to sell vast numbers has decreased significantly. Between 2006 and 2010, only one title managed to sell more than 100,000 copies (NVPI 2010: 1).

2   In the Netherlands the music market'sturn-over dropped to 50% between 2000 and 2010 (NVPI 2010: 1). In Belgium, however, the past years have seen a 21.5% drop, from 183.1 to 143.78 million (combined figures of physical and digital sales for 2005-2011) (Maeterlinck 13.02.2012).

3   In 2011 3.6 billion songs were legally downloaded, while streaming services (Spotify and Deezer in pole position) had 13.4 million subscribers (IFPI 2012: 6 & 11). In Belgium digital sales' share was 13.5% in 2011 (BEA 09.02.2012), up from 10% in 2010 (BEA 24.02.2011). In the Netherlands the share was merely 8% in 2010 (NVPI 2010: 1), but it soared exponentially to 27% in 2012 (IFPI 2013: 27). The rise is also notable in the number of web shops and digital music services: from only 50 in 2003 and 300 in the next year (www.ifpi.org 02.12.2005) to 500 in 2012 (IFPI 2013: 6).

4   In the Benelux (Belgium, the Netherlands, and Luxemburg), Media Market and Free Record Shop are the leading players (although Free Record Shop had to close down many shops in the Netherlands in 2013 following a bankruptcy). In Belgium, the French chain Fnac plays a leading part. As far as retail stores are concerned, an ominous sign was given when Sonica, the biggest in Belgium, went out of business in 2009.

4. From Personal Taste to the 'Right' Taste
The Individual Logic

Early 2009, dEUS receives nine nominations for the MIA, Belgium's Music Industry Awards. In the end, the nation's leading alternative mainstream band gets to take home a meager two awards. By contrast, solo artist Milow pilfers one award after the other right under dEUS' nose. When Milow goes on to win the MIA in the category 'Best Song' for his cover of a 50 Cent number, dEUS' front man Tom Barman loses control. He starts railing against Milow, publicly laughing at him because winning an award with a cover is simply 'not *credible.*'

The infamous moment is typical of the artistic discussion held in the alternative mainstream. It also tells a lot about how the selection process ultimately runs. Selection upon selection, the process is also a matter of taste. Every decision made in the music circuit is based on somebody's personal taste. In the interviews conducted for this study, every first answer refers to taste. People select something because they 'think it's good.' Actors repeatedly put forward taste as the main criterion, regardless of the branches, segments or sections in which they are active. 'If I think something isn't good, you can bet your life it won't appear on our stage. I can be very pig-headed in this sort of thing,' one promoter says.

Judgments about forms, styles, genres and somebody's artistic views are based on personal opinion. Although reasons of taste are relative, they also emphasize the individual autonomy that all of pop music industry's actors possess. As music lovers, these actors argue from an individual logic. Still, the question is this: to what extent do these personal judgments of taste match the standard artistic criteria in the alternative mainstream or the *right* taste? Taking it a step further, the question becomes the following: to what extent is the alternative mainstream prepared to mark itself off against both the underground and the mainstream? Indeed, why is it that dEUS feel the need to distinguish or dissociate themselves from Milow? These questions are of central concern in this chapter. First things first: why exactly do people think that something is 'good'?

The Importance of Personal Taste
Quality Criteria and Aesthetics in the Alternative Mainstream

‖ The Indefinable Feeling

To be able to love a piece of music or a style is a very important motive in the desire or willingness to go to work with it. A booking agent: 'In the end, you go like three to four times a week to a concert, and at that point you'd rather go to a concert you like than to something you don't think is any good.' To many, being able to follow the music they like is ultimately the one thing they derive pleasure from in their work. 'You can only get satisfaction from your job by being able to do enough things you really want to do.' One record manager gives the following apt description:

> I am perfectly able to motivate myself into working with something that will only sell three hundred pieces, but which I think is fantastic. My personal taste is my first motive, and it's something I'll always hold on to. We receive boxes or packages on a daily basis. I'm like a child who gets a visit from Santa every single day. I still buy tons of records; I'll always be a musical glutton. There's one thing I keep telling myself: the day that this ends, when I stop waking up in the morning, asking myself 'What will the postman bring today?' I'll be happy to become a park keeper or so.

When the actors are forced to work with music that they do not like, it can sometimes become a reason for changing jobs. One respondent, for instance, lost his appetite when the distribution label that employed him took on too many dance labels: 'That wasn't my world, and therefore I couldn't sell it.' Another respondent gradually lost his motivation and quit working for his firm when he had to work once too often for The Prodigy, Coolio and The Offspring: 'These are all bands I don't like to listen to, so I was barely able to put my back into it.'

Following personal taste can also balance out other sorts of reasons. Reasons of an economic nature, for example, can be set aside by the pure passion of a music lover. Thus, a booking agent says he will surely take on a very cool band, knowing well in advance that they will not sell out a medium-sized venue: 'Ultimately, it's got to be fun doing it.' A festival promoter admits he allows small bands to play knowing well that they lack relevance at that particular time, just because he likes them. One head of a label emphasizes that he will never sign an artist to his label simply because of sales potential. He only signs them when he would want to buy the record himself, stressing that he does not ask the question about what he can do with it from a marketing perspective until afterwards. These kind of actions could be called *value-oriented*, in the sense Weber gave to it. It is to act from a personal urge based on individual, cultural, ethical and aesthetical values, regardless of utility or effect (De Jong 1997: 116).

Further in the study it will repeatedly become clear that when push comes to shove, when other factors have also surfaced in the selection and when choices induced by position and environmental factors have influenced the decision, personal taste is still the (ultimate) filter. Ultimately, people want to get cracking with music that they also like. A journalist agrees:

> Possible pressure from the social environment? No, that's not what the criteria are about. You're talking factors, not criteria. Not even deciding factors, for that matter. What's essential and will always be essential, is the artistic. Otherwise, I wouldn't have paid any attention to unknown bands like Marble Sounds of Customs. The fact that this could become 'CD of the week,' has to do with one thing and one thing only: the artistic. Believe you me; we won't sell a single paper extra by doing those bands.

It speaks for itself that the pressure of legitimate interpretation is also part of the picture. No actors will easily admit that their personal taste is guided or directed. They do not want to be a puppet, unless they can be the puppet master. In the end, all actors make an appeal to something very legitimate. They appeal to personal autonomy and taste, and they believe it only makes sense that these weigh on the selection. The respondents make this very clear, and repeatedly give evidence of it. As German sociologist Niklas Luhmann coins it in his systems theory, it is a case of an 'expectation-expectation' (Laermans 2010: 224). The actors have an expectation about the expectation that everybody always has of something. As it happens, such an expectation is a Romantic idea. Individual agents are autonomous, stand on their own, and have a taste of their own.

A Good Feeling

It may be true that personal taste is the ultimate filter in the selection process, the question still is this: what exactly do people mean with 'I have to like it, think it is good' or 'it must be good quality music'? What are the quality criteria that exist in the alternative mainstream and how can these guide actions from an individual logic? The first significant observation is that the respondents have trouble describing it, and are fully aware of this. Some do not get any further than 'it is a feeling.' The four excerpts below give a fair idea of the problem:

> **GK** What's it like to like something, to think something's cool?
>
> **Respondent** Well, it's a matter of taste, no?
>
> **GK** I realize it's hard to define what you think or feel when you think or feel that something's good, but can you give it a try?
>
> **Respondent** No, I can't. Because it's very difficult to do... It's a matter of feeling it, sensing it, it's... When do you think something is good, that's... Well, with a track you can have the feeling of 'wow, guys, what have we here? What is this?' Or you can go 'This is okay, this feels good, you can feel it.'
>
> **GK** What is it that you feel exactly?
>
> **Respondent** You can't describe it, it's so... You can sense it, you can feel that this is way beyond just being made to sell, it's...
>
> **GK** What is it that catches your attention? Is it the way they play, the style, or...?
>
> **Respondent** Everything, you know. Also something that sticks, catches on, or something that ... I can't describe

it. I don't think it's even necessary to describe, not with a feeling.

I'm more of a 'feel'-listener. I have trouble finding reasons for liking something. (...) It's so hard to talk about it, everything is very much based on a feeling, very instinctive. Usually I just dive into shallow waters and see where I get. I never plan what I'm going to do. (...) You know what I feel? I feel I'm going to keep saying the word 'feel' for quite some time today (laughs).

To explain about music, why I like it or not, is I think the hardest thing you can ask me to do. I wouldn't even be able to tell what my favorite band is. There are bands I have been following for a long time now and that I think are wonderful, but then again, that's just a feeling. There are jazz or blues bands that I think are really great, while I don't even know the genre very well. At the same time there are also indie bands — a genre that I know very well — I think are really bad. Music is feeling. And describing this feeling is a hard thing to do. (...) I could never be a music critic. The only thing I would be able to tell is 'I like it and I feel this or that,' hardly anything readers would want to read about (laughs).

The only thing you have is the feeling. It is difficult to tell with words why you think something is either good or bad. I find it irritating that I keep on using the same vague terms for something you really cannot explain. It's so hard to explain it. Music is feeling, it's as simple as that.

What these four voices share in their attempt to motivate their selection is the use of cultural *clichés* (the term is used here in a neutral, not a denigrating or belittling way). To like something, to think it is good, is a *feeling*, and this feeling is hard to describe. This is why some also use the word 'intuition.' Many get uncomfortable when they have to motivate their own taste. When a respondent pointed out that bands also need to be good when performing live, he immediately anticipated the why?-question, felt irritation and replied (in a friendly manner): 'You're not going to ask me 'What do you mean with good?' again, are you?

Good simply means 'good,' for me, when *I* think it's good, nothing else.' A striking thing is that concert promoters, among others, do not even think it is their task to (be able to) explain their definition of quality. They leave this to the music journalist. A promoter even said he was not qualified to make an artistic judgment, because he did not have sufficient talent for music and was not good enough a musician to be able to do it.

Examples that Help Express It

The alternative mainstream does not have an aesthetics that is sufficiently clear cut. Nevertheless, the interviewed actors are not obscure or cryptic in their arguments. They are able to illustrate their views with concrete examples. To be sure, the argument is often circular, because the discourse only takes shape when it is linked with examples from practice and situations. The actors use these to support or substantiate and illustrate arguments. By illustrating their argument, they give shape to it. Artistic value judgments are thrown in between, mostly in an indirect manner. To find out how the respondents define 'good music' means to listen to the examples that punctuate or pepper the interviews. Some think Admiral Freebee and Massive Attack are fantastic, while others say U2 has opened their world. Still others think post rock is exciting, while Gorillaz, in turn, is the 'be-all and end-all.' Counter-examples too illustrate the argument. A journalist claims that Within Temptation does not meet his standards of quality, and another actor cannot get it through his skull why everybody is so excited about The National. Comparisons may also help. One actor thinks the new Absynthe Minded CD is qualitatively better than the previous one, and according to another actor, Team William is musically weaker than Triggerfinger. Koos Zwaan's study of selection criteria among Dutch A&R managers of record firms (2009: 32) had the same findings. In the interviews he conducted, actors also viewed the idea of 'good music' as the outcome of a subjective opinion. They illustrated this with specific examples of artists with whom they had worked.

Personal Factors in an Individual Logic

Quality criteria are especially hard to define because they are subjective. This view is a constant in the interviews, regardless of the position occupied by the respondents in the music field. An artistic quality judgment and personal taste go hand in hand.

Universal criteria of quality or of an artistic nature that supersede personal taste are never heard, or only rarely. A journalist thinks objectivity in art criticism is a utopian thought: 'It isn't even something one should try to strive for. The whole idea is pointless.'

The interviews mainly demonstrate that taste is something that is largely interiorized in a physical manner. It is a pre-discursive thing. This, evidently, corresponds with Bourdieu's analysis (1984). In Bourdieu's view, taste is contained in the habitus a social actor interiorizes, making it possible for the habitus to direct actions. It may be true that in matters of taste, there can be no disputes, yet sociology has since long observed that this subjective feeling — that is, taste — is also socially and culturally determined and therefore subject to change. Taste is acquired through upbringing, education and experience, among other things. It is part of a personality or habitus and it provides social actors with one or more 'genre specs' (see p. 75). From the social or cultural background, actors have a preference for, or a feeling with, a certain genre and only that sort of music that is relevant according to their own frame of reference. The music matches their view of music. Therefore, the music can be selected. They preclude, dismiss as non-musical, and consequently do not appreciate, genres that they have no knowledge of and for which they do not possess the appropriate *genre specs*. To recognize or to know something therefore equals to acknowledge and appreciate it. That is how the habitus operates.

In this respect, some respondents refer in a more general way to the frame of reference they have developed or the experience they have gathered. Those who are greatly occupied with music, or have dealt with it for a long period, are better equipped to make assessments. Others also explicitly refer to their upbringing and background. One example is this booking agent:

> I believe this is also simply a matter of upbringing, of your background. Why do you think Godard is cooler than some blockbuster? Because you had an education, because you've picked up certain things from your home, etc.

For reasons of completeness, some elements should be mentioned that are certainly relevant, but do not belong to the scope of this study. These elements are certain personal factors, such as age and generational effects.

The interviews strikingly revealed that actors who have been in the business for a longer period experience a shift in their motivation. The desire to discover new records or to attend as many concerts as they once used to, grows smaller. The sense of wonder that initially existed has gradually been lost. 'Mumford & Sons have stopped giving me the goose bumps,' one respondent says by way of illustration, and another observes that originality becomes relative in the course of time. Apart from artistic criteria, mainly economic standards have joined the picture. One journalist claims he will no longer give up his annual vacation for an opportunity to interview some star artist. As is often the case, these people tend to favor desk jobs. More than often, they also have a family life to which they like to dedicate their time.

Generational effects, for their part, are noticeable in organizations where veterans get assistance from the younger guard, for the first often a deliberate occupational choice which allows them to keep a finger on the pulse. This explains why senior music editors of newspapers often work with young freelancers. For example, a record firm will hire a young A&R manager because 'the drive needs to come from them.' A young promoter testifies:

> I feel I am still stung into action; I am someone who still attends many concerts. When I have missed certain radio programs (such as Select on Studio Brussels), I make sure to listen to them on the Internet. The fact is that I am constantly going at it, and I notice that this way of experiencing the whole thing is different from the way the older generation lives. They tend to make other choices, or in another way. At a certain point, you stop being able to go to concerts every night. Fatigue settles in, you're getting older, you have children. (...) That's why these people usually have a good team around them that still has the desire or the itch to discover things and to bring them to them.

Indeed, the frame of reference is also a matter of generations. The fact that music from the 1980s is 'cool' again, as one journalist observes, is because the *gatekeepers* in the media, as well as the people who run the record firms, were brought up with this music. Another journalist sums it up quite aptly:

When there is a female singer whose voice has an ethe-real touch, a young critic will say 'sounds like Bat For Lashes,' a critic in his or her thirties will say 'sound like Björk,' in his or her forties 'like Tori Amos' and a fifty-something critic will claim it's 'like Kate Bush.'

'Being Touched' in the Romantic Manner

The analysis must now take a few steps back and return to the main parameter for thinking music is either good or not: per-sonal taste. What determines whether something is good music or not is the fact that an actor is touched by it or not. Nearly every respondent describes it in this way. They explicitly state that they only like music when it touches them. 'There has to be a click,' 'It needs to get to you somehow, you have to be caught,' 'It's a vibe, a stimulus, tingling.' As one journalist puts it:

When is something good or not? When it gets to me. And then it doesn't mean a thing if it's innovating, or if it's an expensive record, hip or trendy, whatever. That doesn't interest me in the least. Sorry. Then it doesn't mean a thing to me. (...) Something touches e when it moves me, when it gives me an urge to play the record again. (...) It's art, right, not science. Otherwise, I would have become a business journalist or a math teacher. It's a bit like a football match: (...) team A can have all the opportunities, but if team B scores with just one opportu-nity, it wins the match.

The affection for music is sometimes also indicated with the passepartout of 'gut feeling.' A radio producer:

Gut feeling is a really difficult notion to describe, and actually it's also a fairly ridiculous concept, because it means everything and nothing at the same time. It indi-cates that you, as a music lover, feel if something sounds exciting, that it makes you enthusiastic, by a new sound or a new combination, the way of singing. It has to do with affect. The music has to relate to you or move you, touch you, or somehow blow you right away. Otherwise, I don't think you can talk about gut feeling.

In the alternative mainstream, the vocabulary is an emotional, Romantic vocabulary, not a discursive, rational one (see Meyer 2000: 37-42). People here also express themselves adopting the double view of rhetoric typical of Romanticism: taste is an *internally felt* thing (the individuality is expressed through deeply personal thoughts and feelings), and at the same time it is something that gets to somebody *from the outside* (the individuality is engulfed by the passion, the experience). It is something to which people surrender themselves, something they must undergo, almost suffer (the original meaning of passion). 'It overwhelms me, it happens to me, I am being touched': these are the symptoms, and they 'happen' as if the person was struck by Cupid's arrow. One journalist puts it like this: 'You can really be touched by a piece of music without knowing why.'

In sociology, ANT or Actor-Network Theory is able to shed interesting light on the phenomenon. Works of art are usually viewed as passive objects with which others get going. In Bourdieu's view – they are objects that acquire their worth and reason for existing through social relations. ANT, by contrast, views a work of art as an important, full and valuable actor in itself, not just an (economic) product that moves from one person to another. It is something that possesses a power to which you can only respond. It has an emotional impact, is able to influence people, overwhelm and impress them. Yet it is also able to move them, bewilder them and throw them off balance (Heinich 2003: 50). Instead of looking at what works of art can signify artistically or economically, pragmatist sociologists therefore contemplate works of art because of what they are capable of doing. Music, as Hennion (2001) observes, is not just a static product that is placed on a record, on a music sheet or a concert agenda. It is also an unpredictable event. Music is able to appeal to listeners, and to change them. Music carries people away, has an effect that can be compared to that of drug use: 'a state in which we can be carried away, be taken up by something' (Hennion 2001: 12-13). This, again, is a Romantic idea. In Hennion's view, the experience of music is not an active process which is characterized by the pursuit of distinction (as Bourdieu sees it), or by the measurement of consumption according to predefined 'objective' criteria (education, profession, etc.). It is an experience, in which the person experiencing passively undergoes or goes through the work of art.[1] Listening to music thus becomes an activity that aims at attaining a state of complete passivity. This submission to music occurs in a spontaneous manner, and without taking into account what the establishment or the public at large either thinks is socially acceptable or not. Weber would call this sort of activity *affective (social) action.*

A final point of interest with respect to the Romantic view, and which revealed itself in the interviews, is the way in which the respondents positioned themselves as music fans. In most *popular music studies*, when Romanticism is under discussion, it usually concerns the producer ('the autonomous artist'), and not so much the music lover. In fact, the music lover has the most significance in the interviews. The actors in the alternative mainstream are music fans. Those who work in the music industry, do so in the first place because of their love of music. This goes for all positions and all players alike. Typical is the way in which one respondent reacts when he was casually addressed with the term 'music lover.' He immediately stopped the conversation and set things straight, shouting 'music FREAK!.' Furthermore, the actors also want to share this passion for music with others through the position they occupy in the music field. Even though they do not express this in so many words (for fear of coming across as unprofessional), bringing the music to the public also springs from a mission, 'a calling.' They want to pass on something personal to others, share their taste. They are, in fact, music missionaries. Thus, a radio producer says that he repeatedly plays the music in which he truly believes because he wants everyone to know about it: 'Just like I used to do in the youth club, where I played records to make others listen to them.' A journalist, too, does the same.

> I regularly write about things that make me go incredibly wild, things of which I know that they won't be played on the radio in a million years, but which make me think: this is so beautiful, this must be heard, people must simply be made to listen to this, people need to know that this exists.

To a (Rock) Aesthetics?
The Artistic Discourse of the Alternative Mainstream

A clearly developed aesthetics would appear to be unfamiliar or even unknown to actors in the alternative mainstream. Still, there is 'something.' An appeal is made to the Romantic discourse of 'feeling,' to Romanticism as a physical experience. Actors are very serious about it. Yet because quality standards or criteria are hard to describe, this 'something' is left hanging about hazily, hovering vaguely above music practice. Nonetheless, Chapter 2 showed that popular music studies have put forward clear-cut criteria to distinguish between pop and rock (see p. 62). These values followed the Romantic pattern: only authenticity, credibility, originality and a live reputation can make the distinction from the plain commerce of pop. This study tries to find out whether these values are also very much alive in the (Flemish) alternative mainstream. The questions asked during the interviews remarkably needed to dig deeper and deeper. The respondents are very cautious when it comes to 'big terms.' Yet concrete viewpoints do come along in the stories told. Yet is it enough to serve as a basis for describing what is considered as 'good music' for formulating an (artistic) definition of the music that fits in the alternative mainstream? In other words, is there in the discourse surrounding this music can a specific aesthetics be discerned which is representative or typical of the alternative mainstream?

Authenticity

'My program is about authenticity,' as an interviewed radio producer formulates it explicitly. The importance attached to the authenticity, integrity, credibility and honesty of the musician-performer as an artist, is just about the most central theme in the aesthetics of rock. For all their vagueness as concepts, the difficulty with which they can be described, and the fact that here, too, they are described as 'a feeling,' these notions have a potent effect. They somehow manage to function as a guideline in determining what is artistically good music, in signing or booking artists, in writing about them, or in playing their records.

Thus, a radio maker thinks 'the feel' of the tracks is very important, as well as the way in which the artists make them and how they are occupied with them. A promoter mentions 'the soul' that can be inside the music: 'A band may or may not be your

style, yet regardless the music can be made and played with heart and soul.' In this respect, a journalist emphasizes the importance of the lyrics and the 'penetrating, carrying power of the voice, of the expression.' Indeed often, the voice makes the music authentic, or at least makes it appear so. Following Roland Barthes, Frith (1984: 181) argued that essentially the color of the voice possesses an immediate attraction, apart from the words used or the notes. Rock critics typically talk about the 'grain' of a voice. Other respondents again like to express it with an example. One player thinks Bon Iver is authentic, another mentions the artistic integrity of Absynthe Minded, DAAU and dEUS, stressing the fact that artists should always hold on to a form of stubbornness.

For one manager an important criterion to take a chance with certain artists is the fact that they create their own material, have a vision of their own, and do not simply create something because there is a market for it, without even liking it. This also indicates that authenticity in pop music usually refers to the relation between the artist and the performed material. Unlike in classical music, in the tradition of rock, and especially in that of the singer-songwriter, composer and performer are the same person. Only then does music become a medium capable of expressing the feelings, emotions and message of the artist. The listener gets to know the artist personally through his or her music. Here the idea of creative self-expression and the previously discussed Romantic view of art resurface. Because of this, artists who create and perform their own work will always be considered more likable and credible than cover artists or those who commission other artists to write their songs. Typical, for example, is a journalist who calls the performers of *Idols* 'manufacturable' artists, while in his view a singer-songwriter is 'never manufactured.' Too rational, well thought-out music is also viewed as less authentic. A respondent from a record company says that a 'song smith' who is able to create songs skillfully almost comes across as an artisan with a suitcase. This is considered less interesting than the artist in the gutter who writes his or her songs in a very intuitive manner.

As music lovers, the players in the music field are constantly seeking music that is extraordinary or exceptional, in some way or another. They listen with their heart, to music in which they believe. On the other hand, however, a form of schizophrenia, of disbelief, remains. As professionals, they know what the back stage of the music business looks like and what goes on behind the scenes. They know that authenticity is often just an illusion. One interviewed actor, a journalist, is well aware of the aura of authenticity that surrounds bands as Bon Iver or Isbells:

> Plucking chords somewhere in a shack, penniless, in the heart of winter, in the cold, with numb fingers, piping and peeping along. Oh well, this must be honest and authentic, no? No. No. No.

All this reveals the ambiguity of the statements and the relative nature of heavily charged terms. It does not alter the fact, however, that the actors are sincere and really like the music (the cited journalist does indeed like Isbells). Authenticity is an illusion in which a music lover happily believes. Reason and emotion, head and gut intertwine continuously. The excerpt below (a quote from a record company executive) aptly illustrates this 'believing' state of disbelief.

> Authenticity remains important in music. (...) Whether or not it is an illusion, is beside the point. It doesn't change the fact that you happily believe in the illusion. After all, Tom Waits is also a businessman. A very competent firm surrounds him. The man does not live or lead the life he represents, with grease stains all over his tie. Yet you do want to believe a part of it. I still find it important that you can think that people have made a song of their own, or have achieved something in all sincerity. (...) At the same time, however, it becomes increasingly difficult to keep believing it these days. When I see Aboriginals dragged onto a stage and into the spotlight, or someone as Seasick Steve... There must be thousands like him, if not a hundred thousand. The man with the homeless-guy beard placed on every stage, it's not something I am going to go and watch. I've listened to the record, but didn't think anything of it. This is just one of the lot, one that has been picked out of the many, and then the machine starts grinding. I know how the machine works. The hype works. On every front.

Musical Criteria — Originality, Artistry, Sound Design and Live Qualities

Music must always be 'authentic' first, however vague the term's interpretation. For the alternative mainstream to pick up music, however, something other than 'authentic' is often needed. Points of interest are the extent to which the music impresses the listener as original, how well it is played and how solid it sounds. Musicians appeal to chords, scales, times, specific instrument techniques, equipment, programming methods or recording techniques. Their music could very well be judged on those formal criteria alone. Originality, artistry or criteria of sound design or technique become the focus of evaluation and judgment.

The respondents frequently mention originality as a quality criterion. Music is selected when it is salient, 'fresh' and surprising. One actor thinks TC Matic is original, but Customs a little bit less. To another actor Bon Iver is something he had never heard before. Yet another thinks that there are too many new releases of singer-songwriters, 'things you've heard a thousand times before.' One manager decided to throw in his lot with a particular band because every record the band makes has the potential of being something different, of adding something. 'In the case of other bands you know well in advance what they are going to do, so this won't surprise me on a musical level,' he adds to this. That being said, all respondents do agree on one thing, that there are too few original bands and too many copycats: 'Most records that are being released are copies of things you already know and maybe only two or three in one year are really original.'

Innovation, for its part, is often viewed from the genre's context and from comparisons with other artists within the genre. 'Animal Collective or Antony & The Johnsons, something like that you can sure will jump out,' 'The Opposites aren't that good in their genre,' or De Jeugd Van Tegenwoordig is a new sound and a new approach to hip-hop.' As one journalist puts it:

> Innovation can be discussed from various sides: you
> can look at it stylistically or intrinsically from the music
> itself. Then there isn't much that is really new. But take
> The Black Keys, for example: you can say it's a blues
> band, yet they do link it up to other styles, to electron-
> ics, and in a particular way they manage to sound bluesy

without being your classic, run-of-the-mill blues rock band. Stylistically, you can tell something about it. You may be able to relativize the importance of 'new,' but still there is something to it.

Music can be compared to fellow genre artists, and on a basis it may be labeled as 'fresh' or 'innovating.' A well-founded genre analysis, however, is quite another matter. The collective logic of content, as Gielen calls it (2003: 146), usually does not hold a prominent position in the discourse of pop: looking at the position a piece of music takes in the broader genre story, referring to the history and the conventions of the genre. In addition, originality can indicate great or small differences (Laermans 2009). The interviews are teeming with comments about original variations. Yet hardly anything is said about radical breaks or ruptures. In the alternative mainstream's discourse, innovation usually takes on a conformist, rather than a progressive guise (see Keunen 2002). What's more, this is exactly why questions are raised about the status of originality as a criterion of quality. 'Must good pop music be necessarily innovative?' one respondent wonders. 'I don't think so. I think you can come up with about a hundred criteria which you can emasculate just as easily.' Several respondents indicated that originality has become less important to them in the course of time. This was clearly demonstrated by the negative reactions and questioning glances a participant of a panel discussion I attended received from other people in the sector when he said: 'I like music from the 1980s, at least in the way it was made back then, not in the case of a contemporary copy.' This brings us to the next criterion:

Originality doesn't have to be the main reason why I book a concert. Being top notch in the genre can be enough. Roco Portolatus, for instance: beautiful what he succeeds in doing, but the guy didn't invent hot water.

The quote from a promoter reveals that besides originality, craft is also a criterion. Music that has nothing new to offer, but constitutes a perfect creation within the conventions of a genre. One interviewed journalist was able to explain this in the most well founded manner. In his assessment, the starting point is the personal goal an artist wants to achieve.

One aspect is originality. Another aspect is artistry. You need to look at the goals of a band, attempt to determine the ambition the record sets itself, and then assess how well the band achieved its goal or realized this ambition: what do they want to do and what have they succeeded in doing? When a group wants to be original and strives for some sort of innovation, then you must examine the degree of innovation. When the emphasis is on the craft, you can also assess whether it's been executed well. Sometimes you can have a record which has nothing new to offer, but which is so well-made (...) In this sense, a record that wants to be commercial, can very well be good, in the same way that it can be flat cliché-ridden crap. (...) Therefore, what you need to do is to look at the intention and the ambition that the artists in their context hint at or literally create.

Craft or skill is an important factor in the evaluation. Then again, there are limits to the amount of craft. Not everybody who has some skill in playing an instrument will immediately get praise. Virtuosity, mastering an instrument in the sense of having a perfect musical technique, and quality of a performance are quality standards that hold a prominent position in the culture of classical music and in the realm of traditional art criticism. In the alternative mainstream, however, they are rarely found. When they do surface, they are almost certainly never decisive. In the 1960s (the 'guitar gods' of blues rock) and in the 1970s (progressive rock), however, this was still very much the case. In today's alternative mainstream, these criteria have obviously lost their weight. 'Musical command of the instrument is less important,' one manager confirms. Rock academies and conservatories may not like to hear it, but the fact of the matter is that it is often a disadvantage in the evaluation. Virtuosity can become an obstacle to the sense of musicality and to the Romantic 'feeling.' Too much virtuosity is often easily dismissed as 'musicians' music.' Anti-intellectualism reigns. Any reference to art is a negative reference. This is why actors in the pop music circuit say very little about analyzing a piece of music on the grounds of its intrinsic artistic value. The internal coherence and the aesthetic qualities of the work, the applied formal structure, the schema of chords, the parts and arrangements, the sound colors, the set of instruments, and so on, are barely even mentioned (such criteria pertaining to the musical content fit in with what Gielen calls the singular logic of content, 2003: 145). Now and again somebody will mention a 'good song' or discuss the 'quality of the melodies' in the interviews, but that is the end of the story.

What never stops weighing in the balance, however, is the Romantic bodily experience. The *sound* of the music occupies center stage; the sound is the music's *body*. How something is made, or how it is played, is of no concern. What is of concern is the effect. This reveals that music is an immaterial good, as described by Hardt & Negri (2002: 292-296). It is aimed at operating or manipulating affects, at 'feelings of pleasure, satisfaction, excitement and passion' (Hardt & Negri 2004: 120).[2] This journalist phrases it in the same way:

> Music is a feeling, an emotion. This is the reason why pop musicians make music: to express personal emotions and to touch other people in an emotional way. They never do it to be able to say: 'Wow, that third note sounded really pure.' It is not a thing of mathematics. It is not about how technically perfect a record has been played. Take Leadbelly or Robert Johnson, for example. No perfect recordings, no virtuosos, and yet straight milestones. That is what it's all about, right?

The importance of the 'live' aspect underlines this. Artists establish their name as composers or performers of music, but also as live performers, by way of their concerts. 'Maybe it's even the most important standard of evaluation, that it evidently also amounts to something live,' says a promoter. A strong live reputation can become part of artists' image and determine the opinions about their music. Those artists that are good 'live,' are a step ahead of the competition (often cited in the interviews by way of illustration is Flemish band Triggerfinger). Good or bad concerts can also determine any further selection. A band may diminish the chances it gets by a bad live performance or, conversely, a great gig can make people reconsider their point of view about a band. One journalist recalls how a freelancer who had just run Mika's CD into the ground, made a complete U-turn after a fantastic concert at Rock Werchter. A promoter found that a bad concert at Pukkelpop festival ruined the autumn for one particular band. A manager says that some promoters pulled out after one of his bands did a lousy CD presentation.

There is still one thing that should be mentioned, not because it is important, but for reasons of completeness. Because pop music is also *recorded* music, production value and sound quality have some weight in the selection. Some respondents pay attention to production values and the sound of a recording, but all maintain that it only plays a minor part in the assessment of the music (unless it is assessed employing a different logic: radio producers, for instance, only want to air decently recorded music, see p. 225). A CD that is recorded, mixed and produced according to some standard of industry is actually considered self-evident. With live concerts, a poor sound mix or annoying feedback can have an impact on the evaluation (this may be of concern to journalists).

The Artist as Genius and the Canon

Those who over the years have given evidence of the above-mentioned qualities can secure future selection through their acquired reputation.[3] Occasionally, in the interviews, someone drops the term 'genius.' As was said before, the concept of genius fits in neatly with the Romantic tradition, actively as a general justification for art (what would be the purpose if the truly extraordinary and exceptional did not exist), but also passively as the object of a truly Romantic admiration and love. The Romantic loves to love the outstanding, unusual, uncommon and exceptional. A genius, in our context, is a person of great talent and creativity, an artist who is both authentic and credible, who makes original music, who is perhaps also a good musician, and who is able to shine on stage. The interviews reveal many different voices, each with their own sound. Together they form a buzzing crowd of divergent tastes, opinions, assessments, evaluations, judgments, and justifications. In short, it was a cacophony of selection makers. Yet on one particular subject, these voices sang unison. A name. A name that was truly capable of generating a unanimous love. Mauro (Pawlowski). As soon as his name fell, the respondents became wildly enthusiastic: 'An incredible songwriter, a genius,' 'the most talented Belgian musician of all times,' 'the most charismatic performer we have in Belgium,' 'a musical omnivore,' 'a creative source that never runs dry,' 'Mauro's got it, he's special, and he looks a bit insane.'

In many cases, the deciding element is the belief actors have in artists. With respect to what he calls a singular logic of context, Gielen (2003: 147) points out that such an artist-directed approach focuses on the discography (or oeuvre) artists have built and the reputation they have acquired through it. Although in pop music, a reputation reaches beyond an artist's records, his or her live performances, too, contribute to it. The artists have all been able to develop stories of their own that express their artistic views. These stories actually hand out the listening keys with which music lovers can approach their work. Chapter 2 explained that new works are judged in light of this oeuvre, and it is precisely because of the accumulated oeuvre that new works obtain a relevant meaning. Discography reveals the unity that exists between the works and ensures that the lesser tracks or CDs are still worthy of appreciation. Abrupt stylistic changes in the artists' course can sometimes run into sanctions (this happened to Neil Young, who was sued by his record company for producing 'atypical Young records').[4] These changes, however, are readily accepted when certain events in the artists' life can explain why they are suddenly behaving in such a different way (think of Bob Dylan's conversion, or Robert Wyatt's paralysis). Then the 'deviant behavior' can be ironed out and integrated into the meaningful whole. It explains why an artist's reputation and a work of art's repute can interact and influence one another, as was rightly observed by Becker (1982: 23). Actors will more easily appreciate the work of an artist whom they respect, just as they will have more respect for artists whose work they love.

> If we know that a person of superior ability made a work, we pay more attention to it, so we can see what might escape the more casual inspection we give a work from which we expect nothing special.
> (Becker 1982: 356-357)

Actors tend to judge works in the light of other works by the same creator ('his earlier work is better than his later work'). As one respondent says about the career of dEUS: 'The first three records, those really unlock the awe and admiration in me.'

Actors that look at the reputation of artists may also have eye for the broader history of music and the canon that has developed inside of it. Artists, whose careers are the outcome of years of artistic labor, have more spectacular feats and impact than fledgling artists do (see Bourdieu's long-term production cycle). Icons from music history are quality standards right from the start, and thus acquire their place in the selection more easily. In this way, an interviewed journalist labels Roger Waters and Simple Minds as icons in pop music: 'some things you do because they have their place in history, even if they have stopped making relevant records long ago.' Because of this (yet also because of *re-issues* and documentaries about the big names from history) the canon is constantly confirmed and endorsed. This is what also a record label boss defends:

> I don't think you can simply exist in the now and here. You need historical milestones: The Beatles, The Rolling Stones, The Doors. Cherish your darlings. (...) As it goes in history, they are fairly thin on the ground. How many pharaohs can you still recall? The ones that stick are usually also the greatest, the ones that procured the unity of a nation, the ones that won the greatest battles, and so on. I think that's okay. I don't think that every stone, every little sculpture, every poem should be conserved. Let time take care of the selection. Sometimes this isn't fair or right, and a lesser god may survive by chance. (...) For reasons of self-justification and legitimization, all sciences start with the history of its own discipline. It's the same thing in rock journalism. In itself, I don't think it's something you can bring much objection against.

Evidently, the canon can be up for discussion. Then again, anyone who tries to make sacred cows somewhat less sacred must be willing to accept the consequences. A journalist learned this the hard way when he wrote an article entitles 'The Beatles are an overrated band.'

> Absolutely. Because certain things are expected and thought to be true, like 'The Beatles are the best pop group that ever existed.' Says who? Sure, they made some fantastic things and changed things as well, but not everything they made was fantastic. Imagine me writing this somewhere, against these preconceptions. It bothers me,

the fact that you cannot touch the big names. Dylan also
made crap records.

The Alternative Mainstream's Craving for Distinction

A Separate Segment with a Culture of its Own

Thus the aesthetics of rock, analyzed in Chapter 2, is still present in the current alternative mainstream. Because sincerity, honesty and authenticity remain central values, the segment acquires a cultural foundation of its own. It is the reason why gatekeepers will select a particular type of music and will distance themselves from other segments. A record label boss is spot-on with the following observation: 'This world often identifies itself by distancing itself from the other worlds. Hence, the notion "alternative."' Consider a festival promoter's comment: 'Let other festivals program different things. This is how we distinguish ourselves from them.'

Nonetheless, the interviews clearly show that actors from the alternative mainstream do not feel a great urge to distinguish themselves from the underground, even though they very clearly view the underground as another segment. Some may think the underground too marginal or too *arty farty* for their taste, yet usually the underground is referred to in a positive way (see below). The distinction with the real mainstream, however, is not something they are prepared to compromise. They argue very clearly that the mainstream is a completely different world, 'with very few crossovers' and 'with entirely different *ins & outs*,' *and* they emphasize 'this is not [their] world.' A record label boss claims his firm is strong in making rock bands break through, but has some difficulty with dealing with the real mainstream. His A&R and marketing managers 'do not quite speak the language or know the circuit as well; they have less experience with the world and too little know-how; therefore they are less willing to come and go in the world.' Another record label boss says the same: 'I am incapable of working with flat commercial crap; it's not my sort of thing.' The Flemish radio landscape is also clearly marked by the distinction. One respondent, a radio professional, says there is still a difference to be made between Studio Brussels (abbreviated: StuBru) and MNM:

> You can compare it with cocktails: both stations mix cola in it, but in StuBru's mix there will be a bit more vodka and MNM's mix will have some more sugar. Evidently

the composition of this cocktail is different. The target group that you reach is going to be different too. And luckily so. The difference is in the voice of the presenters, the kind of humor we use, the sort of concerts we sponsor, the type of showcases, publicity campaigns.

It should not come as a surprise that Studio Brussels dumped the broadcasting of the weekly official hit parade, 'Because that sort of music is too far removed from our daily offer,' as the net manager explained (*De Standaard* 16.12.2010). In fact, those who think from a mainstream perspective share this view. Consider the comment made by Flemish female singer Natalia about 'alternative music': 'There is a big rift. Too bad we are unable to appreciate one another somewhat more.' (Vantyghem 25.04.2009) In the interviews, a record label boss labels 'the pop genre' (in which he is active) and 'the alternative genre' (a world he assures he is not well up on) as two distinctly separate worlds:

> When you have a pop artist, then you search and find a repertory that belongs to the pop artist. Then you create a marketing and promotional plan. When you venture into the alternative genre, there seem to be different parameters for assessing an artist. Then the live performances become very important, and 'breaking' an artist can take much longer. It all should happen organically. When you're an alternative artist, then you gradually and silently work your way up via smaller and eventually bigger concerts, and only then, I think, you will want to come up with any records. With pop artists, it's an entirely different ballgame.

Extraordinarily typical is the following observation made by Bob Savenberg (former member of mainstream Dutch-speaking soft rock band Clouseau and manager of every Flemish *Idols* artist, including Natalia):

> The fact is that an artist is a format which you need to put on the market as well as possible. So you need to determine well in advance how he or she will come out. What music do you use? What image does he or she need? (...) I can fairly say I know every little trick in the

book to get a figure in the right spot on the market. Provided I have some sort of connection with the person. And that he or she is able to listen to me. (...) I'm not in the littlest sense tuned in to the alternative circuit. I know very and too little about it, it's not my kind of music and I don't like the attitude thing. I think music and success go hand in hand, and nobody should be condescending about this. (Savenberg, in: Sioen 24.01.2009)

All this tells us that the alternative mainstream is a separate segment with its own proper culture and modus operandi. Yet as was said before, the distinction actors strive for in this world is also ideologically charged. To put it in neutral terms: it serves as a justification (Boltanski & Thévenot 2006). It is not just that people think their music is better; their own values also serve to justify their position and to denounce other segments. The remarkable thing is then that it is not the underground which becomes the bumper, but the mainstream. This is why players in the alternative mainstream in Flanders tend to look down on stations as Radio 2 and MNM, or TV shows such as *Tien Om Te Zien* (a mainstream pop show) and *De Rode Loper* (a celebrity news show). When an 'alternative' artist makes an appearance on such a show, or is heard on one of the said stations, then 'it somewhat devalues him or her,' as one record label boss points out. 'That's not a good thing.' The war of the worlds, the difference between the alternative mainstream and the mainstream, is nicely illustrated by an anecdote told by a manager, recounting the exploits of one of his bands (your typical alternative mainstream band) during a live broadcast on Radio 2 (your typical mainstream channel).

Radio 2 gave the band full airplay. They asked us for their Saturday morning talk show. Some of the other guests were so-called BVs, short for Flemish Celebrities. Ellektra was one of them. She had brought one of EMI's promo people. Ellektra is a Flemish actor, star of a popular soap called *Home*. Blonde bimbo, can sing a tune, did some TV entertainment shows. And EMI, of course, signed her, put her in the studio, made a record, big budget, all the works. So I am there with the band, wondering: 'What are we doing here?' And right in front of us the whole thing turns into a circus. As the band's singer described it: 'Like a tabloid, performed live.' A couple of Flemish Celebrities started quacking, and he had to go and sit at a table with them. Then it was his turn to get a question. And it freaks him out. He's thinking: 'Man, do I really need to answer this? Do you really want to know what I like to put on my fries?' That was the subject, at eight in the morning. Fries. Somebody was making fries, and the question was 'When you go to the fries shop, what do you take with your fries?' Fuck, he said, if I had known this would be the subject, I would have stayed home to play with my daughter. These Flemish Celebrities, on the other hand, they did like to talk about fries. They were there to present their new TV show or something. And they played along perfectly. It's about all they ever do, these guys. Yes sir, it's an entirely different world (...) Later, the singer came up to me and said: 'If possible, this never again.' Well, we don't do this anymore.

The mainstream norms do not correspond with those of the alternative mainstream. Other values result in an adverse, even abhorrent attitude. The mainstream merely serves the purpose of negative reference. 'To us, the whole thing always stinks a bit': these are the exact words used by a manager. Players mainly occupied with the alternative mainstream want to distinguish themselves from what, in their eyes, constitutes the real commercial circuit. Its so-called 'commercial' nature is the most important objection leveled against mainstream music. A manager:

The mainstream has a completely different set of criteria. Not the artistic comes first, but what can be made with it. Unlike in our world, the mainstream only rarely releases something when people cannot reasonably expect that it will do something. That's really the whole premise, and the other criteria are tied up to it. That's why the marketing methods are so different. And when an artist has no hits, they just do some sessions with a couple of songwriters with the hope that a radio hit will come out of it. The mainstream is much more concerned with singles and short-term-careers.

In the interviews, mainstream music is often viewed as music that is mainly created to earn money. This explains why the makers must yield to the broadest possible taste (Bourdieu's account of the large-scale production, or Adorno's critique of the culture industry are close by, see p. 34). The 'typical hit parade music,' one respondent argues, 'is merely a product, which is made in a really fake manner.' Popular Flemish dance act Milk Inc. is a group that is cited repeatedly in various interviews as the textbook example of 'wrong mainstream music.' Consider the following quote:

> Milk Inc. is purely and uniquely the commercial circuit. It's made to sell and be sold, entertainment music that switches off people's brains, pure fun. (...) It's not made to be any good. To me, these are marketing products. Look, Milk Inc. is the flattest of the flattest, thud-thud-thud, I don't think it has any quality whatsoever. I think it lacks just about everything. There's no meat, no blood to it, It's just plain entertainment, that's got a marketing channel behind it.

In one noteworthy interview, a respondent manages to come up with a way of dividing the music world that roughly matches the distinction I have made between underground, alternative mainstream en mainstream. The classification not only indicates the value-related distinction, but also reflects how the musicians themselves view it. On the left side, he places musicians that occupied themselves with doing their very own thing; on the right side, he places those who make music to make money. Between these two poles are the musicians who manage to combine both.

> A band like Isbells is in the left circle, Milk Inc. is on the far right. Artists such as Filip Kowlier and Admiral Freebee are somewhere in between. In their heart they would rather be on the left, but they think: I am able to make a living from this, and because of this I don't have to work from 9 to 5, I am there and I play along.' There are people here whom I find honest, who have my sympathy and who stand for what they do. These musicians still want to do what they want, they will compromise, but not for

a 100%. The bands on the right side go like this: 'Compromising? No problem, as long as we sell more records by it. if I suddenly have to go wear a pink tutu on stage, and if this means I will have more success, then I will do it.' I can give examples...

Those who set these 'alternative' values as the norms, will primarily think from an artistic point of view instead of from angle that solely targets the public. Concert promoters let individual (and equally legitimate, see p. 176) taste prevail over possible cheap success. Thus, the interviewed promoters are well aware of the fact that their public, too, could go out of their heads for Milk Inc., but they will never program the band. 'That would be a bridge too far, that wouldn't be right for us,' one says. 'Although I choose the public at large,' the other complements, 'I do try to serve this public the cooler, better stuff.' Filling the concert halls is not our priority; it always has to fit in the whole picture.'

> We don't program whatsoever attracts a big enough crowd in the main hall. Milk Inc. would also sell out, but we refuse to do this. There is also our artistic line that needs to be right. We'd rather walk the just that little bit more alternative path.

The same idea lives among the written press: 'Milk Inc. is not our thing, not a band with which we would want to associate.' In a more limited way, this may also apply to a major. One actor, the managing director of a major, takes pride in the fact that the musical aspect always prevails, how important the commercial may be as a criterion.

> It must never be too plain. Our firm has always tried to walk the middle road, with better quality. I think we have the image of a firm where there's still a heart for music, and with this I do not imply that this is not the case with the others. I always refer to us as the biggest independent, while Pias is the smallest major, whatever they may claim to the contrary.

The conclusion from all this is that the aesthetics of rock culturally identifies the alternative mainstream and that it forms the basis on which it wants to distance itself from the mainstream. An underground philosophy and a Romantic discourse are employed to attribute a cultural surplus value to the given of the market in which it operates.

The Struggle over Definitions in the Alternative Mainstream

The alternative mainstream's discourse is far from an unambiguous, well-delineated whole. How the gatekeepers in the pop music circuit think about quality criteria such as originality or authenticity is not as innocent as it may look. Here too there are struggles over the 'right definition' of 'good music.' Actors dispute one another's choices of bands. They disagree about what deserves to become the focus of attention and the object of selection, and what does not. The fact that a band is picked up by a number of actors, does not imply that there is a consensus about them in the segment. Examples cited by respondents as negative references illustrate this. Some of the actors do not applaud bands that sound old-fashioned or as clones of another bands, because they do not meet the above-mentioned quality criteria. Flemish rock band Triggerfinger is a good example of this tug-of-war. The band may have had plenty of positive reactions to its live performances, the studio CD faced harder times. Weekly magazine and rock authority *Humo* is said to have ditched the CD ('because they thought Triggerfinger was just another retro band'). Radio station Studio Brussels too posed a problem ('Triggerfinger wasn't much thought of by the people doing the evening programming; they thought it was old-fashioned rock-'n-roll; the result was that the band fell somewhere in between'). One respondent thinks Ozark Henry or Zender is too mainstream, and yet another does not want to hear a single note of De Mens or Monza ('to me it's constantly the same, lacking quality, even a bit cliché-ridden'). Mintzkov is another example of a band that suffered a contradictory, no less grim fate: 'In the Netherlands the band was immediately recognized as a good Belgian quality band; at home, the stigma of dEUS-epigone somehow stuck.'

There can be discussion about the actual application of the shared criteria of quality. This is typical of a cultural symbolic struggle or struggle over definitions, in which much attention is paid to setting boundaries and borders

(Laermans 2010: 181-183): the demarcating, guarding or watching, and possibly altering of the limits that determine what is admitted to the alternative mainstream. The issue then becomes to examine and determine whether music is sufficiently alternative or not, too mainstream, etc. Flemish singer-songwriter Milow is a fine example of such a discussion over definitions cited in several interviews. He started his career like many others in the Flemish alternative mainstream (with a noted appearance in the rock contest *Humo*'s Rock Rally) and grew to become an international star. To many of the interviewed actors Milow does not meet the requirements spelled out in the definition of 'good music' and embedded in the aesthetics of rock (at least at the time of the interviews; the matter whether this is still the case today is left aside here). The reactions are in keeping with one another: 'Not my thing and not the kind of quality direction in which I would like to see the music industry develop,' 'I don't think his music is any fun' or 'Milow may have had his breakthrough, but it does not imply that he can come back just like that.' Milow's aura, too, can raise doubts. Somebody says sardonically:

> I think Milow live is boring as ever. He compensates this by a certain look that causes a hormonal disturbance in young girls. I have seen it happen to my daughter. It is not that serious.

One thing, though, about which all the above-mentioned respondents agree, is that a self-made man like Milow deserves respect, for the way in which he strategically put his music on the market: 'He managed himself, knows how the system works, and has thought out every single step he made. In short, he was very smart in playing the game.' These words, however, only reflect an organizational logic (see the next chapter). When an individual logic is active, the only thing of concern is the music, which is considered too mainstream for the alternative mainstream. Because of this, a manager explains, Milow had a hard time in the first stages of his career:

> There are many people whose taste is alternative at the gates you need to pass in this industry. In the beginning Milow was positioned too 'alternative,' which did not hit it off. He is a child of Rock Rally and wanted to set off

in the alternative scene. What he did was bring a kind of mainstream we didn't have already. There weren't many festivals who wanted to book him. First Studio Brussels didn't even play his music. Milow, for his part, desperately looked for a manager, but didn't find one. He looked for a distributor with the majors, but didn't find one. The industry simply didn't believe his story. Does it make him a self-made man? Partially forced to become one because he wasn't alternative enough for this little world of ours. Belgium is quite a difficult market for this sort of mainstream music, but still he managed to overcome all obstacles. Today allegedly everybody wants to book him. In the music industry, all laws come tumbling down as soon as something starts to work.

The Assault – Criticism Against Leveling out the Music Supply with the Big Players

Everybody who acts in accordance with the values described above faces a genuinely difficult time when some actors choose to go for music that does not fit the criteria and therefore venture outside of the domain of *credible* music. This is certainly so for big, influential players who start to foul their own nests. Managers, record companies and promoters unite, launch an assault and fully engage in the fight over the right definition, over where to set the borders. The case of Flanders proved particularly interesting, as the critical force brought up the leveling out and reduction to the lowest common denominator perpetrated by big nation-wide radios (public 'alternative' station Studio Brussels), influential magazines (*Humo*) and international festivals (Live Nation's Rock Werchter). In their view, these players pursue an insufficiently alternative course. The music they play, review and program has become too mainstream.[5]

The textbook example that is brought to the fore in several interviews concerning the leveling out of festivals, is the fact that Milk Inc. was programmed at the Rock Werchter in 2009. In their eyes, the dance band represented the top of 'commercial' music at the high mass of the alternative mainstream. At the time, press and internet forums were full of voices raising sharp criticisms against this precedent (see also De Meyer 2010: 236-239). It seemed the aesthetics of rock was hit in its very heart. In the interviews, too, the reactions are ultimately in unison.

Why actors think that, on an artistic level, bands like Milk Inc. do not belong in the alternative mainstream, was explained earlier. A record manager feels that the band should be banned from any stage of a festival like Rock Werchter. He draws this comparison:

> I am somebody who feels at ease with a clear-cut menu. If I walk into an Italian restaurant, I don't want any nasi goreng on the menu. I walk into an Italian restaurant because I want to eat Italian food. Otherwise, I would go to a Chinese restaurant.

Others, however, are more violent. Some lash out: 'That's not one, but two bridges too far.' Or: 'An absolute disgrace that such a thing is even possible.' Even those who somehow manage to understand the choice (whether they are connected with the festival or not) are quick to assure that this music is not their personal pick. One respondent even wonders why Milk Inc. 'went through all this trouble just to prove themselves to another group of people.' Still another interviewed actor cites possible strategic reasons: 'The reason why Live Nation has billed Milk Inc. for Rock Werchter? Probably because it will allow them to take their shows into the bigger arenas.' This criticism goes beyond the case of Milk Inc. Players who fail to position themselves as 'alternative' simply *lose* their position and are from that moment on considered 'mainstream.' In the case of Rock Werchter, some are lead to raise serious doubts over the 'alternative' nature of Rock Werchter. 'Rock Werchter has ceased to be a rock festival, it has become very mainstream.' Another respondent admits that this point of view is also an effect of age, of his having become more critical in the course of time. This, evidently, also constitutes a repositioning in the field, by way of assuming a stance that redefines the field:

> Much of what is now called alternative is not alternative to me. I've been there before. Without doubt, it's also a matter of age, so you have to be very careful about this. But the fact remains that I find other things much more exciting. This sometimes comes up when I am with friends, and we start wondering: who has kept a young heart? is it the one that still attends Rock Werchter? I am there, professionally. But musically, there's nothing there

for me discover. (...) Perhaps I am the younger at heart, and not the one who tries to be on that field in Werchter at all costs. For the nth re-edition of Blur, which, so to speak, was actually a re-edition of The Beatles.

For this reason, others think Milk Inc. is exactly where it should be, at a *mainstream* festival like Rock Werchter: 'If they had been billed at a festival like Pukkelpop, I guess *then* I would have been genuinely shocked.' In spite of this, Pukkelpop does not escape criticism, although the target is limited to main stage program. In particular, the fact that the festival programmed Iron Maiden proved problematic for a number of the actors:

> Iron Maiden keeps on making the same music over and over again, and I expect Pukkelpop to bring me something that is able to trigger me, that pushes me on, or is even able to unsettle me or make me scared.
> Iron Maiden, definitely, is the last band and certainly the least to be capable of doing just that. Back twenty years ago, these guys were already a gang of aged icons.

As far as the Flemish media are concerned, especially Studio Brussels gets all the heat. In the interviews repeated sharp criticisms are leveled at the station. In informal conversations, over a pint of beer, in a noisy pub, the frequency of attacks hits the roof. The music that gets airplay on the station is said to be too commercial, too flat, too mainstream, anything but progressive or not adventurous or daring enough. 'StuBru likes to call itself alternative, but it has become a rather bloodless label. It's still mainstream. I feel personal grief over some of the things I hear on the station.' A manager confirms this. Many bands that previously were only heard on mainstream media, received airplay by StuBru. The fact that the station still picked up Milow from his fourth single, is downright proof: 'That is a clear sign of a shift in the media.'

What causes the bigger players to choose a less alternative course, is in the view of most of the respondents merely the fact that the toleration for being guided by market-oriented arguments has dwindled. Studio Brussels is criticized because they are too deeply concerned with ratings. This fixation should never have been allowed to root, not on a government-paid or subsidized network ('Unless they would change the criteria and conceive the programming in a much broader sense'). In addition, the general opinion is that this fall into disgrace would never have been possible in the past. One respondent rounds up the whole process:

> In the beginning Studio Brussels was more of a follower than a forerunner, more rearguard than avant-garde. When grunge, techno, hip-hop and metal suddenly became innovative in the 1990s and a period of turmoil set in for pop music, StuBru initially came up against facts and hard questions: 'Is this what our public really wants during the day? Is this to be allowed on a major station? Only when others picked it up, did they follow, because they were forced to go along. Then the top management changed, new people heralded a period of being reborn, and suddenly the station became a trendsetter, capable of anticipating currents and events. The musical climate, of course, has calmed down, which made it easier for the station to create a distinct profile for itself. Now, however, StuBru has become predictable. It has turned into a station that does what it's expected to do, which is to make sure that the ratings are good. In former times, it was often pure guesswork or the gut feeling, which I find more important. Now, however, they are able to follow the public more successfully. The numbers play a big part. It's an entirely different way of making radio, and it sure is less fun.

Rock Werchter, for its part, is only concerned with selling as many tickets as is unreasonably possible, or simply giving in to the public at large. Or so the criticism goes. One respondent thinks Live Nation wants to think outside the box not because — as the corporate justification has it — young people have stopped thinking inside little boxes, but because their aim is to render the commercial cake as large as possible. 'They literally don't give a shit dumped on the field: sold out is sold out.' From a business point of view, everybody can easily understand such decisions, and this explains why the criticisms are all very relative. Record label bosses with a similar commercial predisposition show some consideration:

Rock Werchter is not a cultural event, but a business and Live Action selects all the acts in order to lure as many people as possible. Not that there's something wrong with that. But what is the task exactly? The task for such a festival then becomes to attract and gather up as many paying customers as possible and this in the alternative format they have chosen. Live Nation makes sure that there is a certain form of quality, that they have the best and the rarest bands. I think they sometimes spice up the whole thing and here and there bill a band as Milk Inc. They had done this before with Faithless, which made them realize that with this sort of public the whole business was like selling hot cakes.

Viewed from an individual logic, everybody thinks the artistic should prevail. Those who really want to be alternative should not allow themselves to go for the big money alone and should be able to resist 'commercial' impulses. As was pointed out, however, this is mainly a discussion about borders, a struggle over the definition of what belongs to the field and what should be kept outside. The intention is to demarcate the borders of alternative mainstream. This implies both ensuring that the upper boundary of what either is possible or not is guarded (therefore, preferably no Milk Inc. on Rock Werchter), and that the lower boundary is set low enough, that is, not too high. As far as the live circuit is concerned, all respondents agree that the situation might have been far worse. Criticism is in the first place raised against the main stages of Rock Werchter and Pukkelpop ('pure commerce,' while the self-image is consistently confirmed as 'alternative'). These bigger festivals also use smaller stages where the aesthetics of the alternative mainstream still occupies — no pun intended — center stage. The media, by contrast, are said to have raised the bar too high and often too quickly label something as niche or underground. One respondent complains about the fact that a Flemish band as DAAU can hardly get an interview in *Humo* anymore. Another one is shocked to see that a quality paper in an article about Dez Mona has no scruples whatsoever to write only about the well-known producer of the album ('And this with a record that had been placed from a highly artistic perspective'). Another paper succeeds in presenting Sukilove ('pop/ rock with an occasional touch of weirdness') as the outlaw in a region of bands that can (scarcely) be allowed to appear in the media. Yet another voice thinks StuBru is far too quick in saying that certain music is 'not fit for airplay.'

Obviously, it not only the fact that there is too much mainstream in the whole picture, it is also the realization that this happens at the expense of what is considered authentic alternative music. The view of the critical actors is that the alternative should have priority. Decisions made on strategic grounds (commercial success) are hackled and the effects these have for the alternative artists who need it are laid bare and denounced. The result is a general feeling of leveling out, of reduced identity.

The Defense — a Changed Cultural Climate

Criticism raised against the media and their possible leveling out is clear proof of a struggle in the field over the right interpretation of 'good music.' It is a constant rock-hard argument over the status quo or upheaval of a tacitly shared, collective pattern of values to which any music must subscribe if it wishes to come up for selection and admittance to the alternative mainstream. These critical opinionated statements are even more interesting when the reaction they unchain is examined. Actors that are under attack, or feel they are under attack, feel the need to defend themselves. What is striking is that they start using a different kind of categorization. While the 'attackers' hold discussions about the boundaries of the alternative mainstream (as an independent music culture with an upper border and a lower border), the 'defenders' question the demarcation line itself between underground, alternative mainstream and mainstream, making a plea for some sort of hybridization or mix. Equally striking is the following: whereas the attack primarily starts from artistic criteria, the defense is more focused on the public. The main argument with which the media and the big festivals counter the attack and engage in battle, orbits around the idea of 'what the public wants,' or the wishes of the people or public at large. They select music of which they think their public will like to hear or see. To this is added the observation that this public is no longer concerned with any distinction between alternative and mainstream. The cultural climate is said to have changed, the role of subcultures is allegedly played out and the traditional mainstream and alternative channels, at least for a part, throw themselves upon the same music.

The discussion runs on three fronts. At the lower side of the spectrum, some respondents claim, the underground of the past has vanished, because the music does not hide anymore in the 'underground.' As was already explained in the previous chapter, it now spreads easily through new online channels on the internet. 'Anybody can now get to whatever record he or she wishes,' a radio man thinks, though this does not necessarily mean that the said music also actually reaches the listener. Some point out that one trend succeeds the other much faster than in the past. A booking agent finds that music which used to be solely destined for a niche and only gradually grew (think of the Icelandic band Sigur Rós), is now picked up with greater frequency, and, above all, with much greater speed. This is why they are knocking at the doors of the big foreign agencies and, consequently, call in at the bigger stages. The tendency is aptly grasped in the battle cries, slogans such as 'underground is the new mainstream' or 'mainstream is the new alternative.'

Secondly, the respondents belonging to the media and the big festivals think the public is open to various music genres from the same (alternative) segment. In their argumentation, they refer to music lovers who like Vampire Weekend, Black Eyed Peas *and* show up at the dance festival I Love Techno, or who like both Deadmau5, LCD Soundsystem *and* metal, or love folk, Nirvana *and* Iron Maiden. From this, they conclude that everything is more mixed or jumbled up. 'This used to be unthinkable, now it's all possible.' 'I think people who are now sixteen or twenty are far less troubled by narrow focus than our generation, let alone than the even elder generation.' The fact that the public listens to guitar rock and techno, however, is not an element in the struggle over definition. This form of hybridization was already found to be typical of the alternative mainstream (see p. 44).

The difference in opinion or point of view actually becomes clear when the distinction between alternative and mainstream is questioned. This is the third and the most important aspect of the discussion. The media and the big festivals assume that the public has stopped making the distinction altogether. Because of this, the interviewed actors who work at Studio Brussels do not think their station or Rock Werchter is less progressive than in the past. They have indeed become broader, simply because people have become more tolerant and like more things.

> This trend also marks the young people who work here. They go to, and listen to everything, Milk Inc. and Pukkelpop. (...) And when we play Justin Timberlake or Kylie Minogue, there's only a minority that reacts.

> There is certainly a sort of openness, glasnost. In Werchter nobody threw any mud at Milk Inc. Unlike ten or fifteen years ago, when it actually happened to Dee Lite.

When young people make faster switches between forms of music, the media must follow the trend, 'unless you want to run yourself into the ground.' It is therefore not really a surprise that Studio Brussels and (commercial station) MNM are drawing closer, a radio producer admits:

> The major problem with all radio networks is that everybody grows a bit closer to each other. It is the same problem faced by politics. We have all become center parties, each with their own characteristics and line of approach. (...) In Flanders, we face the extraordinary situation that we have two pop stations that target young people and the elder people with a young mind. At certain points in time or place, they are able to differentiate, but the fact remains that they are squarely in the center with touching behinds.

A booking agent mentions that because the distinction between mainstream and alternative has largely vanished, more bands are able to get into radio stations or media than ten years ago. Lady Gaga is a good example of this trend: she makes commercial pop music that is billed at Rock Werchter and is able to sell out twice a major arena (Sportpaleis in Antwerp); it is featured in teen mag Joepie, yet at the same time is capable of being found *credible* by both *Humo* and Studio Brussels. Black Eyed Peas, Ellie Goulding, Florence + the Machine and Deadmau5 fit the same picture. One by one, these acts are commercial acts that purport to be indie and *credible* at the same time. The situation here involves artists who belong to both the mainstream and the alternative circuit. This, by the way, is a position that was also included in the segments model (see schema 2).

Some respondents therefore think it is only logical that Tiësto is billed at Pukkelpop and Milk Inc., Pink and Lady Gaga at Rock Werchter. 'It's not because it's called "Rock" Werchter that you can only bill "rock" at Werchter. That's a completely outdated line of thought,' a journalist says. A booking agent adds: 'I think Werchter should simply be a cross-section of what pop music represents at a certain time, which is today, and so everything should be possible.' Quality papers keep an eye out for the real mainstream because a news medium must logically write for a large public and respect (the wishes of) that public. Thus, one paper decided to write about Lady Gaga and Milk Inc. because each is a phenomenon. They are capable of selling out Sportpaleis. Another paper even takes it a step further:

> One of the reasons why I started here back then is to be able to interview popular artists as Britney Spears. (...) Evidently, there is no need to do only the Spears, Pinks or Lady Gagas of this world. But as a journalist and a news medium you cannot put yourself outside of society. Quite the contrary, you should be standing in it with both feet. And a real, arguably essential part of this society are these kinds of phenomena. (...) Our target group is everybody, Everyman and Everywoman, or else I wouldn't be interviewing a schmaltz singer like Dana Winner or somebody as Pink, and restrict myself to the cool, credible, hip acts on the Sub Pop label of today—which we don't do, or at least not exclusively. I don't believe in target groups. The only target group that exists is everybody, because we are a mainstream paper. (...) I like to think that an artist who reaches every single layer of the population, like Britney Spears did at a particular moment consequently also reaches a layer that buys our paper. It's almost logics.

Worth noting is that the respondents take heed to drop any gratuitous remark, or turn a phrase of no consequence, that they feel the need to corroborate their defense with proof-, and in doing so provide an ideologically correct justification. At the radio, actors refer to the listening ratings: 'These clearly show that people tend to like more things.' The composition of the charts is often cited. Because also downloads are now included in the calculation, many alternative music makes it to the charts. As a result, Studio Brussels and its mainstream fellow MNM often play the same records, whereas in the past Studio Brussels would never even have thought of playing music from the charts. 'The charts are now able to give a better, more refined representation of what people like than in the past,' one respondent asserts. A journalist therefore thinks that the distinction between mainstream and underground has somewhat been blurred:

> It's a change of Zeitgeist, as simple as that. The Pixies used to be purely underground, but since Nirvana underground bands too can hit the charts. Foo Fighters, after all, is charts music. The same goes for Queens Of The Stone Age, while twenty years ago this would never have made it to the radio.

Comparing things to what used to be or to days bygone, is a frequently used way of substantiating or supporting the argumentation. There once was a time, when the alternative scene still existed. Actors had to belong to a subculture and could still be 'alternative' by way of statement. This time has gone forever.

> We're in a different societal context. In former times, authoritative media such as Humo were able to create a pro- and a counter-culture. Today, all forms of counterculture have vanished. People determine what good music is on their own, regardless of what somebody claims about what may be good or bad.

To let the taste of the public guide decisions, selections, and actions, is not merely a neo-liberal basic assumption. It can also become a self-fulfilling prophecy. Actors at the supply side advance the theory that things have changed on the demand side. The question, of course, is to what degree they are responsible of co-determining this public taste. Is this not just as well a social construction (see also p. 215)? Although this study is not concerned with the consumption side, and no claims are made about any element of truth of the opinions expressed by the respondents, they do demonstrate a fact of the utmost relevance. Some people in the music industry like to use a high-sounding 'alternative discourse,' employing artistic criteria from an individual logic; others (led by the national media and the big festivals) maintain a discourse that speaks from an organization-al or positional logic. Because of the position occupied by the media and the festivals in the field, and because of the expecta-tions of the organization to which they belong, they are forced to prioritize focusing on the public and acting in a market-oriented way. Not only do these actors argue less on an artistic level, they do not think, either, it is their job to lead the artistic discussion.

In the segment of the alternative mainstream, discussions are not limited to the question of whether the selection has be-come either less alternative or not. The terms 'authenticity' and 'commerciality' are also questioned as criteria capable of delimit-ing and defining the alternative mainstream.[6] The respondents cite the relativity of the criteria on which the aesthetics of rock was built. The alternative mainstream, it is said, does not have exclusive rights on a term as authenticity, and neither on the feeling that lies behind it.

> What is commercial? Everything you can say to de-nounce the music by Milk Inc. can also be said about some death metal band that makes use of clichés and has simple lyrics.

> At the basis lies a similar feeling. (...) Whether it is Edi-tors, U2, Green Day, Dana Winner or something else, is irrelevant. Essentially, it concerns a similar experience. It's about looking up to, worshipping, not getting enough of, and so on.

> To me, authenticity is somebody who believes in the music they are making. Schmaltz singer Frans Bauer is authentic to me if he believes in the sort of music he makes, and if he doesn't do this just to sell as many records as possible. When he sells loads of things with something he truly believes in, fair enough, I have no trouble with that. Maybe I'm naïve to believe that Regi of Milk Inc. makes the kind of music which he fully en-dorses. The fact that the music is a commercial hit will undoubtedly be a great bonus, but I don't think that's the only reason why he makes the music. He makes the mu-sic he thinks is cool, and to him it's never plain flat dance

music. Which is why I think it deserves a place on Rock Werchter. Why not? Next year popular acts like Natalia or Clouseau? Hell yeah, why not? I have no trouble whatsoever with it.

In this case, actors raise objections against an 'elitist' view of art – just as De Meyer (1994) does in the academic discourse. It is a plea for equal rights and opportunities for all music worlds. It does not matter in what segment they are situated. In each world artists try to make something valuable. One single interviewee, a journalist, pushes the view to its limits: he goes right against music lovers or critics who speak or act condescendingly or downright contemptuously about 'popular taste,' and especially against elitist highbrow prejudice or narrow-mindedness. When respected artists make bad records or give a bad concert, he brings up the matter. 'I'm not going to say it was fantastic just because it's the thing 'done' to think highly about certain artists.' He also compensates, by deliberately writing about mainstream artists, regardless of what others may say.

> You don't want to know what this editorial about Milk Inc. (Laughs). It's the kind of piece that people expect to read, except in my medium. (...) And you know what? I didn't even think of this at the time! Afterwards I'm honestly surprised, wondering what just happened. The fact that back then, in 2009, such a discussion was still an issue blows my mind. That the idea of a dance act billed at Rock Werchter can cause such a rumpus and stir up a serious discussion is beyond my comprehension.

This journalist consciously places himself outside of the alternative aesthetics, distancing himself from the 'Old Guard': he recognizes the ideological aspect of the alternative mainstream, but refuses to be any part of it. This might be to provoke people, to make sure the matter is addressed. For our purposes, however, the question is: is this a basic and shared fact of the alternative mainstream's discourse or is it essentially a minority view intended to stir up the debate, an exception that ultimately proves (the validity of) the dominant alternative discourse, the rule?

The thesis that the distinction between alternative and mainstream has vanished also leads us to question the existence of the alternative mainstream as a separate segment. A struggle over definitions and meanings of the fundamental terms can alter the classification schema. Ambiguity, however, is never absent in the statements made by 'opponents.' The fact that the terms 'alternative,' 'commercial,' 'mainstream' etc. are consistently interpreted differently by the respondents, tells us – to use Bourdieu's conceptual apparatus – that there is still an underlying 'objective complicity' to be observed: both orthodox and heterodox actors respect the rules of the game, and ultimately there is a general consensus about the established definitions. The paradox is that the arguments of 'attackers' and 'defenders' are much closer than they appear at first sight. The preceding paragraph showed that the actors did not so much speak against one another as beside one another. The line of approach and way of phrasing things differs. One makes an appeal to an individual logic, the other to a market-oriented logic. Obviously, the conclusion is the same. Both 'sides' ascertain that programming in the media and the big festivals has broadened, that the musical course has become less alternative, and that orientation toward the public has increased. For all their accumulated ambiguity, the interviewees were very clear on one thing, hiding openly between the lines: both camps acknowledge that alternative mainstream is still not the same thing as *real* mainstream. Consequently, both attackers and defenders are still playing with the same ball, using the same set of arguments.

First, the infrastructural difference is a fact. As far as the media and the concert circuit are concerned, every respondent refers to the same players to indicate that the Flemish music circuit contains a clear-cut segment that distinguishes itself from the underground and mainstream circuits.[7] In addition, none of the respondents questions the previously discussed distinction mechanism. The 'defenders' also confirm that still many smaller underground scenes are left.

Apart from this, the interviewed actors are also unanimous on the fact that the public differs from segment to segment. A promoter, for instance, discerns large differences between the public of Rock Werchter and that of Pukkelpop, and between the concert goers who come to see small club concerts in his club (underground/niche groups) and those who come to see bands in the main hall (alternative mainstream).

> This main hall audience never takes in a club concert, the sort of public that comes to see Crystal Antlers or Daan, differs too much, already in age. There is very little overlap. I can see this when I am handing out flyers at our concerts and watch the crowd enter. A club concert requires just a little more from a visitor. The bands are often unknown to them, which is already an extra threshold to pass. Those who are interested need to click on a link in a newsletter now and again, or start a search of their own. It's a much smaller group, whose way of experiencing things is entirely different from those who simply decide on the basis of a newsletter's title whether he or she will come or not, people who say: 'I know a track by them, heard it on the radio, so I'm going.' (...) When we do promotion, we're working in very particular channels, who are not the actual mainstream media.'

Journalists who have no fear of recommending the mainstream also acknowledge that their readers sometimes have different views. When singer Helmut Lotti had his first interview in *Humo*, it caused quite a stir (Sioen 10.01.2009), and another journalist, by his own account, received a lot of negative comments about his article on Milk Inc., in which he was highly appreciative of the band. Such a journalist is evidently the first to realize that 'few of our readers will buy schmaltz CDs.'

As a result, not everyone embarks on the 'popular tour.' On the contrary, Studio Brussels carefully demarcates its domain at the bottom side: the evening programming is still reserved for alternative music, targeted at listeners who want to discover new music. A respondent: 'What is possible here is impossible in other countries. Of all records, 80 % is new and we play things that are not in the playlist. Henry Rollins, Lightning Bolt, it's all possible.' Another respondent, who works at the radio, discusses the daytime programming and offers evidence of how personal taste can surface in an even more pronounced manner: 'I personally think we should be willing to take a little more risks during the day, show a little bit more guts, stick out our necks, and profile ourselves.' This also goes to show that the discussion is alive within the walls of the station itself.

The most significant element that shows how argumentations by 'attackers' and 'defenders' are on the same track, is the cultural aspect. Personal taste, which is the central element of an individual logic, often appears to accord with legitimate taste, the generally accepted 'right' and 'proper' taste. This is not just a matter of culturally shared value judgments; it also involves the desire and commitment to conform to these values. Indeed, it seems that some sort of legitimate classification is always present, and ultimately will be defended, especially when an actor goes public with a 'popular' choice and fears that his or her actions will be viewed as illegitimate by others. When a journalist casually mentions that he used to go and see the popular TV show *Tien Om Te Zien*, he spontaneously erupts in a defense of his action: 'My girlfriend had to be there in her official capacity, and now and again I wanted to be there as well, by way of a reality check.' When a radio producer admits that the records he plays — Lady Gaga, Justin Timberlake — are actually more tuned to a commercial station, he immediately adds: 'These are marginal cases that are acceptable to everybody, even to *credible lefties* (alternative music is often defined as 'leftist,' which is why the alternative mainstream in schema 2 is placed on the left side). One respondent also seemed to be driven to self-defense during the interview, because his station had suddenly started to play a single by an artist who did not have the right 'alternative' look:

> Then I had the sudden feeling that this could be something, a little hit for a broader public, and I said yes. Because it matched up. The later singles, by contrast, we played far less frequently. As soon as we get the impression that this could tip over into wrong connotations, we pull back a bit.

The following anecdote by an editor of a radio show neatly illustrates the instinctive recoil, as he anticipates in his actions the reaction of others who might not find his choice credible.

> I played Spinvis for the first time in an evening program. Upon which the coordinator asked me to bring the number to the play list meeting. At first I winced, fearing that

they the only thing they would be able to do was have a good laugh at me, some Dutchman that will keep on (so)...

Yet another fine example is an employee of Studio Brussels, who admits that Nirvana's 'Smells like Teen Spirit' was not immediately picked up by day-time programming. It was considered too hard. Another employee categorically denies it. 'That's absolute nonsense. We had a firm discussion about it and went on to play it as soon as the single had come in.' What is at stake in this kind of contradictions is that the alternative image of the station must be protected, an element which is of greater importance than the question of who is telling the truth and who is lying. Since the 1990s, StuBru has ascribed itself an alternative image. It does not matter that another employee admits that now a track like Nirvana's would not be played in daytime, because of society's changes. He knows that the 'leftist turn' taken by Studio Brussels in the 1990s was a shift that many foreign networks 'were envious about, consolidating the station's reputation, which survives up to this day.' For this reason, many respondents consider themselves fortunate that Flanders still has a station such as Studio Brussels.

In the actors' statements, ambivalence is almost the rule. For each argument, a counterargument can be put forward. In the end, however, those who claim alternative music is outdated equally maintain that there is still some difference left between alternative and mainstream. Acting from a market logic does not imply that the difference does not exist, but that 'the public' thinks it no longer exists.[8] A quick look at the artistic value judgments hidden between the lines learns that those who adopt the most lenient stance toward mainstream actually speak about the music in entirely different terms. Pieces written about mainstream artists consistently reveal the belief that they are rarely capable of withstanding the test of quality. Daily paper De Morgen writes the following about a CD by Britney Spears: 'Decent inlay, a couple of nice dance tracks. As to the rest of the tracks: much, very much of it is wrapping' (Steenhaut 02.04.2011). The attitude also emerges from the conducted interviews. About Dana Winner, one journalist says: 'You won't hear me raving about her,' while he defines Milk Inc. as 'unpretentious, reasonably flat dance music.' Nevertheless, another journalist recalls that he once ran a concert by Milk Inc. at the Sportpaleis into the ground: 'I think

that's great for our image. A token of honesty.' About Lady Gaga he says: 'I write that on a musical level the lady has accomplished little of what she sometimes wants us to believe or what she claims she has achieved. Now, you tell me, is that a clear statement or not?' Even if the actors assert that they love these artists, they come up with arguments of an entirely different nature. Not the aesthetic or artistic criteria are called upon, but arguments that underline the consumption-oriented aspect, the element of fun that these fleeting little hits can provide. It is an appeal to the functional side of music. Somebody who likes to dance chooses dance music. Others select music because it allows them to blow off some steam. Some select certain music because they like to use it as background music. About Britney Spears' 'Baby One More Time,' one respondent says: 'It's not what I would put on at home, but it's still a top single. You only need to hear it once to....' About Lady Gaga's 'Telephone': 'I am well aware it's a plain single, and that's also what I write about it, that it's flat. Other than that, I have no trouble - they can always play it while I'm on the dance floor.' Furthermore, the 'alternative' press never writes immediately about such pop stars. Reports only appear when these artists have already acquired great fame because the 'popular' press has published a massive number of articles about them and they have become *inescapable* simply based on their global fame (a public-oriented criterion). The chance that this would happen was far smaller in previous times, which in turn expresses the value-charged nature of the process. A journalist:

> In Flanders a certain mechanism was activated which made sure that Lady Gaga was kept out of the picture. At first, nobody really knew what to do with the stuff, and this goes for the totality of the press.

It is also very telling that whenever the actors needed examples to prove or substantiate that alternative music had ceased to exist, the usual suspects always returned (Milk Inc., Lady Gaga etc.; in former times this would have undoubtedly been Madonna). Never is the whole mainstream involved, but very specific cases that seem to have been chosen arbitrarily. The fact is that the anti-intellectualism that I mentioned earlier equally has a lower limit or boundary. Actors may very well claim the lower position of pop music, at the same time this position must never be too low: 'schmaltz or variety are not exactly things that could count on my sympathy.'

The individual logic of taste is different from the organizational or positional. On the one hand, the bourgeois logic of political correctness is operational: actors are hesitant to criticize or exclude something. Among the 'defenders' there are anxieties about possible discrimination, or about coming across as too arrogant or superior. On the other hand, the fact is that what ends up being defended by everyone is the legitimate taste. The actors are preoccupied with avoiding to be suspected of illegitimate behavior, which is why the argumentation may be based on suspicions that are subsequently needed to justify the selected option. In short, those who raise explicit objections against the aesthetics are also those who endorse it implicitly.[9]

Selections made from within an individual logic start from the autonomy that every actor in the music circuit possesses as a lover of music. This autonomy is primarily expressed in the actor's personal taste. People choose something because they think the music is good. To describe what it means 'to think something is good' is a task the respondents fail to fulfill satisfactorily. 'To think it is good' occurs with a framework of reference ruled by the incapacity 'to express that it is good.' Symbolic recognition (or misrecognition) does not function in accordance with an aesthetics that has taken shape. Consequently, an emotional, intuitive, instinctive vocabulary substitutes the rational vocabulary. The discourse is punctuated by constant reference to something that can never be a point of reference in itself, something actors already know about that helps them understand a situation and pass a judgment about it. Music, therefore, becomes a feeling. The actors repeatedly utter the word 'feeling,' and interpret it as a passive undergoing or 'being touched by.' This experience and the idea that certain things must resist explanation and can only be felt, evidently has Romantic roots. The practical examples cited in the interviews allow us to discern some very clear artistic and equally Romantic criteria. Authenticity rules, but also originality, craft and live reputation get positive assessments. Other criteria of art criticism (complexity, virtuosity, instrument mastery) constitute a negative reference, because they are seen as obstacles to the Romantic 'feeling.' Still, the discourse is never free from ambiguity. Those who know the music business' back stage know that authenticity is often an illusion that actors love to believe. Precisely because of this, the conclusion must be that today's alternative mainstream also possesses an aesthetics of its own, which is the source of its cultural foundation.

Via the shared classification schema, the alternative mainstream distinguishes itself from the other segments in the pop music circuit, and individual logic serves as the distinguishing mechanism. The real mainstream is turned into the enemy, against which actors must react. In the segment of the mainstream, commerce is the only thing that counts. In contradistinction with the commercial mainstream, an underground philosophy is employed to confer a surplus value on the market situation in which the actors operate. This does not imply that there is consensus and accord in the alternative mainstream. There is also a struggle over definitions, which itself defines the field. Because 'credibility' is an important value, some really have a hard time when others get involved with 'wrong' (mainstream) music that does not match the value. Managers, record firms and promoters launch a counterattack against the leveling out in the national media and the big festivals. On the one hand, there is criticism against the upper limit: the media and the festivals take an insufficiently alternative course and invest too much in the commercial and market-oriented. On the other hand, the lower limit is set too high (none of the actors is especially keen to label something as niche or underground). Denying this, however, is not what the 'defenders' do. Instead, they question the distinction between alternative and mainstream: it is of no concern anymore to the public at large, and consequently the programming has become broader. The attackers use a high-sounding 'alternative discourse' from an individual logic (in the alternative mainstream the artistic should prevail, not big money), while the defenders act in a public- en market-oriented way from an organizational logic. Nevertheless, when the latter gives way to personal taste, it appears that also from their perspective mainstream artists can rarely withstand the quality test of the aesthetics of rock. This leads us to conclude that both attackers and defenders respect the rules of the game and arrive at the same conclusion. Both put legitimate taste first, ahead of an individual logic. When taste collides with other logics, ambivalence becomes the dominant outcome. At the same time, both hasten to say that there are still plenty of underground scenes and that the alternative scene continues to be different from the real mainstream. For the alternative mainstream, the real mainstream remains the segment to distance itself from, by employing an individual logic.

Notes

1. The habitus Bourdieu has in mind always refers to something that acts from within an active and operational disposition. According to ANT this disposition first needs to be set in motion, an act that always originates with the work of art itself: it is actively doing its job and autonomously choosing its 'user.' When the respondents say 'you can feel it, but I can't put it in words,' it refers to being affected by something that comes from outside and engages in a relation. The disposition Bourdieu discusses is therefore rather a predisposition. This explains why someone is able to love a genre, but still does not love every number that belongs to it.

2. Based on the interpretation matrices distinguished by Boltanski and Thévenot, it could be argued that actors in the alternative mainstream like to dwell in 'the world of inspiration' (Boltanski & Thévenot 2006: 159-164). It is the spontaneous, the irrational, the subconscious, the emotional which people fall for, and they think something is valuable or of worth when it is unique or original, or when it was created by a genius.

3. The interviews also revealed that those qualities are all attributed to record music. Music is chosen because it is released under an indie label, which has become a quality brand thanks to its previous releases (for example, labels such as Bella Union, Sub Pop, Warp, Ninja Tune and Domino).

4. See, for example: www.djbroadcast. nl/features/featureitem_id=1325/ Rivas_Tijdcapsule_Geffen _Vs_Neil_ Young.html

5. In the Netherlands similar objections are sometimes raised against *De Wereld Draait Door,* 3FM or *OOR*. .

6. This is the second element in the war waged over definitions. Besides innocent sham fights over the right interpretation of a classification schema, the disputes challenge basic categories of this applied schema (Laermans 2010: 183).

7. In Flanders, these are the previously cited magazines *Humo* and *Focus Knack*, the papers *De Morgen* and *De Standaard*, the radio stations Studio Brussels and partly Radio 1, the festivals Pukkelpop and Rock Werchter and concert venues such as Ancienne Belgique. For the Netherlands such a list can also be drawn up, featuring the main trendsetters: *De Wereld Draait Door,* 3FM/3voor12, *de Volkskrant, NRC, OOR*, Lowlands, Pinkpop, Paradiso, and Melkweg etc.

8. A possible explanation is that the people working in the music industry (30-ish and 40-ish, a few who are 50-ish) are from a generation with a more alternative aesthetics and that this is less the case with the (younger) public. Yet as long as actors in the music industry continue to think that there is an alternative scene, this remains a social fact. One respondent confirms this, saying: 'That has been maintained artificially, but in itself it doesn't bother me very much.'

9. These contradictions between an explicit and implicit discourse, as well as the ambiguity constantly emanating from the interviews, are lost in the distinction theory. Lahire (2003) has already pointed this out. Contrary to what Bourdieu claims, in his view the habitus does not direct action in one specific direction in any sort of circumstances, since dispositions are only activated under specific conditions. Consequently, the habitus is connected with the situation, always variable and producing ever so different effects. What Lahire suggests, similar to pragmatist sociology, is that the individual level manifests heterogeneous habits and schemas that can face each other in a standoff and can be contradictory. This explains the ambiguity in action.

5. Economic Return and Popularity
The Organizational Logic

> When you only program for yourself, then you should also pay everything yourself. I can't do that. So it's a balancing act. I program a lot that I don't like. The fact is that I'm not obliged to listen to it myself. I can safely stay behind my bar (laughs).

A promoter has the floor, and wants to get one thing straight. A logic of legitimation of his own, as suggested in the previous chapter, is not always possible. It so happens that he, as a music industry actor, also works for an organization. This organization has an objective, and he must tune his selection to this objective. He must act in ways that are both required and desired by the organization.

Decisions, in short, will also follow an organizational logic. According to this logic, two considerations determine choices. The first is economic cost effectiveness. The second is the popularity of the music that is up for selection. Still, in an organization, there are certain marginal conditions and internal processes that can influence the decision. In addition, the organizational and individual logic can be at odds with each other, or they can merge into a compromise. In any case, an organizational decision and personal taste do not always converge.

The Logic of Economic Return

For those who act from an organizational logic, economic criteria are the guiding principles. The organization that employs the actors must be able to survive. Nonetheless, an economic logic in the pop music circuit is not synonymous with the strict commercial pursuit of making as much money as possible. The latter practice evidently also occurs, and may even be the target: a concert promoter or record firm wants to make a profit from selling tickets or CDs. Yet the economic can also be interpreted as 'to reach break-even point.' The notion of *breaking even* is of great importance in the pop music circuit, as also this study shows. The motto is not to cause a money pit. 'At the end of the road you need a break-even,' a promoter says. Often, the viability of the organization is at stake, which depends on the situation (some organizers need more paying entries to arrive at a break-even than others do). Therefore, the economic in the alternative mainstream can refer to potential profit as well as to acting without the motive of profit. In both cases, however, the actors wish for a return on the selections they made. The organizational logic is primarily one of return. It is the situation, though, that determines what is economically cost effective and what term could be set on the return. Sometimes it is in the short term, but more often, the return is set for the medium range. A booking agent formulates it as follows:

> As a booking agent, you are supposed to think about
> where a band should be at any given time in their career.
> It's not so much a matter of 'how much will it make now?'
> than it is a question of 'how much could it make within
> five years?'

This explains why the potential of the choices is important. Acting from an organizational logic aims at investment, on future return. How this manifests itself, differs depending on whether the actor is situated on the input side or output side of the music circuit. On the input side, in the absence of direct contact with the public, this logic frequently relies on a set of arguments grounded in exploitation possibilities and financial feasibility (market- or sales-oriented criteria). On the output side, the focus is on the reach of public, and selections are made based on the target group (public-oriented criteria).

The Logic of Return in the Selection of Input
Potential as a Criterion

A Cost-Effective Artist for a Cost-Effective Organization

Industry actors who sign artists to fill a managerial position, release records or look for concerts for them, may allow artistic criteria or personal taste to determine the choice right from the start. All respondents think it is important to become enthused by the music, to 'be able to feel' the music. Yet it is also obvious right from the start that the individual logic is not enough. Consequently, a significant adjustment is made: at the end of the line, the artist must be economically cost-effective or profitable so that the organization can also be viable. On top of the individual logic, the organizational logic sets things straight. An artist manager and a booking agent testify:

> My criteria of selection have changed in the course of the years. Something has been added. Sal(e)ability is important and has become a criterion that carries far more weight than in the beginning. (...) I'm looking for something that can exist autonomously, is capable of surviving financially, for its own sake and for ours: in short, bands who will be able to pay my assistant and me.

> Because I don't get subsidies, it has got to bring in money. Especially with domestic artists: only half of them go on tour, and if you're inclined to emphasize that, the need for a return becomes absolute. Honestly, I have to make a living with it. If I have to invest time in something, then it must be cost-effective, which is certainly possible on the condition that they play a lot.

In the case of the three studied positions on the input side of the music industry (management, record companies and booking agents), the potential economic return of artists who are signed is of obvious and crucial importance. In post-Fordist times like these (see p. 87), it is imperative to look at the salability and exploitation possibilities of artists and their music. Is there a public for this? What potential markets can be penetrated (in marketing terms: product/market-combinations)? Can a record company work with the artist? Can the media be warmed up to the band? Can the act persuade concert promoters or organizers? Are there any singles on the record? The series of questions is endless. 'In every case, a complete picture is drawn,' one manager says. These last few years, the live story has gained in significance. Now that CD sales are falling, selection by record firms requires a band to be able to deliver strong live performances on stage. A label boss explains:

> It's an important factor in signing bands, and this is my commercial side: I can like a band on the basis of what I've heard, but I really also need to know whether they are any good live. (...) We sell a portion of the CDs after the shows. When the concerts stink, people aren't going to buy the CD.

The reason why the focus on the commercial potential of the band or artist carries such weight is because it is a choice that can be made long before the band or artist has achieved anything. Music needs to be good (artistically), but much more important than this consideration of personal taste are the possibilities: what can be done with the artist in the given term? Only when artists prove to be marketable in one way or another, will the organization also reap the financial benefits and survive. The potential is preferably realized. 'A band has got to show a clear-cut growth curve,' a record label boss says.

Subsidies may provide a backup for small management firms (see p. 254), yet it is remarkable that the logic of return and cost-effectiveness has taken possession of all actors, both smaller national players and greater international figures. Economic criteria and sales-oriented thinking are inevitable. Ultimately, the commercial aspect is a reality that cannot be ignored. A local division of an international major:

> The commercial aspect certainly is a factor. (...) We draw up a marketing plan based on how much we can sell. This means making sure that there's something left when our promotional budget is 'this' much, and we'll need to channel 'that much' to the London HQ. The fact of the matter is that you need those revenues.

Evidently, the size of necessary income is different for large record companies than for smaller ones. A small firm has fewer overhead costs and therefore needs fewer sales to achieve a break-even than a large firm does. 'To me a record that sells three hundred items can be a success,' the owner of small record label says.

The inevitable effect of the return requirement is that bands deemed non-profitable are often left aside, out of necessity. Managers argue: 'Some bands are so specific it's really impossible to work with them,' and 'If it's not marketable, I won't do it, I can't afford being frivolous. We're an agency, a mechanical structure.' Among the record firms and booking agencies, the message is this:

> In the past we would've gone for a band that's good but just not suited for radio. That's become more and more difficult these last few years. In times like these it's got to pay to do something. And if we still decide to do it, we'll put less time in doing it.

> With some bands you simply know that it's not going to happen. I may like the music, think it's really intense and so, but sometimes the music is too alternative for the market, which makes it impossible to make a living of it.

> Many foreign bands could work in the club circuit, and if I really wanted to do it, I could take on 30 of these bands. The thing is you put an enormous amount of time in it. To limit yourself to bands that play only twice a year, is only possible when you're an not-for-profit organization. (...) In the end, it's evidently also a job, economics, and business.

Underground as Negative Reference

When it comes to evaluating music, the alternative mainstream adopts the aesthetics of the underground. Underground is a positive reference in artistic and content-related elements. It is striking to see, however, that when economic motives are involved, underground becomes a negative reference. The interviews reveal that actors in the alternative mainstream want to handle their job in a professional manner. It presupposes a certain gravity. About business, actors are serious. Underground activities are a hobby at the most, something actors do after hours. It explains why managers think that bands that are unmarketable and therefore not viable may have a reason for existence, but are not really the thing they personally want to do. To limit themselves to booking only five concerts and selling a couple of hundred CDs, is not a target for any actor that focuses on the alternative mainstream. The following excerpt from an interview with a record label boss sums it all up. However strong his underground-minded love for music may be, he is never alienated from the economic reality:

> I'm not going to sign a band that is not marketable. I'm not an elitist in the sense that I think 'the more obscure, the better,' and then go on to produce a hundred CD-Rs, if you know what I mean. At home, I have a bunch of obscure, strange things that I like. But you won't see me starting a thing with it on my label. I don't have the energy for it. (...) It's not that I feel too good about myself to do it. I just want to get the maximum out of my bands and if possible sell a million records. Then again, three hundred pieces would also be great, you see? The more, the better. Not because I want to behave in a purely commercial way and nothing else. No, when I like a band, I also want to find out what I can do with it. (...) It's a hobby, and it's also serious business. I don't do whichever group is possible. With every single release, accounting keeps an eye at the number of pieces I have to sell. It's not just mere guesswork.

Following the theory proposed by Boltanski and Thévenot (2006: 133-138 and 143-144), it is fair to say that professionals in the music business venture upon the test of the market. Those who enter the world of the market are prepared to accept the challenge and let the market test them. The framework of reference and the logic of justification require actors to refer negatively to the underground. As will be explained further on, it also becomes a way of learning how to cope with the uncertainty associated with every investment. In addition, the attitude conceals a kind of toughness. Whenever something does not work, it is considered a failure. Success is the proof of professionalism. To the actors involved, it can be a factor of recognition, indicating that their reputation as an entrepreneur is growing. In Bourdieu's terminology, it is a form of accumulation of a particular kind of symbolic capital, to wit, *professional* capital (see Vanherwegen 2008, the term will be explained later). Capital can be acquired and accumulated by way of the market test. The latter then also becomes a test of personal professionalism. Players in the alternative mainstream get satisfaction from their toil when success is achieved in the long run, when their artists grow 'from nobodies into commercially viable and thus profitable groups,' as one booking agent says. Another booking agent and a promoter illustrate this:

> The coolest thing you can achieve as a bookie or agent is that you can start with a band by doing a couple of support acts for a hundred bucks in a few bars and sell out a main hall three years later. That's what makes the job fun. When you have thirty bands you like, but you haven't seen any development in five years: that doesn't appeal much to me, personally. The fun thing about this job is that you can develop small things, then hopefully see them grow, and realize you've made your little contribution to making it happen.

> I like to think along about a local thing and together with the booking agent look at how we can develop it: which festival we'll do, when the clubs, etc. I rather do that than one-off things. It's more important to live the story. It's obviously nice when you see a band grow in which you had faith.

When these statements are compared with those by people who resolutely go for the 'showbiz' mainstream, a striking similarity can be observed. There too people do not just experience the joy of working. They also get a personal kick when commercial success is achieved. Upon being asked how important it is to be touched emotionally by music, a record label boss says:

> I think I am moved in a certain way when I see a potential in somebody, when I can provoke a progress with someone who is talented and is just starting, and when I can also turn it into a commercial success. That, I think, is what is expected from me and at the same time

what I get a kick from, or at least that of which I can feel whether I am on the right track.

In any case, the alternative mainstream is characterized by a junction of the cultural and the economic, by the corresponding logics of justification, which match the dualism in which they are caught: for the former, actors lean towards the underground, for the latter towards the mainstream.

The Logic of Return in the Selection of Output
Range of Public as a Criterion

Those who operate on the output side of the music circuit also think in terms of cost effectiveness and return. Here music is presented to a public. Consequently, public-oriented thinking is a priority: a promoter wants a good crowd in his venue, a radio station wants a sufficiently large body of loyal listeners, a paper or magazine wants readers and subscribers. Looking at the public as the main focus of what you do, means making an assessment of what this public wants (ways of thinking and planning on the basis of a target group) and whether it is possible to reach a sufficiently large public (thinking in terms of popularity and economics, on the basis of cost effectiveness). The question then is: will people like the selected music?

Concert Promoters: A Good Crowd in the Room
(Public-Oriented Out of Economic Motives)
However great the desire of concert promoters may be to include their personal taste and love for music in their programming, in the end their organization must be able survive economically. As one respondent aptly sums it up: 'Even somebody who does this purely out of love for the music will want to attain break-even at the end of the night.' Organizing concerts is inextricably connected with financial viability, and this equally applies to people active in subsidized organizations (see below). Because a concert organizer gets his income out of ticket and beverage sales, this financial viability is automatically dependent on the public turnout. Organizing a concert only makes sense when, depending on the size of the venue, there is a sufficient crowd present, 'otherwise it's just sad for the band and our wallet.' Economic motives are the priority.

> With large venue concerts the commercial considerations are obviously much greater (...) In those cases it's not like with small club concerts, 'wow, we've got to put this on stage,' but rather 'well, this could work' or 'that's something that could attract the local crowd.' That's why we didn't do The Opposites. I personally like the group, but the choice here was public-oriented: I didn't think it could draw enough people, because people aren't that much into hip-hop.

In order to attract a large enough public, now and then actors need to put aside their personal taste. In any case, the two elements go hand in hand, which leads to conformism. 'That's the choice we face,' an organizer says, 'either stubbornly do your own thing, follow your personal taste, and take all the risks that go with it, or look at the ticket sales.' Nearly all organizers literally declare that it does not matter whether they like a band or not, as long as there is a public for it.

> It makes no difference to me whether I personally like Absynthe Minded or not. You just ask yourself if that's something our public wants to see and then put it on.

> When I want 16-, 17-year old kids on (sic) my festival, then I don't need to bother them with my personal taste.

This also reveals a big difference with the underground. There the fact that something draws a good crowd is not a reason for programming. Someone in the underground corner phrases it in this way:

> That's one choice, but it's not mine. If you choose like that, you've become a salesman, and that's not the reason why I started a club back then. I have to be able to stand behind every single concert, without any compromises regarding the content. A club can never become a 'venue,' or else it would mean that I get up in the morning to go to work.

The Radio: Target Group/Listeners Ratings/Public Support

The radio stations that play a leading part in the alternative main-stream belong to the public broadcasting networks (BBC in the UK, Studio Brussels in Flanders, 3FM in the Netherlands). Because their functioning is primarily financed by tax funds, one would expect economic motives to carry less weight than with commercial companies. Yet the national stations, which are partially also dependent on complementary advertising revenues, adopt the same public-oriented way of thinking. Radio-makers want to serve their target group, and listener ratings are a barometer of success. A record company manager says: 'They need listener ratings and therefore they choose music which they think their public will like, they just have to keep their audience happy.' That is why public-oriented criteria and an organizational logic prevail among the national stations, as was already established in the previous chapter. Artistic quality criteria are immediately linked to the target group: in order for something to be played on the radio, the primary question is whether there is an audience for it ('can we do something with it?'). Whether the music has a public support and is radio-friendly becomes the standard line. A respondent provided the following definition of the perfect radio single: 'A single people can hear many times without growing tired of it.' All radio-makers argue that a number needs to have a sufficiently large public support or potential, if it wants to be on the radio. 'It's a matter of necessity, when you don't want to be working outside of reality,' one respondent claims.

The selections made by the public stations are therefore largely determined by the fact that they are mass media. The radio-makers confirm this. They are forced to take into account as many listeners as possible, which is why the public at large becomes *the* target group to focus on. The logical choice is the taste of the largest common denominator, the average taste, banning all extremes. 'People with a broad interest, who are interested in music, but do not fanatically want to discover new things,' is a description given by one. Another puts it as follows:

> People tend to forget that we are working for a very large public. Radio is a mass medium and so you automatically look and go for the greatest common denominator, which enables you to satisfy as many people as possible. You

try to make an estimate of how many people will receive the record well. You know well in advance that Chinese metal has little public support on Studio Brussels. (...) You need to find the limits, where people start switching to another channel or when they are hooked. In any case, people increasingly less tolerate heavy music on the radio. That's why we examine how we can acceptably include alternative music in that mainstream of that day without snubbing or brushing off people. StuBru's size is a disadvantage. The group of people that listens to it will be much larger, certainly in the public spaces out there. If you put your head on the block for a number like 'Born Slippy' (Underworld), then you know that a number of people will be snubbed, because it's not radio music.

It explains why a station such as Studio Brussels will rather focus on the average listener and not on the music freaks or *'credible lefties.'* They, so the line of reasoning goes, will find what they need somewhere else. 'We aren't concerned with the real underground, it exists detached from everything else,' an employee says. Another even asks himself whether it is the public station's task to approach the small niches and put money into them. 'These odd 5000 people find all the music they want on their own, through the internet. Working for a larger group has the benefit of cost effectiveness, but it means that you run off the smaller things.' Although this too is a self-fulfilling prophecy (by not playing underground, underground stays underground), it certainly reveals that in the landscape of radio broadcasting the distinction between underground and alternative mainstream is also structurally delimited. Underground or niche music may be represented in the evening programming, but:

It's got to stay radio, you can't chase people away. The evening programming has the task to signal things, and afterwards people can hear it elsewhere. The radio functions less a source of discoveries. Real music freaks never listen to the radio. (...) The genre programs of the past are gone because people won't sit down anymore for a whole hour to listen to hip-hop. These things are easily found on the Internet.

Specialized evening programming also takes into account the public support of certain music. There too actors are forced occasionally to put aside their personal taste.

> I'm a fan of The Fall, but I can't put that in the program, because the group has lost its relevance, has no public support. Or sometimes the music is too extreme and not radio-friendly enough. You need to be able to put aside your own opinion and personal taste to put them in the bigger picture. I don't like everything that is aired in the evening programming, but at least I know it lives among certain people, that it has public support. Then I'm certainly going to play it. You can feel that it has quality, even though it's not your taste. It's a matter of finding the right balance.

The fact is that this has become a general principle. Personal taste plays a part in everybody's choice, a radio coordinator says, but it can never have the greatest weight: 'You have to take into account what the general, average taste of your target group is, and be aware of the fact that this taste does not always match your own taste.'

Public-oriented thinking also affects the format of radio programs. Every program has its own profile, and the selected music needs to fit in ('something for the morning slot or something for during the weekend').[1] For reasons of optimal rotation of records, the Flemish public network (VRT) uses the software program 'Music Master,' which is programmed by the person-in-charge. On one given day, he or she places a track from the playlist in the morning slot. On another day, this track is appears in the afternoon slot. In the case of the pre-defined formats, there is a difference between the day and evening programming. In the evening programming aesthetic criteria can still play a part, and music that is 'more difficult' can be presented within the limits of the station's signaling function. In daytime programming, the main intention is to appeal to a broad public, requiring the music to be sufficiently accessible. 'Otherwise people would pull out,' a respondent says. Two others explain:

> The program's format is in the back of your head. That's the first selection. Some things won't work in daytime,

but do work in the evening. During the day, the public is much larger, and people's state of mind while listening is different. The evening simply offers more opportunities. Serving the listener extreme metal at 21.15 won't work either. It's all about administering the right dose.

Not everything can be played, because every radio has its own format, depending on the hour. You have to ask yourself what music you can play on what specific time of the day. There are genres you can't listen to in the morning. I do believe in some sort of soundtrack to somebody's life. There's a kind of morning, noon and evening rhythm. They're all different experiences. That's why you need to program cleverly. You just weigh it out, how many new records you can add to your playlist, how long they need to be played, depending on the public that is listening at that particular time and its specific wishes.

Written Press

Just as in public radio stations, in national papers and magazines economic motives are also more indirectly active (except perhaps for free monthly publications like Belgium-based *RifRaf* or Dutch *LiveXS*, which live off ads). Music is merely a part of the whole paper or magazine, and not the most important, at that (the cultural pages are never in the front of the paper, and within the culture section is pop music but one element). Yet here too journalists need to serve their public, allowing economic motives to play their part. In an informal conversation, a former journalist of a big newspaper told this author the following: 'You ask on what the selection is based? Well, I can sum it up in one sentence: to sell more papers.' In official interviews, revealingly, the tone is more differentiated. 'I need to find something good on a level of quality *and* it needs to be able to appeal to a broad public. Those two need to be united.' Still, the factor of public has the deciding power. *Servicing* of the public can determine the selection: as was mentioned before, actors inform about groups which they think the public will find them interesting. Then personal taste is easily put aside. 'That's not the case with reviews,' a journalist says, 'but it certainly is with interviews.'

Although this study limits itself to two so-called 'quality newspapers,' just as with the radio stations the message is that papers are mass media and therefore make a different selection than niche media do, because they need to service a broader public:

> I sometimes write about things that they're good, while I personally don't want any of it. I think this is something you simply need to do. It's because of the sort of paper for which I write. An underground magazine or a paper focused on one specific public probably has less need to do this. In the case of our paper, this is impossible, it's much broader. (...) You can say that I look at what's popular, but I can't take myself as a criterion, see? I don't match the profile of the average target public. I hear too much stuff, am too heavily occupied with it to be of typical taste.
> There are things I am forced to do because the industry, no, not even the industry, because the public at large, the mainstream public for which I write, expects me to do so. Specialized magazines like *Gonzo Circus* or *RifRaf* make an entirely different selection than we do. (...) because you are writing for a mainstream public, a number of things is expected by this public to be covered, such as a Metallica, Mika or U2 CD. Popularity is one of the factors; I would be lying if I'd say that that's not part of the game.

A paper or a magazine has a profile and an image, and the choices that are made must fit in.

> My line of reasoning takes the perspective of making a magazine. We need to be able to stand behind as a magazine. (...) Every magazine has its own identity. The bands you want to present need to fit in with the identity you want to give to your magazine. It is actually by making that choice that you can create the desired image for you magazine.

> The first point of interest is: what does the reader want? You have an idea of who this reader is and what he or she expects as far as music is concerned. What you then do is work towards that idea, in a way you want to serve the reader. That's why there's very little coverage of metal in

our paper because we assume that metal does match our image. This image is determined by the group of readers and by the paper's tradition. And then there are the hidden lines of approach of the person who decides, that is, me. (...) I write about folk because nobody else does it and because it is somewhat associated with our paper, it matches in a certain way. (...) Somewhere in a newspaper you need to write a series of stories in the course of the years that manages to drag along the readers (...) and I assume that in the long run the public knows this. Then you have to bring on the new things there because the public, the customers, is counting on you to do that. And in our case it's not from metal that they expect this.

Coping with Uncertainty
Popularity Criteria as Risk Reduction

An organizational logic dictates selections that can guarantee the survival of the organization, that can ensure economic profit or — in most cases — a break-even. However, as was argued before — and this is a central element in my study — economic return is always uncertain. To assess well in advance what (in the long term) might be profitable, is difficult, if not impossible. Consequently, the industry and the media search for ways to reduce the risks. In chapter three, I already discussed the strategy of record firms that engage in overproduction in the hope that at least a number of titles will be successful. Another aspect is to look at the popularity of the artist that must be selected or the kind of music he or she makes. Putting aside any artistic judgment, the actors are led by the market value of the music. Describing the logic of justification with Boltanski and Thévenot (2006: 178-185), actors inhabit the 'realm of fame,' which applies when recognition among the public or in the public opinion govern the common ground actors can seek in order to argue, evaluate, judge, justify and legitimize. When putting back the 'pop' in pop music, the original meaning of 'popular,' 'of the people,' remains an important criterion.

Both the input and output side of the music circuit are highly sensitive to the matter, even though the criterion is most clearly visible in the media. 'Radio is a reflection of the artists' popularity among the people,' a person-in-charge of the radio. Popularity starts with current affairs, with actual, hot relevance. The artist's news value is the source of every form of attention. Releasing CDs, going on tour, are news facts that have the potential of bringing him in the public eye, in the media. More, any non-music-related rumors and sensational stories, whether blown out of proportion or not, have the power to do this ('Artist X again committed to rehab clinic'). The fact is that music only seems to be relevant when it has a topical, current interest, a news value. The interviewed media professionals all agree that there has to be a persuasive, current reason for publishing something.

> You always need a solid, fresh reason to bring something. The days that just the record could pull it off, which is a rare occasion, are over. Concerts are very

important. If you can get on Rock Werchter's bill in Flanders, you have a clear advantage to be selected, because a lot of readers are interested in such a news item. (...) Pukkelpop too is very gratifying, because it allows us to put forward more new bands...

Any good story that accompanies or surrounds artists, and consequently the media attention and name recognition that it entails, increase their value as current hot items. Those who are popular will be able to appeal to a larger audience or public, which, in turn, entails more buyers, concert visitors, listeners, readers, etc. This popularity does not need to match the current news value. It can also be timeless: established artists who have become classics remain wanted as long as their fan base is large enough. Each time, however, a logic such as this, based on popularity, is a vicious circle: following selection, you can build a certain reputation and become popular; this, in turn, ensures repeated selection, which leads to still greater popularity.

Name Recognition and Previously Built Reputation

Known artists get picked up much faster. Their previously built reputation guarantees much easier selection. Popularity in itself can constitute a reason to program a concert or give a band a record contract. In some cases, these choices can coincide with personal taste, but this is far from always being the case. Certainly not on the marketing side of record company: attempts will be made to sell weaker records of known artists as great albums.

I may think a new Robbie Williams record isn't as good as the previous one, but this man has performed twice here in a football stadium. Obviously, I won't be the one carrying the flag that says: 'This record isn't as good' Then you just do your job and get the promotion and marketing running. Because there always is an nth number of hardcore fans.

Especially the media are highly sensitive to an artist's name recognition. Rothenbuhler & McCourt already established that a single gets even more radio airplay when it has recently been played before (Bennett ed. 2006: 312). The selection made by the media often relies on the same vicious circle: those who are already known remain the focus of attention, thus still being better known. What is concerned here is the fame of the artist — his popularity as a public-oriented criterion — and not necessarily the previously acquired artistic reputation and the Romantic view of the artist that was discussed in the previous chapter. The media, in fact, never deny this. Quite the contrary, actors openly admit that such an organizational logic influences the individual logic. In the interviews, all radio- makers readily admitted that they look forward with just a little bit more interest to the new Daan, Muse or Bowie record. They would be quicker to play a number by these artists, precisely because it is Daan, Muse or Bowie. They confess they are milder for the *core* artists, and that they only allow these artists an instantly high rotation. They even call it an illusion that an artist's name would not be of any consequence. The written press too subscribes to this logic. 'Really important releases' by 'artists you already know' or by 'the great artists within the pop-rock genre' are immediately reviewed. 'I just have to do it,' a journalist says.

The respondents seem to take it for granted that this name recognition plays an important part. Artists with a large fan base simply have to be played. They must get print coverage, because the public demands it. One journalist even agreed to an interview with a famous film actor that had released a CD (Hugh Laurie, better known as Dr. House), without having heard a single note of the CD, for the sole reason that he was a famous person. If there is a public for a given artist, he or she has news value. 'We are a news medium, and therefore news value, which is to say 'the big names' are an important criterion.' News value has no relationship whatsoever to journalist's personal predilection or fondness for the music. It is completely detached from personal taste. That is why a respondent speaks of the 'inescapability' of a band: 'there is simply no getting around it, because it's exceptionally well-known.' Even if the said artist has made a record of lesser quality, the potential of a public remains an important criterion.

> If Admiral Freebee had made a weaker CD and you
> know that many listeners are interested, you still going to
> play the record.

> A bad record by Metallica will still be reviewed. A big group that has acquired a reputation on the basis of the past, and still has that reputation (at least in the eye of the public at large, and not necessarily in my opinion, not in the case of Metallica), then I'm still going to do it. When I get a chance at interviewing Metallica, even if it's a bad record, then I' still going to do it. When they are here to do a concert, I cannot let it pass: I will review the concert or send someone to do it.

> If Lady Gaga's new CD isn't that great, we'll still going to put it on the list because Gaga currently has an inescapable news value. This has also happened with Madonna, that were thinking 'God, we really don't think it's that great,' but we'll do it anyway.

Conversely, an artist can become less popular in the course of time, which can cause the news value to drop, making him or her les relevant to the media.

A rather perverse effect of the sensitivity to name recognition is that an artist's previously built reputation can turn against him or her. Whoever has a wrong, tainted image jeopardizes his or her future. Certain negative conditions can impede selection. Music that in itself would be perfectly capable of being appreciated does not even make it to the CD player of the evaluating actor. As was established by Rothenbuhler & McCourt in a study of commercial radio stations, new releases are often categorized based on the first impression, and afterwards they never leave the category to which they were assigned. Following a classification, certain artists are immediately rejected 'because they were categorized outside of the format' (Bennett ed. 2006: 312). This practice is especially prevalent with music that is perceived to be too underground or too mainstream. In the former case, it is immediately assumed that the music is 'too hard,' 'too monotonous,' 'too difficult' or 'too jazzy.' In the latter case: popularity in the 'entertainment' mainstream can have a negative effect on selection in the alternative mainstream (which again illustrates the difference between those segments). Even if these artists – in an exceptional case – want to make an alternative career move, they are not immediately credible. A radio-maker:

For our listeners to get any interest in that, they'll have to come up with something very serious. The fact that Leki, for example, actually was an artist for a commercial station like MNM, initially played against her. An Idols finalist has been proposed to us repeatedly, but this guy drags along the Idols image, and he keeps making music that does not fit the profile. (...). There are other examples of artists who want to make a switch in their music career and who get desperate because nobody goes wild for what they offer.

As was already mentioned in the previous chapter, to give in to the taste of the public and put aside personal taste for that purpose, comes across as illegitimate behavior. This explains why here too the respondents repeatedly throw in artistic criteria to justify their actions. On the one hand, radio-makers claim that such well-known artists most of the times actually release good radio singles. On the other hand, they put this mechanism into perspective. The developed popularity of an artist does not in the least entail that he or she will be selected again no matter what happens, or that everything he or she puts out will get an equal amount of media attention. In Flanders Studio Brussels claims not to have played all singles by Moby or Pearl Jam, or local stars such as Daan or Absynthe Minded (the same number of times): 'A bad single stays a bad single, no matter what.' One journalist stopped writing about John Hiatt and Randy Newman because he could not see anything new in it, although their concerts sold out and there actually was a readers public for the artists.

Here as well, this defense encounters criticism on the input side. 'When Muse brings out a new record after two years, it'll be hotshot. Studio Brussels is prepared to do anything for this,' somebody from the record company says. Others confirm this:

> Radios sometimes claim that they judge a song by its merits, and that it doesn't matter whether it's Bono or Madonna... Bullshit, of course. The new Lady Gaga will be played, even if she'd sing it in Mongolian. Those superstars can release whatever they want — not forever, but for quite a while. And the media are there to follow. (...) But of course this is so, that's how mainstream becomes mainstream, and stays mainstream.

There's a lot of pure commerce involved. The press also prefers to write about Franz Ferdinand instead of covering a small band that isn't known, because everybody knows FF, so that more people will be reading it, hence more paper will be sold. When I put out the offer of an interview with Franz Ferdinand magazine *Humo* answers within three seconds. (...) *Humo* needs to be sure that they have interviews with bands that are big. If they'd cover alternative, small bands every week, a number of people would stop buying the mag. (...) Everything is intertwined. There's a kind of opportunism active on both sides, everybody makes use of everybody.

Because of this, it may seem that certain favored bands (such as Daan, Gabriel Ríos or Admiral Freebee among the Flemish artists) have a subscription to media attention. 'Bands that are big stay big, because they have an audience and no radio is going to leave them aside,' is how a person in charge of promotion describes the vicious circle.

One consequence of this mechanism is that new or young artists are having a harder time to be included in the selection procedure. Radio-makers and journalists freely admit this: 'Obviously it's harder for a new artist to get a chance and keep one's footing among these big productions like U2, Daan or Ríos.' 'For young bands the bar is set considerably higher.'

A 4-star-record by Bonnie Prince Billy or The Bony King of Nowhere will get in, a 2-star-record I find a bit harder to do. Or even worse, the debut of a band nobody has ever heard about and which hasn't particularly blown me out of my socks.

It is true that we are not looking for obscure bands, less known bands, bands that play in small back lots and perhaps make good music, but that have no support or don't have a record out. You can't do anything with those.

Yet here too people do not want to have said that new artists won't get a chance. In the interviews, the actors illustrate with numerous examples that there is still relatively much interest in young talent. This mainly concerns smaller articles and CD reviews, because to qualify for an interview 'such a young band does not have a good story to tell.' At the same time, journalists also know that 'now and again you need to give your public something new in order to be considered a trendsetter.' A radio coordinator sums it up:

> I always tell artists: that's not a wall, it's a threshold. And this threshold is lower for an artist whom our listeners are watching out for; for somebody whom we still have to introduce to the listeners, the threshold is higher.

By way of comparison: at a smaller music magazine which still has stronger ties with the underground circuits, lack of space is less an issue, and actors do not make a fuss of giving a chance to a lot of unknown music. A journalist:

> We can still run 150 reviews in one month and not a meager 15 like the rest. I don't want to fill these slots with the bigger names. I prefer to reserve some room for the younger and more innovative stuff. This cannot become a mag where there's nothing to discover. That's not our job.

Having said this, giving carte blanche to well-known artists and snubbing unknown artists is very hard to justify, not only to the whole of the music field, but also especially to oneself. Nobody wants to be a puppet that only does what it is told to do, that much was already clear. Whether the actors are puppets or not, the fact itself that they want to justify choices that may seem illegitimate, may indicate that there are certain rules of the game that have grown in the field.

Trends and Zeitgeist

Popularity is not measured by means of the artist's name recognition alone. Music that fits the Zeitgeist and the trend of the hour is also an indicator of potential public success. A record label boss, for instance, knows very well that he managed to sell thousands extra CDs thanks to the folk trend one of his bands started. One manager likes to call it 'the momentum' and thinks it is the most important thing one needs to be able to really score. The questions are these: How do trends and hypes alternate? How can music attract attention among all the oversupply? How can it possibly announce the newest hot stuff? A festival organizer phrases it as follows:

> To be relevant to the particular moment of time is an important criterion. That has always been the case. Absolutely. It's always been like that. The sound must be right, at this very moment. (...) In 1994 our festival was one of the first festivals in Europe or even in the world to put dance music on the bill (with Underworld). You could feel that it was something that was brewing in de underground and therefore you gave it a stage. (...) By taking a look at the bills in the course of the years, you can measure the Zeitgeist; what was significant back then, what was the sound at that moment.

This sort of argumentation is ranked by Gielen (2003: 148-150) under the collective logic of content, since the focus here is on the artistic context of a work of art (to look at other works of art, at genres and styles, at artistic conventions). As a result, selections often follow the dominant artistic tendencies. 'As a radio station you cannot afford to be blind to this,' it is said. This judgment is detached from the artistic criteria that an actor would apply if he were to follow his personal taste and act from an individual logic. The selection or rejection here is based on the consideration that the genre an artist brings is popular or fashionable. Then, music is relevant. You can notice this from the revival of music from the 1970s, both the harder guitars as the softer singer-songwriters (nu-folk). Two respondents comment on Triggerfinger: it is less original, but 'people think it's fantastic.' Consider the excerpt below about the folk revival, where the journalist admits that he can only start writing about a band like Mumford & Sons when he thinks there is a market for it.

> **Journalist** You can hardly call Mumford & Sons really new, but in the context it is something new. The new thing is that British folk is suddenly hip again among a young crowd. Then it is not the music — largely somewhere between The Pogues and The Waterboys — that is

new, but there is indeed a reason for 'there's again a great appetite for this kind of music.'

GK You are talking about trends.

Journalist But then it certainly is a new trend. (...) I saw it coming and in the case of Mumford & Sons I was really early to get on the wagon. At a certain moment, the story is ready to be exported, and you can start writing about it.

GK But how do you know?

Journalist You can feel it. There are a number of signs. The Mumford & Sons record was produced by the producer of Arcade Fire. When you compare it with the Noah & The Whale record, you can feel that this record has that explosive quality to it, that majestic sound that is the in thing now, where people fall for. Call it the U2 sound, the sound that gives the intimate a kind of stadium appeal, which makes it possible to bring the intimate to a stadium level. That was exactly what Noah & The Whale didn't have. And that's why such a band, or Magic Numbers, for that matter, isn't able to make it very far. I have that feeling and it turned out right: it goes up to a particular venue or festival, but it stays small (...) At this particular moment there is a need for a very enthusing, optimistic, even inciting sound. You can see this: Arcade Fire's success is really something, I think, that they managed to switch almost overnight from a medium-large to a large venue. Fleet Foxes, the same. In addition, since a few years you have the rise of the harmony. You can detect it all in Mumford & Sons and then you think: these guys can fill in the gap that was left open by The Pogues back then and never really was filled by anyone. On top of that, there was that small hit. From nowhere it dived into the top 10, like Underworld who came from dance and made a pact with rock. At a certain moment, you can feel it: this band is going to do it.

Being able to ride the Zeitgeist is a selection criterion. Still, because ambiguity is the chorus line of the pop discourse,

the criterion is immediately put into perspective: sometimes this argument is decisive, but not all of the time. Thus a promoter says that good songwriting must be possible as well, just as timeless music, as that made by The National or Nick Cave.

‖ Popular Musical Style Properties

How then must music sound or be produced, for it to be considered 'radio-friendly' or public-oriented? Are there any constants to be found, for which the gatekeepers think that there is a public, that listeners or readers want to hear, that have enough exploitation possibilities etc.? We can ask ourselves if there are also particular formal properties of style, which do not necessarily represent the personal taste of the gatekeepers, but which are needed for the music to be selected from an organizational logic.

Can the interviews show what music needs to meet certain conditions? Obviously, this has to be deduced from what can be read between the lines, because these properties, too, resist accurate description. The most important condition is that the music has to be a *song*. For anything to be picked up, it has to have a traditional song structure (stanza-chorus and containing vocal parts),[2] 'because most people are able to manage this.' This goes especially for the radio. The respondents think a number is 'radio-friendly,' 'radio-phonically nice' or a good radio song,' when it has a 'charming chorus,' does not disturb people when it's in the background and when it does not tire out. It has to be accessible, and it should jump out.

> The selection is based on the song; it is absolutely song-directed. The traditional song structure is more accessible. A number needs to make you prick up your ears. It should jump out. After you've listened to it three times, it should be in your head. Of course, this is a matter of feeling, but it has to be an attractive melody, and there should happen something in it. When you start looking at your watch after a minute and a half, that's not very promising.

These are the elements needed to play a song in daytime programming. In evening programming song-directedness also prevails ('because it is always practical to have songs on the radio'). The decision-makers in the record business are equally guided by the song. They anticipate the selection by the radio (see also p.329). As one record label boss points out, the potential of a number is assessed based on its quality, but *De Afrekening* never leaves the back of his head (the Studio Brussels charts put together by the audience). Other actors in the record circuit follow:

> Of fundamental importance in an artist's chances of being picked up, is whether his number is indeed song-directed or not. Without traditional songs, nobody can break through. There have to be vocal. Somebody must sing. An instrumental hit is nearly impossible. It does not get in *De Afrekening*, and even in the evening programs, they won't keep playing it. (...) Good song lyrics? Perhaps these are important to the credible press, but the public couldn't care less. Only the trigger counts: a piece or melody of fifteen seconds that appeals to people, a hook. Then I will focus on a song, and then I have the will to work on it. A number must trigger me. That's how I know that I can play the public I want to play. Those fifteen seconds are very often what makes things work.

Sometimes potentially successful music is also described in general terms, or by making use of examples of bands. The word then is 'emotional music,' music that contains an overwhelming emotion that everybody recognizes. A record label boss and a manager:

> It's what I call a StuBru sound, invariably the same sound: Coldplay, Radiohead, Air Traffic, Starsailor, and The Kooks to a certain extent. Or call it the REM, U2 sound: the big emotion. You don't have to understand it in order to still grasp that it contains a baroque, overwhelming emotion. A bit like Bono's flag-waving. You had the same thing with the Simple Minds... You recognize it.

The Bony King of Nowhere: that's emotional music, capable of appealing to a large public — just as feel good music. But there's little connection with artistic criteria. It's pop music, a CD you can give to your mother as a present.

In all these cases, the actors focus on those musical properties that will help to reduce the risk of the decision. Some of these properties are perhaps timeless; the pop music circuit's actors never choose anything other than song-directed, catchy music. The minimal condition for selection could therefore reside in certain general genre conventions that are typical of the alternative mainstream. This, of course, does not mean that these style properties are not bound by time. The idiom of the song has been dominant throughout the history of pop. Still, non-song-directed music sometimes undermined this supremacy (see Keunen 2002). In the second half of the 1990s, for example, the aesthetics of rock was virtually dead. The alternative mainstream was teeming with electronic dance music that would have none of songs. In the 1970s, the traditional song structure was undercut by a generation of progressive rockers, while ten years later guitar solos were declared taboo. In hip-hop, musicians ask themselves over and over what beats are popular and therefore acceptable. The musical properties of potentially successful music are subject to trends. Yet certain genre preferences keep their footing. Just as in Chapter 2, the examples cited in this chapter reveal that the alternative mainstream does not think highly of genres such as metal or R&B.

All this implies that those who make music that does not match the dominant idioms of style, and who deviate from the songs, by definition will have trouble in being picked up. A manager tells the story of the Flemish band DAAU. By their uncompromising, self-willed attitude in the pop music circuit, they shut themselves out and vanished back into the niche again. 'Had they continued doing what they did on their first CD and had they had a slightly more commercial attitude, their future and their bank account would have had a different look.' Even dEUS, he says, could have meant more internationally, had they worked a little longer on a single, reduced it to an edit of three minutes, superimposed the vocals a bit more and omitted the break at the end where they play the number into smithereens.' Becker (1982: 129) already discussed this: you can disregard conventions, but it will cost you more money and effort to achieve something. Those who want to sell more need to comply with the conventions and make concessions. If the music sounds too different, it needs to be adjusted when it wants to be picked up. Flemish bands such as Motek and Dez

Mona are good examples provided in the interviews of music that initially deviated too strongly from the standard and afterwards, thanks to another musical development, became more accessible. Motek (temporarily) made a breakthrough when they interpreted post rock in a poppy way with the single 'Tryer' and managed to trigger the radio audience that normally would not be occupied with that kind of music ('instead of becoming a post rock band, they became a post rock pop group,' their manager says). Dez Mona was only signed by their current label when the music became more song-directed. Besides, when the bands (or their management or record firm) are not prepared to do these adjustments, there is still the radio which will do it for them. For tracks that are too long to be played on the radio, either the stations ask for an edit or they make one themselves.

Generally, it can be argued that artistic criteria that are formulated from an organizational logic are complementary to the alternative mainstream's aesthetics of rock. They do not necessarily run parallel and reveal largely a mainstream attitude rather than an underground attitude. Whereas the aesthetics of rock referred to underground qualities, this time around the music is viewed from a mainstream perspective. It also reveals that the alternative mainstream is situated at the intersection of the underground and the mainstream. From an individual logic, they are pulled out of love toward the former, but the organizational logic pushes them back to the latter. Thus, an artistic judgment always receives an economic reflection. It makes the classification actions difficult and leads to an ambivalence that is embedded into the segment (Bauman 1991).

The Creation of Popularity

The alternative mainstream does not simply look at what is popular. It also has the ability to make music popular. Promotions may be instigated by the concert circuit (a new band getting a good spot on an important festival is one example) or by music publishers (get recognition for numbers by using them in films, series, games and commercials), but it is especially the radio which can influence the public taste. The written press may write an nth number of times about artists, the impact of the articles is different from the impact made by airplay. By frequently playing the same number, the radio co-determines what is popular. This factual observation proves to be inherent to the way in which the radio carries out its programming. In the preceding section, the argument established that radio, as a mass medium, does not want to be a platform for as much music as possible that the radio-makers like artistically, but for music that the suitably broadest public possible loves. The radio wants music that has public support, music that is popular or can become popular. Consequently, radio-makers are very careful in drawing up a playlist and in determining the rotation of records. They want to give a number a radio life, make it known to the public, so that that same public will recognize it.

This is the reason why all programming starts from two principles. On the one hand, the playlist for daytime programming is composed adopting a much sterner selection, only granting a limited number of songs a high rotation. In Flanders, at Studio Brussels, it amounts to five new records per week. Some respondents descry this as a clear sign of reduction to the greatest common denominator, the leveling out. Furthermore, these chosen few do not simply receive a high rotation; they are left in the playlist for a long time. For a minimum of two months, the time it takes a number to be really well known with the public. This means that radio-makers must push aside their individual logic (personal taste) and yield to the organizational logic. At this point, the radio-makers also want to defend themselves.

> When you're in the music business, you do want to hear new things, just to keep it exciting. But the listener is not that fast. He or she will hear a number, or start to like one, when we are already sick and tired of hearing it. If it takes off at that point, you have to play it another three months.

> I'm absolutely convinced that we — the people who are really occupied with it — are weeks ahead of the listeners who do not pay attention. Only after six weeks or so, when we are starting to doubt, people pick it up and begin talking about it. The average person does not listen to a station for more than two hours a day.

> Thinking that certain numbers are too long in the playlist is a reflex typical of a musician or a music lover,

people who listen in a wholly different manner than the average radio listener. I really think we tend to overestimate our public.

That being said, radio-makers are well aware of the fact that playing a record too often can destroy the number. Radio programming thus becomes an operation of seeking a balance: 'I have to keep playing a song until it is just not worn out,' a respondent says. That is why the actors remain sensitive to the comments and feedback of the listeners. If needed, the playlist will be adjusted. By doing so, a practice is installed, which gains in frequency. It consists in the introduction of a number in the playlist in low rotation. It is a test run, to see if it causes a ripple, both inside ('Listening to a number for 30 to 50 seconds on a playlist meeting has a quite different effect than when you hear it on the radio'), and outside, among the public, the listeners:

> As a playlist editor, you can feel whether something
> has potential and needs time to grow, like for example
> Yeasayer. When you play it and you feel it sticks and it
> continues to jump out, then we go for a longer spin. But
> I check the blogs every day and look at the reactions the
> listeners send. Sometimes we just stop playing a number.

The modus operandi national radios have developed assumes the abovementioned vicious circle and the self-fulfilling prophecy: they want music that is popular, but at the same time, they are active in the process of making the music popular. Because of the stringent selection, the radio makes, airplay is almost certain to have an impact on the reach of public. The effect of this on the selection by the music industry seems to be a logical consequence (see Chapter 7). Yet a selection or non-selection is never final. It is the task of the radio to play 'what occupies the listeners at that time,' so the line there goes. It explains why the initial decision can be reconsidered and revised, in both directions. A selected number can be rejected afterwards, or a non-selected number can still be picked up. The latter scenario occurs when a number achieves a public success that was unhoped for. 'Sometimes *De Afrekening* is a signal that we should check things again, to see if we should revise the decision and actually play it,' one radio-maker says. According to another, a number that has vanished from the playlist can crash into the charts a couple of months later, which ensures that it will be played again. Later success can also have consequences for earlier numbers of the same group that were rejected at the time. A compiler/producer:

> 'Velvet' by The Big Pink was only picked up by the evening program, in daytime nobody wanted it because it was too fierce. Then along comes the single 'Domino,' which becomes a small cult hit, climbs high in *De Afrekening*, and it's catchy, and so it's also played in daytime. Then the record company re-releases the first single, and now it's on the daytime playlist. I think that's too bad. You can create a distinct profile for yourself as a station with this.

By Way of Conclusion
Experience Must Help

In order to dam in the risks of their decisions, the actors look at the popularity potential of the music that comes up for selection, and the reach of public. To determine, or make sure, that they effectively reach that public, the media keep a close watch on the listeners and readers ratings. Otherwise, the actors hire agencies to do general market research, and then let their choice be guided by the results. Based on these studies, profiles are established in order to be able to describe the target group. In Flanders, for instance, Studio Brussels is the station for younger people, while Radio 1 aims more for the thirty-something and forty-something. In-depth research about tastes of their public is lacking. The available data do not always say anything that can be clearly isolated. Some of the respondents admit that the target group is also a 'feeling for,' a 'hunch' or even 'mere guesswork.'

Precisely for this reason, the main factor in coping with uncertainty is found elsewhere: in experience. Over the years, the actors have learned what it is to live in an economically uncertain context. They know that they take risks, but from experience, they learn how to better assess what choices either should be made or should not. Successes from the past can become a guideline for future decisions (Bauman 1991: 2). The respondents define this as 'assessment capability,' the 'instinctive sensing whether there is a public for something or not' or 'métier.' One radio-maker argues: 'Hear a number, and regardless of genre know whether it's a perfect radio number, will appeal to a large or small public, suited for every moment of the day.' Here professional capital is called in, the special kind of symbolic capital. Somebody's reputation as an entrepreneur is closely bound up with the amount of professional experience the actor has been able to build in the specific field' (Vanherwegen 2008: 84). The extent of professionalism that he or she can put forward serves to decrease uncertainty. A record label boss on the matter:

> It's a bit like in fashion or in paint retail: you feel what color is going to sell this year. It's the same with music. You can feel it, after some time it becomes a craft. (...) There are certain things we listen to reduce the risk factor. It concerns the song, somebody's appearance, his or her background, the possible collaborations you can do, a tour. All these sorts of considerations. When you're talking with somebody about an album, all these matters shoot through your head. It's on your mind, you think it through, and with all the experience you managed to acquire through the years you are going to take a decision.

In addition, when new trends are in the making, it is the selectors' task to assess the value of the trend from their background of experience. One promoter says that when The Drums and Fleet Foxes were rising he 'felt' that the current would make it. A radio producer and a journalist:

> When you listen to extremely many (sic) records, you sort of slip into a situation where you have a kind of instinct for what is possible and what is not. You do it so often and you have done it for so long a time, that you're simply able to see things much faster than others. To be sure, I don't have it for all genres – I don't have it for hip-hop, which is why I put somebody else on hip-hop – but I kind of have it for pretty all melodic genres, because I have the largest background. I have an extra sense for this sort of music. It's difficult to grasp into words, but sometimes you feel: this is going to be something, the time is right and ripe for it, I get why this sound on this moment in this world works:

It all depends on your frame of reference. The farther you can go back into your experience, the more you will be able to put it in some kind of perspective. And the more you are able to assess whether or not it is going to work, because you can compare with other music.

The combination of dealing with uncertainty (a clenching of the gut) and making an appeal to experience (a feeling for) can best be grasped by the words 'gut' and 'feeling': a gut feeling. The previous chapter already argued that this was a rather vague passepartout. Then it was put forward to describe somebody's personal taste ('to like something that is good'). Several respondents, however, describe a gut feeling not only as an artistic appreciation of what is thought to be good. It is also connected with a practical awareness or sensing of the viability of music. Because the actors cannot make the gut feeling part of the discourse, they demonstrate the intuitive nature of it (gut feeling implies 'without giving it much thought,' 'not having to think it over). This, of course, points to the presence of a habitus, and, more particularly, of an actively guiding professional habitus. The habitus gives social actors a situational 'sense of practice' (*le sens pratique*), which enables them to exactly know what they have to do in a given set of circumstances (Bourdieu 1989: 64-65). The practical sense contains both symbolic and economic elements, as is illustrated by these quotes from individuals in the concert circuit:

Gut feeling? It's your own will and want, an affective thing. To put a part of yourself in it. But I have learned to distance myself, because otherwise it doesn't work. At the same time, gut feeling is also that the concert has to match the music club's profile, that you are able to find an audience for it, that it feels okay financially.

Gut feeling is primordial. It's the subjective sensing of yes or no, finding something fantastic or innovating, and emotionality. It's musically content-related. But it is also infused with years of experience: having seen the band once before, knowing the record and being able to situate it, knowing the network around the artist (what booker, etc.). Beside this, there is the reality check, a checklist of practical things such as: will the venue be free on that date? Is there still enough budget? Can the band enjoy sufficient popularity? Gut feeling and reality check have to go hand in hand, or else the venue goes bust and out of business.

Gut feeling is the combination between finding something cool and 'this just might grow into something big' or 'with this we can take a few steps further.'

The gut feeling may be very strong, the amount of experience and professional capital accumulated great, the decisions will always remain uncertain. Years and years of experience and paying plenty of tuition can build up the intuition, and make it grow. Yet an actor can never be completely certain (Laermans 2004: 15).

Marginal Conditions for an Organizational Logic

Those who work in an organization need to have an eye for economic cost effectiveness and the strategies of risk reduction that go along with it. Apart from these, there are also a series of marginal conditions involved: practical and logistic, artist-bound and content-related criteria that co-determine the choice. Aspects as these are of the utmost importance for the daily work practice, and hence also for the selection, but they are not related to the process of symbolic meaning making and therefore are no part of the core of this study. For reasons of completeness, and because these are necessary marginal conditions, the matter will be dealt with briefly.

‖ Practical and Logistic Criteria

Some criteria that co-determine the selection are of a practical nature. To organizers, this can be the infrastructure and the location of the venue, as well as the available tour data. In the media, a chronic lack of space can determine the selection.

The Concert Circuit – Infrastructure, Location and Tour Data

As a promoter, you obviously need to have the right infrastructure for the sort of bands you would like to be able to book. The fixed venue can be too large or too small for certain bands, hence it will not be offered by the bookers. Location, too, plays a part. Big cities have a larger potential public. Consequently, they are offered more opportunities. Here lies a difference between domestic and foreign artists. According to one programmer, visitors would not be willing to travel more than 30 kilometers to see a local band. Foreign artists present a different case, and the capital cities (Brussels, Amsterdam) get first choice. This is so because the international agents would rather have it that way. Secondary in line are the other bigger cities (Antwerp, Ghent and Louvain in Belgium, or Rotterdam, Utrecht and Tilburg in the Netherlands). Promoters from these bigger cities are aware of their privileged position, and those working in the smaller cities sometimes have trouble accepting this. Reality rules, however, and they simply have to reconcile themselves to the factual situation. They can succeed in doing this with the necessary professional capital.

If I were to work in a big city, I would look at bands in a different way. The same band is able to draw as many as four times the crowd they attract in the smaller cities and communities. (...) I often see bands in the concert halls of the large cities bands of which I think: Damn, I would have loved to have them.' On the other hand, I am realistic enough to understand that these venues can also take more from the bookers. If I were a booker, I'd also put my bands in the bigger cities, because there's a greater chance of success. (...) I don't blame the bookers. They too have things to account for to their agents. Otherwise, these will say: 'You didn't do a good job.'

Those actors who want to program foreign bands will have to know whether the bands are on tour (unless he or she has enough funds for a one-off, or is able to work with other organizers to set up a tour of their own, which would make the concert financially viable again). Festival organizers have the additional task to 'get lucky': to know before anyone else whether a group is looking for a concert date, and to make sure that there are no other candidates at the particular time. On other moments — when their bill needs to be fixed — the same promoters are under pressure of time, which can lead to the prices going up.

Lack of Space in the Agenda, in the Paper, on the Bill, etc. Sometimes just the oversupply is to blame. When there are already many commitments (a paper may have agreed to several interviews), the slots for bands run out quickly and all at once the whole bill is blocked and there is not a single place left. Then, regardless of the quality or success of the artist, great opportunities are neglected, new offers turned down. Lack of space is indeed an important argument. Two journalists declare that, each week, their paper has only room for 5 to 8 CD reviews, and that the number of concert reviews is limited. With regard to the radio, it is common knowledge that the number of slots in daytime rotation, as well as in evening programming, is (too) limited, and that the number of releases is too large to be able to have everything spotted or enjoying attention. One journalist adds a psychological aspect to the deadlock: too great a workload, too heavy pressure of time and too little free space left in the head.'

Artist-Bound Criteria

The Artist's Personality and Motivation

The contact between managers and artists is usually much more intense than the mostly fleeting contacts an artist has with persons from the media or the concert circuit. For the artist manager an additional criterion joins the balance: is the artist a person who is easy to work with, both on a personal and a business level? The interviews show that managers as well as record firms look at the personality of the artist in relation to his music. Are the artists sufficiently ambitious? Are they motivated? Do they have the will to go for it? Are they willing to make sacrifices for it? Are they not over-occupied with other things that will steal time from their career? Do they offer a perspective on more than one project? Are their career dreams realistic enough? Are they available (for concerts, promotion)? The questions never end. Managers also check how artists deal with business and administration duties. Such qualities are a complementary condition when a cost effectiveness logic is involved, and they determine the possibilities for prolonged collaboration. In the case of one small independent every *signing* is allegedly preceded by a long talk in the pub:

> You may very well have made a fantastic record and you may be a good live band, if our conversation of a couple of hours leaves me with a feeling of 'Oh no, not cool,' then I'm not going to do it. And again here the opposite applies: the majors would probably do it. They just think: 'we're going to sell lots and lots of this.' Not with me, I mean it. I only do bands with people I think are cool. That's very important to me, or else it won't work.

Nationality as Criterion of Selection

The nationality of artists can play a part in the selection. It can be a statement to choose consciously for domestic talent. Music clubs often include it in their business plan. In addition, very nearly all journalists say they like to give preference to the local artists: 'Our sense of being involved is evidently greater. We are also more important to them than to a fledgling English band.' The choice for national or regional can also be inspired by practical or public-oriented considerations. Domestic artists are easily available and are sometimes so popular that they attract a public as easily. Still, because everybody can book them, foreign artists determine the color and the tone of the programming.

For the public network in Flanders, interest in national artists is established in the managerial agreement with the government (Flemish Government 2011), in the form of mandatory quota: 25% of the broadcasting time (taken as an average for all networks together) must accrue to Flemish music productions, while for Radio 1 also 15% must be in Dutch. This should never happen at the expense of quality, a prerequisite the producers find rather difficult to meet. In order to achieve these quotas, the bar has to be lowered considerably for Belgian bands. Again, that is what the radio-makers argue in chorus. Domestic bands are positively discriminated. Sometimes this affirmative action can go horribly wrong, a few respondents claim. Qualitatively lesser numbers must get frequent airplay to arrive at the quotas. This leads to the artists' 'burning up.' In addition, the affirmative action is never a guarantee of success for younger bands, since – as was said before – the public prefers to hear what they already know: the better-known fellow citizens.

Content-Related Criteria

The Significance of a Good Story

The written press is constantly seeking the story about and around an artist. If the artist has swum some difficult waters and has experienced the hard knocks of life, a story will be written and published all the more swiftly. 'When you want to enthuse people or issue a warning, you need to pay attention to that sort of thing and push the frame of reference wide open,' one journalist explains. To some *the* story, if it is *a* good story, is the most important criterion to do an interview with an artist. If there is no story to tell, a CD review is the most that the artist will get.

> We're a magazine, and we sell stories. (...) We need to bring a story that is well-constructed, where there's meat and dirt to be discovered. (...) Whenever I want to read a music story, I too want to read a story. I don't want to know what guitar he used during the concert. I want to know how things are with his wife, or – again an exaggeration – what particular drugs he used to take.

When there is no guarantee in advance that something good will come out of it – a story – journalists are never squeamish about putting an invitation or proposal aside. If the record company has granted him only 20 minutes, or is he is unable to talk to the front man of a band, the coinciding negative elements can result in a 'no.' Hence the tendency and preference to write about domestic artists: a reporter can write better stories around them, there is more time, more space. To give the whole thing a touch of exclusivity, the journalist will not hesitate to visit the artist in the studio during a recording session, or to accompany the artist or a band on a tour across Flanders.

Conversely, it is also possible that the story suddenly presents itself and a decision not to do something about a group is revised. One journalist decided to go to a concert by Don McLean when he had heard that McLean's band would not make it in time because of the Iceland cloud of ashes. This forced McLean to play solo, in a very difficult position. 'Then there was a story to be told.'

Variety in a Program – Variation in Content

Actors are always ready to ascertain their own personal taste as a guiding principle. They are also the first to realize that too much of the same is to be avoided at all costs. Especially when there is a need to work on a public-oriented basis and you have to consider the selling possibilities. Variation in content and spreading in time are necessary. The choices have no connection whatsoever with popularity and artistic quality. The matter has then become one of the right music at the right moment. Promoters will be quicker to refuse when they have already booked (too) many bands in the same genre. On the CD page of his or her paper the music journalist can 'trade one of the three proposed electronic music CDs for a country rock CD, or he chooses something else when he is under the impression that he has written already too much about a certain artist who is coming up. Customer benevolence, one journalist calls it.

Criteria of Technological Design of Sound

The quality, qualities or certain properties of the way in which the sound of a recording was engineered equally have their part to fulfill: standards of sound design and engineering must be up to major radio level. In short, it has to be well enough to be played. All radio-makers who were interviewed confirm this. Industry people who are to offer the record to the radio people will therefore perform a careful check-up. With subjective quality assessment or any artistic judgment, this criterion is most definitely not concerned.

Internal Organizational Processes

Group Processes

The pop music circuit is flooded with self-employed, freelancing sole breadwinners, mostly, but the gatekeepers of the alternative mainstream very often perform their function inside of an organization, working in close team context. Organizations, according to sociology, are durable social relations. Within these, various group processes can influence the selection process. The first environmental factor is the direct surroundings or environment itself. Who is taking the decisions in an organization, how does the decision develop, are there internal tensions?

The first and principal thing to note in the interviews is the social validation of the selections: most actors put their choices to the test, deliberate and negotiate them within the walls of their organization. Thus, an A&R manager of record firm will place his choice before the managing director or the person in charge of marketing. Programmers of music clubs have internal and external advisors to assist them — even though they possess great liberty in their choices. They gather with the colleagues and consult each other as a team, and external experts are asked for their advice on specific concepts of music that the programmer knows very little about. In music clubs with a younger programmer, there is a notable difference. Sometimes the programmer has to bang his fist on the table and take a hard line, then painstakingly convince the artistic and/or business manager of the importance of a risk-carrying concert. In the written press, the editor of the music pages seeks assistance for general reporting among the freelance journalists, who get assignments or propose items, and thereby may exert an influence.

In larger organizations, several persons may be assigned to do one single function. A large club may have several music programmers (as is the case in Brussels-based Ancienne Belgique). Live Nation can have several bookers. A radio station can have quite a number of program editors or producers. The organizational logic dictates that there is group consultation and deliberation. The playlist selection at the radio, for example, is a team effort. There is group discussion and collective decision about the records that are to get airplay or not, must get more or less frequent playtime, that are up for daytime rotation or destined for evening programming. The interviewed radio coordinators explain that they prefer to let these decisions come about via (rational) deliberation. Because all are present and together, 'they can keep a close watch on one another. This, it is believed, is 'the most democratic and objective way possible to come to a decision and do justice to the whole procedure. As in every group process, however, the weight of the various participants is not equal. In this respect, Laermans (2010: 262) notes that 'in the making and taking of binding decisions on collective terms it is not uncommon to see interpersonal differences enter the game, causing an independent social dynamics.' Those who bang their fists hard enough on the table, can hit lucky. A radio producer says:

> Somebody should film the playlist meetings. (...) Some stand up rock-hard, for what they think and are able to found and ground their opinion or view. Perhaps I myself have been too soft in those situations to really push thinks through. Take Sufjan Stevens, for instance: I had brought it up at least twenty times, but nobody could get it.

This social valuation of selections clearly indicates that such selections are never made in a void. In addition, other players have to be taken into account. In an organization, the model of collective deliberation and consultation ensures mutual adjustments of individual taste. It could be argued that the internal organization operates and functions as a community. Shared conventions are at stake in the negotiation, but they also work as the regulating principles, with the common purpose of coming to an agreement.

Instead of participating in deliberation, the different employees may work on their own little island, and be pitted against one another. Apart from symbolic processes of community, there are also economic market principles that determine an organization's modus operandi. Unity, community, mutuality and collectivity, and consensus are intersected by disagreement, competition and rivalry. It is not uncommon for organizations to see tensions rise between different sections or departments. One respondent recalls how the gloves came off inside of a certain record label when the distribution department (including promotion) differed on the approach of a band with the label department (including the group's manager). Tensions rose to a critical point ('It was never ever any good, they were constantly rude to the promo team, and it was awful'). Another interviewee compares his former workplace (a big record company) with his current employer (a small record firm):

> Structurally speaking the difference is very great. It is the reason why the work floor atmosphere is much nicer here. We've all become friends, and I have a very pleasant relation with everybody. At my former company, this would have been out of the question, and that isn't meant as a reproach. That's just the way it is with a mega firm. There were people I had never met. As in every big firm, people are constantly competing with each other, and the musical vibe that's active is completely different (...) A big firm has this pyramid structure which you cannot ignore. It has several bosses (head sales, head promotion, head this, head that...) who dispose of a team and who have much higher salaries. In such a firm you start by working for zilch for a very long period of time, and if you happen to get your career opportunity, you can end up with a better job and you can start filing your personal claim for more money . And suddenly you realize that you're making ten times as much as the people who are not doing your former job. You really need to want such a thing. I think it's not cool.

Internal competition can also arise between the bookers of a major agency may, as one respondent says about (the head of the Belgian section of) Live Nation:

> He's a champion in silently influencing people, without having to use much (sic) words. He's a super commander, a dictator who doesn't dictate or do anything to enforce his will. You just know or feel what he wants. As chief, he determines the house style and is able to put pressure on his staff. Every booker has his or her own territory and sometimes they try to steal things from each other. He incites them to do so He can be very cunning and sly, but he is one of the best promoters in the world, and perhaps you have to be cunning to be able to do it that good as he

does. When he succeeds every time to be top of the class, and knowing that he has this little, divided country, that's a clear sign that you're delivering top notch work.

The quote also illustrates that every organization has a person with ultimate responsibility whose decisive view will weigh with or against selections. In the written press, a senior editor of editorial coordinator ties the Gordian knots, in radio stations it is the person in charge of music or the station coordinator who has final responsibility with respect to the station's line of music. This person responsible for the final stage of the selection oversees the common agenda and the group processes, but takes heed not to grant him- or herself too much power. This programmer, who supervises other persons, sums it up: 'All offers have to be run by me, but I am just a key figure or pivot in the entire programming team. We have a democratic regime in which every programmer can be totalitarian.'

In international organizations, another internal factor is of key influence. For international *signings,* the local branches are merely a serving hatch or conduit. The selection has already been made abroad. 'We just carry it out,' a record label boss says. Another one confirms this:

> When you're with a major or a company like Pias, obviously there is an international offer, which has been A&R-ed abroad. These artists are already signed, and we are just customers or buyers. That's why the largest department in a firm is the marketing and promotion department. (...) When an artist sells a couple of million records and holds the #1 position in the Billboard-charts for weeks, it's logical that we take a look at that and that this artist is on top of the pile. I would be very bad at my profession if I would say: 'I think Katy Perry for example is but a drab little Trudy and that her music is for girls of fourteen.' No, that's not my job. When Katy Perry has a hit, than clearly this is supposed to be my job.

With a small distribution firm, it is a different story, at least partially. The Belgian person in charge of a Dutch mother firm says:

I don't get instructions or pressure from the Netherlands,
I do whatever I want. Naturally, I consult with my colleagues. For instance, I'm not going to say about Antony
& the Johnsons: 'I don't feel like doing it.' I just do it. But
then again, there are lot of examples of bands that come
in and that I think are fantastic, and I really want to go
for it, while In the Netherlands the word is: 'We don't feel
much for it, but go on and do it anyway.' That was the
case with 65daysofstatic: post rock doesn't work as well
there as it does in Belgium.

Internal Organizational Conflicts Between Logics

Organizations such as a record company, a booking office or a
concert club are solely occupied with music, which is why you
can assume that they all work towards a similar goal. In the case
of the media, and especially the written press, it is indeed a different story. On the one hand, the music editor is only one of a
newspaper's editorial staff, and usually not the most powerful; on
the other hand, papers also have a marketing department and a
chief editorial staff who do not necessarily follow the music journalist's individual logic, acting mainly from an organizational
set of objectives (selling more papers). Adopting the model of
the 'economies of worth' proposed by Boltanski and Thévenot, it
could be said that the chief editorial staff and marketing department inhabit another world or realm than the music editor: the
first think from 'the world of profit,' the other (at least partially)
from 'the world of inspiration.' Because what is of worth or valuable in one world can be unknown or entirely irrelevant in the
other, conflicts may arise. Decisions are thus not only made in
a personal vacuum. Other worlds are also in the game, and they
sport other principles.

Clashes with the chief editorial staff are therefore not uncommon. They have other interests and want to publish articles
that appeal to a broader target group or they fear that the music
editor does not deal with the average reader's profile at sufficient
length. A journalist comments:

What they think is that you are just doing your own thing
and only cover those bands you like yourself. (...) I also
have to explain why I do Joanna Newsom, and among

> the editorial staff, there's not a single soul that is able to grasp the line of reasoning. To them it's simple: do all concerts in large venues, do the big events and everything that's a hit. When I did a big piece on Jeff Buckley in the paper, the chief editor said: 'Who is he again?.' Anyway, they tolerate what I do, and I just have to deal with the whole situation. (...) I honestly think Clouseau is not a typical band for our paper, even if it's a typical Flemish band. Still, this is a highly sensitive issue at our paper. The chief editorial staff is convinced we should bring Clouseau very big and that we're spot-on in our target group there. Personally, I don't believe this at all. There are many popular acts that the chief editorial staff would like me to write about, but where I dig my heels in, or just put a CD review in and write that it's very bad.

The marketing department of a paper or magazine also holds another position within the organization than the music editors. It can mount special commercial actions with concert promoters or record firms, and often with music to which the journalist does not necessarily want to pay editorial attention. Yet these activities are said to have little or no journalistic consequences. The interviewed journalists all agree not to feel any pressure from the market department. The music editor may not always be aware of an action, but usually his or her opinion is asked whenever special actions are prepared (such as a series of live CDs, free tickets or streaming of concerts).

> They come knocking at my door asking for advice for the free tickets and the streaming, 'whether it's worth the while.' And that's why we did a streaming for the Black Box Revelation and not for Admiral Freebee, which was also on offer and would have been a lot more lucrative. (...) Besides, they don't have to do what I say, I only give advice. Which is normal, because those marketing people aren't busy listening to music all day.

Another journalist says every marketing promotion is discussed with the editorial staff 'in order to see whether it could also be interesting editorially speaking, and if we don't support it, the whole thing is buried.' As far as the interviews are concerned, music editors are never forced to write about anything. There are examples of CDs which were presented as gifts along with a paper, but which were never reviewed by the editor because they were 'too awful.' When a medium has a sponsor deal with a festival or a concert hall this does not immediately result in journalistic coverage. The interviewed journalists emphasize that they often deliberately ignore concerts that are sponsored by their paper, or, conversely, that they write about concerts without any sponsor deal. One actor expresses his motivation: 'Simply because I have a great deal of sympathy for certain festivals.' Yet music journalists have the opposite view. Because editors are asked for advice and because the marketing department usually follows the advice, 'we have many actions that are in line with what we do on the editorial level.' Furthermore, 'we write more about the festivals that are sponsored because the bill is more in keeping with what we bring in the course of the whole year.'

Nevertheless, here too, socially acceptable behavior can occur. One interviewee said: 'Sponsoring is a devilish thing.' It smells too heavily of an economic logic, to which actors do not want to yield (at least not officially). What the organizers have to say, however, is quite a different story. Off the record, and viewed from personal experience, the truth is that there is a link between sponsoring and editorial attention. The explicit conventions do not always run parallel to the implicit ones (see also Chapter 6). What's more, the journalists sometimes admit that a decision can be revised under the influence of marketing actions.

> A paper needs to sell and there are marketers who keep an eye on this and who want to be able to recognize something once in a while. So you have to make sure that there are also popular things to be covered, insofar that these have something interesting.

Thus, a newspaper did publicity for a concert by Faithless that could be followed live on its website via streaming. Initially, the paper's music editor did not want to write about the concert because he thought there was nothing new to tell. He expressed his opinion from an individual logic. His editor-in-chief, however, pointed out to him that it would strike the reader as odd that a newspaper advertised for weeks about a concert and then did not write a single word about it when it was over. The editor thought he had a point there. The clash of logics was solved by a compromise:

> I placed a large photo with a tiny little article under it written based on the stream. By doing so, I still had room to do a review of the first Belgian concert by We Have Band, which I did find interesting. And this is important to me.

Apart from consensus and competition, a third mechanism is active: the compromise.

Compromises Between Individual and Organizational Logic

From Equilibrium to Economic Dominance

To select is to combine personal taste with organizationally induced choices. One journalist summarizes it as follows: 'I think
we do a number of things we simply have to do and a number of
things we absolutely want to do.' Especially on the output side
of the music circuit, this is a constant given. The media make a
mix of new and established names. 'This balancing act between
mainstream and the more *left* is just the interesting part of it,' a
radio-maker says. A newspaper editor thinks this:

> On those two pages I try to make a mix of what needs to
> be done (news value, the big names) and next to that the
> accents we personally want to lay on certain things. (...)
> It's a system. You're just working along with the industry.
> You can try to go against it, but if you decide to be a total
> troublemaker and be entirely contrary, you're writing
> above the heads of the readers, which is not the inten-
> tion. When you just completely go with the flow, you're
> just like everybody else. What matters is to find a kind
> of balance between keeping your own identity, your
> individuality without losing sight of your aim, which is to
> write for a large audience. Actually, that is the most im-
> portant criterion of selection: finding the right mix.

With concert organizers, this also translates in a mixed
programming: a mix between specialized niche programming on
the one hand, where artistic motives and personal taste are prevalent (usually the smaller concerts or special events), and music
for a broader public on the other hand, where these motives are
less fundamental or decisive (usually the bigger stages). A festival
organizer starts from what he thinks are good names on a substance level, but at the same time he looks for crowd pullers that
can make him sell enough tickets. 'In the end, the balance must
feel right,' somebody says. When both can be combined, satisfaction reaches the highest level.

The respondents usually view this as the filter of the individual logic that is being released onto the organizational
logic (either inspired by the pursuit of distinction or not). Then

personal taste kicks in, but just as well the actors' sense of being 'called,' out on a mission. It explains why a journalist says it is his ambition to let the reader discover new things, and why a radio producer wants to put 'a special bit in the mix now and again,' every now and then play something that manages to surprise people for a brief moment or which can highlight the station. In the words of a festival organizer:

> I'm a music freak and it is still my hobby. When I think something's awfully bad, I won't do it. (...) It's not because it can draw a crowd, that I have to program it. I leave that to other festivals. They can do it. (...) I've done many things of which I knew well in advance that there wouldn't be a soul to come and see it, but which I think are fantastic. Briskey, for example, I don't know if you even know them... (laughs) (...) The fact that I haven't made any compromises in this, has made the festival to what is today. And I'm not talking about wanting to be an elitist festival, which I don't want. But still, it resulted in us being a different kind of festival, where bands think it is cool to play and which they personally think is a cool festival. (...) The combination of Everyman with music lovers makes sure that you can run a festival with a good draw. When Everyman does not know band X, but the music lovers are there to attend, then you get an ambiance that incites others to come and see it, which makes you end up with something cool. That's what I want to show to people: that there's more in the world than Milk Inc. and the likes. (...) I strike the happy medium between popular and cool. With a cool, exciting bill that's well worth seeing, one that sees both the average man and woman as well as the music lover right.

Selections in the pop music circuit are made from an individual and an organizational logic, but the two are never acting separately. In most cases elements from both come together, get intertwined according to the situation, and ultimately result in a selection. It fits in with the thesis that the alternative mainstream operates at the intersection of cultural and economic principles. The logics could be said to be complementary. Still, following Boltanski and Thévenot (2006: 277-282), it is better to call them 'compromises between logics.' A compromise is always the outcome of a negotiation, but does not necessarily mean that both components are of equal value or worth. In the pop music circuit, the relationship between the two logics depends on several factors, yet each time it is an economic assessment: at the end of the line, the organizational logic weighs heavier. Most respondents easily put the share of personal taste in their choices into perspective. They even think 'that you cannot go too far in this.' Taking decisions from personal taste in the pop music circuit is more of a desire than an established fact. It is the cherry on the cake. For actors to survive, however, they must put aside their personal taste and look at the potential or targeted public. The most striking element in the interviews is that the (implicitly) employed artistic criteria are often linked up with criteria that are rather of an economic nature. Albeit that the artistic is the starting point, when music is not cost effective or too loss making (based on profit, exploitation possibilities, reach of public, etc.), it will have a hard time being selected. This partly explains the ambivalence that exists in the discourse. In this way, a programmer says that his music club was too underground before his time and that he rather would play a central part in the city's music life. Another programmer says his festival is not 'heavily alternative,' he could not neglect the region and should always be able to fall back on the Everyman. A journalist, for his part, says he actually wants the reader of the paper to discover new music, but that he embark on this early, but should give the reader time to catch up.

Consequently, the gatekeepers on call take less risk than they personally would like. Especially the concert circuit provides many examples. An organizer talks extensively about the financial problems he used to have and how he had to be creative to keep his head above water, by organizing business parties, among other things. The number of concerts where organizers can actually do what they want is but a small fraction of the entire programming (and sometimes is dependent upon subsidies, see further on). Consider the following excerpt:

> If of the estimated 70 or 80 people only five would show up every time, then I would have to start watching what I do after only a few months and I could not just decide to do this new fantastic band which makes an experimental sound with wooden spoons which I happen to like. (...)

If I was to put my 100 favorite bands here, which nobody has ever heard of, after two years my house would not even exist anymore. It would have been two very cool years for me personally, because I would have been able to see everything that I ever wanted, just like those five other people who thought the wooden spoon with the experimental sounds were wonderful and would have had the tine of their life. But the fact is you don't get any further with that: It's simply impossible to do a concert like that every week. You simply can't afford it.

It follows that a compromise need not always entail a consensus. It can also bring forth rumblings and tensions. The same interview attracts attention because of this:

It is unfortunate that you have to put a limit to it. (...) Before I started to do this job, I had pictured something completely different. I thought a much larger part of my time would be spent on tracking down new music, but that is not the case. If I could choose I would have it differently, but that doesn't work. (...) That is a reality that I have had to face. Sometimes I think 'the programming by the Brussels-based AB is fantastic,' but if you know that even they had to scale down the club concerts, that says it all, doesn't it?

Or, as a festival organizer observes:

Little mad things like doing small bands and provide an extra tent for it, does not bring in anything. Not professionally, not financially. (...) It's a pity, but we cannot afford to do this, the cost of doing a festival such as ours is simply too great. And the fact is you don't get any extra visitors by doing it.

The question then is how actors in the pop music circuit deal with the tensions that ensue from these compromises. In the next part, the analysis distinguishes three attitudes that emerged from the interviews. In the first, the economic dominance is approached from a professional attitude; in the second actors try to convert economic surplus value in artistic choices; in the third, they hope to be able to do it by means of subsidies.

Professional Attitude as a Basis

Giving in to economic reality, making it impossible to do what they want, can indicate illegitimate behavior to which actors have resigned themselves. Yet this is not always perceived as a problem. A previously mentioned quote by a programmer provides a possibility: 'I program a lot that I don't like myself. I'm not obligated to listen to it myself, I can safely stay at the bar.' The success of a good concert night out does not depend upon a decent artistic performance alone. From an organizational logic, it is also successful when it is organized well, when there is a good crowd in the hall and when the audience has enjoyed it. A festival organizer notes:

> Music is a party, right? Music is an experience, is having fun. All this fuss has no purpose, if you ask me. People come to a festival for a total experience. (...) That's why we put a lot of energy and a lot of money into our sets, in our environment, in the atmosphere.

The fact that actors have to put aside their personal taste is just *part of the job*. For those who have sufficient professional capital, it will be easier to do. This capital provides a sense of pride at achieved success. This was already cited with respect to a successful investment in a group. The same goes for the turn-out. Being partially forced to perform certain selections, should not always be detrimental to the joy or pleasure actors find in their job. Actors can also have fun with organizationally inspired choices. 'It can't be wrong to have a good crowd at your festival,' an organizer throws in. Two colleagues add:

> To see 60,000 people go crazy for 50 Cents at my festival gives me a tremendous kick. Just as when a music lover comes up to me saying he has discovered a small band in the little tent, which he thinks is fantastic.

> I can also enjoy the sight of 800 people going berserk in the main hall, even if it's not a band whose record I would

play at home, even if it's a different experience from when I would be watching a club concert for 50 minutes with smile from ear to ear on my face.

Allowing personal taste to outweigh other considerations, after all, is also not a guarantee of enjoyment in one's work. 'If I would put on ten bands that I think are fantastic and there's no crowd, I wouldn't be happy either.' In addition, the interaction that exists between the organizational and the individual is a complex process. A remarkable phenomenon is that personal taste can change due to the position an actor occupies within an organization, due to the group process that exists within it or due to changed interests. One of the respondents, for example, was rather negative about a certain group during the interviews, but today the same person is that group's manager, and his initial value judgment has changed. Another respondent corroborated this phenomenon when this author presented him with a personal experience:

> **GK** As a record label manager of Zomba I used to think the somewhat better things among the garbage Zomba released were really good, whereas today I wonder 'no way that I could have ever thought this was any good.'

> **Respondent** We had the same thing at our radio station. And you tend to affirm each other in those choices, right? There were things that jumped out between the regular stuff, but when you listen to it today, you wonder: 'What was this actually? Has this ever meant something?

The same occurs, in a somewhat different form, when music that has been picked up by the industry and the media, is suddenly assessed as good music. The fact that it has been picked up, is viewed as a form of recognition, as a proof of the music's quality. This author experienced it personally during a jury deliberation for some pop prize. A discussion arose concerning a band that enjoyed a lot of media attention at the time. One of the jury members (who, by chance or not, was a radio producer) said: 'The fact that the band is in the spotlight can only have happened because the music is of good quality.' This sort of reasoning fits in perfectly with the cultural cliché that 'talent always manage to surface.' The artistic relevance of music is thus identified with being successful.[3] A radio producer agrees: 'In my opinion, quality always rises to the surface, sooner or later, if it's really good.'

By way of illustration, it must be noted that this professional attitude is shared by the alternative mainstream with the mainstream. In the alternative mainstream, it is accompanied by an artistic love for the underground (which provokes the customary ambivalence). In the mainstream, the economic arguments prevail. For this study, this track was not really examined, but elements of it were revealed in the interviews. Upon being asked whether his personal taste is of any significance in the selection, a label boss whose heart is with the pop mainstream replied:

> No, because then I would unilaterally impose upon people what they should buy. I simply don't want to do that. That's not what we're here for. We're an entertainment company. It is my job to develop qualitative content, make it available and in the process make some money as a record firm. (...) I am responsible for the 50 people that work here. These people have to be able to go home with an easy conscience and say: 'My boss isn't somewhere in a casino enjoying himself, he's thinking about everything, there's a plan being made. And the plan is this (he shows the charts): these names highlighted in yellow, those are the hits we have in the charts. That's an indication that you are in fact doing something good, because otherwise you wouldn't have so many hits. It's just about doing your job, about the profession. You have got to be driven and willing to win. I mean, if you would be playing in a football team tomorrow, you would want to make as many goals as you could, right? But if you work for a record company, or a book publisher, then for some of the press that's suddenly not done. Why not? Isn't it cool to work for a record company that scores the most goals? (...) You've got to want to be the best. I'm passionate about doing business, about music, about winning and about this team spirit. I just want to make sure we're the best with our team: sign the best records, the most effective, promote these in the best way possible and make sure we get to number one. That's what we do. That's a way of life. Are we enthusiastic or what? (laughs)

From a strictly commercial logic, commercial success is synonymous with quality of music. In the television documentary *Belpop* both the producer and the record label boss of the popular Flemish group Clouseau commented on their second CD being received less well than expected: 'But it did sell a lot; in the end, the sales figures prove that it's a good record' (Wille and others, 25.10.2010).

At the opposite side of the spectrum – in the underground – people occasionally have difficulty accepting such an intensely professional attitude. One respondent testifies:

> This is the reason why we don't work with majors on a regular basis. If you hear these stories, it gets very frustrating. Only the big stars have priority. The rest must be ignored, so to speak. I know of a promo guy who wasn't allowed to spend much time on PJ Harvey and Queens of the Stone Age. That wasn't interesting enough, it didn't sell enough.

Deploying Commercial Surplus for Artistic Choices

Economic factors determine how the pop music circuit operates. Music clubs can let just a small part of their selection depend on purely artistic choices. The combination with economically cost effective concerts is needed for the survival of their overall activity: risks in a smaller hall can only be taken because of the profits made from a number of sold out concerts in a larger hall. 'This basic line of reasoning is the same for everybody else,' one organizer says. Another organizer adds:

> By programming a well-known name at our festival – even though it may not be the coolest name there is – we can sell some extra tickets and do cooler stuff on other days.

Concert halls have yet another strategy to finance their activity: by renting out their rooms they can take a greater artistic risk at other moments.

The same goes for the bigger players, for whom economic profit is a clear-cut motive. A piece of the profit can be invested in a programming section with a more distinctly artistic profile.

This allows big festivals such as Pukkelpop or Lowlands to select alternative music with full force. A program director of a music club and one of a big festival:

> A commercial main stage is good for the alternative side stages. (...) When you want to give all these small bands a chance at performing, you just need the big groups. Otherwise you can't afford to do it. I don't have any trouble whatsoever with someone buying a ticket for Metallica and on their way to the beer tent including two or three other things.

> The economic assessment is of a super importance for us. The main stage is then the absolute priority. Snow-Patrol isn't my personal taste either, but without it we can no longer do the small tents. That's the philosophy behind it all, a full 100%. (...) And, at that, even if we're already there financially, when I bump into something which I think would be crucial to put on the bill, then we'll do that. Cool and beautiful of the festival that it wants to keep doing that. Of course, this will never go at the expense of things, I mean, we're not talking about more than 10,000 euro.

In each instance, the logic of economic return or cost effectiveness can make room for an individual logic. How much room is made for such choices depends on the volume of business, the turnover: those who have sufficient means, are able to invest occasionally, without having to deplete their profits. The interviewed bookers sell big shows to compensate for the little ones, or to allow an artist in their artist roster who is not viable ('Somebody has got to nurture this artist, although I have little room do so,' one booker says about one particular artist). Management agencies can afford to work with smaller artists thanks to the commercially successful artists. In this way, the Flemish rock band dEUS made it possible for their management agency to work with less viable groups such as Evil Superstars, Kiss My Jazz and DAAU. This also used to be the philosophy of the major record companies, to reserve a nest egg or some funds for *development*. Those days are gone, although it may still occur.

From time to time, we have these promo visits here, and then I think, wearing only my financial hat: what a waste of time. Still, I keep doing it. We always try to create some room for the things we personally like and are willing to back. That's how I got in the business in the first place. I was hired as a product manager and I got the chance of doing Jesus Jones and EMF, invite Marc Almond, the things I was fond of myself. Blood will tell, now as good as in the past. I still think that having a guy like Richard Hawley here for a day and a half establishes the company's image vis-à-vis other labels, which perhaps play a rougher game. Sometimes it really doesn't have to get any crazier than that, but you still do these things.

In bigger record companies, economic criteria prevail, yet here too the compromise is common. Apart from the alternative mainstream, the major goes for the commercial mainstream successes. These revenues are a necessity for a multinational. A record label boss:

We're not averse to these successes, and I don't look down on them. With Fiocco, 2 Fabiola and all that stuff we did some wonderful things commercially. Hits are hits, it's what pushes along a record company.

Are Subsidies an Economic Safety Net or an Artistic Playground?

Another factor that reduces the risk and the economic dependence, are subsidies. Clearly, the government is not a part of the music industry. Nonetheless, it does establish the legal framework, as well as having the power to intervene in the market and make adjustments, favor particular artistic choices and in doing so have an impact on the selection process in the alternative mainstream.[4] As far as the situation in the studied region of Flanders is concerned, the interviews reveal that subsidies in the field are deployed differently, depending on the type of player and the size of the subsidies. In each case, though, it involves a surplus. Adopting an economic line of reasoning, the idea is that subsidies allow players to think artistically and take financial risks somewhat more frequently. Yet in pop music, subsidies actually function as an economic lifebuoy, rather than as an artistic playground. Two organizers comment:

> Subsidies determine what we do. Although you are only able to build the line of programming because you can take financial risks, we still aim for a break-even with every concert we do. (...) The total loss then needs to be covered by the subsidies.

> Subsidies are a vital condition. You may take things as business-like as possible, without subsidies you can't carry it. Unless you want to work on a strictly voluntary basis.

In the concert circuit, a large organization such as the Brussels-based Ancienne Belgique can count on larger means than the smaller clubs. Officially, AB is an Institution of the Flemish Community, and in this capacity it directly receives a greater portion of subsidies. The public capacity allows it to have a subsidy for management costs as well as an artistic budget (which it uses to organize festivals such as Domino and De Feeëriën, as well as other projects of its own). Here too, the line of reasoning is similar to those of the previous quotes:

> Because we received more subsidies, I can do my own thing more frequently and set up all these projects that make me fly. (...) But even with an organization like ours, every show is carefully measured. Without subsidies, the artistic, small-scale, loss-making part would be smaller; with more subsidies, we would be able to make choices that are even more radical.

The other music clubs, whether or not they are members of the non-profit organization Clubcircuit, do not have a separate artistic budget, according to the interviewed programmers. In these clubs, subsidies are mainly employed to be able to finance the regular activity of the organization — even they are granted on the basis of artistic criteria. The costs primarily relate to personnel, followed by infrastructure and other fixed costs. This is what every respondent says. 'Even if you cannot write this in a file for subsidies,' somebody adds. Nevertheless, because the fixed costs do not need to be included in the balance of every concert separately, it indirectly also benefits the artistic activity.[5]

Some clubs distinguish between concerts in the large hall or in the club. As a rule, the first need to be self-supporting ('for this end, subsidies should not be used'), whereas in club concerts investments are made:

> Bands I really want to put my foot on, something that I really want to do, even if I know that they'll only draw 40 people. (...) Then you weigh the pros and cons: is this worth using the subsidies, giving this group a chance so that they'll be able to grow?

In Flanders, even alternative management agencies can be subsidized, which is unthinkable in many other countries. The fact that the regional decree for the arts speaks of 'alternative' management agencies, evidently tells a lot. The same situation recurs. Subsidies are used to pay personnel costs, which makes it possible to take a chance with risky bands. Without subsidies, one manager claims, he would merely be able to work with bands like Triggerfinger, and not with artistic showpieces like Dez Mona or DAAU, bands that cost money. Another manager says:

> Thanks to the subsidies, you get the freedom to think more artistically and are able to take on a greater diversity of bands. Here the artistic section breaks the surface: we choose projects that we really like (personal taste) and that are having difficulties in the market. If we didn't give this sort of bands the attention they need, they would start playing less, producing lesser results. We also have bands that cannot find a booker in a context of market economics, because their bookings aren't self-supporting. So we take them and for doing that we receive subsidies. Without subsidies, none of them would be able to go abroad and play foreign venues.

Thus, subsidies can help to make choices that are more artistic. These, in turn, can then have an impact on the selection process. However, the respondents claim they never make selections with the purpose of getting possible subsidies. Their line of reasoning is quite the opposite. They want to develop a good activity and want to be judged positively based on their results.

Another striking thing is heard from the management agencies: in the long run, none of them want to continue working with artistically relevant (and therefore suitable for subsidies), but economically little cost-effective groups.

One manager thinks that when working with certain groups fails to deliver in the long run, these can no longer claim subsidies, and any activity with them should be ceased immediately. According to another, such a band would then start to resemble a kind of theater company: 'A few people who get paid and who must get the thing to run: is the game then still worth the trouble?.' This marks a striking difference with the subsidized players from classical music, for example, who are able to survive because of subsidies, who think these subsidies are an acquired right, and a token of (artistic) recognition.

Nonetheless, in the Evaluation Committee for Music — the committee that advises the Minister in Flanders, of which I have been a member for twelve years — similar arguments are often heard. There too the line of reasoning is that management agencies can only be subsidized by way of start-up, and that this should be temporary. The viewpoint starts from an artistic choice: 'commercial' music must be capable of keeping its footing after some time. As a result, the committee is very suspicious of popularity as a criterion. I remember something a committee member said about a festival: 'If even I, who am not in the least occupied with pop music, know most of the names on the bill, then they simply have to be very popular and commercial.' This explains why a respondent said: 'The alternative mainstream is required to prove itself more than other manifestations of culture and too rarely is it considered art.'

This also reveals the difference in logic between the music sector and the government. A comparative assessment of both parties' line of reasoning shows how they speak a different language, evaluating from: 'the government (including the committee) supports pop music because of its artistic value (market adjustment).' Better, the selection of those who are subsidized, and of the amount of subsidies, is grounded on artistic criteria. The field of music, by contrast, does not always survive the economic laws of demand and supply. Completely detached from what is considered 'artistically relevant' by the government, the actors of pop think in terms of economic criteria and they usually view subsidies as some sort of relief in economically difficult times.

In addition, another argument is involved. In the pop music circuit there are mixed feelings about governmental support. For example, upon finishing the interview, a respondent said jokingly: 'I'd rather done this conversation in the evening, after hours, and not during the day, like the subsidized.' It is a value-laden statement. Pop music needs to have a certain rock & roll dimension and subsidies are capable of ruining that. This idea lives among both subsidized and non-subsidized actors. It probably explains why an organizer says: 'At this moment, personnel already work twice as hard as they are paid, but it keeps the juices flowing and whets the appetite, so we don't become civil servants just siting out their hours.' A record label boss claims that, if he were to receive subsidies, he 'would have a much easier time working, with respectable pay, but that this would perhaps make him less sharp.'

In the field, however, tension can be noticed between similar organizations where one does, and the other does not, get subsidies or support from the government. One respondent has stopped filing for subsidies, 'because we'll never get any, since they think we're too commercial. Isn't that an absolute disgrace?' Whereas to some (the subsidized) subsidies are a reward, others think they are an unnecessary evil. Still other organizations – not only the larger, more commercially oriented players, but also the smaller ones that have to stay alive in the free market – have harsher words: to them subsidies are falsifying the market, producing unfair competition (see also Valckenaers 2009). The following statement by a record label boss speaks volumes:

> I am 100% opposed to subsidies. Subsidies ruin everything. It's the cancer of being creative. Why? Because you're competing against people who try to get by organically or in some other way with means that are normally not available. Which distorts the whole picture. (...) Everything that's subsidized, is artificial.

Obviously, subsidies can have also favorable effects for a few respondents that are not subsidized. A multinational like Live Nation, a corporation that lives off economic factors, is able to benefit indirectly from the subsidies in the concert circuit. 'That's true,' one respondent admits. Another explains:

Live Nation may be able to tell that they manage without subsidies, but actually they are able to profit from a subsidized circuit where they can launch groups, and it's only after these have gone through the circuit that they put them in the big venues and in the festival bills. On top of that, they have the commissions, which also enable them to make money.

In the other camp, the story goes like this:

That's true, but the fact is that this also applies to every booker. Of course, there's the subsidized circuit on the one hand and Live Nation on the other hand, and subsidies are partially there to promote concerts that you wouldn't be able to do without subsidies. (...) Take Antony & the Johnsons, for instance, now it's an act that can sell two to three thousand tickets. I also don't think that it's the job of a subsidized club to do those bands as well.

Whatever it may be, in the alternative mainstream, subsidies make sure that the individual logic can survive in a professional context where organizational interests are constantly demanding attention.

Although the individual logic of legitimation may translate into a logic of justification that mobilizes personal taste as a common principle for making choices and selections, it is not because they work in the pop music circuit that actors are always able to follow their own taste. Actors also belong to organizations, which have specific goals to which they need to adjust their actions. In addition, they often work in a team or hold positions that can only be understood in a specific relation with other employees of the same organization. The group processes that arise function as a social valuation of the selections made. Yet they can also be the source of conflicts, when different roles and expectations clash.

Economic criteria are the main directional indicators in an organizational logic. Still, an economic orientation in the alternative mainstream does not necessarily lead to great profit. Viability, survival and break-even are words that also apply to the organization. The selections must ensure that the organization, which employs the actors, is able to survive. The organization logic, therefore, is mainly one of cost effectiveness. It is aimed at investment and future return. However, what is economically viable, and what time limit should be set for this, is determined in accordance with the situation. It differs depending on whether the actors are on the input side of the music circuit, or on the output side. With actors on the input side, who have no direct contact with the public, an organizational logic often relies on a line of reasoning based on potential options for exploitation and long-term financial feasibility. Those who operate on the output side of the music circuit and want to present music to a public must adopt a primarily public-oriented line of thinking.

This explains why actors during the selection process are sensitive to the popularity of the artists who are to be selected, or of the music that the artists make. They proceed to evaluate music based on its market value, without by definition taking into account artistic motives. Popularity can be a reason for programming a concert, signing artists to a label, writing about their music, or playing it on the radio. The artists' previously built reputation facilitates the selection. Well-known artists stand a better chance of being picked up faster, which results in newer or younger artists having more difficulty to enter the selection procedure. Equally, music that fits in with the

Zeitgeist and the trend of the hour is an indicator of potential public success. Besides that, certain formal properties of style of the music can be more popular than other properties. Songs, with a traditional song structure, for example, are still dominant.

For the alternative mainstream, the underground is a positive reference as long as the selection involves artistic, content-related elements. It is striking to note that as soon as economic motives break surface the underground becomes a negative reference. Actors in the alternative mainstream want to engage in their profession in a professional way, that is, with certain seriousness. It is an understandable effect of an increasingly uncertain economic return. Experience and the professional capital that has been accumulated from this experience, need to reduce the risk and instruct actors which choices either can or cannot be made.

The fact that choices can also be organizationally inspired automatically means that these can clash with the individual logic and personal taste. Provided they have the necessary professional capital at their disposal, the participants in the field are able to live with the economic dominance in the selection process. In addition, when the organization manages to invest in risky choices thanks to profitable activities, or when subsidies provide help in doing so, the artistic logic can merge with the organizational logic, and a compromise can be reached.

Notes

1   According to Boltanski & Thévenot (2006: 203-211), the practice of linking music to external formats, functions or goals is typical of the 'world of industry': by means of schemas and models, efficient, functional and good organization is achieved.

2   I like to call this a horizontal construction of a piece of music (stanza alternates with chorus on a timeline), as opposed to a vertical construction (multiple layers on top of each other, as is done frequently in electronic music, psychedelic rock or post rock). The term song only refers to (vocal) music that is constructed horizontally.

3   This was also pointed out by Boltanski & Thévenot (2006: 294-296): the contention 'true talent will always emerge in time' is the outcome of a consensus between 'the world of inspiration' and 'the world of fame.'

4   For information purposes, a brief overview of the situation is in place. In Belgium, culture is not a Federal matter. It is the regional Communities that have the authority (there are three: the Flemish, the Walloon and the German), which makes it the responsibility of the Flemish Government, more specifically the minister of culture. The main decree regulating matters of culture is the Decree for the Arts, which, in the case of pop music, makes it possible for music clubs, festivals, management agencies and artists to receive structural or project-related funds or subsidies (either for the full operation of the organization, or for specific projects, for CD recordings or international tours, etc.). The minister and his entourage, a politically representative cabinet, determine policy. The practical implementation of the Decree for the Arts lies with the Arts and Heritage Agency, while the Evaluation Committee for Music works as advisory board for the minister. In the Netherlands, the minister or secretary of state for Education, Culture and Science makes the policy. The allocation of subsidies is put into funds: the Dutch Fund for Performing Arts is responsible for the allocation of subsidies. For about 45 stages (the core stages) the fund can arrange to cover deficits (to a certain degree, the losses made by programming Dutch groups are refunded).

5   There are obviously also small clubs which would sooner connect with the underground and which dedicate the whole of the subsidy to the artistic component. This marks a difference with the alternative mainstream, according to one programmer: 'This kind of luxury and freedom is ours to enjoy, and subsidies are the means that allow us to keep investing in it. Without subsidies I would be doing it in squatting rooms, with crates of beer as a stage and a crooked P.A.'

6. Between Trust and Distrust
The Positional Logic

Years ago, this author worked in the music industry as a concert organizer and thought it was good strategy to ask the records labels of certain booked artists for promotional support of their artists' gigs. This often involved artists who had had their CD releases quite some time earlier. The request usually prompted a predictable reply: 'Sorry, we did our promo campaign last year, at the time of the CD release. We can't do anything now. Our priorities lie elsewhere.' Disappointment invariably turned into annoyance when, on the day of the concert, faxes started rolling in from the labels, with names to put on the guest list. Later this author became label manager with a record company and found himself at the receiving end of the requests for promo support. The reply sounded strangely familiar: 'Sorry, I did all the press at the time of the CD release. Right now, I'm unable to arrange press attention. I'm working on other artists, and they come first.' The disappointment at the other end of the line also rang a bell.

The anecdote illustrates how actions can be explained through the positions occupied by the actors in the field of pop. Positions can determine choices independently of the actors who hold the positions and make the choices. As was uncannily demonstrated by the two different parts this author did actually play, personal identity has little effect on the routines or practices that are set in motion when the positions interrelate (which, in the anecdote, also meant sending a fax with one particular name for the guest list).

Actors who make selections in the alternative mainstream cannot always let their personal taste determine their choices (individual logic). At the same time, they cannot simply make sure that the choices will benefit the organizations to which they belong (organizational logic). The position the organization in turn occupies in the field of music, can likewise determine the selection. In these cases, people act from a positional logic.

A Network of Relations Based on Trust

Linked to the positions actors can occupy in the circuit (positions of programmer, journalist, manager, etc.) are certain *roles*. Each of these roles is different, because each time another market, another public or another opponent is involved, engaging the actors in a different way. 'Each party has its own agenda,' a manager says. 'Strictly speaking, all actors simply play their parts, end of story. Ultimately, the job of record label bosses, by their own account, is to sell records and not to be enforcers of good taste.' Likewise, bookers just need to sell concerts and make a turnover, as this respondent affirms:

> As a booker, I place concerts, and that's it. I don't sell a product, don't do promotion or management. I don't know most of the journalists, because it's not up to me to go and plug the records. That's not my job.

Radio producers and journalists only want to make good radio or write well-read articles. They want to introduce music that they think their listeners or readers will appreciate, and therefore must get to know. 'Record companies sell records, we sell a magazine,' a journalist says. A radio producer argues: 'We don't put anything on the playlist just to allow artists to make money.' Possible consequences that actors can have for other positions are by definition inessentials. Especially the media do not dwell on the impact their airplay or articles may have (such as more concerts and a bigger fee for artists, a bigger records sales figure, more revenues from copyrights etc.). 'That's not my job ,' 'We don't bother ourselves with that ,' 'That's not what we work on ' or 'That's not our main or first concern,' are lines used by all respondents who belong to the media. For journalists, the story is told as soon as a piece has been published. Then they proceed to the next band. One respondent frames his thoughts as follows:

> When you're President of the United States, you don't stop every hour to think about the fact that what you decide has an impact on that many Americans. Maybe it's also a matter of not wanting to think about things too often.

However different the line of reasoning in each position may be, and whatever the opposing interests are, actors need to cooperate with one another. The couple of dozen players that is important in the Flemish or Dutch alternative mainstream need to turn to one another. Their interaction determines the selection. This is a social process, as was already established in Chapter 2. Between the different players, habits and routines may form and grow that facilitate selection. At the same time, these are generally taken for granted and therefore hard to change. This chapter attempts to uncover these conventions. It will focus on the explicit norms of legitimate interaction, and on the concealed, implicit norms. The ambiguity between unilateral and bilateral or mutual dependencies is the connecting thread in the story: when certain power relationships govern the positions of actors, the latter engage in a continuous fight to preserve their independence. This duality reveals itself when an examination is made of the way in which actors develop their networks and put their accumulated symbolic reputation into the interaction with the other positions, of the effects these interactions have on the selection process, and of the influence or pressure that other actors exert in the same field of pop music. Because of the difference in power positions, certain players are able to force a selection on other players, prepare deals or revise decisions (voluntarily or under coercion). This, of course, fits in nicely with the aspect of struggle that Bourdieu identified as typical of positional relations. Working *with* each other can sometimes turn into working *against* each other.

Trust and Mutual Dependence — Explicit Norms

Social Capital and Trustful Cooperation

Networking is a trendy term. It describes in a single word the essence of the current post-Fordist society, in which a new network-based form of organization has substituted a hierarchical work structure.[1] Like anywhere else, work in the music industry requires networking. It is of great importance for players to become acquainted with as many actors as possible. A booker confirms this: 'I know all the promoters and concert organizers, down to the middle of nowhere.' In a small region (such as Flanders or Belgium and the Netherlands), this networking is an easy task. Most of the actors run into one another at concerts, in the VIP tents of festivals and rock competitions, where they talk, have a drink, and socialize. These contacts have their digital counterparts on Facebook. Like any other business sector, the music circuit is marked by the practice of 'we know each other's ways.' A promotion manager explains:

> I know everything and everybody. That's exactly what doing promotion is all about. These personal contacts are the most essential. It's twenty years of experience, you see. I am willing to hand over my address book to anyone, but it wouldn't do anybody any good. It's all about knowing people personally, about knowing how to know them. (...) Like spending a night out together. It's a thing many people have.

There are strong ties between the people inside of this network, relations that go much further than the business element alone. Remarkable was the frequency with which the interviewed actors talk about others in terms of 'is a friend of mine.' Evidently, the quality of collaboration may vary from person to person, but 'the personal bond is of the greatest importance,' because 'people have to hit it off.'

Networking involves maintaining personal relationships, keeping people as friends in order to get more results. Actors mobilize and invest *social capital*. Bourdieu (1989: 132-133) famously identified it as the more or less extensive networks that actors develop, the number of connections and relations they have (acquired and accumulated) in the social world, or even the number of 'sleeves that can be pulled.' Important aspects in accumulating social capital are the ability to convert incidental relations into durable relations, to invest in relations that rely on mutual respect, and to maintain and nurture these without interruption. Players with extensive networks get more things done, are able to turn this to their (material or symbolical) advantage. Hence, the importance of informal talks at the bar back stage during concerts. As Bourdieu (1990: 99) pointed out, small gifts of modest worth, easy to give and to get, similar to a treat, can reinforce and consolidate friendships. An organizer puts it as follows:

> Why does the whole gang of Belgian professionals go to Eurosonic in Groningen? To go out and have a beer to-

gether, to strengthen the ties. Those who don't take part, place themselves outside this small world. After three days of Pukkelpop or Rock Werchter you leave and realize you have barely been able to see a band, but have had a talk with everybody in the VIP tent. That's just the way it is, it's part of the game. Because of this great bonding with others, it will be easier for me to get certain bands.

These relations are situated in what Luc Boltanski and Laurent Thévenot call 'the domestic world' (2006: 164-178). Central to this world are personal relations, relations of frequent and individual contact between actors. Such relations are characterized by trust and confidence, respect and responsibility, by harmony and continuity. They are social conventions, which actors respect in order to be accepted and respected, and which they reproduce in turn through these relations. Their most important quality is the very fact that they are relations of trust. In this way, they constitute an explicit convention. A programmer, for instance, says about a booker: 'That's someone you can really rely on.' He talks about 'a blind trust that has never been betrayed.' Even the agreement a small label has with a major, is more than just an official license deal, 'it is a relationship of trust where I get to have carte blanche and can think along with them.' Trust, after all, is not only the basis of cooperation; it is also the foundation of all economic relations. It is a condition – better, *the* condition - for the ability to close deals in a market economy, 'a lubricant for cooperation and (economic) exchange, which (...) facilitates social traffic' (Abts 2005: 3-4). The most important function of trust is the reduction of complexity and uncertainty, which was discussed in the previous chapters. 'Without ever being certain, it allows us to take risks and deal with an unknown, uncertain and uncontrollable future.' (Idem., 5). It explains why cooperation is also a form of strategy, because actors need to be able to trust one another in order to produce results in the medium-long run. Putting aside the point of struggle, the music circuit revolves around one thing and one thing only: doing business with the right partners. A booker testifies:

> You can't do it on your own. I need to have the feeling that I'm not the only one pulling the cart, because otherwise I won't do it anymore. Therefore, you need a

record firm, management, organizers and other contact persons. When we work together — we, that is the venue's programmer, the guy from the label and me as the booker —, then you can be an asset for a group, a surplus value. Then they will be able to get a full house. You have to try to come up with a good story, which allows you to tell the organizer: 'this is a new band, they're on this or that label, listen on the Internet, and the guy from the label is in on everything.' (...) You have to see what the record firm is going to do as far as promotion is concerned. You have to consult each other, have a look with the organizer at everything that's possible.

In the end, one programmer says, there is a common goal: 'We all want to give a band the best possible launch, or get them one step closer to what they want to achieve.' This explains why the actors have a mutual relation of 'checks,' as another actor phrases it. One promotion person points out that colleagues occasionally ask for advice. Journalists traveling to New York, for example, ask which concerts he thinks they should attend, or programmers who consult him on what new bands are really worth the while. In his view, this is what forms the basis of handling promotion. It is to consult and convince people, in order to draw up a plan and make sure actions can coincide. It is also the reason why he will never exert any pressure.

I don't put pressure on people; you can ask any journalist if you like. When they really don't like a certain record, I'm not going to be the one who'll convince them. I can't blame them for that. You don't have to put them under pressure. Instead, you need to value them for what they are.

This relation of trust makes it possible for actors in the music circuit to have privileged partners. A number of festival programmers make it a habit to go to concerts together and afterwards discuss their projects: if one of them is currently entertaining a bid on a particular band, the others will abandon any plan to do the same. This is not merely an agreement that has grown spontaneously; it is also part of the explicit convention discussed above. The same goes for music clubs in their mutual relations.

They confer on offers, fees and ticket prices. Obviously, there can be competition among them, regarding the size of the public to reach, or about certain genres. Yet because all clubs have their own profile, emphasizing their own content, they do not focus on the choices others make, but on the central concern of cooperation. 'The in-crowd has been the same for fifteen years, and although everybody certainly looks after their own interests, we're not going to run one another out of business,' one organizer says. A colleague adds:

> We need each other; you can feel that. I think we have a very good front here. There's plenty of discussion among us: we ask about each other's fees, ticket price, and the size of a crowd. You know this about the other organizers. You know what the others want to work on, what they think is important.

One booker, however, points out that good relations with an agent or an artist will result in a reduction of possible competition with other bookers. The mutual bond of trust will keep an artist from switching too quickly from one office to another, although occasionally this will certainly happen. These relations of trust may grow between the actors and the artists themselves, and the personal ties may favor further selection. Usually, an artistic criterion lies at the basis of such a mutual bond, like the shared confidence in the artist. Thus, programmers continue to follow their favorite artists. This, for example, is the case with the respondent who invariably gives carte blanche to the artist Mauro. Still, it is also possible without any artistic motives. A booker, for instance, claims that he will always continue to work with a certain artist, even if this artist makes a lesser record, 'because of the relation and bond of many years between me and the artist. I am extremely fond of the guy, and in such case the question whether I like it or not is irrelevant.' When actors know and trust each other, better cooperation is possible. A person responsible for promotion compares a 'good' artist manager with a 'bad' one:

> Some managers act in condescending ways, or they are troublemakers that are never satisfied. They use psychological pressure, which is counterproductive. Others come up with plenty of ideas, are always the

first to consult, thinking along in a constructive manner. This is what motivates me.

Evidently, good cooperation may also wither and die out. One programmer had a significant share in launching a particular artist. The latter dumped him as soon as he became a national star. He started working with the big bookers, performing in the big concert halls: 'Then he didn't need me anymore. Consequently, all contact simply evaporated.' In addition, all actors tend to have somebody with whom cooperation is far from optimal. Because the supply of music and the number of players are large enough, this does not matter much. 'Once in a while you can very well lose one or two,' one programmer says. On the other hand, when the rival party is still needed for good functioning within the circuit, the relation of trust must be restored anyhow. When things are not going so well, convention dictates that both parties should work on reestablishing trust. A promotion person talks about somebody from the circuit:

> He thinks of himself as God, and I collided head-on with him. Nevertheless, I learned to deal with him. It took some effort, but in the meantime, I can get things done with him. Maybe I'm a hypocrite, or an opportunist. I'm aware of this, but I've learned not to shy away from it. If you lock horns with somebody, they will always turn on you.

Mutual Dependency and the Symmetry Norm

Cooperation through trust is an explicit convention in the music field. It gives the music circuit the apparent quality of a social community. The image, however, is less idyllic and considerably more ambiguous than it may appear at first sight. Possible relations and imbalances of power that govern social interaction here will be discussed further on. First, with regard to the everyday relations, some nuance may be in order.

Some fine-tuning is possible by means of the already mentioned *filter/flow*-model. The framework here will consist in applying the model to the relations cited most frequently in the interviews—on the one hand, the booker/organizer and booker/agent relationship within the concert circuit; on the other hand, the relationship between the record firms and the media. The filter/flow-model takes a one-way communication as its starting point. It explains why in the concert landscape international agents come before national bookers, and bookers before organizers. It also throws light on the reason why in the world of records the media (often) follow the record companies' supply.

As far as relations between bookers and programmers are concerned, bookers precede organizers in the chain, and the first are able to control the supply to a certain extent, pushing the organizers in a somewhat dependent position. To be more specific, the bookers are the ones who make the first selection, and the organizers are left the choice of following this first selection or disregard it. The interviews show that this is still an accurate description. A programmer is being ironic, but no less sincere, when he says:

> You are lived by (sic) the market system, at least for a part. You cannot change this. My function is that of go-between: you get all sorts of things offered or you don't get anything. The booker selects and the organizer says yes or no. There's really nothing much creative about it (laughs). Bookers operate differently than used to be the case; they are the ones that pick a venue and a programmer. It's really not the programmer who picks the booker. It's actually a receptive thing: accepting the offer of the booker.

To a certain degree, the other interviewed actors agree on this. 'That's the way it is,' one says, 'denying it would be foolish.' 'Certainly when it comes to the big venues concerts,' another adds. Most of the organizers do not see anything wrong with it. On the one hand, the supply is so large, and the number of bookers with whom collaboration is possible so great, that an organizer is still able to make his or her own selection. In fact, organizers tend to collaborate with every possible booker, depending on the offer.[2] 'Certainly, Live Nation is the primary partner, but it is far from the only very important one,' a promoter remarks. Besides, all respondents seem to agree that organizers are still able to put accents in their programs, regardless of the offer. They can start their own projects, or go on a personal quest for the ideal bill that will realize their special project (special thematic evenings, festivals around new currents, multimedia projects, etc.). 'You make it as creative as you want it to be,' one respondent argues. A booker may go to extremes in pushing forward his things, yet the organizer actually (and usually) remains free to choose whatever he or she wants. The filter of personal taste is always present. It explains why the organizer is not simply the bookers' plaything. All organizers emphasize this in the interviews: when they really do not want something, they stick to their guns despite possible pressure, and do not program it. Positional independence therefore remains a decisive force in the process.

The relationship booker/organizer is mirrored on the international level in the relationship agent/booker. Here too the booker may appear to be a simple intermediary for the supply of foreign artists put forward by the agent. One booker admits that he does not have to make a deliberate effort to look for new, smaller acts, because recent developments show that the big agencies he works with also started to pick these up. 'And because you try to serve these agents, you automatically start working on the smaller things too, just because there is an already existing relation.' At the same time, this booker says he collaborates with several agents, claiming that there is always room for one more.

> On the other hand, I am still looking for new things myself, and in doing so I get in touch with new agents. There's certainly plenty of room for that. (...) Whenever I find something new or pick up something, say via the Rough Trade Shop or Pitchfork mailing, I'll look for the agent myself. On a yearly basis, I add an x number of new agents to my list. Sigur Rós's first show, for instance, I booked directly with their label Fat Cat, because at the time there wasn't any agent yet. Therefore, it's not as if the whole structure is fixed to the gilts, that it's all on the Bryan Adams or Rolling Stones level, or that only ten agencies remain.

Although it remains an open question whether the deciding power of the individual programmers or bookers is limited to the 'small' artists and does not apply to the bigger names, it is all the same ill advised to speak of a one-way traffic or communication. It is perhaps the most forceful criticism that can be raised against the filter/flow model. The fact is that this kind of 'social bonding' typically involves actors in a state of mutual dependency (Laermans 2010: 17). This produces a two-way traffic.

A festival organizer, for instance, says that because of his fine collaboration with bookers he is able to get the bands he wants, and that he is always in a position to negotiate with them about fees in a constructive manner, to keep prices within a reasonable limit. Agents and bookers, too, listen to each other:

> It is not because an agent says he wants two concerts in Ancienne Belgique that you automatically have to do this. Such decisions are made by mutual agreement. You can have your say in this. You can object: 'Don't you think it's a bit a bit quick, wouldn't it be better to do some more small clubs first? It's actually a dialogue. On the other hand, when an agent wants us to do the figures of a concert's costing on 14,000 tickets instead of the 10,000 we had in mind, it's always possible to negotiate. Even if this is easier said than it is done.

Organizers and bookers, indeed, are not simply intermediaries or conduits. The mechanism of cooperation and mutuality still stands. Interaction here is regulated by means of the symmetry norm. This is also noticeable in the relationship between record firms and the media, although it is nothing remotely like the relationships inside of the concert circuit. Whereas in the concert circuit the live performance career of an artist is the shared starting point, record firms and media tend to have opposite interests due to their positions held in the field. The media want to report about new music in an independent way and keep an eye on their target group. Record firms, by contrast, are interested in getting free promotion for artists. Still, here too there is a need for collaboration. The promotional campaign of a record company is largely run through the media, while the media need the record companies for new CDs, interviews with the artists and special competitions or give-aways to win over readers and listeners (by handing out concert tickets, CDs, exclusive trips abroad, T-shirts and other *goodies*). In the filter/flow model, communication runs from the record firm to the media. According to Hirsch (1972: 654-656), attempting to influence the decision of the gatekeepers in the media was one of the strategies developed by the record industry enable it to function in an uncertain environment. Target-oriented promotions set up by the record companies are therefore a part of their marketing campaign and are financed by these firms. In exchange for this, the medium sets up a promotional radio campaign. This may seem at first sight like a bribe, because in the eyes or ears of the listener it is not the record company but the media that aims to sing the praises of something. The media, however, categorically deny that they merely submit to these actions, claiming they do not discriminate between the promotions that are included in their programming. This is confirmed by the way concert organizers say they go about give-aways:

> StuBru won't give away tickets for any old event. They've already said no to certain things for which I really hoped they'd do a give-away. They only do so for artists that fit in with their programming, that belong to their playlist or have been on it in the past. They will never do it for something completely unknown.

The media emphasize that such actions never influence selection, because they unleash a filter onto these. Promotional activities are only set up after the media have made their own selection and only involve artists that have survived the selection. Radio producers emphasize the fact that they only do promotions with artists they are already playing. They look at what is interesting for their station, never the other way around. The media actually only take up the music industry's offers when there are shared interests. 'If it's not a win-win-situation, we won't do it,' is how the convention is described by a person in charge of a radio station. A journalist agrees:

> A good interview, a good agreement is a win-win-situation. It is a good name, at a good time, brought in the paper in a good way, which allows both the firm, the paper, the artist and the public to benefit, to gain something. It is good for the artist's credibility, exposure for the record firm's product and good entertainment for the readers, who are able to read something about the band they think is cool. In the best case, all of this coincides.

The media do not merely want to report about music. Because they are engaged in a competitive battle with one another — see p. 296 — they also want to promote themselves. For this purpose, they need the artists for whom the record firm wants to secure press attention. Radio stations, for their part, follow the marketing proposals as long as these involve well-known artists, from whom the station itself can derive benefit. Three radio co-ordinators explain:

> Radio purports to create new names, yet at the same time you want to ride along on the wave of the success that's already there. Music is also publicity for your station, and for that you need big names. When you are able to offer a concert trip to the States, you also promote yourself.
> A meet & greet or concert trip to Paris for a band nobody knows, isn't interesting for us. For special live sessions, we'd rather go for big international artists instead of putting some new little band whom nobody has ever heard of. Otherwise, we don't waste a publicity spot on it.

> If we think a band is an asset or surplus value for a net and they can come over and do a showcase, then we will certainly spare no expenses and hook a campaign onto it. This reinforces the image of both parties. Hiring an advertising agency to translate our station's feeling, would otherwise be a very expensive undertaking, while we can do it just as well by way of some action campaign set up around an important artist.

For their part, at the other side of the table, the record firms are well aware of this. 'Everybody can organize competitions and give-aways, but the impact this will have is inevitably tied to the band's popularity. A radio station understandably prefers getting tickets for Moby than for a lesser known artist,' a promotion manager notes. As a result, record firms consider this: 'You have to think with them, think from inside their radio show, about what is interesting to them and where there is opportunity for collaboration.' Thus, a promotional activity will never have any influence on the decisions made in the selection process, the media spokespersons argue. The deontological balance, after all, is of greater importance.

> We will never link up an action to the playlist, because that would be a kind of payola. That would make it possible for the record firms to buy themselves into the

playlist, and that's clearly at odds with the independency of the editorial office.

Journalistic independence is considered a great good. A radio coordinator asserts that he never lets himself be influenced by anyone that starts singing the praises of particular music. Music gets airplay because it is good per se, not because it is good for people's careers. Positional dependency, as this seems to show, is still tolerable. The fact is that the relations of dependency are not asymmetrical, but symmetrical, and each party is able to maintain its independency. This constitutes the core of the symmetry norm.

To Give and to Take
Implicit Norms

Besides explicit norms, there are also implicit norms. Precisely because a positional logic is primarily focused on trust and symmetry, other conventions have developed simultaneously in order to be able to deal with the possibly applied pressure of one of the parties. What are at stake are implicit, unspoken expectations that are part of an informal professional culture. This *working consensus* implies that pressure is legitimate when it is 'friendly' and is integral to the relationship of giving and taking.

Friendly Pressure

Nobody in the pop circuit will deny that there is pressure. When actors work together with someone in a relation of trust, and everything seems to go fine, they do not perceive pressure as pressure. 'They certainly try,' says a program director, 'but I myself am never under pressure to place things I don't want to.' The respondents interpret this as 'friendly pressure' and think this is largely a self-explanatory thing. After all, it is the booker's job to get bands placed, or the task of the record firms to force through media attention for their artists. A radio producer argues: 'Because record firms also invest money in an exclusive studio session on the radio, they will try to get some return for this. But I don't feel this as pressure. It's just good collaboration.' Indeed, good understanding forms the foundation. The actors never perceive the implicit professional practice as a breach of the explicit norm. 'Everybody has something to buy or to sell,' one manager claims. 'And you try to get the most out of it. Just standing by and watching it happen, saying 'Too bad, I got zilch,' that's not our job, is it?' An organizer and a booker shed light on both sides of the same relation:

> There is some soft pressure to program less interesting bands, but that's actually their job to do so. (...) When you work with bookers on a regular basis, this kind of pressure occurs in a friendly way. The personal ties with the booker are important. The offering does not always happen based on rational arguments; it can also be out of sympathy for a certain program director.

> When you have a good relationship with a club and you've been working with somebody for ten years without a glitch, then once in a while you can be so bold to ask: 'Look, I'm really in trouble here, I can't find anything for a particular band. Could you find a spot for them, as an opener or so?' However, I look upon this as a human relationship, not as putting pressure on a club.

It also explains why organizers do not necessarily have to make concessions to remain on good terms with certain bookers, as long as the relationship is free from noise. Not even with Live Nation. 'I've known these people for fifteen years,' programmer says, 'so it's not necessary to do certain concerts for me to be able to keep the bond alive.' Live Nation shares the feeling:

> Remain on good terms? My impression is different. I think they also try to remain on good terms with the other bookers. For example, there's a number of Belgian bands I have trouble finding shows for. In such a case it's not as if a festival will welcome me with open arms and place a band on the bill just because it's Live Nation that asks them to do so. Even if I would probably place the big names with them. I think most people. I think most of the people are sensible enough to decide first and foremost based on what they themselves think is good. (...) For example, I have Leftfield at a festival, which to them is a headliner, and I want to put Stijn with them, but in the end their program director doesn't want to do

it. Obviously, I keep pushing, but no means no: the program director doesn't want to do it. Then I just say: Fair enough, I'll find other festivals for Stijn.

The same — in the relationship booker/organizer — goes for the so-called *package deals*. In this form of conditional sale promoters who want to add a band to their program are forced to take another band (that they do not want) in the same deal. Here, the pressure exerted by one party is less innocent. Both sides, however, deny such practices. The interviewed bookers admit that they will try to include another of their artists along with a request for booking, but all of them claim that this is merely a suggestion, not a requirement. 'There is never any pressure on my part; it is not something that I demand,' says one. 'That won't work,' another notes. The organizers, on their part, confirm this (at least initially, see p. 291): 'I am not aware of this,' 'This is never a gift for anyone.' Again, this only works if there is trust between both parties. 'You have to nurture it, let it grow,' says a programmer. 'In the beginning it is difficult, and you have to work with the crumbs, make concessions.' In the end, however, those who commonly work with bookers, get the upper hand.

You Scratch My Back, I Scratch Yours

Because people trust each other, and because the pressure is 'friendly' and the dependence mutual, the actors resort to helping one another. Any good relationship needs to grow, but it also needs to be maintained. Therefore, certain selections are made deliberately. Nearly all respondents consider helping another as a game of give and take. This allows a programmer to agree more quickly on something less favorite when a booker previously offered something good. Two organizers and a booker explain:

> That seems normal and logical. If they can offer you a very good name, why should not I be able to do something back? You scratch my back, I scratch yours.

> When a booker takes really good care of me, I will also do my best. That's helping each other, right? If I can do someone a favor, I will do this happily. Why not?

I try to develop some mutual exchange, be on good terms with the organizers, and take good care of them. Because if you know that somebody takes on bands of yours that will lose money anyway, you must make sure that sometimes money is earned. For example, someone did some of my small bands in the spring, and I thought that was really cool of him that he agreed to do them. And I tell him that: 'If you do these, you're really doing me a favor.' Later, when a particular artist insisted on playing in the AB, I put that concert with him. Then I'm not afraid of rubbing it on, so to speak.

Because a specialized music magazine such as *RifRaf* increasingly gets its necessary advertising revenues from the concert circuit, the mag also started to write more frequently about the music clubs. 'As a result, you will do something in return more easily,' is what the people from the clubs say. At the radio, a record company setting up a good marketing campaign is viewed 'as a gift from because we already decided the play the record, independent of what the company would want us to do.' This corresponds to what anthropologist Marcel Mauss (1990:9) already observed in the 1920s: a gift always presupposes an obligation to give something in return. Mauss studied the way in which exchange mechanisms create social relationships that are durable, because of the fact that when a gift is made, there is always something expected in return. In this way, an organizer explains why he programmed The Disciplines: 'Because I still owed that booker one.' Because actors start from the principle of mutuality, this implicit norm can be called the reciprocity principle: those who give something must receive something in return afterwards. Bourdieu further developed the theory, stating that a gift can also be a strategy. It may establish relationships of solidarity among peers or equals, yet also engender relations of dependency. Because, as Bourdieu writes:

> A gift that is not returned can become a debt, a lasting obligation. (...) Until he has given back, the receiver is 'obliged,' expected to show his gratitude towards his benefactor or at least to show regard for him, go easy on him. (Bourdieu 1990: 126 en 106)

As long as the recipient does not meet this expectation, the giving party can maintain a degree of dominance. Then the relationship becomes strategic in the medium-long run, or better: it becomes a relationship of investment. During the interviews, off the record examples were given of festival organizers booking a group at a (too) high fee, not because the festival needed the group, but only because it wanted to be on good terms with the agent in order to be able to get, for example, Bruce Springsteen. All of this comes down to creating the necessary goodwill with the goal of being able to influence the future selection. I personally experienced the practice during my activities as a label manager with Rough Trade, and some respondents confirmed this: in marketing actions, for instance, part of the competition prizes (T-shirts , DVDs, etc.) do not ever reach the public; they stay in the editorial office, reinforcing the relationship, creating expectations for the near future. For the same reason, record companies' actors in charge of promotion offer specific interviews to the media.

> If I can put journalists on the guest list, or arrange an interview with a hip artist, or even pay a trip abroad, they will be happier than when I try to do the same with a less famous name. Because they feel they're somehow chosen, they will be quicker to do me a favor with a smaller band. There's nothing wrong with that, it's just more relaxed. The collaboration is different: if you can do more for them with things they think are cool, they will be more inclined to do something in return with things I think are cool.

> For groups that are now the hype of the hour, I'm still going to offer interviews to the small magazines and webzines, even though the labels clearly state in advance: 'only the most important media and no more webzines.' Then I tell them: 'Hold on a minute, these people have helped us right from the start and wrote about these groups when no one else was interested.' So now and again, I'm going to reward them.

That is the essence of acting from a positional logic: to select is to give and take, and it is motivated by the expectations that accompany it.

From Implicit Expectation to Explicit Agreement, and Back Again

The exchange principle is not only found in the norm of reciprocity. Sometimes implicit customs lead to explicit agreements. Then formal deals can be negotiated. The fact is that sponsor deals or exchange agreements in connection with marketing campaigns are contractually confirmed economic transactions (such as the structural deal Live Nation has with all the networks of Flemish public broadcaster VRT). Depending on the promotional activity — so says a radio controller — the contract states how much the return of media attention includes, by means of spot campaigns, announcements, and so on. If a festival wants a live registration on Studio Brussels, the festival has to pay for it, yet it gets a lot of promotional attention in return (in addition to the broadcast itself, spots on radio and television). Sometimes the deals are of a more informal nature, not through a contract but merely verbal. When a record company offers an exclusive interview or a scoop to the press, there is always some form of return agreed upon in advance: not so much free advertising, but a competition linked to the article, or a prominent announcement (in the newspaper or magazine, on their website or in their newsletter) or a place on the cover. This is quite logical, the label boss thinks:

> Then we say, as the record company, 'Okay, you get it first, but then you need to show us.' Because I know that what I lose for B, I need to win back for A. A may get a scoop, but in exchange they have put in the whole works: cover story, or an inlay on the front page, repeated in an appendix, and obviously a review, preferably at weekends and not on a Thursday.

Because the record companies decide on who gets the interviews, the media try to work out deals to be ahead of the competition. 'There are some who go as far as to drop their pants to get all sort of things done,' one journalist notes. He, for his part, insists he would never go that far. At the same time, he admits that for every new release by dEUS he makes an appointment with their manager to discuss things and work out a deal. 'The purpose is to exchange ideas and see what we can do with the release in order to come up with a better story.' Such explicit agreements go hand in hand with an informal professional culture. Deals are negotiated in order to rule out any asymmetrical exertion of power. Thanks to the existing mutual respect, there is always room for everybody to have a say in things. A programmer comments on the evening programming by Studio Brussels: 'I work closely with the producers of these programs, who also think along.' Or when a record company places an ad in a magazine and expects an interview with an artist in return, the magazine can come up with a counterproposal.

> If the record company proposes a group that we don't like, I give tot for tat: 'I'd rather not do this group, but I would like to do something with that other record you have.' Sometimes I tell them to count me out for certain things, but then I immediately suggest something else to keep the goodwill and collaboration flowing.

Both the sense of independence and the norm of symmetry, which was discussed earlier, remain intact. The negotiated deals form no impediment to the informal culture of giving and taking. The relationship of trust between organizers, record companies and media is always present, and every party wants to uphold the bond. A radio coordinator:

> It is natural that we also want to do fellow organizers a favor, because it also happens that they give us a double ticket if the concert is already sold out. This occurs without there being any agreement on the matter. It makes sense for a good relationship that we do such things.

Penalties for Violating the Norm of Reciprocity

In sociology, 'norms' constitute concrete rules of action or conduct which may be institutionalized into 'customs' or 'conventions.' When they become institutionalized, they acquire a coercive character: in case of violations, sanctions may be imposed. In practice, this appears to be the case with the norm of reciprocity. Whoever puts aside the norm of give and take, can expect a penalty. This was repeatedly expressed in the interviews, though, not by accident, off the record. A booker's request to give one of his bands a good spot on the bill was denied a number of times by one particular organizer. Later, when the organizer asked the booker's

group for a pub concert, the booker returned the favor and also said 'no.' 'Then I play the game hard: if he can never do me a favor, I'm not going to do him a favor.' When a record company refused to collaborate on an organizer's project, and the firm later needed the organizer for a particular group, the programmer said: 'This is not the way things are done. As far as I'm concerned, the group is not going to appear there.' A magazine once saw a record company withdraw an ad because it refused to do a particular interview. And on the management front, there is a story about a manager refusing to put a number by a certain band on a magazine's compilation CD: 'Just to give the medium a sign: 'if you won't do anything for the band, we will do nothing for you'.'

When agreements are not respected or the presupposed return is not delivered, this may have repercussions for the future. If a particular medium has been granted a scoop, but fails to do anything with it, the record company, for example, may offer the next scoop to a competitor. Or when a medium refuses to do interviews with young artists, it risks being excluded from interviews with bigger artists. The same applies when a record company grants a scoop to one medium and another rival medium breaks the imposed embargo. Then it is possible that the record company - as was told by a journalist who claims to speak from experience — will deny the transgressor interviews in the future or cancel other outstanding commitments (such as a previously arranged interview). In one particular instance, and to great dismay of the press,[3] management and record company even established a fine of 25,000 euro for any medium that did not respect the embargo set on dEUS' CD *Vantage Point*. One of the respondents revealed off the record that the medium, which broke the embargo, did indeed pay the fine (in advertising space).

Conversely, the media also possess the means and opportunities to impose sanctions. Sometimes journalists can fight with equal weapons. When a journalist is not allowed to interview a particular artist, or when a record firm is as foolish as to offer two media the same scoop, the journalist, or his or her medium, can simply ignore other artists of the same record company: 'In that case, the game is on, and I play along.' When a magazine runs many interviews linked to the same record company and the latter shows no intention of buying ads, it will certainly alter its policy towards the company and reduce the number of interviews or coverage of the company's artists.

Positional Influence and Legitimate Pressure

Working in the pop music circuit, occupying different positions, each with their own agendas, presupposes relations of trust. Doing each other a favor, occasionally handing out a present: these are instances of kindness and friendliness, and as such innocent. Because the exerted pressure is 'friendly,' it is also legitimate. The tenet of independence is never jeopardized. Still, this does not mean that every actor or position carries the same weight in the field. One actor, or one position, may affect another. I examine three types of such positional effects: first, the weight of an actor's social capital, next the symbolic capital the actor has accumulated, and finally the economic power the actor is able to mobilize.

Social Weight

Whatever the degree of individuality of a selection made by an actor, the music circuit's other actors may consciously or unconsciously leave their mark on this selection. A first form of positional influence is an effect produced by social capital, a term that was previously discussed. Social capital is essentially accumulated because social networks generate value. The composition and magnitude of a person's network can lead to striking effects of interaction. This study shows that a player will be quicker to listen to someone he or she knows in person. Within the interaction between organizer and booker, it is true that when a befriended booker proposes something, he is able to get more done than a stranger would. The interviewed bookers offer countless examples of the ways in which their networks allow them to find easily enough, and especially *good*, concerts and festivals for their groups. Even more, they are able to do so for fees that are high enough.

> The more contacts you have, the easier you will sell. A minor booker needs to do hard labor in order to place his small groups for small fees. (...) Some of these personal contacts go back twenty years. It's plain to see that this plays a role. You know whom you can offer something, and before you know it, you have your number of performances. Sometimes one simple phone call is all it takes.

When you've been around a while, you know your people, who you're dealing with.

Bookers, for their part, will also be more inclined to follow the propositions made by international agents with whom they have established a good relationship than with others that have never crossed their path. Consider what this booker has to say:

We have an internal policy to further help agents
with whom we frequently collaborate, simply from a
business point of view, since you work frequently with
these people.

Similarly, good contact gives a head start in the interactive relation between record firm and journalist. A promo person notes that at least a couple of times per month, when preparing his press mailings, he puts a big exclamation mark on a CD that he thinks is good: 'So the journalists will know that I recommend them something special.' Because this occurs selectively, the action has sufficient credibility and is able to produce effect. A journalist admits that it is the tip by the promo person that made him go check a title:

Turned out I found this record to be so incredibly good
and fantastic that I immediately gave it five stars and
made it 'CD of the week.' (...) Every week I have at
least 40 CDs to listen to. It's impossible to do each and
every one of them, there are only 24 hours in one day.
The chance of finding something that's worth the while
becomes twice as large when you work together. My 24
hours, those of my colleagues, he promo guy, friends: I'm
open to everything. If I wouldn't do this, I would assume
to be Mr. Know-it-all.

The working principle here is complexity reduction, a typical function of trust that was already discussed. A&R-managers of record firms also mobilize their professional network when making selections. This was beautifully demonstrated in Koos Zwaan's doctoral study of career success among Dutch pop musicians (2009: 30-32 and 120), which used in-depth interviews to examine the selection criteria adopted by A&R managers of record companies. Zwaan found that A&R managers are only convinced of the quality of both a new artist and of his or her music when legitimized by the opinions of the other music industry professionals in his network. Demos do not constitute a sufficient basis for gathering the necessary information about new, promising artists, and are not enough for an artist to be noticed and picked up. The selection depends on the persons who introduce the novelty (managers, bookers, journalists, among others). A&R-managers receive positive signals about artists possessing something that makes them unique in two ways. when he or she is mentioned by different people, independently and simultaneously. On the other hand, when an artist is introduced by someone belonging to his professional network, the information which this established is more valuable to the A&R than if this were done by an anonymous source (as is the case with a demo).

In general, this point of interest involves the influence on decision-making gin selections that emanates from the actor's social context, his or her position in a network. Gielen calls this the 'logic of collective context.' The determining factor in deciding on what either constitutes art or not is not the intrinsic value of the artifact, but the place where it is located' (Gielen 2003: 151).

Symbolic Weight

Actors build up networks, which leave a mark on the selections. In addition, actors can accumulate credibility within these networks. 'The world of management is mainly about personalities, detached from the agencies that employ them,' says one manager. Social capital is thus converted into symbolic capital: the professionalism an actor possesses and the right contacts he or she disposes of, can yield symbolic profit. The actor acquires a reputation or 'name,' and gains a stronger position in doing so. A promotion manager argues:

> This is what I tell my artists: I cannot guarantee that you will get into the magazine *Humo* or that you will play in Ancienne Belgique. But I can trigger things, talk to the right people, and hopefully get something done. Because I do believe that I have influence. (...) To journalists I'm like a breath of fresh air, compared to some of my colleagues, usually twenty-five year old blondes who work

for majors. Each Friday they report to their head of pro-motion, who then asks them to try calling Humo again. I think it's a very different way of working.

Through their symbolic status, record label executives and artists managers have an influence on selection in the media. They can procure special attention for their artists, or even have an initially negative selection reversed into a positive one. One radio producer freely admits:

> It often happens that we listen to a song again and that the song ends up in the playlist anyway, because the label or manager asked us to check it again and offered solid arguments to do so. Because the pluggers keep emphasizing this, we have come to realize that we literally mean the difference between life and death for many groups. In a case where there is legitimate doubt, this can certainly be of consequence.

The previous section suggested that actors would sometimes be 'quicker to listen.' This effect is also triggered by the good repute or prestige certain players have gained. This booker explains:

> An agent who never fails to provide bands that have genuine quality, and tops it off with good promotional support, will certainly speed up any decision I make about the bands he proposes. With a guy like this, you know where you are at, what he has done in the past and what new plans he has in store. That is really a strong element: the person who's behind it, his credibility.

A positional logic will motivate actors to accumulate symbolic capital. Just as the size of the social capital does not simply depend on the size of the mobilized network, but also on 'the amount of [...] capital each of his acquaintances privately owns' (Bourdieu 1989: 132), so too is an actor's symbolic weight as he becomes connected with a high-value player whose general capital is high. Such a player can be put into action strategically. Thus, the research revealed that the media would be more inclined to give a new artist a chance when this artist is signed to a label or a management that houses several successful artists. A label boss and a manager discovered that they had gained importance as players because of this:

> When you have made your name with one group, people look at you with different eyes. The questions keep coming: 'What's next?' Now, when my label comes up with something new, everybody's immediately interested.
>
> It certainly had an effect that these groups were offered by the same people. Now, when I call up people about a new band, and they liked my previous offers, the bookings start pouring in. It does help, no doubt about it. Visibly, this works as a reference.

In this way, record labels have the power of *labeling*. They grow into a respected quality label. The artist, for his or her part, also holds the power to invest symbolic capital in other artists. If they let themselves be led by him or her, the gatekeepers will be more inclined to listen to the newcomers and, consequently, be encouraged to pick them up. This, for instance, is what happened with Damien Rice and the Mexican duo Rodrigo y Gabriela. Or take the story of Selah Sue and Milow told by two respondents: Louvain-based music club Het Depot discovered Selah Sue during their Free Stage. Milow heard her and took her on as supporting act. Nobody was working with her, and yet everybody was able to watch her, thus becoming part of a career launch. A manager, who explains the story of DAAU and their close connection with the Antwerp music scene, provides another example:

> DAAU made name thanks to a strong live reputation: four men playing classical instruments, starting off in a very obstinate and naïve way. They knew nothing about pop music, and yet somebody set them free, straight into the rock circuit. And there was something else. They were connected. They had a link with dEUS. DAAU and dEUS shared the same management. DAAU did a cover of 'Suds & Soda' which ended up on the B-side of the dEUS-single: things referred to each other. At the time, there was a spotlight on Antwerp and on all the bands the city harbored, because of dEUS.

This is the reason why record companies or managers hire a famous producer or guest musician for a young or less known group, or send a band off on a tour as opener for a more reputed group. The better-known group acts as a conductor of symbolic capital, or as Gielen (2003: 66) puts it, as 'aura-infecting agent.' The same mechanism also applies to organizers.

> With smaller foreign groups that may have opened for Kings of Leon, you can use the story to program them at your festival. Then you feed off the Kings of Leon story, rather than using the group's own story.

When an actor's social capital changes, its symbolic effect can also change. The interviews that focused on the relationship between bookers and agents provide some fine examples of this. Agents are only as strong as the artists they have in their stable. When a group hires an agent to represent them, the accumulations of capital reinforce each other. Groups sporting a high repute also grant their agent the same standing, and agents harboring important groups can give back support to less important bands. In this respect, a booker speaks (off the record) about an agent who used to be ignored by everybody ('hold your head in, see how you could avoid him'). When he signed on a major act, everything suddenly changed. A booker initially would not have anything to do with a particular has-been female artist, until she ended up with an agent who had some big acts under his wings: 'suddenly, the artist's name skyrockets, and he or she is promoted to priority number one.'

Social capital, according to Bourdieu (1989: 133), can be accumulated by way of individual actions, but also through membership of a group. In this case, too, a symbolic capital transfer may take place: the status associated with the group is granted to the actor. This author personally experienced the phenomenon as a member of the Flemish governmental Committee of Evaluation for Music. People know who is who and will approach each in a different manner. This can induce them to do strange things. Indeed, this author's occupation as a label manager for Zomba lead Flemish King of Schmaltz Eddy Wally to believe he could secure him a breakthrough in the United States! In the interviews, a booker comments on how actors adopted wildly varying attitudes toward him depending on the positions his career had led him to occupy — initially as an indie booker, then as a booker for a major agency, and finally back to being an independent booker:

> When I went working for that big firm, I was extremely annoyed because people who had simply put me aside all those years, suddenly came knocking at my door. Now that I've moved on again, some people just dump me again. They just leapt on me because I worked for the firm. Then again, in the eyes of others I'm back in favor because I left the company.

Conversely, someone can acknowledge the symbolic weight of another actor and mobilize this for a personal strategic action. This is clearly demonstrated in those moments when record companies and managers, on the occasion of fresh artists and releases, attempt to warm up key-persons from the media and the industry, bustling and pushing them to listen to the music. Thus, managers and bookers can give a preview in the hope that this will influence later decision on selection. A manager:

> I had invited the man who, at the time, was music coordinator of Studio Brussels to the studio, where one of our bands was recording a new album. It so happened he liked what he heard. The fact that the final decision maker was won over will undoubtedly have played a role later, when the single came out and ended up in the playlist.

For the same reason, a label boss has lost all faith in traditional, collectively targeted CD presentations:

> It packs a lot more punch to approach everybody individually. Invite someone to a rehearsal and grab a bite afterwards, together with the artist. Journalists and radio producers are very sensitive to this method, whether they deny it or not. If you ask me, that's the approach to pursue. It's labor-intensive, but in this way you get an individual story. (...) You just gotta make sure you know the key partners and who you want to influence in a positive way, without putting a knife to their throats.

So symbolic capital leads to remarkable interaction effects. As was famously theorized by Bourdieu, symbolic bankers invest symbolic capital in order to procure a reputation for artistic products. The result is the consecration cycle that is set in motion. Zwaan too, in the previously mentioned study (2009: 120-122), argues that the reputation of individual musicians largely depends on the reputation of the intermediaries who represent him. The results of his inquiry are consistent with previous studies in the US and the UK in the 1980s and 1990s (including Negus 1992). This leads him to conclude that conventions and practices within the music industry show strong similarities, both historically and geographically.

Chapter 4 already showed that symbolic recognition in the alternative mainstream is not established by means of an elaborate, fully developed aesthetics. A number of categories remain obscure and ambiguous. Precisely because it is a hybrid of the cultural and the economic, symbolic recognition in the pop music circuit looks quite different. Everything here is conditional upon the actor engaged in the recognition, the size of his or her network, and the symbolic weight he or she carries. It prompts us to refine the notion of 'professional capital' cited in the previous chapter. The term was used to indicate an actor's professional experience in the music circuit, which would offer support in dealing with uncertainty. The term primarily referred to any actor who keeps a close watch on economic factors such as cost-effectiveness, or the target public. Professional capital, however, can actually also be symbolic capital in the strictest sense: the accumulation of prestige from the knowledge of music and from the recognition as a music expert. A 'good' professional in the alternative mainstream possesses healthy commercial insight, but equally sports a symbolic personality or aura. Just like the alternative mainstream itself, professional capital contains both a symbolic and an economic component. When the combination is highlighted, professional capital in this sense could be denoted as *alternative mainstream capital*.

Economic Weight

Depending on the positions occupied by the players in the field, they also gain economic power.[4] Thus, each respondent knows that a major record company will have less difficulty in setting up a marketing campaign with the media than a minor firm, since a radio producer prefers to organize actions with popular artists who are usually signed to the bigger companies. A person in charge of promotion affirms he used to have little means of pressure when he worked at a small firm. In his current firm, however, 'things are much easier because I have a lot more big names in the catalogue.' All radio makers agree that small labels only get into the niche programs and will obviously have a hard time giving away a trip to the US. Despite the fact that they initially minimized the effect (see p. 258), whether a major brings music to the media or an indie will indeed have a different effect. It explains why small firms almost obliged to beg to get enough interviews for starting artists or to find a place for niche acts. As an independent distributor observes:

> I don't have as much power as a major, because frankly |I don't have that kind of change. I think I'd hardly be able to do it. (...) For a difficult, new little band I can't find a soul who's willing to do an interview, yet from time to time I have a hyped artist, and then everybody wants to get in.

The same goes for the other media: major channels simply have more opportunities than small channels. When a record company has an exclusive interview to offer to the written press or when it is unable to get more than a few interviews for a big international group, the prizes almost invariably go to the most influential media, that is, to those with the largest circulation and, therefore, with the largest public reach. A promotion manager and a magazine coordinator testify:

> Making everyone happy is simply impossible. You cannot but disappoint people. That's a terrible thing to do. I too have landed in the system where I have to choose. The logical thing is to go to *Humo* first. And if there's one to spare, it's *De Morgen*, sometimes *Focus Knack*.

> The market in Belgium has disintegrated to such a degree that these bands limit themselves to one or two interviews and that's it. When *Humo* and *Focus Knack*

are among the candidates, we know we can forget about the whole thing.

All interviewed journalists are well aware of this, and none are more conscious of it than the people from *Humo*: 'They all want to get into *Humo*. I often get priority even when I don't ask for it.' The effect is another way for smaller media to become economically dependent. A music magazine such as *RifRaf* relies on advertising by record firms and organizers:

> *RifRaf* is a free magazine, we are independent, and not subsidized. The only source of income is advertising, and everything stand or falls with that. (...) We try to take care of advertising record companies, just a bit better than we treat those that don't. We are forced to do that. Because losing those is definitely not an option. Or else we can just shut down the whole thing. For us, it's a constant struggle to survive. If all your advertisers drop out, for whatever reason, then it's over and out for us. It's as simple as that.

Record companies take advantage of this, because they know that players who never buy an ad in *RifRaf* will also have trouble offering interviews. Consequently, says a promo guy, 'if there is a bigger budget for advertising, it's easier to get interviews.'

In the concert circuit, the player with the largest capital can push through his or her choice with greater ease than other players, and thus impede or even block the choice of others. Less substantial organizers may be jealous of the larger piggy bank, subsidies or sponsorships other players dispose of. For example, a respondent says he can merely look on, as a 'competitor' he is able to fix a group in one single day and for twice the normal fee. As a result, certain festivals can find the door standing wide open to ask, and get, exclusivity in a specific time and region. One organizer remarks: 'If a group asks a lot of money, the concert must be exclusive. Unless they deliberately ask less in order to be able to perform on several festivals.'

Live Nation in particular has complete supremacy over the horizon of concerts.[5] All respondents view the US-based firm as the most powerful player, and therefore inescapable. 'The company has a controlling presence in the sector,' one organizer claims. Tall trees, however, catch a lot of wind (especially off the record). A regular criticism voiced by some players in the field of pop, which is in turn refuted with examples by others, is that groups for which Live Nation acts as the booking agency more easily pop up in line-ups for Live Nation festivals, at the expense of others that must be booked by Live Nation from other bookers. 'That's 15 % booking fee saved, and wholly understandable,' one respondent said. But because Live Nation occupies different positions at the same time, the people who work for the company are evidently the first to realize that this makes strategic selections far easier than it is for others. Live Nation is able to give its own groups better circulation, and therefore gains the ability to guide their live career.

> Suppose 29 festival spots are filled, and the last spot is for one of two acts you think are equally good and are able to draw an equally large or small crowd. Of course, I will choose the agent with whom I have worked for over a decade. Also because I know that I will be able to build something with this act after all's said and done, which pays off in the long run. I think this is self-evident, goes without saying. You should not exaggerate this structure, but it's something that will continue to have its effect. Because you know that a spot at Rock Werchter or at I Love Techno will be a step forward for the band. (...) Obviously, that's a strength. These festivals are an important pillar, where you can introduce a band to a large audience. You will certainly try to develop a group in which you believe by way of Werchter or I Love Techno. You can call this a privileged position, a luxury, and I admit it's a cool tool to work with.

Some respondents also raise the matter of the other privileged position all major booking agencies share: apart from booking groups, they also organize concerts of their own. Live Nation can always choose to offer a group to an organizer as a booking agency, and in doing so cash in the usual booking fee without running any risks, or rent the same venue and organize the concert on their own (thereby taking all the risks, but also making maximum profits when the project is a success). In this way, a certain artist venturing upon a comeback was first offered as a test case to Ancienne Belgique, one respondent says confidentially, 'because if it failed, they would still be able to claim the booking fee.' The people from Live Nation, by contrast, claim the agents often urge them to organize it instead of selling it as a booker to somebody else. As a respondent says: 'Because he knows we're in control of a well-oiled promotional and marketing machine.' In such cases, the symbolic weight of the agent kicks in. A consequence of this position, according to an organizer, is that Live Nation also has less trouble in arranging a tour for a small band than a small booker. 'When it is offered by Live Nation, programmers spontaneously give it better chances.'

Resignation and Understanding through Professional Capital

In any case, the cited examples of positional and economic power never cause any trouble. Few are willing to lose any sleep over a medium throwing a deal with a record company or a manager to be the first to write about an artist in exchange for an agreed promotional return. When a record company gives an exclusive interview to the media with the largest circulation, the journalists of the affected media may be disappointed, but they accept the situation. When concert organizers fail to secure a concert and have to let it go to a colleague, they too reconcile themselves with the selection. All understand that there are marginal preconditions such as location (see p. 222) or that bookers freely admit that they give a group to an organizer who will take them further than others. The fact that Live Nation also books many small bands is not something that will come between smaller bookers and their sleep. Moreover, the fact that it exploits its controlling position at festivals such as Rock Werchter and Pukkelpop — although the latter is officially an independent festival, rumor has it that it *is* a Live Nation festival — seems a perfectly logical thing to the majority of actors in the field who raise objections. These are, after all, the most important festivals. More, bands are dying to play at these festivals. The size of their fee will never become a matter of discussion. In short, a certain form of resignation can easily be observed. This also suggests the presence of professional capital. Those who want to play the alternative mainstream game must know and recognize the business. Players need to collaborate and close deals. Consequently, they are obligated to try to help their persons of confidence and occasionally give something up for the sake of the 'good relationship.' A booker explains why he has a hard time saying no to an agent:

> These personal contacts remain important. As long as you take care of those, you're the booker that the agent will want. That's business: putting something on the market as well as you can, and do the best you can...

A programmer sums up the impact of Live Nation: 'It's part of the game. That can be frustrating, but you cannot lose any sleep over it. Or else you'd better choose a different business.' 'Live Nation's wanting to control things, that's simply what the market is about,' another respondent says. It explains, in spite of constant criticism, why players continue to play the game. Another programmer:

> Live Nation is the most important, essential for every programmer in this circuit. If you mess things up over there, you can kiss your thing goodbye. And if organizers refuse to work with Live Nation, you can tell from their programming: you're just limiting your own options without ever harming Live Nation.

This clearly suggests that there is an inequality in the field. The field is stratified based on the amount of social, economic and symbolic capital. However, contrary to what Bourdieu's analysis claims, this is not contested in the pop music circuit. Quite the opposite, it is generally accepted. It is even assumed and expected, as an explicit norm. It is a legitimate form of power and 'powerlessness,' because there is still enough room for the norms that were discussed before. Also, these very norms are the answer to the social, symbolic and economic inequalities. Since the pop music field has a de facto inequality, the need for symmetrical and reciprocal relationships is very real and there is general expectation of these norms.

Elements of Power and Illegitimate Pressure

At first, the story that was gradually outlined in the interviews appeared to be one of symmetrical relations of trust, in which personal logic (taste and independence) was safeguarded. The music field is actually governed and regulated by the explicit and implicit norms that were discussed. On further consideration, and knowing the empathic claim of the respondents that 'nothing bad ever happens,' it is again both tension and ambiguity that strikes the observer. Positional inequality can sometimes lead to an imbalance of power. Bourdieu's analysis cannot and must not be put aside too quickly. Competitive field mechanisms and power factors may also be present in the pop music circuit.[6] Indeed, the relations of trust do not say a word about certain parities existing between the partners. Selections that are made to maintain these relations of trust, and which actors can still personally put their backs to, may also become forms of selection pressure. Then it is the power of decision-making in the genuine Weberian sense is involved: the ability to push through personal will within a social relationship, even against resistance (Laermans 2010: 267). Those who have power, will carry away the spoils. Those who are put under pressure are left without freedom of choice and forced to set aside selection criteria.

'Friendly' pressure becomes 'real' pressure, symmetrical power relations become asymmetrical. In this way, a hierarchy may arise between the relations: one actor is, or unilaterally becomes, dependent on the other. Though it is rather the exception than the rule, as will become apparent later on, these effects of the field structure can also provide illegitimate pressure and violate the symmetry norm. Violating the reciprocity norm was clear: those who do not *give* anything, will not *receive* anything next time. In the case of a symmetry norm violation, a penalty is difficult, if not impossible. The fact is that imbalance of power is difficult to put aside. This can be inferred from the violent reactions that often color the interviews. In addition, these violations were almost exclusively told off the record. It is no coincidence then that those who speak candidly in the interviews are without exception the 'victims.' To release certain information, however, is apparently not without danger. It could make the work floor relation even more difficult. Possible discontent is not voiced publicly, which somewhat betrays a resignation in 'fate.' This was often heard during the talks: 'We all know *it* happens, but no one can or wants to prove it.' Someone made the following comparison: 'It's a kind of omertá, like doping in cycling.' This too tells much about how the field works. There is a double standard: besides the official, there is also the unofficial.

Imbalance of Power in the Concert Circuit

Limits to Personal Freedom of Choice and Faits Accomplis
Crucial in the relations of trust that form the basis of networking in the pop music circuit, is the belief that either one of the parties always has the option to say no. In this, an appeal is made to the position of independence. It is from an individual logic that personal taste is invoked as the filter of the last resort. This individual freedom, for that matter, is itself not limitless. The position in the field allows others to exercise power. The interviews show that actors cannot always have their own way. From time to time they are purely intermediaries used as conduits, or forced to yield to the 'demands' of others.

Organizers experience their dependence on bookers as powerlessness. It is not always possible to refuse to accept an offer from the booker. Occasionally, a proposition can be turned down, 'but I cannot do this ten times,' or: 'If you say no too often, the booker will stop making offers.' 'The fact of the matter is that the bookers, for their part, are under much greater pressure from the English agents.'

The truth is that in the agent/booker relationship is particularly where the imbalance of power emerges. It was indeed not by chance that nothing was written about the personal filter of the booker in the preceding section of this book (6.1.2). The relations of bookers with agents are different from their relations with organizers. Whereas by definition a booker works together with several organizers, an exclusive collaboration may very well exist between agent and booker (in every country an agent can indeed seek one single booker who must find the necessary concerts for the agent's artists). In that case, bookers are quicker to follow the agent's choice even if this choice clashes with the booker's personal taste. 'I can hardly do every single group a particular agent offers me except one,' says a booker. Another booker adds:

When by chance an agent whom I frequently work with, offers something that's not really my thing, I cannot really say straight out: 'I think that's crap.' This is just part of the job.

There are also agents who offer their groups to different bookers and exploit the competition that exists between the latter. 'It's actually all very pragmatic,' an organizer said. 'The booker who does the best job, also has the best ties with the agent.' Whatever the case may be, sometimes it just will not come to anything but one-way traffic. The artists' rosters which international agents have at their disposal put them in a position of power which reduces local promoters (including Live Nation) to mere following. Agents can charge bookers with the task of arranging or organizing concerts for their groups. It is a story many actors had to tell. An example:

There's an unwritten law at Live Nation. It says that the firm must do everything in its power for artists who are in the top 5 of the agent, no matter how bad they are. (...) When the big boss of such an agency writes an email to Live Nation's boss in Belgium or the Netherlands saying 'It's imperative that this group plays a key festival in every market,' the only thing Live Nation can do is say yes.

This, as the three respondents indicate, explains why Rock Werchter always has a certain number of groups in its line-up who are only there because the agent wants it so, even if they are barely able to draw a crowd. As far as the big festivals are concerned, it has become increasingly hard for booking offices to decide which groups they will put on the main stages.

For the big foreign artist the Belgian or Dutch bookers are wholly dependent on the foreign agents. The artists will only appear here when those agents want them to and when it fits in with the tour schedule.

It is the foreign agent who says top-down: 'This year I'm coming with that group, and you make sure that they'll be here or there in the summer.' These days, festivals have no say whatsoever about the line-up of the groups, which band to place after which artist. This is already decided for you by the agents: 'I believe my group should be before or after that headliner,' regardless of what reality lies behind the group and what number of tickets they are able to sell. It's something you can observe more and more.

To allow personal taste to play a part in such cases is never under discussion. In other examples, it was not so much the absence of any personal contribution as the feeling to have been presented with a fait accompli. This, for instance, is possible when a booker plays clubs and festivals against one another. All programmers who were interviewed had their own experience of a group that was not offered to them or of a group for which they made a bid, but which was ultimately (for whatever reason) placed by the booker with some other organizer. This, quite naturally, causes frustration. Especially when the negotiations have reached an advanced stage, some players can indeed lose some sleep over this sort of thing. Consider what happened to one programmer with a particular group: 'I made a bid for them at a time when nobody even knew them. Then came the breakthrough, and they just slipped through my fingers. I still catch myself cursing at that.' Frustration is also rife, several respondents declare, when a booker offers a programmer small, uninteresting stuff, when he is leading all the bigger names toward the big venues and festivals. In such cases incomprehension is the normal reaction, because the duped actors believe the choice is not always to the artist's advantage. One programmer sums it up in a few words: 'A rule of *fair play* does exist, but it is not always respected.'

Organizers can also find themselves facing 'done deals' in their relation with the media. For some announced concerts, one organizer says, the attention of journalists can only be obtained on the condition that there would be a give-away promotion. Another organizer notes that live capturing has become so important for festivals that a radio station has managed to make the festivals beg for it (and, as a result, also pay for it). This too can provoke powerlessness.

Abuse of Power?
Illegitimate pressure mainly pops up when one party, engaged in a social relation with another, thinks the other has made unjust use of an acquired positional dominance. When the interviewed

players brought up such cases, a flood of abuse usually followed ('that guy's the mafia,' 'it's impossible to work with that asshole,' etc.). These situations usually involve bookers who exert pressure to place particular groups, demand a certain fee or impose package deals. This is often the outcome of unfair negotiations about fees (a group has no fixed fee in the music circuit, given the fact that everything depends on_supply and demand; every concert therefore presupposes negotiations). A programmer recalls that he agreed to take on a group for a certain sum at the incessant insistence of a booker, but suddenly saw the booker demand twice as much for the same concert when the group had become more popular. When this author was an organizer, it once happened that he had booked a group by verbal agreement, yet the group suddenly decided to switch bookers, causing the negotiations to start all over again and the fees to rise dramatically.

In conditional sales these tensions may also rise. In accordance with the implicit norm — as was explained in 6.1.2 — the actors claim this should not and indeed does not happen. Still, they confirm in the interviews that such practices do occur occasionally, mainly with smaller festivals (which have only one sole event per year), with younger organizers who do not have a solid network, or with certain dance events. 'You can tell by the bill,' a programmer says. 'They get a good headliner, and beside that group they're forced to put on two or three things.' One booker also admits this, yet more geared to a give-and-take-relation:

> When a festival gets three or four good foreign names, you ask him to take on another small group, or next year, you tell him, he'll need to look for his foreign groups elsewhere.

From time to time, in actual practice, the norm of reciprocity is pushed aside. For the protection of the respondents this study must be intentionally vague, but the interviews uncovered stories about bookers actually forcing organizers to accept pure package deals, even threatening with extreme sanctions those organizers who refused to go along. In these cases, abuse of power affects the selection with full force.

Another source of discontent which emerged from the interviews was experienced with bookers who hide themselves behind the agent (and thus, it is implied, behind the artist) with the aim of obscuring other interests. Off the record examples were given of situations where a particular organizer made a bid for a group, the booker then kept everything on 'hold,' only to let the organizer know that the artist and the manager were not interested. Another respondent explains this as follows: the booker simply does not let the agent in on the bid, but rather wants to organize the concert alone or in co-production with a fellow organizer. The said organizer, it is true, cannot really claim to know this, yet he does feel twice duped: not only does he not get the group, but neither will his venue or festival become known to the agent; any future collaboration is thus effectively thwarted, obstructed and made harder for all.

Live Nation, for its part, is rumored to play all its master cards with the sole aim of further developing its position of power. Some think the organization wants to clog up the market by also taking on a great number of small bands ('in doing so they'll be able to keep the market under control and even secure themselves an open field'). Others view the co-productions Live Nation likes to set up with medium-sized festivals as unfair competition. Because the organization shares in the profits, it intentionally gives some of its major groups to those specific festivals, thereby making it harder for other festivals to come up with a strong, tight program.

Competitive Disadvantage

The latter example is a fine illustration of the competitive disadvantage players can incur as a result of the economic and positional power of other players. The actors then get a feeling of dependency and powerlessness as a direct effect of occupying their position in the field and of observing certain mechanisms unfolding around them. For example, some organizers complain that the competition between the major booking agencies causes the price of some groups to rise sharply. Keeping the phrasing as general as possible, it can argued that this is true when booker X tries to rupture the ties between an agent and booker Y: with the purpose of winning over the agent, booker X can try to sell one of the agent's groups, which are normally handled by booker Y, to an organizer for a higher fee than usually is the case. Consequently, booker Y must go along with the incremental bidding to secure the contact with the agent. In both cases, however, the fee goes up-and-up.[7] That this is a violation of the norms, as is evidenced by the off the record responses that followed. Due to tough economic competition, organizers cannot complete the intended selections.

Among organizers as well the competitive struggle can lead to dependency. The blurring of norms becomes the crucial process. Cash-rich organizers of substance, who juggle with excessively high fees, do not meet their commitments or respect agreements: the agreement, for instance, to abstain from any bidding on a certain group because a colleague is already working on it, or playing solo slim when there is an agreement to do a joint bid. By doing so they violate the conventions that have grown in the field. Not only is this said to disrupt the good relations between colleagues, it is also believed to destroy the market and cause the price of particular groups to soar. Because of this, organizers are said to keep their agendas hidden from each other: 'It may certainly be so that we know each other very well and frequently have a beer together, still we do no tell each other everything we are doing. You never know if somebody is going to steal one of your groups.' Another respondent adds: 'The bookers use this to pit people against one another. Having said that, sometimes it truly is a little game.'

Internal Competitive Struggle and External Pressure
Relation Written Press/Record Company

In the interviews, one respondent tells the story of a record company which refused to continue sending promo CDs to a press medium after a bad review of one of their artists. Yet another respondent said that a record company — by way of conditional sale — had asked for an interview on the condition that next time it would be the other way round. 'This is not said in so many words, but it is insinuated, between the lines.' Indeed, abuse of power also exists in the relation between the written press and the record company.

Nevertheless, the relation is also marked by another striking phenomenon: the intersecting of an organizational logic with the positional logic, which closely connects with the 'competitive disadvantage' described above. From an organizational logic and in view of a return, actors want the best for their organization. This can be obstructed and impeded by the competitive struggle between similar positions all pursuing the same target.

It follows that the logic of cost-effectiveness does not only play its part in the actors' own actions or their own selection, but also in the interpretation of others. Especially in the written press, in its relation to record companies, this is a particularly effective element. To the press, interviews with more well-known and (in the eye of the beholder) relevant artists are important for maintaining the bond with the readers. But when interviews of the same kind start appearing in the same kind of media at the same time, then one medium will be unable to distinguish itself from another. By means of an exclusive interview or a scoop the distinction can be made, and this explains why the logic of cost-effectiveness described in the previous chapter acquires special urgency.

Between the press and the record company deals are made to ensure that the selection for this or that artist depends on whether the medium can be the first or the only one to write about it.[8] After all, viewed from a competitive position and the urge for differentiation, one medium needs to come up with a stronger story than the other. This is why they all want to be the first. Otherwise, the respondents argue, it all makes little sense.

> Because you are a news medium, and because the circumstances have led to your being confronted with another medium that is allowed to bring an article at an earlier time than you, a reader might be right to assume that we are behind, chasing after the facts. And that's not my job. Because you can bet your life that the same people will read different media. That's just how it is.

> For a cover story, I prefer to be first. If we would do Joan As Police Woman this week, and find out that the story was run somewhere else a week earlier, then half of the fun is definitely gone. What I really don't want to do is to ruminate what the rest has already brought. At that point, I have already lost interest.

Because the media that focus on the alternative mainstream fish in the same pond, they are divided among themselves and engaged in a perpetual competitive struggle: pressure, tension, frustration and lack of understanding are common properties. In Flanders, the battle is mainly fought between the weekly

Focus Knack (the entertainment supplement of *Knack*), daily paper *De Morgen* and stand-alone weekly *Humo*. Several respondents comment: 'If one of them does something, it automatically means the others won't.' 'The battle for release data and scoops is being fought more fiercely than ever before,' 'It drives me absolutely crazy,' 'They're like cats and dogs, the whole time snapping at one another, or simply being a nuisance.'

That this may be a sensitive story is clear from the contradictions in the statements. One says (obedient to the implicit norm): 'It's still a matter of give and take. When I'm the first to receive something new from the record company, I know I'll be second somewhere soon.' Another, by contrast, comments rather negatively: 'When they're not the first, they'll give the record companies a mad call. When something has been put under embargo, and one of the media chooses to ignore this, the others may suffer competitive disadvantage, a factor that places a business at risk for losing customers to a competitor.' The 'offender' says: 'If I find out someone is going to publish an interview in the beginning of the week, I would be an utter fool not to run it in the weekend before.' The fact that this practice occurs under the guise of 'freedom of press' can seriously get on the nerves of some colleagues. The internal competitive struggle and division among the actors of the written press can therefore easily tip over into insult and gossip, of which some of the interviewed actors gave examples.

Here, the internal competitive war is fueled by external pressure, which originates with the record company. Because interviews are thought to be more important than CD reviews (the piece will cover a far larger space, usually includes a picture, therefore means more free promotion), the company will try to manipulate the press and influence the selection. A journalist:

> Of course a record company still has the power to do so. It would be very naive to deny that we are but a link in the promotion chain. Of course we are. Part of the supply comes from the record company. No matter how, an interview in one of the major media is free publicity, much cheaper than placing an ad, and much more effective. Because it is a piece of journalism, it will have a greater credibility, and will not be perceived as advertising. (...) The fact that I am part of the record company's market-

ing campaign, does not bother me in the least. As long as the record company will not tell me what I can or cannot do in the interview.

Journalists want to maintain their independent position. Because CD sales continue their free fall, the record company will increase its attempts to pitch into both the position (as a reality) and the conviction (as an illusion). 'Friendly' pressure turns back into 'real' pressure. Two journalists comment:

> It's pure lobbying and pressure, more than anything else, and more aggressive than before. They really want more return on investment.

> The pressure has become much worse, you know. And you really feel the weight on the shoulders of the promo guys when they call me. I feel the pressure that's put on them by the A & R, the marketing manager or the label; I feel that there's already been a serious talk, over at the record company. (...)The gloves are off, because things have got to work. And it's a fight till the finish. That needs to be rammed down the throat.

The record companies readily admit this: their activities are a lot more focused than in the past, while the oversupply pushes them to aim on certain titles. 'When you've finally made that choice, you're going to apply just that little bit extra pressure, which is more than the media care for,' a label boss says.

Though this section is about the written press, the pressure is also said to be felt at the radio stations. Following the explicit conventions, as was explained in section 6.1.1, radio producers emphatically deny that a marketing campaign results in more airplay. But this too may be an expression of socially accepted behavior. In informal conversations, after all, the players often affirm that there is a direct connection between marketing of record companies and 'airplay' (which must not be confused with 'playlist'). Plenty of examples are given in the interviews. A radio producer says the record companies will go to all lengths to have their products selected, and 'by funding campaigns, they are able to put the offer in.' Another admits that a record accompanied by a give-away promotion (and the frequency of announcements) will be played slightly more often. Yet another one tells the story of a group that was initially only played in evening programming, until the record company put up a promotion to support it..

> And then this thing is sent to the public, four or five
> times a day, until it rises to the surface. But not without
> a push from the record company, which ties in an action.
> That's how it works.

Let us now go back to the written press. When the respondents are cautiously sounded on their stances towards scoops and embargoes, the interviews become the scene of a cat-and-mouse game: journalists believe the record companies are playing the various media against one another; the record companies say they can do little else because the media are the ones who ask for scoops and embargoes. The two parties blame and contradict each other. Consider this particular exchange between a journalist and a record label boss:

> This pressure from record companies is no fun at all, and
> impossible to deal with. You don't want to hear about
> the number of fights I've had with record companies. (...)
> They are the ones who constantly pit the main media
> against one another, that's absolutely true. Especially
> when local artists are involved. When a new record is
> released, they sometimes close a deal with a magazine, or-
> dering us not to publish anything about the artist before
> Tuesday. So what this magazine wants us to do is to wait
> and respect some right of first publication while the old
> bloated cow wallows in its exclusive. That's like telling 1
> of 8 athletes in a 100-meter run to go ahead and find him-
> self a good spot at the finish.
>
> It is true that we work with scoops, but it goes without
> saying that we were not the ones who asked for it. Record
> companies are whores: we just want everything with
> everybody. (...) There's no question about it that they are
> the ones who ask for it. We do it under pressure from them.
> Because they are the ones who want to sell more news-
> papers or magazines. They want to know when another

medium will publish, so they can outrun them and be first. And then out of the blue the other party goes 'We're pulling it back in...' Kids, that's what they are.... I truly refuse to believe that readers buy this paper or that magazine because it was there they read the first thing ever about an artist, nor do I believe readers will cancel their subscription because another medium was ahead of the magazine. Besides, it's a fairly ridiculous battle, no? Doing everything you can to be first. Pray tell, who in the world has ever bought all newspapers and magazines at a time?

Truly remarkable in this interaction between the record circuit and the media is that the battle is waged for all the world to see. Apparently the game of exerting pressure is indeed played 'with the gloves off': it is easier to tell 'on the record' in this context what was still 'off the record' in the previous section. As was already observed, the pressure here is of a different nature. In contrast with, let us say, a festival that is more dependent because it needs the right groups, when the media do not get the scoop or when they are blocked by an embargo, it is actually the oversupply that makes it easier for them to say no, and to do this in a more hard-hitting way. A record label boss puts it as follows:

The media are poised in a position of power. They can either say 'I'll do it' or 'I'm not going to do it.' And then they are pitted against one another by the record companies. But also relative to each other. (...) They are very clear about it, holding a knife to the throat: 'I won't do it if another one gets the scoop.' In my book, that's a threat. (...) The whole principle obviously originated from their internal differences.

Almost all journalists provide several examples of 'saying no' during the interviews. Each time it boils down to the same thing: a medium will not run a story about a group when another medium was given the scoop by a record company or had already written about it in a prominent way. 'Then I simply don't want it anymore, and I say: "fuck off",' one respondent says. 'Sometimes you need to tell them to,' another says.

> I'm quite categorical in this. The supply is so gigantically vast that you can afford to make choices. The advantage of having less space than you used to is that you are able to be even harsher in making selections. The harder the pressure, and the more they blackmail, the less I'm inclined to roll over. (...) It's not my job to do a story days after it's been done elsewhere. I don't believe anyone should go along with such practices.

The organizational logic urges actors to want the best for their readers. When this choice is on a collision course with the interests of others, attempts are made to eliminate the rivals (by closing a deal for an exclusive with the record company). When this fails, or another medium is ahead of them, the actors say no and look for something else. According to the respondents, alternative items can include a deal with foreign papers. Interviews with renowned artists can thus be published without any intervention from the record companies. Another option is to write a piece about a group without having to conduct an interview with the said group. In this way, the independency requirement is again guaranteed.

By Way of Conclusion
Distrust versus Fair Play

A typical example of internal differences and tensions in the music circuit is the clash between a radio station and a rock band discussed by three respondents. The group had already gained a solid reputation, but received very little airplay because the radio station did not think the music was good enough. At one point, a single did manage to get into the lower regions of the playlist. The group then proceeded to play at various parties of the station (as it turns out, also at a convention), but soon after that, the single vanished from the playlist. The group was stunned, the group's entourage dismayed: 'We actually did everything in our power to develop a good relationship with the station,' and 'When radio stations stop picking up singles, the whole story comes tumbling down like a house of cards, and that is nefarious for this sort of group.' The station was subsequently put under pressure by the entourage ('Or else we won't do anything ever again for you, now and in the future'). It paid off. The number was back somewhere below in the playlist. Good public response even turned it into a radio hit. 'The radio station had to follow, not wholeheartedly, but simply because they had no other choice,' one witness argues.

From the anecdote can be inferred that one party thought the mechanism of give and take had not been respected and that sanctions should be imposed for violating conventions. The said party mobilized its accumulated symbolic capital, while the radio shifted from saying no; a judgment made and situated within an individual logic, over starting to doubt the validity of no, to saying yes, a judgment made within an organizational logic. Different interpretations and clashes of the logics adopted in the field thus create tensions. Niklas Luhmann argued that investing in relations of trust remains a fragile and risky business (Abts 2005: 5-7). Actors never know what they will get in return, and whether it will be of the same order of what they had put into it. Exactly because confidence is based on expectations, it remains something of a wager or gamble. Breaking the word or promise, betrayal, and abuse of power, may cause expectations of trust to take a sudden turn and reverse into expectations of distrust. Violating the norm of reciprocity was a clear example of such 'breaking faith,' whereas 'abuse of power' is a violation of the norm of symmetry. Boltanski and Thévenot (2006: 176-178) pointed out that the 'domestic world' can be seriously jeopardized by gossip and hearsay, quarrelsome individuals and indiscretion. All these elements are revealed by the interviews. This may cause resentment, and the accrued and necessary relations of trust may receive debilitating blows.

To what extent these relations of trust can tip over in distrust, however, is difficult to establish. In the interviews, any possible unilateral exercise of power by those involved is either denied, referred to strictly off the record, or ends in beating around the bush. This fact is evidently inherent to in-depth interviews: there is always a gap between what is said explicitly and the implicit argument participants develop. What is nevertheless clear is the range of attitudes assumed by respondents toward any possible imbalance of power. For example, when an organizer is faced with demands from a booker which he views as unfair (such as an excessively high fee), he has two options. If the group is necessary for his club, festival or event, he must accept the booker's dominant position. If he has alternatives, he can disre-

gard the demands. As was already established, the media have an easier time taking the last option than is the case for the concert circuit. Even then, if maintaining the relation is indispensable for the future, it may be imperative to restore trust. Apart from this, the maturity, responsibility, reputation and professional capital of the 'dependent' party will play a part. In the beginning of a career in professional music, the need for compromise and concessions is much higher. In the course of time, actors may allow themselves to take firmer positions. As a journalist says:

> I never argue with record companies, go ahead and ask them. I just say no. And they know that. I think they got to know me and that somehow they respect me. Record companies have trouble put the pressure on me.

Still, one of the main findings of this study is that even in situations of inequality of power a norm of fair play is still active. It explains why respondents speak of abuse of power and 'things that simply can't be tolerated.' After all, what is at stake here is the validity of norms, of views and beliefs about how things *should* be. Inequalities in the field are accepted, the systematic appropriation of power to the detriment of others is not. As long as the conventional ways of interaction and cooperation are not outnumbered by individual incidents and practices of an intolerable kind, the relations of trust will not take a turn toward distrust. Then the rule of exception applies: pressure is possible and allowed, but such illegitimate behavior should remain the exception at all times. Ultimately, the actors need each other. One festival organizer rightly puts it like this:

> A booker knows he simply cannot dump all the leftovers without offering something good in exchange. It is all the same not in his best interest should a festival go out of business, because it is still his market and our commission invoices are the ones he's counting on.

In terms of reasoning, one manager sets the record straight:

> Because we live in a small country, there is still plenty of comradeship and solidarity among colleagues, and we are

still far from the game of power that is played abroad. Take for instance the issue of conditional sales and package deals, or the problem of putting the pressure on people: of course, it happens, don't be silly. But is there an alternative? That's just the market situation of different parties and stakeholders who all have a different agenda, and it is fair to say, I think, that the game is played properly. The simple fact is that people are obliged to work with others in so many capacities, you are not in a position to avert the frustration of one group on to the other, because they are also people whom you want to get along and move forward with. It is this awareness that often sets relations right again. In theory, the situation could be the object of gross exploitation, much more than is the case right now, but the fact is that it doesn't happen.

The conclusion then is that actors merely wish to find 'the right balance' in every situation. 'You win some, you lose some,' is a piece of wisdom all programmers express at one time or another. 'Sometimes you have to watch and let groups slip by, but then you tell yourself there are also gifts on the horizon,' says one. 'If there's a certain equilibrium and you notice others envy you, than things are fine,' yet another smiles. One journalist comments on the pressure exerted by record companies: 'I'm not happy about it, but it's just the given world in which you happen to be caught. We need each other; *it's a give and take.*' All this shows that the described relations of trust mainly function in the medium-long run. As long as there is fair play, and as long as the gifts are still on the horizon, the relation of trust is saved and safe. As such — and this has been the subject of this chapter - the relation is again governed by the norms that have been culturally constructed, and not by chance, just for that purpose.

Whereas an organizational logic starts from the relation actors have with the organization to which they belong, the positional logic refers to the place held by the organization (or the type of player) in the field. Depending on this position, the logic can get a different interpretation with every new situation. The motivation underlying a particular choice varies with every position and every other context, since there is always a new market, another public, or a different opponent to deal with. Nevertheless, actors need to work together and find cooperation, whatever the opposite interests that are engaged. In the interaction, both explicit and implicit norms can be distinguished.

Perhaps the most important explicit convention that obtains in the field is that relations of cooperation are also relations of trust. 'Knowing many people' in itself is not enough. People have to be able to trust one another. The positional logic drives the actors to make deliberate choices with the purpose of maintain good relations. An explicit norm is that these relations are based on a mutual dependency that allows everyone to safeguard their positional independence (the norm of symmetry). Implicitly, the norm of reciprocity is paired with it: positional equilibrium is a game of give and take. For example, concert organizers will now and again program a less loved or wanted group in exchange for their bookers' commitment to deliver a sufficient number of — what in their view is considered — relevant groups. Another example is found in deals made between record companies and the media that are conceived from a projected win-win situation, that is, good promotion for the label's artist as well as for the medium itself. For this reason respondents do not feel any pressure in the decision-making process. They interpret it as 'friendly pressure' and think this is no more than usual, because in the end they are allowed to make a free choice.

Be that as it may, in a network not everyone carries the same weight. The extent to which actors can have influence depends on their weight in social, symbolic and economic capital. A notable interaction effect is that actors are going to listen to someone with whom they maintain good relations or who convey credibility. In addition, those who have greater economic power in a network, acquire (the) power to select. The result is a generally accepted state of inequality in the field. This obviously can have illegitimate effects. Imbalance, and possible abuse, of power puts pressure on the norm of symmetry. Sometimes one player is simply obliged to follow the other, or they are engaged in an internal competitive struggle. 'Friendly' pressure then becomes 'real' pressure, and trust can turn into mistrust. In these cases, positional actions include both the attempts made by actors to render other actors dependent and those made to protect their own independence. Yet as long as unilaterally dominant relations of power remain the exception, a dynamics of give and take is sustained and the sense of fair play keeps up in the storm, the relation of trust will still hold.

Notes

1   In this respect, Boltanski & Chiapello (2005) speak of the 'projective city,' the seventh in the model of cities or polities (cités), to which worlds (mondes) correspond where higher common principles provide common ground for justificatory practices. It is a supplementary contribution to the model presented in Boltanski & Thévenot (2006). The 'world of the project' deals with networks, with setting up social connections that are necessary for realizing projects.

2   In Belgium, these are Live Nation and their rivals (Greenhouse Talent, Gracia Live, Jazztronaut, L&S) and small, independent or local bookers (Peter Verstraelen Bookings, Busker Bookings, Rockoco, Quiet Concerts, Toutpartout, Nada Booking, Progress Booking, Stage-mania etc.). Apart from Live Nation/Mojo Concerts (less significant as a booker of Dutch acts), the booking market in the Netherlands is inhabited by Double Vee Concerts, AT Productions, Paperclip Agency, Agents After All, Boom! Agency, Tornado Concerts etc.

3   A striking observation is that in the commotion caused by embargoes such as this one, only the record firm or the management is attacked, while the group is kept out of range. Bourdieu (1993b: 278-279) already pointed out that this is part of the rules of the game: even when artists are in it for the money and the success, it is crucial – also for the art dealers – that they emphatically deny that they are doing it for the money, and even that they expose the strategies of the art dealers ('money-grubbers'). This sort of censoring back and forth, which artist and art dealers carry out, evidently serves to mask the economic motives operating in the art world.

4   Bourdieu's discussion of the cultural field is inescapably linked to the (symbolic) negation of economic capital and relations of power, and therefore also of any form of organizational logic. In the pop music circuit both negation and recognition of economic power are caught in peaceful, yet always ambivalent coexistence. All actors engage in an economic market where music is traded. In the economies of worth of Boltanski & Thévenot (2006: 193-203), with its worlds of higher common principles (to which correspond political cities or polities) competition is the common higher principle of the world of the market, which thrives on financial interests and economic rivalry. Opportunism is never far away: actors must go with and capitalize on whatever presents itself, find or create a hole in the market, and distance themselves of emotions.

5   In Belgium Live Nation is not only a booking agency, employing some eight bookers who sell big and small artists to about every concert organizer in the country, it is first and foremost a concert organizer for all important big venues (Forest National, Sport Palace Antwerp, Ancienne Belgique, Botanique etc.). It runs its own major festivals (Rock Werchter, I Love Techno) and – as some respondents tell off the record – organizes other festivals in co-production (Pukkelpop, Les Ardentes, Dour, Graspop and Suikerrock are believed to be on that list, but there is no official information about this). The situation in the Netherlands is highly comparable. Live Nation/Mojo Concerts is also owner of Lowlands, North Sea Jazz and Songbird, has managerial interests in Pinkpop and partly controls Heineken Music Hall and Ziggo Dome. Internationally Live Nation Entertainment, the American multinational, determines the long and short of everything, sets up global tours and acts in managerial capacities for international. The corporation is – following the merger with Ticketmaster – also world leader in eCommerce/ticket sales (nl. livenation.be/about).

6   The mechanism of 'give and take' described above fits in with Bourdieu's theory of fields in which the 'dominant' are pitted against the 'dominated' in a constant struggle (over the definition of the field): relations founded in the economic are disguised by symbolic actions that must legitimize the arbitrary, asymmetrical relations of power (Bourdieu 1990: 123-127). This is what he has famously called 'symbolic violence': the exerted pressure may invariably appear 'friendly' and

resemble 'give and take,' and the appreciation, trust, personal loyalty and prestige which the 'giver' acquires thanks to his action is never something more or less than the symbolic capital of someone who holds a better economic position.

7   The bookers can actually also hurt themselves as they trigger the pressure of having to repeat the painfully high bid in the event of a next occasion (when they, or somebody else, want to organize it on their own). For this reason, some bookers may actually propose to organizers not to pay too much. 'But not all bookers are willing to do this,' a respondent comments.

8   An exclusive is usually reserved for foreign artists, whereas the scoops primarily involve the bigger domestic artists (when the item is put under embargo for others: they have to wait until the first interview has been published).

7. The Social Process of Second-Order Selection

In the summer of 2012, Foo Fighters descended on the Low Countries, playing live at two big festivals: Lowlands in the Netherlands and Pukkelpop in Belgium. For days, weeks and even months, the event was 'the buzz of the year.' The band, headliner at both festivals, gave stunning, unforgettable concerts. The hymn of praise that followed was universal. Every single paper, every magazine, every radio station, every television crew, every online medium and very nearly the entire Facebook community thought the performances were first-rate.

There is not a shred of doubt that the concerts were 'unique' and 'powerful,' and every value judgment about the band's performances will surely have been sincere. Yet the speed with which, and the massive scale on which, the good news show spread, was remarkable, to say the least. It almost seemed as if each player simply took over the other's opinion.

This particular phenomenon is striking, but far from uncommon. It bears all the properties of second-order selection or second-order observation:[1] actors observe the selection made by fellow actors and proceed to determine their own selection based on this observation, either consciously or subconsciously.

In the case of an individual, organizational and positional logic, the actors' judgment is the starting point, whether it is induced by social and economic factors or not: the logics involved are those of legitimization that the actor uses to justify actions and make a selection. This is done based on personal taste, or whatever the organization the actors belong to or the position occupied in the music field suggests them to do.

Yet the selection of cultural products can also be induced by observing others and taking over their choice. Here the motor is not a specific logic of legitimization, but a mechanism that affects the decision and is colored as well as intersected by the previously described logics. Because selections are influenced by the contacts and interaction with others, this second-order observation is a social process. The previous chapter looked at social relations on a particular, even private level (for instance, between one specific booker and one particular organizer). This chapter, by contrast, puts the interaction on a collective level, where decisions can have an impact on further selections.

The chapter is thus concerned with the ways in which the music industry and the media rely on other people's opinions in an attempt to reduce both the complexity of the offer and the risk of the decisions they need to take. In such situations, media attention assumes overriding importance and calls the tune. Actors from the music industry look for their own assessment to what circulates in the media, while actors from the media, for their part, affect one another's choices. Through these mechanisms, a collective support base of 'relevant music' takes shape, which paves the way for conformism.

Dealing with Oversupply
Complexity Reduction

‖ **Opinion Makers as Symbolic Guides in Times of Oversupply**

It is impossible for actors in the professional field of music to command a bird's eye view or at least keep control of everything that goes on, online and offline, in music. Today, the flow of music is an endless series of releases and concerts from fall until spring that only stops to leave the summer to a chain of festivals that bill new and old in as many slots as possible. Hypes are created on and off, platforms for presentation of music seeking a wide variety of mobile-users come and go, web shops sell in both downloading and streaming format. Chapter 3 already showed that there is actually so much going on, that so much is headed straight for the music circuit's gatekeepers and drones, challenging them so quickly and deeply in their basic patterns of classification, that they inevitably must run into trouble when they need to make selections. By looking at others, taking over their criteria for selection, or simply obeying their value judgments in blind trust, the actors can somewhat disentangle a hopelessly confused and confusing state of demand and supply, which has become oversupply and overstock. Observing certain gifted, even visionary key figures can indeed be helpful in making the right selection. Their symbolic capital transforms them into symbolic guides. The interviewed actors labeled them as 'catalysts,' 'opinion makers' and 'gatekeepers,' to whom they willingly submitted their independence by allowing their musical tips to influence them. 'In order to be able to see the forest through the trees, you need certain well-established opinion makers,' one actor voices the general opinion, 'much more than ever before.'

If this is the case, second-order selection is an explicit convention. The previous chapter already touched upon the influence of symbolically important actors, yet concerned itself with actors in cooperation, helping one another on a common ground of trust. In this chapter the actors do not engage in cooperation, but simply obey the substantive judgments of opinion leaders with the goal of enabling themselves to make better choices, that is, secure selections. Evidently, this task could also be fulfilled by friendly contacts in the music circuit. In the previous chapter, a respondent brought up the relationship of mutual 'testing by criterion' that existed among the players. The majors or bigger record companies also employ such confidential advisors, on the understanding, as one radio playlist editor remarked, that they have excluded the niches from their field of operations. 'Niche music has ceased to be a core business of the big firms. All initiatives that involve investing time and money are banned. Small labels, their distributors and their employees, on the other hand, are still a source of information. Such role models or reference-individuals can actually also be unknown, unsung voices in the music field. As Laermans (2010: 255) points out in this respect, the mass media (including the internet) have a significant role in this. 'In a heavily "mediatized" society, a society which allows the various mass media to have a great impact, the act of comparing oneself and, respectively, identifying oneself with unknown others, can indeed be a crucial social mechanism.'

The Internet as First Selection

It is obvious that new groups, which have not yet caught the attention of the actors in the alternative mainstream, elicit an especially urgent need for reference. As a result, the players direct themselves toward underground feeds. All respondents agree that the Internet is beyond question the main input channel. Thanks to the digital revolution information channels have mushroomed. 'The time when a handful of sacred magazines were the only source of information is gone,' says a respondent. The players who are active in the Flemish music circuit choose to follow, or are guided, by music which circulates and finds diffusion on various websites (webzines, blogs, social media, forums etc.). These online mobile locations are also overwhelmingly foreign — something that is apparent, for instance, in a small region like Flanders. In any case, such sources are becoming increasingly more important. In this study, Pitchfork was the most frequently cited online location, closely followed by Stereogum, Metacritic and Hypemachine. 'There's even a button that's called "popular," so you know what is being downloaded a lot,' a radio producer says. Sometimes the media hire special freelancers whose only task is to keep an eye on new groups, 'read the blogs that attract the music freaks, then single out some of the most promising events or acts and possibly lift out something really significant.'

When an actor must actually observe, seek and find what is brewing and prevalent in certain groups, he or she will have a

stronger motivation to pay attention to them, thereby facilitating the process. In the case of the media, the search for new bands is never induced by the prospect of pleasure new music brings to society or by the contribution it makes to culture. One journalist calls a spade a spade arguing that it is not in the least about the desire to *discover* new bands, yet about being able *to present the discovery* (to the public at large), and being the first or only one to do so: 'Let's be frank, we are A&R managers.' In practice, to discover something personally is in most cases indeed synonymous with being the first to pinch something from another and start working on it as if it was a personal find. As the saying goes, it is better to be a good copycat than a bad inventor. Nonetheless, and in spite of the fact that the players in second-order selection choose to look to others for solutions, and willingly obey the judgments made by the community, the quest made by journalists and radio producers for uncharted music is a personal journey. It leads them to the underground media and opinion leaders from the niche, while they act from an individual logic of personal taste. The Internet works as a giant channeling hub. It is a meeting ground for music lovers that will start the valuation game, an observing post for music industry scouts who want to figure out what novelties will make the music lovers tick. In addition, it is a new-blood post for artists who are fresh, whose values are up for testing and who long to have their values evaluated. Finally, it is a platform for a privileged group of deserving artists. These ones will move up and get past the gates. The significance can be read from the evening programming of the music channels (for example, Studio Brussels programs such as *Select* and *Duyster*).

> The Internet is the most important pipeline, a regular live feed, where you can watch what is vibrant, vital and alive among the music lovers, and check whether it's something that indeed looks worth the while. Every day I check the blogs, since these are especially of interest for late evening or night radio programming. I also dive into a large collection of links and online locations that were sent to me by the said music enthusiasts. Because the offer is so vast, the first thing you do is have a look on the net at the things that are starting to draw people, or not only starting to draw people, but are also starting to make people want to come back. If some band, or a kind

of music, suddenly surfaces in many different places at the same time, you know that this band or music must be very much alive and kicking in a certain group and that it can perhaps receive a support base among the music freaks. At that point, I think, you are obliged as a radio station to pay attention to it. In terms of new releases, trends, artists we try to be on top of everything as fast and as close as possible. The things you run into on the blogs are certainly things you will check out, because it is usually a sign that it can't be bad. Unless, of course, the whole thing is a hype that's been prepared and orchestrated by the record company or the management.

One other reporter, for his part, relies on the Internet to struggle and plough his way through the rest of the offer, the tons of CDs that still need processing after the first CDs have been selected based on the criteria that were discussed in the previous chapters. The Internet, he says, 'allows you to get in touch with a huge variety of opinions.' He mentions Metacritic, a website which gathers reviews from all major, and dozens of other, US-based sources (from the *L.A. Times* to *The New York Times*, from *Variety* to *Village Voice*), as well as players such as Pitchfork. These sources make up an evaluative list, in which all reviews and overall end judgments receive a metascore: it means they are effectively ranked from top to bottom with a score that reflects the value judgment made in the piece. Lists may start all the way up, from an exalted green score of 100, and then descend into an alarming red, where the weak scores hit bottom on zero.

To listen to the loads of CDs that end up in the residual category is simply impossible, because in the time I'm supposed to catch up, I keep receiving dozens of CDs. Then, I admit, I simply type in the names on Metacritic, and I listen to anything that scores above 80%. When twenty U.S. media, ranging from highly alternative to highly mainstream, from intellectual to commercial, give an overall favorable assessment and rate a record as 'this is a good record,' I will listen to it. In this way, selections aren't mere guesswork. No doubt, I will miss a few things we were actually supposed to do, but hey, I'm far from perfect, right? I'm fairly convinced that I'm still quite ethical in my way of doing things and that I'm doing the best that I can.

Not only have the media paid attention to these new sources of information. Concert organizers also rely on them. They look at line-ups abroad and draw up their wish list by way of the Internet. One programmer even thinks the Internet holds the most vital information because the magazines are often behind, compared to what goes on online. A second reason is that 'you know those Internet sources also turn other music lovers in a particular direction.' The same holds for bookers:

> There are a number of websites, newsletters and blogs where I'll have a look first, such as Pitchfork, that's right, and the Rough Trade Shops in England. I tend to follow them intensely, just to be well up on everything very quickly and to be able pick up certain things. If you feel that something's brewing in England or in the States — and in such cases this is still on a very modest level - chances are it'll be here soon from across the Atlantic or the Channel. It even looks like this happens a lot more than used to be the case. Is it because these things are more readily accessible? Because people are able to check everything quickly now? I'm pretty sure journalists, bookers and organizers are not the only ones who will follow this.

In addition, the public can make itself heard through the Internet. As was mentioned in Chapter 3, music also circulates via the social media. The choice of the 'unknown public' is a source of information for national actors. 'Very important, for example, is the number of likes something receives on YouTube,' an organizer and a manager affirm.

The Underground as Guiding Environmental Factor

Besides the Internet, the written press is still very much a source for manhandling the multitude of publications, and the vast number of foreign magazines in particular (see p.320). Many respondents in Flanders and the Netherlands read the influential magazines, which are overwhelmingly written in English: They do this to see if they can get a story out of certain artists. Consequently, these magazines contribute their share to the decision-making process.

'I also read loads of magazines, I devour them,' says one journalist says. 'In the UK you have so many specialized media, some of which easily offer 200 reviews per issue. I will read every single one of those 200.' Domestic underground media can also see to this initial attention (webzines such as Cutting Edge, Enola, DaMusic, KindaMuzik, and specialized magazines such as *Gonzo Circus* and partially *RifRaf*). The journalists from the alternative mainstream consult these 'to see if they haven't missed something,' one promo person tells. 'People who do this sort of thing are exactly the people with the highest motivational .'

Getting attention in the said sources, both online and printed, has its desired effect, which is why the record firms will also make use of them. One promotion manager recounts that he suddenly received many questions for one of his bands when their CD became 'CD of the Week' in the Rough Trade Shop in London. Another one testified that all journalists wake up with a start when he is able to send them good reviews from Pitchfork or *The Guardian*. *RifRaf* too can have this telltale or detector function:

> By deliberately putting an unknown group on the cover, other media will also notice this and have a listen to it. In this way, I think, the record firms are also able to see us, checkout what we're doing. This is why we're often allowed to do an interview with one of the smaller things up to a couple of weeks before the actual release. I think especially the small record companies does this on purpose to open the eyes of the larger media, certainly when it's our cover story.

Complexity reduction is thus the reason why people from the music industry and the media follow the underground's opinion leaders. These underground channels are an environmental factor that contributes to the selection. As is often the case, the actors rely on the same niche media to be knowledgeable. This may push the selection in a particular direction. A booker puts it as follows:

> Such a thing may start out from a small club of music lovers and industry people, whatever you want to call it, who have an imprint for this stuff, are hot on new things. They are pinned down on a number of websites or media that they think are good and in many cases, these will

actually be the same media. This is true, no doubt.

Groups that are in the spotlight or become the tip of the hour in these media are subsequently allowed to present themselves at showcase festivals, such as Eurosonic Noorderslag in the Netherlands, or Glimpse in Belgium. Later, they might even appear on the bill of the bigger festivals. It is then that selection as a social process can begin. The VIP tents of the festivals become the buzzing ground, and the actors start giving each other tips, or they hear their colleagues spreading the word: 'Be sure to check out alt-J or Django Django!' 'Then you go check it out,' one organizer rounds up. 'And so the news will spread even more quickly. Afterwards you notice that everybody starts posting the clips on Facebook, or is listening to the same thing on Spotify.' And so the music becomes music 'which is tipped *via-via*,' in which the observation stays a certain course. This could be called a specific form of the consecration cycle, where the symbolic capital of the first affects the selection by the other.

Mutual Influencing and Conformism in the Media

Chain Reactions in the National Media

The fact that the gatekeepers of the alternative mainstream allow themselves to be informed by the opinion leaders of the underground, still does not mean they will actually do something with it. To follow current affairs in music is one thing, to start breaking a lance for it and granting new music nation-wide attention is quite another. Then somebody must be willing to make the first move. In the case of the media, some journalists and radio-makers may do so in the pursuit of distinction, aiming to demonstrate or give proof of their function as discoverers. By picking up new music that others do not know yet, they can set the tone for their medium and distinguish themselves from other media.

Those who are the first to report about certain artists will later be able to tell they had a hand in making the artists. 'To *make* someone' is recurring jargon in the select world of music. As a journalist points out with regard to Mumford & Sons: 'We were the ones who made them, right? We were immediately on to them.' A radio maker speaks about '*making* a record' in the case of The Big Pink and De Jeugd Van Tegenwoordig. Some actors in the media will indeed make a song and a dance of 'being the first.' Yet scoop function, discussed in the previous chapter (see p. 296), is part of a positional competitive struggle and is induced by an organizational logic. Here the matter concerns the accumulation of symbolic capital. Still, the number of journalists that listens to underground telltales and actually acts upon it is believed to be limited. One respondent stresses the point, off the record, mentioning individuals by their full name: 'There are only a few who dare to stick out their necks. The rest will do so only when they are able to follow those individuals. You can count the real music freaks and culture vultures in the important media on the fingers of one hand.'

This element is crucial in the social process discussed here, because when the selection of one national actor is taken over by the other, a second form of second-order observation comes into being. At the radio, this is primarily noticed when music moves from evening to daytime programming. Two playlist editors give multiple examples of music that was first played in the evening programming (Yeasayer, Sigur Rós and in past times dEUS, Nirvana and Underworld), and was later retrieved – 'when there's a broader support base' –in daytime programming. The editors of the daytime playlist partially look upon the evening programs as test cases: 'It is there that we try out things. If there's quite a reaction, we can also play it in daytime.' In the written press the same movement can be observed, when a small review develops into an interview.

Second-order selection can be detected when a medium copies reporting by another medium. This can cause a chain reaction. Others can then follow the searchers in the niche, yet the effect of their discovery is dependent upon their power in the field, their symbolic capital, or better: their professional or 'alternative mainstream capital.' The fact is that this second-order mechanism mainly occurs when one of the major media chooses for something, and this sparks the interest of other media. One person in charge of promotion says:

> *Humo, De Morgen, De Standaard* and *Focus Knack* are the main players in the Flemish written press. They are also important because they influence other journalists. When one of them writes about a CD, everybody will want it.

Laermans (2010: 41) calls this 'the carry-away effect': a first group of 'believers' wins over others. Just about every respondent is able to cite an example. One particular manager talks about a group which *Humo* and *De Morgen* refused to write about:

> And then *Focus Knack* started raving about them. It pulled them all in. You see this often. They are opinion makers. Once a start has been made... People are waiting for someone who sticks out his or her neck and sort of gives the green light.

Another manager initially ran into a *no* with his group at the radio, until a leading newspaper published a 5-star-review: 'After that they started playing two numbers, one of which got the highest rotation.' Richard Hawley benefited from such a newspaper, one label boss affirms. Because of a review, the label resumed work on the artist, with success: other newspapers, radio and TV followed.

> The record had been out for five months and there was very little . At a certain point, nobody wanted to do anything with it anymore. Until an important newspaper wrote a raving concert review, entitled 'The most beautiful 90 minutes ever.' It prompted the rest to follow. This was a piece of promotion we had nothing to do with and hadn't lobbied for. We never saw it coming. But it helped, I can tell you that.

Nevertheless, people in the pop circuit are reluctant to ascribe a symbolic power to themselves. As one journalist notes: 'It's not as if I'm saying: "Yoo-hoo, look what I've done!" It doesn't work like that.' Another one downplays the fact of wanting to be 'the first' by referring to the promotional activities of record companies. The latter regularly organize press days or junkets, where several interviews are done at the same time, 'making it impossible to actually measure the impact,' he says. In addition, the scoops are often pure luck. One newspaper did not have a review of a particular concert for the simple reason that the freelancer had been wrong about the date: 'And then this is read by other papers as if he had been the first and we simply followed him.' All respondents agreed that sometimes one medium, sometimes another is the first to pick something up, or that everyone may well be working on something at the same time. A radio- maker says: 'There are plenty of examples when a radio station started playing a record without anyone ever having written one word about it. And vice versa!' Another one agrees: 'Sometimes it's just a matter of luck.'

In any case, it is striking to see that journalists can be 'awakened' by this social process. Two promotion managers recall numerous instances of journalists requesting a promo CD that was sent to them several weeks before. They had not listened to the music, but only swung into action when they had read something about it elsewhere.

> Only this week, The Antlers became 'CD of the Week' in one of the leading, important magazines. All of a sudden, I got calls from four other journalists who wanted to have a review copy and who had forgotten that I had already given them one a month ago.

Taking Over Foreign Hypes

Second-order observation is not merely a dynamic game between national actors. It also occurs when all eyes are focused on what is going on across the borders. For small regions like Flanders/ Belgium and the Netherlands, the mechanism is even essential. This time the object does not concern the previously discussed first attention with foreign niche media, but the alternative mainstream abroad (with Great Britain leading the rest). If an artist receives exceptional praise there, all continental players across the Channel will prick up their ears. Especially British magazine NME, and public broadcaster BBC (with the annual *Sound of* list) are explicitly labeled as influential by almost all respondents. The journalists do not consider the fact that these foreign media are closely watched as something to worry about. Not one of them denies that they are keener to listen to artists as a direct result of these foreign players' selection. Three respondents testify:

> The *Sound of* list is good. If there is something listed there that we are unaware of, we will certainly look it up.

> It is an incentive, a reason to go check it out. I certainly consider it, and I will run some sort of blurb, because there's always some sort of hype that makes it across. In these cases, the news value of the CD elicits coverage.

> Take the first record of the Arctic Monkeys. There was so much fuzz and buzz around the record that people already knew the band before they even heard the music.

> When NME, Q and MOJO tip certain music, there's always a buzz and I will evidently listen to it. (...) I think that this is a determining factor in about eighty percent of the CDs that are discussed. The average journalist is primarily engaged in following whatever is receiving special attention abroad.

A radio producer observes a difference between the mainstream and the alternative mainstream: 'Hit stations only look at the charts, while we tend to focus on *the credible* press.' The same mechanism, for that matter, can be found in the concert circuit. Foreign media guide organizers also let themselves. One of them argues: 'You need to read everything. If a group in England surfaces, and manages to impress a couple of people, you can be dead certain that they will eventually cross the Channel.' A booker confirms this, adding that the influence from abroad does not solely originate with the media, but also with the agents who work with them—an observation which is in line with what the previous chapter showed. 'A great deal is sent over from England, or from the States, because that's where the agents are, who just dream of imposing their will.' Consequently, second-order selection can also originate with these actors.

Whatever the extent to which the actors in the small music field of the Low Countries have become consumers of UK- and US-based fads, there were quite a few respondents who raised objections against this subservient following of hypes, against believing the hypes, and especially against *believing* the foreign hypes. Such criticism, however, is almost exclusively heard among actors belonging to the record companies, management or concert circuit. They raise the issue of dependence, advocating a more autonomous stance. Their arguments emphasize that actors fail to take a sufficiently critical position, rely too much on the British press, and are tricked into 'hyping' and publicizing too many foreign groups much too soon. The quotes below amply illustrate the frustration:

The hype is created elsewhere, by the combination of the label, agent and, to a lesser extent, the manager. In my frustration, I say: 'We are dumb enough to go along.' Why? Why is it that Hanne Hukkelberg has an international deal while An Pierlé not? I do not understand this. The XX: fine by me, but why not another similar group? If a small label that has a quality label works long in advance, with a well-hyped club concert, with all digital sites and the support of NME, then everyone will start working on it. (...) And so the record label Domino can go on tour receiving pats on the back for Arctic Monkeys, the first so-called Internet group.

Everyone knows how important the UK is. Look at Sigur Rós: Without the support from England, they would never be where they are now, not as an band from Iceland. (...) Sometimes I'm baffled by how it works, how uncritical it all happens and how random it is. This year [2009, GK]: La Roux and Florence + the Machine, it was a self-fulfilling prophecy. In the beginning of the year the bands were put in the *Sound of* in the British press. This is the only reason why StuBru in Belgium also tipped them. Then the CD is released and NME gives it five stars, because for six months they have been telling that this is going to be the new hype. And at once everyone here thought it was fantastic. Moreover, everyone actually thought it was fantastic before the CD was even out. By definition, everything that comes from across the Channel happens in the same way. (...) That's why I think that Pitchfork is so important, making it possible for us to know what's cooking among the U.S.-based little bands, and not just among the American bands that are hyped in the UK. Previously, we always had this U.K. filter on U.S. bands.

To those involved, the influence of foreign alternative mainstream media does not come across as illegitimate. 'Has it ever been different?' one journalist wonders. 'I also can't tell if there's anything wrong with it,' says another one. 'Those foreign journalists just do their job like we do. Everybody is fed by the record companies.' Yet another says: 'That's simply the way it works. Foreign papers and magazines have the advantage that they are able to get a CD much earlier than we do here in Belgium.'

Whatever the case may be, at the time these matters may be discussed, the initial decision has already been taken elsewhere. Actors just follow role models, the channels that they trust. A self-fulfilling prophecy works best if the prediction originates with actors who emanate credibility. As Laermans (2010: 41) argues, it is often not the content of the prediction, but the social prestige of those making the prediction, which clinches the matter. When this prediction comes true, this prestige will only grow greater. This is what he calls the 'social circle of belief.'

Conformism

Chapter 5 explained that the alternative mainstream is a space where journalists and radio producers select on the basis of what they consider relevant for their national target audience. The fact that this relevance is bestowed upon music can also be the outcome of a systematic takeover of other actors' selections. Journalists, after all, are keenly aware of what other media do. Radio producers see what is very much alive in the written press, and vice versa. It fits in with Gielen's 'collective context logic,' because in the realm of this logic 'field actors keep an unremitting eye on each other, while their decisions are attuned to one another' (Gielen, 2003: 61). This causes second-order selection in a field to result in conformism. In the case of the radio, Rothenbuhler and McCourt use the notion of the *consensus cut*: records are only being played at the time everyone is playing them (Bennett (ed.) 2006: 315). Because everyone is looking at everyone else and taking over each other's selection, a 'spontaneous' consensus arises about what music is worth getting attention. Even though everyone applies a personal patch of nuance, it seems as if only one overarching (group) selection has been made. A journalist says:

> Between the media, mutual influence is much more frequent. Because the offer is greater and because as a journalist you only have so much time to make a selection, as well as increasingly less space to place reviews, the sum total will automatically be that many people end up with the same result. Because if you have five slots to fill with reviews, you have no choice but to put in at least two of which you can be certain that everyone else will have them too. You can always fill one or two slots based on the image

you want to cover, but then it is remarkable that so many media appear to target the same groups.

What sometimes comes across as conformism, but is not necessarily so, is the search for confirmation. Actors compare their own selections with those of others, to make sure they have not lost sight of anything and have not made any mistakes. One journalist, for instance, says that kindred magazines endorsed his choice of Joanna Newsom, whereas some freelancers may give four stars to a CD about which he will not find one piece elsewhere. The way actors seek confirmation with others is particularly appaent at the end of the year (Brennan 2006). Those who deviate rather too heavily from this cannot be said to keep a finger on the pulse.

> Control is something that I reserve for the end of the year, when it's time for the lists of the year: then I'll have a look to see if we have had them all. There's a kind of meta-feeling hanging about, of 'these here have been the most important.' You may have mixed feelings about this. It seems there are people who agree on everything. But if that's the case, everyone is basically writing the same as the other, and you are merely following the creed.

To follow this creed is also considered a sign of professional capital. A good journalist follows that which should be followed.

> I strongly believe that our assessments of this are generally good. Of the groups that broke through in the past few years, we missed very little. I'm not saying we don't make mistakes, but in general, the margin of error is very small.

When confirmation effectively becomes conformism, the remarkable effect can be that actors revise their initial decision: music that was first rejected is picked up again. This often happens when something is successful abroad or is tipped by leading foreign channels. When journalists start putting in requests with the record companies for the same promotional CD that was already sent to them earlier, this often happens when a group that was initially unknown suddenly becomes a hype abroad. For the same reason, one manager says, distribution firms often only begin working on a title at that particular moment. In some interviews certain actors said about radio stations — albeit off the record or in informal conversations —that this explains why a previously rejected record can still end up in the playlist. Nobody wants to say it aloud, but respondents do indicate that there are frequent cases at Studio Brussels of persons in charge of music blocking music until they learn that the music is a hype in the UK. One week, certain acts can be dismissed as 'alternative crap' or 'corny' stuff; the next week, they can be picked up anyway 'because it's in the BBC playlist.' 'That's common stuff,' one respondent says. 'These people are your typical ratings and lists people, who keep an eye on everything, both domestic and foreign.' Another respondent says that some playlist editors are not heard when they come up with a proposition at the playlist meeting, but that afterwards the blame will be laid at their door for having missed the boat. It is clear that in these cases, as pragmatist sociology will argue, people alter their frame of reference depending on the situation and thus revise their decision. Something is first rejected based on an individual logic (the initial situation), but following a hype created abroad (the new situation) this decision is revoked and revised from an organizational logic. 'This music is hot, so we must go for it.' A choice that was initially legitimized in an individual manner consequently becomes a social or collective choice.

Second-Order Selection as Risk Reduction

The Media as Attention Machine

For those working in the music industry, the result of making a selection is invariably uncertain. The previous chapters showed that the players develop actions to reduce uncertainty, for instance by relying on their professional capital and building relationships of trust. There is, however, yet another way for them to reduce the uncertainty: second-order-observation, which is a strategy adopted by organizers, managers and record companies in order to reduce the risk of their decisions by looking at what receives a lot of attention in the media. The actors look at the media because the public also looks at the media, or more correctly, because they assume that the public indeed looks at the media. This is a reductive equation: media attention is viewed as synonymous with public attention. Once the media have made their selection (which is partially also an instance of second-order-observation), that selection may start weighing on the selection by others. Even more, it will soon be clear that the effect of media attention on decisions in the music industry is not to be underestimated.

One notable trait of concert organizers in the way they make a selection is that they look to the media in order to estimate the potential public reach. 'Without airplay there is very little chance that you'll have a venue concert that works well,' a programmer says.[2] Two festival organizers confirm this view:

> To people, a festival is quite an experience. They will go to a concert to be able to clap and sing along. You should always consider this. When people recognize songs that are played on the radio, they get a good feeling from it. I think that's important. Popularity is an important criterion. (...) Besides, this also applies to Rock Werchter. Nearly everything that is billed there, must have been played on the radio, must have hits.

> When I choose groups, media attention is always an important factor, either airplay, or what has been written about it (...) If two groups are of the same quality and one receives media attention and the other doesn't, I will choose the first. We don't do a group without media

attention, because in those cases there's only very few people who will come and watch. I don't gain anything by doing it, and neither does the group (...) A radio hit is something that simply needs to be there. Only then the people really want to see it.

Obviously not every selection is guided by current media attention. Established names, groups with a long reputation, have less need for media coverage because they have received it on several occasions in the past. For niche programming in small clubs or the smaller stages of festivals, this is also less important. In those cases, the logic of the underground kicks in. 'For bands that I put in the club, I don't always look at the playlist,' a programmer says. However, for the larger stages and the 'bands of the hour,' media attention is crucial. The same goes for the marketing and promotion set up − at the input side − by record companies and management agencies for their groups. When they sign new artists, there is often no question of media attention. Still, the potential for it can already play a part in the selection. In his study of Dutch A&R managers Zwaan (2009: 33) determined that record companies keep a close watch on media politics, because these remain crucial in the circulation or diffusion of music: they want music that fits in with the profile of the media, which could get into their playlist. In this study, a label boss puts it like this:

To the general public airplay on the radio remains the main gateway. All the rest is merely support. Which is why you start to think in terms of the formats the radios use. (...) The first step is the battle in the media, starting with the radio and then a bit of press. Evidently, things depend on the target audience. If you're talking about Studio Brussels, you're dealing with a relatively young audience, people who have their laptop or smartphone tuned to Radio One, and their radio on Radio Two. But these people don't read newspapers or magazines, they don't care, and they're probably right. Actually, Internet is everything and nothing. If you put aside the internet, radio is still #1, I think. When push comes to shove, radio is much more important than the written press, which matters to the older reader who may have to work more than other people, who doesn't listen as much to the radio, or maybe plays his or her own selection like I do.

It is typical that the same record company boss also defines the markets and target groups on which his firm will focus by means of radio stations.

> The entire network and the community that surround a radio station form what you might call the market. In Flanders this is manifestly so. Each radio station represents a different market. With the culture and the people who work here, we focus on Studio Brussels and Radio 1. Which is commercially not always the most sensible thing to do. Because in that case, you'd be better off with the market that exists around MNM and Q-Music.

The respondents view radio as the most important link in the chain. For the alternative mainstream, TV has a significantly lower importance. In the interviews, only few references were made to typical music channels (MTV, TMF or possibly JIM). 'This kind of music doesn't get a great deal of chances on these TV stations,' one manager comments. 'They have no role to play anymore,' says another respondent. The impact of TV is situated on a different level: TV is essential for circulation, for moving up to the mainstream. Musical guests of popular TV shows (talk shows, quiz shows, etc.) have an instantaneous opportunity to present themselves to a mass public. This, for example, is what happened to the lead singer of Flemish band Das Pop. By participating in a popular quiz, he became a Flemish celebrity. As he personally testified in a newspaper: 'The theaters are full, the tours are sold out. There are certainly quite a few among these people who before the show didn't even know we existed.' (*De Standaard* 21.12.2010).

The Impact of Radio Airplay in Flanders - The Case of Studio Brussels

Artists who want to make it in show business need public exposure and media coverage. In the music business, the key to success is radio airplay. It is this simple fact that determines the way in which the mediating industry actors will work on, around and with a particular band. This is the digital age. Is it not remarkable, even peculiar that in Flanders a traditional radio station like Studio

Brussels[3] continues to be a dominant point of reference and catalyst? The interviewed actors all agree that the station plays a crucial role in the careers of those Flemish artists who are active in the alternative mainstream. The station decides whether they will be able to break through to a broader public. This manager is very clear about it:

> When you wish to become something in the Belgian story of music, you need to get into the daily rotation of Studio Brussels. If you don't succeed in climbing on board, the attention you will get by playing will be limited and you will simply stay 'promising.' Bands may have raving reviews, but without StuBru hits they will never be a 'made' band, and reach the level of established groups. In its genre, StuBru is the almighty god.

Airplay is what determines the opportunities for concerts. When artists want to make it to the better spots and be on the bill of the bigger festivals, they must be heard on the radio. This is perfectly obvious to all managers: a single on Stubru is what it takes to convince organizers. Promoters are very explicit about the fact that their target group consists of Studio Brussels listeners, and that this why they keep an eye on the playlist. Consider the words of this programmer:

> Our venue's profile is StuBru. Any group, who manages to get airplay on the station, has an immediate advantage. StuBru means a window to a live audience, full stop.

The bookers are of the same opinion. In order to place groups and sell many tickets, airplay on Studio Brussels is indispensable. 'There's really no alternative,' one respondent says.[4]

An additional argument in this story is a listing in *De Afrekening*, the hit parade or Top 100 chart that is drawn from votes made by StuBru's listeners. Even though the impact and significance of this alternative chart will be downplayed further on, record companies grant a Belgian group immediate and higher priority if it has a number in *De Afrekening*. Festivals, for their part, base their choices 'in the spring on everything that has made the list,' one programmer claims. A label boss claims it even goes further than that:

> The effort we have to put in getting a group booked after they have made it to *De Afrekening*, compared to the effort we used to invest before the group hit the chart, is colossal. Even though StuBru doesn't have the highest ratings, *De Afrekening* is still the barometer for all those surrounding the station: the live circuit, the journalists. *De Afrekening* works from the 10th place and then bookers are able to use this, as from the 5th place on clubs and festivals will be present themselves. Organizers that initially rejected offers for 400 euros, will afterwards come begging for five times that sum. They really use *De Afrekening* as a barometer.

The bookers confirm this. They look at the list on a weekly basis and use it in the story they tell as bookers.

> I don't even need to take the list with me, since every organizer knows whether or not a group is in *De Afrekening*. The fact that you are in it as a group will no doubt get you a lot of extra bookings.

Apart from this, airplay is also said to have an effect on CD sales. Some respondents claim that in Flanders, and in these days of crisis, CDs can only be sold if they get daytime rotation on Studio Brussels. Consider this promotion manager's words:

> If what you have is only good written press, this doesn't mean you're straight away good to take off. Perhaps you'll sell a couple of hundred records, but bingo? I don't think so. You've learned it the hard way yourself, haven't you, with Briskey [this author's band, GK]: you're well received, you get into the leading press, but that alone won't make you sell loads of records. You always need the radio. (...) But if you only get airplay in the evening programs, then you don't get any further than those odd thousand music freaks in Flanders. That's not a basis to grow from, right? What you need is to be played in daytime.

Besides Studio Brussels, Radio 1 is also a station that elicits the careful watch of the actors, although some respondents think this is already a different segment. All respondents, however, are explicit in affirming this: 'commercial' radio stations such as MNM, JOE fm or Q-music are to be ignored (the same goes for the Netherlands, where 3FM is crucial to any breakthrough in the club circuit, whereas 538, Q-music and Sky Radio belong to the other 'side'). The 'real' mainstream media, therefore, do not work for the alternative mainstream.

The Impact of the Written Press in Flanders — The Case of *Humo* and the Rock Rally

Besides the radio, the written press also has some impact, which was already clear from the foregoing. One label boss says:

> A small review of a Belgian band in *Humo* does not translate into more CD sales. But if you're 'CD of the Week' in *Humo* — and the same goes for *De Morgen* or *Focus Knack* — you can hear the roll of drums. A large interview in *De Morgen* also has a greater impact than a regular review.

With respect to the Flemish written press, the respondents consider the weekly magazine *Humo* the most significant. In addition to general news and a TV guide, the magazine pays a lot of attention to 'alternative' rock music. 'I too will rise to the bait of worshipping *Humo* as the holiest of things,' a record label boss says, 'but the simple fact is that it's the most important player and that you simply must try to get into it.' Attention paid in *Humo* is not only of consequence in the yarn told by the bookers, it is also important in winning over others. 'A good review in *Humo* is of great importance in convincing others,' says an organizer. One manager argues: 'Such a review won't make you sell more CDs, but it can play a role in the perception of the group and urge the doubters in the industry to go and check it out anyway.' In those cases, it is social prestige and the symbolic capital of an actor that will play a role, combined with the concomitant carry-away effect. Newspapers too, for that matter, have this influence. 'The number of readers is not the only criterion, it's also what kind of readers,' a journalist remark.

Humo can also punch an impact thanks to its Rock Rally (which may be compared to De Grote Prijs in the Netherlands).

All respondents agree that this is the leading rock competition in Flanders. Rock bands that wish to get somewhere have no other choice but to participate. Even though the contest is all about live concerts, it mainly thanks its impact to the media attention paid to it, in the first place by initiator *Humo* itself. The magazine really wet-nurses the finalists and gives full coverage week upon week, several respondents are keen to observe. The people at *Humo* think this is quite logical:

> In a way, you commit yourself to these bands when you put them in the finals. If you think something's good in the beginning and it goes on to develop well, it can also stay a selection. Otherwise, it's a once-only thing and you shouldn't pay too much attention to it. That would be a little bit dumb. (...) You know the said groups better, that's a fact. When I receive a CD by a finalist, I tend to think: if these hadn't participated in the Rock Rally, I probably would have been less quick to listen to it.

In addition, it is said that *Humo* writes ostensibly less about groups that were not in the Rock Rally and in doing so enlarges the importance of the competition. One manager notes:

> A Belgian group will be in *Humo* primarily when they have participated in the Rock Rally. Other bands will not particularly be thwarted or hindered, but I have never received any back support from them unless they are inescapable and have had several singles in *De Afrekening*.

Apart from *Humo*, other media such as *De Morgen*, *De Standaard* and Studio Brussels provide extensive coverage of the event. 'It gives a group a platform,' one manager says. 'The whole press writes about the circus.' Whoever gets into the finals of the Rock Rally is not only certain of a great deal of media attention, but also gets an unmediated opportunity to present themself to the music industry. The Rock Rally acts as a collective ritual for those who work in the industry. From this gathering of the clan a lot of record contracts and management deals originate, according to the interviewed managers. There too the social process of selection is started. When the CD is released afterwards, the group again gets media attention. 'Then, evidently, we're going to watch carefully if they do well,' a journalist says. Furthermore, it will be easier for the finalists to get concerts, as the managers, the bookers and the organizers all agree: 'If the CD will be a fact, as an organizer you simply need to jump on board of the train.' A place in the finals of the Rock Rally can, therefore, deliver name recognition and can contribute to the desired uncertainty reduction. The Rock Rally, after all, plants the first seeds and thus helps in creating a vibe around a group. In this sense, a programmer asserts that he too can be an extra link in the chain for a group, yet to launch them is not something he will be able to do, 'whereas the Rock Rally can do this for a band.' But to put things in perspective: 'To make it to the finals in the Rock Rally does not guarantee success, but it certainly helps.' In the end, in any case, airplay remains vital, most respondents think. This is something the people at *Humo* are well aware of: 'You may very well get coverage in *Humo*, but without airplay ... You also need to have airplay.'

Power or Perverted Effect?

It is a truism to claim that press attention is crucial for an artist's career. An American study from 2012 by the reputed agency Nielsen showed that radio remains dominant as a source for discovering new music. Moreover, and surprisingly, with a score of 48% radio would seem to leave other channels of discovery such as the Internet etc. far behind (Nielsen 2012). Previously, it was observed that rock academics have concluded in numerous studies that the media in pop music are the main gatekeepers and meaning makers. These facts are also confirmed in the conducted research. It is true that the traditional music industry has come under pressure from the digital revolution, and that alternative ways of developing a public have been added (see p. 111). Nevertheless, in order to get national attention, and consequently force a breakthrough in the alternative mainstream, the established channels (media coverage, the right concerts and contacts) remain as important as ever. This is at least the case for the actors in the alternative mainstream itself, ensuring that it remains a social fact. In the selection process, the eyes of the actors are set on the media, specifically focusing on those channels that constitute definitive features of, and most prominently give shape to the alternative mainstream — as was cited numerous times in this study. Because of the importance that is attributed to these media, a distribution of symbolic capital arises to which actors reconcile themselves, but which, as will soon become clear, is also questioned. The fact is, there is a perceived influence: if you watch an actor a great deal, and think this actor exerts an influence, he or she will indeed have a great deal of influence. It is a typical example of a self-fulfilling prophecy. It also explains the (relative) position of power occupied by Studio Brussels in particular inside of the Flemish alternative mainstream.

Actors attach importance to media interest in order to make their choice less risk-prone, in an attempt to reduce risk. An artist's popularity or name recognition, which functions as a selection criterion, does not merely possess an economic or quantitative aspect. The social factor is also active here. The point is that this or that artist is talked about, that it is clear who is the talk of the town. In Laermans' view (2011a and 2011b), this is typical of the 'attention regime.' It is a property of our contemporary information society. Because of the excess of information, attention needs to be continuously stimulated, and in this, the media play an important role. In this way, something can increasingly get more attention and acquire a broader 'support base.' The interviewed actors therefore look at the media as an attention machine and assume that this attention also has an effect. Even though there is no watertight guarantee that artists whose name is circulating in the circuit also have an easier time attracting people (there are always examples that prove the contrary, see below), the assumption is that it does help. It is in this manner that every actor interprets the information derived from the circuit based on his or her accumulated professional capital. More than anything else, it is a game of observation and, at the same time, of participation. Exactly this is what enhances the effect. This is also clear from the following comment made by a manager:

> The majority of the public needs a guide. They ask that someone else acts as the filter and makes the selection. As a result, this is *Humo* and Studio Brussels and not some weirdo from Finland who teaches you a thing or two over the Internet. If you're not among those, you run into troubles and are unable to move forward, and people start cursing. The fact is that you cannot but play the game.

Breaking Through in the Alternative Mainstream

By way of second-order observation, the players in the music industry take the media and such media can take over one another's judgment. That may generate a snowball effect. As each selection entails ever more other selections, when everyone starts to watch everyone else, with interactions between media, record companies, managers, bookers and organizers, a collective game arises of mutual influence and certain effects of accumulation may come about. Because this social process is also a consecration cycle in which the gatekeepers in the music field give meaning to music and musicians (this is why they were called 'cultural intermediaries' in Chapter 2), there is also an impact on the development of artists' careers. If we want to examine these effects, a shift takes place in the perspective of this study, which will thus draw to its end.[5]

Convergence and Coincidence of Attention

The influence one single player could have on the rest, is relative. But when all attention coincides, an influence can indeed be observed. Then an artist can gain enough popularity to break through in the alternative mainstream. This is also how the media view things: for a strong effect, you should win over as many main channels as possible. In the words of a journalist:

> You are a cog in the whole machine. (...) I think the media are too fragmented to really have a great effect. It does have effect when a release has ten interviews coming up in the same week, the number is also picked up by the radio and the clip is shown on TV.

This is why a marketing manager says that running promotion in Belgium and the Netherlands at the same time is both 'incredibly easy and incredibly difficult.' Because you have only a few crucial media to take care of, you need to try to convince only a few journalists.

> And then the rest follows. But if none of those four journalists of the written press is with you, you have nothing in Belgium. It happens frequently that my foreign labels ask me to account for the fact that I simply

haven't got anything. This is something that happens, you see?

When it does happen that all players are going along, it may give rise to a hype: one is the first to discuss it, then another follows, and all of a sudden, everybody wants to hear and see the same music. A hype, therefore, is more than merely some media attention. An artist or act is on everybody's lips, which certainly has an effect on concerts. He or she is asked for radio sessions, charity, special projects, and so on. It is the finest example of an accumulation effect. About the impact on concerts, an organizer says:

> When a group's presence in the media is very frequent, not only on the radio, but also in the papers and magazines, the direct result of this is that the ticket sales will rise. One single review is not going to make any difference, but if it's everywhere, you can bet it's going to have an effect. For example, when Admiral Freebee appears in every magazine, there would really be a problem if we didn't get everything to sell out. Most of the visitors, who come to the big venue concerts, are people who listen to what is said in the media and are prompted by it to attend the concert.

A hype is not only the effect of a shared selection; it is also the source for further selection. A hype makes others jump on board of the train. A festival organizer admits being susceptible to a hype, because the audience 'is going to check it in advance, because they've heard that it will be cool, that you simply have to see this, and so they really want to go.' Concerts too can lead to new concerts. As one record label boss told about one of his groups being billed on a festival:

> There are also people of the club circuit present and these could persuade themselves of the fact that this was something good. Precisely because of this, you'll get calls from organizers who initially refused to do the group. Consequently, it is a reinforcing fact. One thing reaffirms the other.

Only when interaction arises between attention in various media *and* good concerts, will the second-order selection and its impact grow. For illustration purposes, three managers will tell (part of) their story with a few successful Flemish groups (Mintzkov, Customs and Isbells, in that order). While they are at it, they provide a look into the ins and outs of the Flemish music industry.

> The first singles by Mintzkov, in the wake of the Rock Rally, didn't get much airplay. 'Mimosa' (2004), by contrast, got a lot of airplay and became an audience favorite. The result was that our public became broader and that we got easy access to festivals (Lowlands and Dranouter), something we would have never had without the Rock Rally and 'Mimoza.' (...) The second CD in 2007 made it three times into *De Afrekening*. This shows what StuBru's support for the group has been and that the public followed up on that by voting them into De Afrekening. Back then, Mintzkov was the group. We got excellent reviews in *Humo, Knack, De Morgen*, later the CD became the highest Belgian CD in the year lists, and we had a really great show at Pukkelpop. In that time more people converted to being a Mintzkov fan than there ever had been before.

> Customs was first spotted when they won a competition that got support from Studio Brussels. The station then put the group below in the playlist. The playlist editors gradually started to put the number in the list. When, for instance, the music coordinator hears that the niche editors keep programming the track, he can give it a chance in the daytime rotation. Even though Customs didn't immediately skyrocket, at one point the big shots were there: front page in *Focus*, ' CD of the Week ' in *De Morgen, Humo*, the single got into *De Afrekening*. And then everybody wants to go along, and the taps are open. We didn't ask for it. It just happened, based on getting twice into *De Afrekening* and being the talk of the town. As a result all the popular TV programs also wanted the group in their show. Suddenly, all the players are present. Now StuBru already wants to know what the next single

is going to be, in view of the new *De Afrekening* CD. People are anticipating what is still to come.. As soon as you have two singles, you're there, and you only have to keep on working with support.

One of *Humo*'s journalists came to pick up some records at my place, heard Isbells' pre-mastered CD and was deeply impressed. When the first single came out, he immediately put them in the listening list and announced the album. When the CD was released, he wrote really super review. *De Morgen* too ran a raving four-star review, *De Standaard* paid a visit to the singer's barn for a full-length interview, and *Humo* did one as well. This was all within three weeks following the release. So everyone already had this feeling ... Then I went to the radio with the single. Radio 1 immediately went along; StuBru waited for a week, but then made it Hotshot. Hotshot! That's when everything took off. (...) And StuBru didn't dump Isbells later on. The group did a studio session and played at all the station's major events. The record sales and concerts took off. There was a simple reason for it. The number was in the top of StuBru's playlist, and in *De Afrekening*. Those are the things that attract the organizers' attention. As for myself, the bookings ran without a hitch. Actually, I didn't have to look for anything at all. I simply said yes or no to requests. (...) And all this when I initially thought to have signed your typical niche group. In any case, Studio Brussels was the catalyst in this story. Absolutely.

Strategic Selection

Those who want to build artist careers in the music industry — record companies, managers, bookers — always have one thing in mind, that the choices of all relevant actors must converge, correspond or coincide. This is why the actors' selections are also strategic selections. Each time the actors examine what strategy works best. This is based on two things: making full use of the network, and making sure that all noses point in the same direction. A typical example: during the interview I conducted with an actor from a record company — the location was the Ancienne Belgique terrace in Brussels — he started talking about a specific

group. It happened so that a few moments later the booker of the group walked by. 'Pukkelpop has been confirmed and there are options in the AB and two other concert halls,' he said. Upon which the respondent replied: 'They're 'CD of the Week' in *Humo*. Now others will wake up. So that's launched from now on.' Such situations are part of the music industry's daily routine. Bookers think and work in the same way.

> If you want to build up a good live reputation, you also need to think strategically. Strategy is important and sometimes even more important than the fee. You have a good concert when there's a large crowd, when the press is present and in the correct room — otherwise you can count me out. It is not a matter of playing as many times as possible, but to play on a beautiful moment, on the best location, or as supporting act for a good group.

For record companies, such a strategy forms the foundation of the promotional campaign. As one respondent puts it: they will go and talk to the key people well in advance, will regularly send out press releases, unblock new tracks free as appetizers for the CD, try to have all the interviews published at the same time around the release, ensure that there is a tour following on the release, and so on. By doing so they hope to somewhat reduce the previously described uncertainty:

> Already from the start of the campaign, you get these first comments from people who are curious. You begin to feel that there's something in the air and that things will work out: then you start to build something up. It makes it less of a lottery show. By occupying yourself with it in an organizationally sound way, you increase the chance that something will be viewed as important.

For the same reason attempts are made to push through the move from evening to daytime programming, or make a small review by a freelancer grow into an interview with one of the senior editors. A label manager therefore prefers his groups to be able to grow organically, in a natural way from the bottom up. 'You have to make sure that you have that first inflow and that it jumps over, catches on with the rest.' Another record boss translates this into marketing terms: the effect that a record company wants to achieve with its campaign, is that the public will eventually grow to like an artist even more. The way to do this is by contact conditioning.

> You look for a marketing mix and try to make it thicker. Radio is an important part in the gateway, but you also try to reach people via TV and the written press, on the internet, on the shopping floor and in the general street scene. (...) What you will try to realize with such a marketing mix is that people say: 'Artist X is really breaking through now, there's a lot more going on around the man.' That's based on nothing, that's marketing. As if I were in the store and thought: I should really have that brand. But who says that it is a better brand? It's never been proven scientifically. It's just a brand that's better known, more popular. Which is really not the same as better. Name and fame is the core business of marketing. Fame is trust, and trust makes people bind, and think it's better. In the case of music 'better' is 'more lovely, more beautiful.' (...) And that's of course exactly what we want to achieve. That someone opens the newspaper, artist X; and that he looks in a magazine, again artist X. Then there's a reaction: 'Maybe this guy has made a good record.' That's what you want to make happen. It's possible if you can deliver different kinds of stings. to play a record once is not enough for airplay. Contact conditioning, that's what it's called.

In order to get this effect, the record company and the management often venture upon very deliberately sophisticated actions which will make the media supposedly discover the music by themselves, or which will create the impression that the music is bobbing up spontaneously from the social network sites. A manager:

> People want to be the ones who decide themselves. That's why it's a good thing when, for example, an artist's breakthrough is said to have originated from the internet. We can also intentionally wait with the release of the record, and first put the artist on a small festival stage: there the media people are free to discover him themselves and launch him as 'the next big thing' in the press.

> How the business deal with an artist came into being,
> is not part of the subsequent story you want to bring to
> the outside world.

Evidently, this remains an ideal. Whatever the strategy followed, the outcome will always remain uncertain. Everybody has examples of groups for which the same arsenal of media was mobilized, but where things faltered and did not work. 'Then an act may get stuck in a little corner,' a record label boss says. Typical is also the promotion manager admitting that he is still not able to assess what is possible or not on the radio, even after twenty years of professional experience: 'That's still the greatest mystery.'

Interlude

Dropping Out of the Rat Race

It is fairly obvious that those who want to build an international career, will need to succeed in all these steps in every new country that has to be conquered. Moreover, in every country the artists should be able to rely on the same kind of network. However, being able to push beyond national borders is not always a guarantee for lasting success on the home front. Second-order selection can actually also explain the dynamics in the segment model, as it was introduced in this study (see schema 2). In the foregoing, examples have been given of how groups can break through in the alternative mainstream. The fact is that a breakthrough only accrues to a lucky few. Because the media and the industry swear by a rigid selection, they cannot pick up everything. Most music remains stuck in the underground niche in which it originated. It used to be that artists were trapped in their own village; today they are drowning in a globalized oversupply. Groups that are only active in an underground circuit usually find very little resonance outside. In such cases, it can be a good first step for them to do their own promotion (consider, for example, Milow, who already had a basic public before he broke through). Apparently, a breakthrough is only realized by way of the traditional media and industry. As a result, one manager argues, there is a problem with the upward flow of the groups: 'many groups get stuck in the club circuit and are hardly able to draw a crowd of 500 people for a concert.'

A group may very well have a once-only spot at a big festival, and as a result, they may get extra press attention around that specific time. For a group to develop a more solid artistic career, however, and consolidate into an established value, this attention needs to be renewed repeatedly, and new second-order observations need to take place over and over again. 'Sometimes it's simply not in the cards, and the projected growth can suddenly hit a ceiling, simply because the music isn't suited for it,' an organizer says. It certainly explains why groups that have been picked up can disappear from the sphere of interest. If there are no new hits, or due to a failed concert on an important place, because of discussions on forums, or of changed trends, following negative press reports etc., the vibe can vanish. Then the media attention and the concert opportunities start to fade away, and the entire

selection carrousel can grind to a halt and stop spinning. An example is Motek. Their success story was finished after one hit single. Because there was no second single on their CD, several respondents argue, the group ended up back in the niche where it came from. 'Then such a group costs too much money and isn't able to draw a crowd anymore,' one programmer argues from an organizational logic.[6] From a career perspective, one manager says in a more general way, it is therefore never any good for a group to climb up too quickly and immediately get to the biggest stages. 'Because if you can't continue to live up to the expectations, you can be quickly back to square one.' He also points out that some things are released far too early on the public.

> Artists should actually skip the first record and be stern with themselves until the music is perfect. This is often not the case, and then the entourage starts complaining that nothing is working and that the music isn't picked up. Then they start pointing the finger at the press or blame the 'power games.' But you can't use the holes in your business model as explanations for things that fail to work. It's also about the music itself. When something's not good, it won't stand out among the rest.

No matter how, because of a lack of second-order selection, an artist can end up a step lower in the alternative mainstream or in the underground, or, at best, end up in the waiting room of the alternative mainstream (temporarily disappear from attention in order to play back along afterwards). Then again, it may just as well be a conscious choice to stay in a niche circuit. DAAU is a good example, their manager says: a non-rock band with classical instruments which still made a name in the rock circuit (as was said before, thanks to the dEUS-connection, among other things), only to vanish again from there briefly afterwards.

> The group got a major deal, even more concerts and attention from the press. Yet Studio Brussels chose to ignore them. DAAU saw its moment of glory on the other side of the street, but there were trucks driving in between. (...) The group was too stubborn and too quirky for the plan Sony had drawn up for them. They had the feeling of being caught in a trap and were disappointed that promises were broken.

Although they are often forced to do so, groups such as DAAU may in fact choose for a career independent of the traditional industry. They forget about wanting to break through to a wider audience and look up the niche. They direct themselves toward the Internet communities, and evening programming on national radio becomes the highest attainable in the typical alternative mainstream media. In *Art Worlds* Becker (1982: 34-35) pointed out that making unconventional works is not impossible, but only harder to do, and that it will take more work, effort and time. When artists create works which the existing established institutions have no clue what to do about, these works stand no chance of being exhibited or distributed. Those who choose to ignore the existing aesthetic system will run into trouble. However, they will have gained the greatest artistic freedom.

The Ambivalence of Second-Order Selection

‖ Dependence versus Independence

Whatever the importance of second-order observation in the selection process, and whatever the number of examples cited in the interviews by the respondents, the statements they make are invariably ambiguous. Sometimes this is merely out of ignorance. Among different respondents, opposing statements are heard, perhaps induced by different experiences. Take, for instance, what is said about the impact of a CD in a leading magazine. 'A good review in that magazine means a couple of hundred extra CD copies sold,' one respondent says. Another contradicts this: 'This used to be the case, but not anymore. The monopoly such a magazine possessed in either allowing groups to break through or not has been heavily truncated.' Usually, the earlier described relation of tension that exists between dependence and independence induces ambiguity in the alternative mainstream. After all, second-order selection can come across as illegitimate behavior, as a sign of dependency, and no actor will be in a hurry to display this publicly. The result is that actors wish to defend themselves and will never admit that they adopt or copy something indiscriminately. In these cases, socially desirable or acceptable behavior is what counts: respondents are reluctant to admit that their opinion is co-determined by others, which explains why they emphasize their individual logic of legitimacy. This independent position and autonomous freedom of choice will be defended with tooth and nail.

The Filter of Personal Taste

The most common means of defense consists in emphasizing personal taste. The legitimate filter of personal taste is applied without pause on social factors. Personal taste is pushed forward as the absolute basis that serves to demonstrate that an actor is staying a headstrong, self-willed course. This can be observed very clearly when those media are discussed that let themselves be influenced by other domestic and foreign media. Actors will check out what is hyped abroad, but not without a critical assessment of the music's quality. Almost all respondents confirm that they keep a close eye on the foreign media, but promptly add during the interview that the selection is only adopted or copied when they also think the music is good — and this in accordance with the aesthetics that was discussed earlier. Because personal taste, a singular taste of one's own, is predominant, the actors do not perceive themselves as blind followers of hypes ('If it's no good, I won't play it,' a radio man says). This, again, is authenticated and substantiated with numerous examples. Respondents claim they often just ignore such foreign groups, but that they occasionally review them, for example, 'to warn the reader about the record, that it's not worth its money.' Even then, ambiguity can be heard in their voice, as is the case with this festival organizer:

> Of the *Sound of*, there are five that are on our festival's bill. Yet not because we follow the list indiscriminately. In those cases, the agent also has a bit. And I still hope that bands get into those *Sound of* based on quality. (...) I personally think we are critical enough. I don't think we take over everything just like that. We do it partially, but Avi Buffalo for example: I happened to stumble on them on the internet and I booked them. Now it turns out the NME is writing pages about it. Then I think that's so much to the good. But I've also booked groups which I'm the only one to like and which are only able to fill half of the small tent. (...) Maybe I'm contradicting myself, but I don't think this is something which I will consider very much in my bookings. Whenever I believe in something, I book it.

The same is heard in Flanders with respect to Rock Rally finalists. Initially, finalists have a news value for all members of the press. When they release a CD, however, it is the artistic judgment of the evaluating individual that prevails. One journalist puts it like this: 'Why is it that we choose to go further with one finalist and not with the other? Because we think the story of the first is somewhat more appealing.' Alternatively, a programmer about booking yet another finalist: 'The Rock Rally may have played an instrumental role, but they certainly have good little singles.' The fact that the individual judgment is central to every action is also demonstrated when journalists, for example, claim they often write about artists who have no media attention yet, or before they are hyped by others: 'In those circumstances, I only follow my own taste.' As was said before, to select, however, is primarily a story of *and-and*, and therefore inherently ambiguous. The excerpt from an interview with a programmer below bears witness to this. In it, the constant back and forth, the give and take between personal taste and external influence is beautifully expressed:

> **Respondent** I'm also not always immediately convinced of something. While this'll get four stars everywhere and is discussed on every single blog and site, and on StuBru as well, I, for my part, still need to be convinced and am not inclined to put it straightaway on a stage.

> **GK** When can you be convinced?

> **Respondent** Sometimes it can take a long time, by putting a lot of time in it, trying to get a grasp of it. But by doing so I have also missed things, such as Arcade Fire: At first, I didn't have the feeling.

> **GK** What will you allow yourself to be guided by?

> **Respondent** For that purpose, I read the proper magazines and sites. I also have my friends whom I'll call for advice, people who are on to the Zeitgeist. This sort of thing really influences me. I need a second opinion. It happens quite a lot that I'm in doubt. This second opinion can also be my girlfriend, but that's often not enough.

> **GK** In your case you will revise your decision because of an influence from outside.

> **Respondent** Certainly. At that moment, I will have heard the group's name a few times already and you feel that when the group will get response anywhere, when their music will be on the right blogs, there will also be an agent ready to jump on it. You're able to see this so much faster than others are. Then you know that something is going on. When you see it live afterwards, you're thinking 'Ah yes, this is so right.' With The Drums I also wasn't the first to go along right away. Then you see them live: that guitarist, that live sound, that front man of whom only once in two years a

specimen is born. Then it gets to me and then I get it.

GK So you still give a group you didn't like at first a chance and then you think they're all right.

Respondent That's weird, right. Well, I don't know, I'm running into trouble here ... With women, things are not always love at first sight, you need to have a chat first. And it's not as if my pals must come up to me first and tell me that it's a first rate vamp. Of course, you allow yourselves to be influenced by the views of others. I too am no longer able to keep track of everything. Who is?

Counterexamples

What the actors love to add to this – an equally popular form of defense, for that matter – are counterexamples. Against each statement about how the music industry works, the exact opposite is raised as a counterargument. In a discourse that is constructed with practical examples, this is also the most effective way to offer justifications. Consider, for example, the point raised about *Humo*'s Rock Rally. To be the winner of the finals is now said to be far from a guarantee for public success. A programmer asserts: 'Take Charlie 45, who have never achieved anything.' Vice versa, one booker says, 'You can name ten examples of Belgian groups that were able to break through without the Rock Rally.' When *Humo* is confronted with people from the industry who argue that artists or bands will have a hard time getting into the magazine without some connection with the Rock Rally, one of the *Humo* people answers:

> That's what the record companies keep telling everybody. It's those who can't get in. And there are more than enough examples to prove the opposite: The Bony King of Nowhere, Selah Sue, Hooverphonic.

The link between airplay and concerts is also believed to fail. Both concert organizers and radio people offer examples of artists who were played frequently, but went on to sell very few records or did not appeal to the public. Then again, they also point out the opposite: artists that are only occasionally heard on the radio, yet still manage to sell out concert halls. Rock trio

Triggerfinger is the most commonly cited example: a group that was not picked up by the radio, but managed to become popular thanks to a strong live reputation. 'Triggerfinger is the living proof that people are able to build up on their own by means of their concerts,' one manager says.

The duality is also very typical when it comes to taking on foreign hypes. The respondents then give examples of groups that were praised abroad (Pixie Lott, Viva Brown, Little Boots, Kasabian) while they never managed to gain any footing in Belgium. The reverse movement is also possible: hype in Belgium, but not in the UK. The respondents perceive this as a sign of the autonomy and headstrong nature of the Belgian decision makers, who are able to indicate and choose what is good independently from the foreign hypes. A journalist cites Editors, a radio producer The Streets, and a record boss pulls out a range of examples from the cabinet:

> Groups like Radiohead, Air Traffic, The Kooks, Starsailor and Coldplay had their first gold records in Belgium, without these ever being pushed from across the Channel, because they were less hot at the time. We gave them everything we had promotionally, without the same having happened in England, or somebody giving the example. Even though it will often fail because it doesn't come from over there...

Minimizing and Denial

Another form of defense is to minimize the fact that actors take over or copy each other's selections, or even deny that it happens. Thus radio-makers claim they are not influenced by the playlist of other stations ('Obviously we will have a look at it, but they will never be of any deciding influence to us,' one of them says). One respondent manages to deny the impact of the Rock Rally by referring to his failing memory: 'By the time those finalists bring out a CD, I have already forgotten that they ever were in the Rock Rally.' One journalist maintains that it is impossible for him to be influenced by colleagues, because he 'does not know in advance who is doing something about an artist.' Yet another is convinced that radio has no influence whatsoever on him.

> I rarely if ever listen to the radio; I don't receive a playlist, not from the official hit parade nor from

De Afrekening. I really take pains to guard myself against it, because the chance that you will allow yourself to be influenced is indeed very real. Which is why there's often a very peculiar course we embark upon, of things that are very much picked up on the radio, but are ignored by us, and vice versa.

This might be a sign of socially accepted behavior, as is evidenced by the fact that some only confirm what they are trying to deny. Because different respondents argue, and this is still a form of defense, that they, for their part, do not follow the foreign media and blogs, but that their younger colleagues and freelancers do. Thus, a radio- maker says that taking over hypes is something for the evening programming and that this is not an issue in day-time. Second-order selection is often also put into perspective by dismissing it as 'something normal,' without far-reaching conse-quences. In this respect, actors think it makes sense that people in the industry constantly look to one another. It is part of the actors' professional capital. It belongs to the role they play in the field. A radio coordinator:

Absolutely, the opposite would be absurd: locking our-selves up and from our ivory tower only program the stuff we really like. We need to look at what's going on, at what we think the populace will want to hear, but also at things that are written about in the newspapers. Evidently, we look at them, but they will never determine what we do. (...) We're not on an island. Adopting a pro-fessional attitude, we look around us. (...) It speaks for itself that anyone can be influenced, just by having a sim-ple talk or by sticking out your head. But in the case of radio makers this effect is merely unintentional. Of that I'm certain.

In the same fashion, the fact is also denied that taking over each other's selection must at a certain moment lead to everybody covering the same artists. 'That is a specific property of the news,' a journalist says, because the occasion or cause is the same for everyone (release dates, interview days, and concerts). 'Besides, if it's a good record in the first place, isn't it natural everybody wants to do the same interview?' another one completes.

The Relativity of the Impact of Media Coverage

Earlier in this study, we showed how great the impact of media attention is estimated to be by the respondents. Actors in the music industry allow themselves to be guided by it. The choice of radio producers and journalists is taken over in the second order by concert organizers, record companies and managers. Nevertheless, this is by no means an explicit convention. Just as in the previous section, here too the recognition of the impact of media attention is ambivalent. Dependence is pitted against independence. Yet whereas in the previous section the notion of independence was the chorus, this time around the chimes of autonomy ring far less forcefully.

The best example is again *De Afrekening*. On the one hand, some are very clear about the importance of the list; on the other hand, its impact is questioned (mainly due to the hazy way in which the list is compiled). Festival organizers are remarkably Janus-faced about it, blowing hot and cold at the same time: *De Afrekening* does not always work, but it is still the list to follow. At one particular time in the interviews, two organizers firmly denied being guided by the list. At another time, when they were asked about the reason for putting the group Motek at their festival, they admitted that this choice was based on their ranking in *De Afrekening*.

> Motek was programmed as a substitute. A very opportunistic choice, because they had made a name thanks to *De Afrekening*. Sometimes it happens, but not all of the time.

> Of course, otherwise I would not have done that. I think Motek's cool, but it's far from easy music, right? If they hadn't enjoyed even the slightest media attention and I had programmed them, they would've been lost on stage, and nobody would've come to see them. Fortunately, they had a single in *De Afrekening*, which is why people want to include it while they're at it. At that particular moment it's an ideal situation: that this was precisely the reason why I was able to do a cool little band like them.

Organizers quite predictably question the impact of *De Afrekening* when it involves niche-oriented programming (every club programmer, for that matter, denies that it has any impact). Then again, for one particular segment of the public — which is rather sensitive to the alternative mainstream — the list is still viewed as a barometer. A programmer sums it up: De Afrekening does not always work. But in many cases it simply does.'

More generally, this ambiguity applies to the relation between airplay and concerts. As was mentioned above, concert organizers claimed by way of counterexamples that a group was also able to build a career by playing a lot and at the right locations. Nevertheless, here as well it is striking to see that when the actors intend to generalize from these examples, the argument is put into perspective. Both programmers and bookers claim that good ticket sales are possible without Studio Brussels' support, but 'then it's pure agony,' and the groups who are able to do so 'remain well in the minority.' In addition, they believe the exception only applies to foreign groups. To Belgian artists, Studio Brussels is still more of a determining factor. Alternatively, as this programmer puts it: 'Airplay is not always guaranteed, but many times it is. In the big picture, it works.' As far as a large concert hall such as the Ancienne Belgique is concerned, the ambiguity is shared:

> The Ancienne Belgique has the effect of a multiplier: if you pass our selection, you're launched. Look what happened to Stijn, Bony King Of Nowhere, Admiral Freebee and Joost Zweegers. Obviously, we cannot simply make or break an artist. AB may be a fine pick-up platform; the eventual breakthrough, however, is realized by Studio Brussels.

The ambiguity is found among the media-makers themselves as soon as they start to reflect about their own influence. Accordingly, a journalist is not convinced that a piece in his newspaper is able to have much impact. At the same time, he says:

> Sometimes I'm proven wrong and I notice that it does produce results, especially on the level of . As was the case with Jóhann Jóhannsson or Craig Armstrong, or José James whom we were the first and the only to write about, but who was able to play to a full AB. So it must have some affect. (...) Because we pushed Arsenal so hard, they have had two fantastic summers. In the heat of the moment you're not

aware of this. It's only afterwards that you hear that this has a gigantic effect on the inflow of bookings.

The interviewed radio creators, for their part, think you should not exaggerate the effect of airplay. Having said that, and still in the same interview, they realize the radio is a co-determinant factor in shaping public opinion, that their selection affects the name recognition and concert opportunities of an artist, that radio is necessary for pushing music toward a breakthrough, and that things are a lot harder for groups that never get any airplay. As this respondent comments:

> It would certainly be sad if a music station like ours would have no influence whatsoever on the pop scene in Flanders. If that were true, we would be doing a poor job. To be included in the playlist is a form of recognition for a band, it contributes to the perception of a group. (...) Chances are created because you enable a larger public to get to know this band. This is a secondary consequence of the fact that you are either played or not. I guess it will have an effect, and that this will mainly count when it concerns a place at the festivals. (...) It goes without saying: the more you are in the news, the more popular you become.

The words have just left his mouth, when he feels forced to add: 'But this is not always the case. We assume that it works, but it's not always so.'

What all these examples have in common is that the alternative mainstream recognizes certain symbolic power relations, yet is not equally comfortable with them. The proper autonomy cannot be relinquished, and the urge to behave in a socially accepted manner is here too (as in the previous section) the direct reason why a defensive reflex pops up.

Second-Order Observation and Conformism

Actors who appeal to other persons' selection wait for an opinion leader to pick something up. The risk then lies wholly with the 'symbolic banker,' who is the first in going all the way with a particular artist. Therefore, it is a step not easily taken. However, what is equally crucial is to avoid being too late or wait too long.

Therein lies the danger of second-order-observation: to delay a viable decision on a selection until has become impossible as soon as the snowball has grown too large. When there is a hype around a group, for example, organizers will be more willing to place a bid, but sometimes the market value has then become so large that that group is now effectively unaffordable for them. A festival organizer:

> If the bid has gone up from 1500 bucks to 25,000, you can be dead certain you're (too) late. Or when a group plays on Eurosonic, and it's no secret that all of Europe's biggest festivals will be there to have a look, then I won't, or shouldn't, even try to place a bid.

In the latter case, reasoning from an organizational logic establishes the economic impossibility to pursue a particular selection. That being said, reasoning from a positional logic can also endorse the actor's actions (or lack of action) as motivated by the pursuit of distinction: a state of still being *able*, but no longer *willing* to select because others have already identified with it too heavily or in too great a number. Journalists, for example, believe they are too late in their selection decision-making when their main competitors have already published a piece about an artist. Consequently, it is a matter of jumping on board at the right time. To be avoided at all cost, however, is *missing* the train. It appears indeed that the alternative mainstream is governed by the latent unconscious fear of falling by the wayside. Actors do not want to lose face, and abhor the idea of being seen by others as somebody who is no longer 'on it' or 'in the game.' The reason is that this comes across as incompetence, as a lack of professional capital. It is diametrically opposed to a certain professionalism that everyone in the world of pop is eager to demonstrate (see Chapter 5). To be 'in the game' is an expectation connected to social position. Failing to meet the conditions can lead to loss of professional/symbolic capital, or to informal sanctions (backbiting, or malicious gossip, is one example).

This invisible normative structuring of behavior gives rise to the impression that everybody is evaluating the same thing, and happens to make the same selections. The social context generates great pressure on the actors to keep the middle ground, to go along with the prevailing trends and to position them in a conformist way. Certainly in the case of the success stories, this apparently generates an overall effect that shifts everything else into the background. Selection criteria can also be socially shared logics of argumentation and justification, and this confirms, in Bourdieu's terms, the doxa and the rules of the game. Nevertheless, as cited on several occasions, in the music scene such conformism is happily denied by relying on the individual logic of personal taste. The result is that actors say yes and no at the same time. They long to be original in their choices, yet also do not want to be behind and miss certain music.

However, the relationship between an individual and a social logic of legitimization is more complex. After all, someone's personal taste can also be changed by social factors. The Actor-Network Theory provides a good point of view. According to this theory, a network is a process in which actors take over the action of another (!), push one another in doing unexpected things and in the process also distort and change the message every time (Latour 2005: 38-40 and 131). Such a process of 'translation' is also noticeable in the pop music circuit: music changes in meaning depending on the actors who are committed to it (Hajdu 2002). As a result, it is suddenly seen from a different perspective, and found to fulfill artistically (in the terms of the ANT: it gets *attachments*), even by people whose genre views are wholly different. When at the end of the 1990s dance acts were finally programmed at the big rock festivals, the rock-loving music journalists too were suddenly won over and claimed to like the music. Moreover, thanks to his success the respect for Milow has only been growing. Isbells manager had the same experience: even people who normally do not like this music genre, are now fully behind the group.

> The music industry teems with people who once started out of love for music, but who in the meantime have shifted focus to how they will get backstage at Rock Werchter. Many people of my generation have important jobs and thick wallets, but don't ask them what they like listening to. And evidently this year every single soul in the music industry has asked me the question: 'Can I get the Isbells CD from you?' Isbells is release number 25 on my label. If you ask me, maybe they can try listening to the other artists as well. That is, if they want to. No, these guys are not interested in the rest. Of course, everyone has heard Isbells: 'OMG, wicked record!.'

In an informal conversation following the interview, the actor also talked about someone from the industry who initially did not want an Isbells CD, but who, after three weeks of media attention, all at once wanted to be on the guest list. 'Yes,' the man admitted. 'I am but a camp follower, a hanger on.'

Recap 7

Cultural products can also be chosen by looking at how others select. Usually actors will do this, consciously or subconsciously, either for the reason of complexity reduction, or with the intent of finding a way to deal with oversupply. Niche media on the Internet are, in particular, the first step to get to know new music. From there the selection can float over to other actors. The first logical place where it may come to rest is the media: in their search for music that they deem relevant for the target public of their own nation, journalists and radio producers often consult others. The fact that music acquires this relevance, may be the result of a gradual assimilation and appropriation of other persons' selection: for reporting on things one medium looks at another medium, and as soon as the door has been set wide open, others will jump right in. In small regions like Flanders, the mechanism holds true especially for foreign artists. The greater the praise for a group by certain prominent media abroad (with the United Kingdom in pole position), the faster certain actors across the Channel will prick up their ears.

The practice of observing the media is just as common in the music industry. Concert organizers, managers and record labels rely on whatever receives attention in the media, assuming it is indicative of what is living among the target public. With a view to risk reduction and sizing up 'the bands of the hour,' airplay is the most important indicator.

Second-order selection can have a domino effect. When music is tipped through the grapevine and all attention converges, this affects the development of artists' careers. Attention emanating from one single is bound to fall short in the realization of any hoped-for success. However, when all the main channels are on it and all is set for an interaction between both attention in various media *and* good concerts, this is bound to have some influence. In this way a collective support base of 'relevant music' is created.

The pop music discourse is nevertheless marked by considerable ambiguity when it comes to acknowledging the influence of media attention and any subsequent impact on artists' careers. The actors tend to downplay these elements, put them in a situational perspective. Both industry people and the media are convinced that ample airplay and reviews do not always guarantee success, and that, conversely, musicians can build a live reputation without airplay. This ambiguity is mainly dictated by the need for justifying choices that may come across as illegitimate. As a result, an appeal is made to the ultimate filter of personal taste. Actors will check out the things other actors put to the fore, but not before the music's quality has stood the test of (individual) criticism. Still, the idea of external influence is also denied, or refuted with counterexamples.

Even though actors love to minimize the fact that they take over each other's selections, they still tend to feel horrified at the possibility of being (left) behind and fail to pick up particular music. On the one hand, the social context creates great pressure to stay in the middle and go along with the ruling trends. On the other hand, the actors will emphatically deny such conformism. In short, a double-faced, dual attitude is typical of the circuit's (public) discourse.

Notes

1   The term is borrowed from German sociologist Niklas Luhmann (2000) and refers mainly to the ways in which people look at works of art. To Luhmann, a work of art is the result of close-knit observations (first order, between artist and work of art). These observations, in turn are observed by others (second order).

2   This fits in with the *'shriveling* of the music offer,' as one manager calls it: only the (radio) singles are picked up, not the rest of a band's music. The development is fairly typical of the 'iPod generation,' and actually a step back to the period before 1967, when singles were more important than albums.

3   The 30-year old station started off as a regional (Brabant-based) division of the bilingual national public radio and television broadcasting company Belgian Radio and Television (called BRT in the Dutch-speaking, Flemish part of Belgium, and RTBf in the French-speaking, Walloon region). When Belgium became a federal state, with three autonomous regional governments, public broadcasting became one of the de-nationalized services, under regional authority. Studio Brussels is now a Dutch-speaking station of the Flemish public radio and television broadcaster VRT.

4   This author experienced something similar, be it on a smaller scale, during his personal musical career: when one single from the debut CD ended up in the daytime rotation of StuBru and Radio 1, bookings for club concerts and festivals came pouring in spontaneously. After the next CDs, which had no airplay worth mentioning, but received better reviews in the specialized press, this gradually decreased.

5   Evidently, it is impossible to determine the causal effects of this on careers (structure) based on logics of selection (culture). It would require more specific quantitative research, comparing clearly described variables about the type of magazines that write about the artists, the type of booker who works for them, etc. What is possible, however, is to take the reflections made by the interviewed music industry players and adopt the perspective of second-order selection to examine how this congealing of selections and the development of artists careers is perceived. This also illustrates the circular movement in Bourdieu's analysis: the experts 'know' what the doxa is, and by knowing it they are shape it at the same time.

6   The personal musical career of this author provides another good example: following the release of the debut album, the group Briskey was briefly picked up by the alternative mainstream, only to disappear again from the segment when the musical climate changed and the group changed course artistically, resulting in less airplay and concerts.

8. The Selection Triangle
Conclusion

> Alternative mainstream... That term really nails it. We all know its two composing parts. And we all know the question that accompanies it: which weighs heavier in the balance?

The above statement, made by a particularly lucid programmer, sums up the spread-eagle position in which the alternative mainstream segment of the pop music circuit seems to be caught. In the segment two logics intersect, a cultural and an economic logic. Sometimes the players that populate the segment make an appeal to the mainstream (the more commercial), sometimes it is the underground (the alternative) that is the point of reference. Alternative mainstream players are national actors in the music industry and the media, and they determine a significant part of the current affairs in music. By selecting certain music, they also grant the music a label of quality. This is the reason why the alternative mainstream is essentially a cultural construct. The goal is to distinguish the 'superior' or 'qualitatively better' forms of pop music from the 'inferior' or 'commercial' variants. This is done by the attribution of positive and negative values that are borrowed from the Romantic tradition (for music to be 'good,' it needs to be emotionally authentic and artistically original, thereby ignoring commercial intentions; 'bad' music is emotionally dishonest and fake, cliché-ridden and shallow, because its sole purpose is to gain money). Chapter 2, as well as the research, showed that such a discourse really exists in the music circuit. The rock press defines it in such a way, and the industry allows itself to be governed by the distinction. At the same time, however, alternative mainstream thrives in, and because of, a given commercial market situation, which is precisely why the Romantic values (and the discourse of an/the underground) need to occupy center stage, since they must grant the music, rendered inferior by the commercial context, a special meaning and added value.

At this point, a theoretical recapitulation is in order - of the logics of selection and of the main chorus in the discourse that was the object of study: making choices in the alternative mainstream is a balancing act between dependence and independence, which is why these choices are fundamentally uncertain and ambiguous.

Paths of Selection in the Alternative Mainstream

Social, Economic and Individual Choices

It is almost natural to view the selection of music as a primarily social process. The findings of this study reveal that the artistic value of an artist and his or her work (in the singular) do not suffice to gain recognition or prestige. The latter values are the result of a collective action, a view that is standard in classic sociology of culture. Especially the social context and the actor's network have influence on the decisions involving selections. In these cases, the positional logic has the upper hand. Actions arise from the position occupied by the actor in the field of pop and from his relation to other players. In the second-order selection, too these field mechanisms come to the fore, because the actors inside the field are constantly observing one another and mimicking one another's decisions.

Selections in the alternative mainstream are also economically induced choices. Because the actors in the pop music circuit venture into an economic market where music is traded, they also select from an organizational logic. In other words, they act in a way that is acceptable or appropriate for the organization that employs them, thus ensuring this organization's economic survival. This underlines the importance of public- and market-related factors in the process of selection.

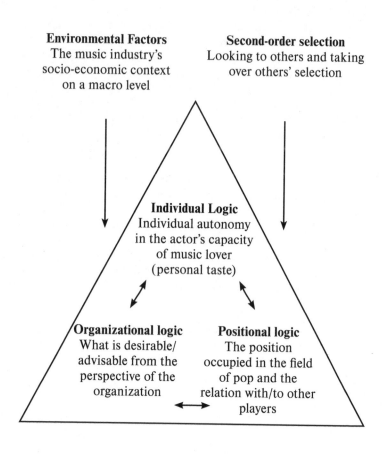

Schema 3 *The Selection Triangle in the Alternative Mainstream*

One significant supplementary contribution to classical cultural sociology lies in the importance attached to individually induced choices. Selections cannot be solely attributed to social or economic processes. This study also shows the importance claimed by individual autonomy. At the basis of each decision is personal taste, and in the process this autonomy continues to affect selection as a filter. In the individual logic of legitimacy, especially great weight is carried by the position of music lover which actors in the music circuit inevitably occupy. Here, however, the vital vocabulary is not one of rationality, but of emotionality. Taste is an indefinable feeling, a stimulus that overwhelms the mind. Again this is a Romantic thought and double rhetoric which typically goes along with it is deeply ingrained in the players in the alternative mainstream: taste is not merely a subjective thing (personal taste), it is also a state of 'being touched.' It is a force that enters from outside and which only you can respond to. Therefore, collective processes are only one part of the story; the impact and the content of the actual works of art that circulate in these processes, is another. These aspects are summarized in Schema 3: The Selection Triangle.

Uncertainty and Risk Reduction

The digital transformation of society, taking a dramatic turn with the digitization of audiovisual objects, has enlarged, expanded and accelerated the potential circulation of music beyond comparison. It is now infinitesimally easier for artists to produce and distribute their music outside the traditional gated channels, and find an audience among the new online and mobile masses and their social networks. This open source and open access development has drastically limited the power of the industry to create and manipulate its own outlets and markets. As music comes and goes much faster than ever, the oversupply of the past has become a *hyper*supply, while CD sales have been in constant free fall. All this has dramatically amplified the pressure engendered by the music circuit's selection process. The professional actors are left with very few indicators as to the actual reach and return of a product, and have less knowledge in advance about what will either work or not. Apart from these marginal conditions on the macro level, and because selection is also a social process, the decisions on the medium level are constantly crossed and intersected by those of others. In short, the economic return of the selection is more uncertain than ever.

More than ever, actors seem to look for ways of reducing risk. At the same time, this is nothing new. Music industry actors have always been highly aware of the uncertainty involved in making selections and acting adequately on the choices made. Although awareness of uncertainty is here to stay, the pop music has gradually developed routines and conventions that can provide a feeling (or illusion) of safety and security. First, a positional logic induces actors to try to enlarge or accumulate social capital. The social relations they establish need to be relations of trust, of cooperation on good terms with one another, promoting mutual understanding and goodwill. Because the network consists of people with different degrees of charisma and credibility, choices can be made more easily by going straight for the actors with the largest accumulation of symbolic capital. Yet actors can also engage in second-order observation, choosing unknown symbolic guides who do not belong to the actors' personal networks (such as the underground media, national colleagues or the leading international press). Complexity reduction spurs actors from the media on to take over assessments and decisions of other media willingly and eagerly. Actors from the music industry, for their part, are equally happy to look for authority judgments in the media and thus set aside their personal autonomous choice. The idea behind this allegedly is that this is exactly what the public does, enabling them to choose based on what the public knows and wants. The media are viewed as an attention machine and actors look for those persons or things that are the talk of the town. Also, risk reduction leads to conformism, the urge to be *on* to things, rather than be *behind*.

This, of course, leans toward selecting music because of its popularity, a criterion that can only apply within the frame of an organizational logic. By starting out from already successful artists and genres, the potential success evidently becomes greater. On top of that, the media are in a position to create this popularity by way of their playlist. Record companies still have other tools for reducing uncertainty. Overproduction, oversupply or excess of supply is one of them, that is, to increase output and releases in the hope that at least some titles will be profitable. Reaping the benefits of the extended back catalogue, milking the notion of re-releases, is another. In general, however, the necessary professional capital helps to better assess the risk.

By taking economically realistic decisions and by many years of professional experience, actors can employ the organizational and positional logic to play safe and find better ways of dealing with the economic uncertainty that each investment entails. A professional attitude and entrepreneurship are indispensable to the players in the alternative mainstream.

The Pressure of Legitimate Actions and the Ambiguity of Decisions

Defending the Legitimate Taste

Following conventions or trying to reduce risk often means that actors have to push aside their own personal preferences. When a programmer wants many people in his concert hall, personal taste is probably not the advisable standard to pursue in your actions. In the same way, the media need to ignore personal taste when they let the public guide their thoughts. Actors who look to the media for their decision, establish popularity as a criterion or let themselves be guided by other symbolic guides, can only conclude that the selection does not always match personal preference. In other words, the organizational and positional logics can sometimes collide with the individual logic.

That being said, the negation of personal taste can resemble illegitimate behavior. This can be deduced from the respondents when they spontaneously seek to defend themselves in these cases. As they hold themselves accountable for some reason, they seem to have two options of acting in their defense. First, the illegitimate behavior is put into perspective, or it is even denied. The justifications they put forward are threefold. Media attention is not always a guarantee for the success of an artist ('a group can also sell out a concert room without airplay'). There are well-known artists who, nevertheless, are *not* selected, or young and unknown artists still get a chance. Foreign hypes are not followed in each and every case. The actors prefer to substantiate this by means of counterexamples. In doing so, however, the ambiguity in their statements surfaces most conspicuously. They are both confirming and denying the matters they address, simultaneously asserting that one aspect is important *and* that another, quite opposing thing carries great weight.

Secondly, a decision previously taken by actors can subsequently be revised (or reversed) by looking at it from another

logic (in that case, the ambiguity is not manifested in a simultaneous way, as in the first case, but sequentially). This happens often with choices that come across as illegitimate and were made from a positional and an organizational logic, or from a second-order observation. The choices are then interpreted in a new, different manner that permits them to appeal to an individual logic. When actors allow themselves to be guided by the selection of domestic or foreign reference persons, they claim to do so only because of two things: one, these reference points have stood the test of quality; two, these channels have also and already made a first selection in terms of quality. When actors give way to popularity or the 'taste of the public,' they claim to do so because they personally like the music. When actors are quicker to lend an ear to artists with great name recognition, they claim that they will always set aside and ignore 'bad records.' When actors adopt a conformist attitude and wish to be 'onto' things, they add that they also want to be original. By laying out artistic counterarguments, they restore the connection with socially acceptable behavior.

Independence versus Dependence

The significance ascribed to legitimate taste points to the presence of a cultural opposition, or even contradiction, in the pop music circuit. It is in the love of what *they* view as authentic (rock) music that actors in the alternative mainstream differentiate themselves from the (pop) music of the mainstream, which, again in *their* opinion, is commercial and therefore illegitimate. To put it in another way: those who think from a purely market-oriented perspective render themselves unilaterally dependent on the economic context. It is precisely the apparent independence of this economic context that was said to be typical of the alternative mainstream's Romantic rock aesthetics. The contrast between independence/dependence thus forms the heart of the discourse, distinguishing legitimate from illegitimate practices.

In addition, this contrast is not only cultural in nature, but also social and economic. All social relations in the music circuit bear its marks. As long as these relations start from trust and a mutual dependency, legitimacy is never compromised. However, when actors have no choice but to go along with others, when 'friendly' pressure becomes 'real' pressure, they lose their independence. There is actually nothing wrong in being quicker to listen to actors with a certain amount of symbolic capital. Yet when their positional influence leads to the copying of someone else's selection without any form of critique, the autonomy that defines an actor is lost. Individuality is a higher, if not the highest good. Actors must remain credible, and most certainly not reduce themselves to puppets.

The contrast between dependent/independent also determines the discourse when social relations acquire an economic dimension. Actors keep their autonomy when an economic deal with others proceeds from exchange agreements (give and take). The fact that organizations with loads of accumulated economic capital (the big booking agencies, festivals and record firms) have advantages, may still be considered legitimate. By contrast, when pressure is exerted unilaterally, the mood changes from resignation to indignation, and the criticism of illegitimacy is raised, because one party becomes economically dependent on the other. The research shows that indeed actual dependencies and inequalities of power can be observed in the alternative mainstream.

Making selections from an individual logic is not the only way to obtain legitimacy. This can also be done by adopting an organizational and positional logic. The fact that actors are unable to follow their personal taste because of the practical marginal conditions of an organizational logic (a venue is already taken; a lack of space in the newspaper; the need for variation in content) does not imply straight away that they act illegitimately. Nor are they caught in illegitimate action if they cannot carry out their intended choices on account of insufficient economic capital or the organization's requirement of cost effectiveness and efficiency. Even conformist choices can be legitimate, because they show the presence of the desired professional capital. This explains why actors keep an eye on economic return and assume a professional attitude. Actors enjoy the satisfaction of the success they have achieved. They are quite simply proud of it.

By way of a general statement, the following could be said: a similar and homologous dichotomy characterizes cultural and social, as well as economic practices; the difference between legitimacy and illegitimacy is the difference between independence and dependence, between individuality and external pressure.

Selections Determined by Situations

These dichotomies run through every selection and form virtually a basic vocabulary of the alternative mainstream. There is a continuous interaction between the two poles of opposition, which can lead to tensions. The fact is that certain patterns of expectation are attached to the positions held by the actors. The general, never lessening expectation is that actors act in a legitimate and socially acceptable manner. For example, when the media fail, against all expectations, to make artistic choices and merely follow the supposed target group (organizational logic), they will be held accountable (as in the struggle over definitions which was discussed in Chapter 4: managers and record firms raised criticisms from an individual logic). However, it is because of this legitimacy pressure that media are subsequently able to switch back to an individual logic (defense of the choice by means of artistic criteria). It also goes to show that the tension between legitimate and illegitimate acts can drive actors to revise the decision or switch between logics of legitimacy. In fact, justifications in the alternative mainstream are determined by the situation: they depend on the current situation, an argument also made by pragmatist sociology; the choice, moreover, is never final.

There are no unambiguous rules that can explain why actors sometimes act from the music lover's point of view and position, and sometimes act from an economic perspective or from a specific social relation. Depending on the context, the position, the opponent or the moment, actors choose off and on, on and off one particular logic and then another. When programmers do not have financial reserves to act on an individual choice (ambivalence in role taking between an individual and an organizational logic), the situation may change for two reasons. The first is that they possess a commercial surplus resulting from choices in the past based on the organizational logic. That this what allows them to go ahead anyway. The second is that they receive subsidies, which allow them to do so. Then there is again room for an individual logic. Conversely, too, a selection that was previously rejected because it did not tally with personal taste, or because there was no 'support' for it) can be revised for a few reasons. Here, the first is that the music suddenly gets ample media attention or is highly recommended by a role model (from a second-order observation an organizationally legitimized choice is made). The second is that the choice is required to maintain a relation of trust (positional logic). A choice that was initially legitimized on the basis of an individual logic then becomes a social or collective choice. The context of selection is different, allowing a different logic to thrust itself on the actors. Selection paths, after all, are little else than the ceaseless reinterpreting of possibilities of choice. As was represented schematically in the selection triangle, artistic, social and economic criteria interact in order to arrive at the final selection. The relative weight of these criteria and the proportional relation between them is constantly changing.

The Supremacy of Personal Taste
Deep within the alternative mainstream, a collectively shared belief in legitimacy exists. As a rule, individual, independent actions are valued higher. It is no coincidence that decisions that do not start from this common principle are often mentioned off the record. Officially, even before the categorical denial of possible concessions made, the actors deny the existence of external pressure, or the possibility of this pressure having an effect. There also seems to be a hierarchy in this legitimacy, which may indicate the presence of a characterizing realm of value. In the end, after all, it is love of music and personal taste that are considered the highest good. Organizational and positional choices of second-order selection, as was already made clear, can also be legitimate, but when they are, they always are significantly less so. This is clear when the statements by the interviewed actors become ambiguous. The ambiguity is at its highest whenever personal taste is at stake. Even better, this hierarchy of legitimacy *explains* the ambiguity.

Personal taste is never just *a* taste. Indeed, it bears close resemblance to the aesthetics of rock described in a previous chapter. It is through the adopted and collectively shared views of how music is supposed to be, that the alternative mainstream distinguishes itself from other segments in the pop music circuit. In this way, players are not supposed to work openly with the sole purpose of serving a public or pursuing financial gain, which in economic relations is quite simply the starting point. Moreover, at the end of the ride, actors should always give account in a personal and artistic manner. The Romantic idea of 'the autonomy of art' is very much alive in the alternative mainstream: the symbolic prevails over the economic.[1]

Then again, all this concerns values and valuation. If, in practice, the symbolic is deployed as a way of obscuring economic and social aspects, it comes very close to the ideology of rock discussed in Chapter 2. The research indeed showed that the positional and organizational logics are the ruling logics, the ultimate 'reality check,' as one respondent dubbed them. If an individual option inflicts too much loss, nobody will choose it. Those who want to survive will put their individual taste aside and focus on the potential or intended audience, on what is profitable for the organization, on what valid inside the small music business, on the choices induced by social connections, on internal organizational processes, on marginal conditions of all kinds. In many cases, actors in the music industry immediately couple artistic criteria with economic and social principles; on top of the individual logic of legitimization, actors apply an important organizational and positional correction. Making decisions from personal taste is therefore more a wish than an established fact in pop music circuit: it is the icing on the cake.

Therefore, to select in the alternative mainstream is a balancing act. It is a compromise between what one wants and what one needs, between 'alternative' and 'mainstream.' Actors are always seeking a balance between the names that seem imperative from the organizational and positional logic, and the music they like and would choose from an individual logic. Yet, regardless of the difficulties in making it happen, all actors equally want the sort of hybrid outcome that highlights in a sufficiently prominent way the personal touch they took care to add. This is why even choices dictated by position or organization will always be legitimized by means of the individual logic. To be sure, the players never cease to hammer it home that their personal taste is the highest good, whatever the magnitude of the impact made by the social process of meaning creation and selection, or whatever the extent to which the economic climate and other environmental factors are able to influence the selection. This ambiguity, in turn, betrays the hierarchy of legitimacy: making selections is an interaction between the three major logics; organizational and positional criteria are dominant and relentless in tying the Gordian knots of selection; in this, the individual logic remains the direction indicator go round and ultimately *the* legitimate criterion.

This is what makes professional capital so important to those who work in the alternative mainstream. Actors not only gain a better knowledge of how the business works and how to work in the business, how to keep their organizations running and how to close deals; those who have sufficient professional experience, undergo less pressure from the symbolically and economically more important players. Professional capital also has a symbolic component: the expertise of music connoisseurs that actors have been able to develop, both in the short run (by being the first, understanding the importance of the scoop), and in the longer run (by gaining credibility and reputation in the business). Because the alternative mainstream is situated at the intersection of the symbolic and economic, actors who possess enough professional or 'alternative mainstream capital' will have an easier time giving and taking, compromising, finding a balance between the two poles. These actors will be better at playing the game between independence and dependence, without being robbed of their individuality. However, tensions and clashes among logics or between legitimacy and illegitimacy, will never disappear. Working in the alternative mainstream remains an uncertain, risky and consequently ambiguous undertaking. The future is never a closed book. Now and again, the sky will be anything but the limit, but there will most certainly be gifts on the horizon. The one telling the whole story—this author's story, which has come to its end — is the manager with ankle-deep roots in the music circuit who spent three hours talking through questions and rounded off with a punch line: 'The conclusion? Is that I haven't got a clue.'

Notes

1   This is not much different from Bourdieu's view: the negation of the economic that is inherent to cultural discourse is also the negation of dependencies. The same 'discourse of independence' profoundly marks the alternative mainstream.

Postscript

THANKYOUVERYMUCH

This book evolved from the doctoral research I conducted from 2008 to 2012. The road to a Ph.D. can be lonely, and it requires confidence in decision-making, in *choosing* to choose and to select. Thankfully, I was not alone when it demanded the confidence to make the *right* selections. A word of gratitude is therefore in place, a salute to the guides and fellow travelers who helped me to complete my journey.

The first 'thankyouverymuch' goes to Rudi Laermans, who managed to be more than merely a Dissertation Director. Twenty-one years after he became tutor for my Master's thesis, he was again present for my Doctoral dissertation, not only sharing my passion, but also helping me take it to a higher level. The numerous and long conversations we had were interesting, enlightening and always enjoyable. Rudi, quite simply, *rocked*. He rocked my mind and work, acting as a (rock-) steady GPS when I had trouble finding my way.

When Pascal Gielen, my Dissertation Co-Director, invited me to participate in the Arts & Society Lectureship, he provided the spark for my doctoral study. By graciously sharing the plan he drew up for his own doctoral research he gave me an invaluable head start. For this, as well as for his constructive feedback, I owe him a big 'thankyouverymuch'.

The Arts & Society Lectureship took place at the Fontys School of Arts in Tilburg, the Netherlands, where I am lecturer at the Rock Academy, as well as associate lector for the entire program of music studies. During a period of four years, Fontys granted me the necessary time to do research. I must thank directors and colleagues Alexander Beets, Chantal Rothkrantz, Ivonne van de Sanden, Hans van den Hurk, Gerard Boontjes, Bertus Borgers, Raf De Keninck and Rien van der Vleuten for their unbridled faith in me.

Equal support and flexibility came from my colleagues at the Belgian institutions of higher education where I teach. I extend profound gratitude to Gert Stinckens at PXL Music in Hasselt, Jan Bulckaen and Martine Ketelbuters at Erasmus School Brussels/ RITS, as well as Wim De Temmerman, Leon Lhoest and Maarten Weyler at Ghent School of Arts.

Amsterdam-based publisher Valiz was willing to take on the English translation of my book *Alternatieve Mainstream: Over selectiemechanismen in het popmuziekcircuit*. I sincerely thank

Astrid Vorstermans and Pia Pol for their confidence in the project. Thanks to Jo Smets for the English translation he did a great job.

I would be nowhere without the people who agreed to be interviewed, the actors in my play, and all the others with whom I had the privilege to talk. I am deeply indebted for the patience with which they answered, or even endured, my (often-covert) research questions.

A very special 'thankyouverymuch' goes out to my family and best friends (they know who they are).

Finally, more than anyone else, I must thank Libelia, my mainstay, anchor and crutch: my reality check, my soundboard, my wife.

Gert Keunen, *July 2014*

Respondents

Riet Coenen
at the time of the interview:
Music programmer, music center
Muziekodroom (Hasselt)
currently:
Assistant booker, Live Nation
(live entertainment, concert
promotions, venue operations,
ticketingsolutions, ...)
formerly:
Booker, management agency Keremos
(Ghent)

Peter Daeninck
Artistic director, festival Lokerse
Feesten (Lokeren)

Eppo Janssen
Programmer, festival Pukkelpop
(Hasselt)
Music producer, radio station Studio
Brussels (radio program Duyster)
Music producer, radio station Radio 1
(radio program *Closing Time*)
Deejay
formerly:
Programmer, music center Trix
(Antwerp)
formerly:
Program collaborator,radio station
Studio Brussels

Wim Merchiers
Artistic director/business manager,
festival Feest in het Park
(Oudenaarde)

Mike Naert
General manager/musicprogrammer,
music center Depot (Louvain)
Deejay
formerly:
Marketing manager, record company
Atrecordings.com
formerly:
Tour manager, pop band The Radios

Kurt Overbergh
Artistic director,concert hall
Ancienne Belgique (Brussels)
(person-in-charge of developing
artistic policy, budget management,
subsidy files, etc.)
formerly:
Press officer, record company Rough
Trade
formerly:
Booker,avant-garde rock/jazz bandX-
Legged Sally (UltimaVez, company of
choreographer, photographer and film
maker Wim Vandekeybus)

formerly:
Freelance journalist, music magazine
RifRaf

Patrick Smagghe
Music programmer/co-ordinator/
artistic director, music club 4AD
(Diksmuide)

Eric Smout
Music programmer/co-ordinator/
artistic director, music club
Democrazy (Ghent)
Member of the Board, non-profit
organizations DOK, Glimpsand De
Beloften
formerly:
Music programmer/artistic director,
music club 5voor12 (Antwerp)
formerly:
Music producer, radio station Studio
Brussels
formerly:
Music producer, radio and television
broadcasting company VPRO
(Netherlands)
formerly:
Freelance journalist, daily newspaper
De Tijd/Cultuur
formerly:
Collaborator, music club Pacific
(Antwerp)

Jeroen Vereecke
Organizer, festival Boomtown (Ghent)
Artist manager/co-founder,
management agency Rockoco (Ghent)
Owner/programmer, music café Video
(Ghent)

Roel Vergauwen
Booker, Live Nation
Programmer, Live Nationfestival I
Love Techno
formerly:
Booker, The Foundation
formerly:
Freelance journalist, magazine *Gonzo
Circus*

Peter Verstraelen
Owner, independent booking agency
Peter Verstraelen Bookings (general
direction and bookings)
formerly:
Booker, festival Rock Werchter/
booking agency Live Nation
formerly:
Owner/booker, The Foundation

Respondents from the record circuit and artists' management

Patrick Busschots
at the time of the interview:
Managing director, record company Universal Music Belgium
President, music producers' rights management company Simim
formerly:
Owner, BMC (Busschots Music Compagny) Publishing
formerly:
Owner, record company ARS (Antwerp Record Store) Entertainment
formerly:
Owner, record shop ARS (Antwerp Record Store)

Christoffel Cocquyt
Artists' manager/co-founder, management agency Gentlemanagement (Ghent)
formerly:
Artist manager, rock/electronic band Soulwax/ 2ManyDJs
formerly:
A&R manager, record company PIAS

Eric Didden
Artists' manager/co-founder, management agency Gentlemanagement (Ghent)
formerly:
Artist manager, management agency Mad In Belgium
formerly:
Artist manager, management agency Musickness Management
formerly:
Promotion manager, record company Rough Trade
formerly:
Promotion manager, record company Boudisque

Christoph Elskens
Label owner/artists' manager, record company Noisesome Recordings
at the time of the interview:
General editor, webzine *Soundslike*
formerly:
Purchasing agent, wholesaler Sonica
formerly:
Owner, record shop Music Mania (Louvain)

Erwin Goegebeur
at the time of the interview:
Chairman/head A&R, record company EMI Music Benelux (operational person-in-charge EMI Belgium and Netherlands)
formerly:
Freelance journalist

Geert Mets
Label owner, Zealrecords (A&R, production, promotion, bookings)
Promotion manager Belgium, distribution company Konkurrent (press, radio, TV)
formerly:
MD/A&R, record company R&SRecords
formerly:
Head of label management, PIAS Distribution
formerly:
Warehouse collaborator, PIAS (leading independent music company, consisting of [PIAS] Artist & Label Services, record company [PIAS] Recordingsand [PIAS] Cooperative label licensing division)

Maarten Quaghebeur
Artist manager/business manager/ co-founder, management agency Rockoco (Ghent)
Organizer, festival Boomtown (Ghent)
Owner, music café Video (Ghent)
President, federation of music managers MmaF Belgium

Jasper Wentzel
Promotion manager -Flemishmedia, record company PIAS (Brussels)
Deejay
formerly:
Person-in-charge of promotion - Flemish Media,Bang! Distribution
formerly:
Promotion assistant, music center Kinky Star
formerly:
Freelance journalist/editor-in-chief, magazine *Gonzo Circus*

Respondents from the media

Philippe Cortens
at the time of the interview:
Program producer, radio station Studio Brussels (evening programming: *Select*)
Program producer,radio station Klara (*Laika*)
formerly:
Collaborator/co-founder, radiostation Fm Brussels

Karel Degraeve
at the time of the interview:
Co-ordinator of editorial staff and person-in-charge of music, weekly magazine *Knack Focus*
currently: Assistant general editor, weekly magazine *Humo*
formerly:
General editor, weekly magazine *Knack Focus*
formerly:
Copywriter, NewscoProductions (RMG)

Pascal Depreeuw
at the time of the interview:
Music co-ordinator, weekly magazine *Humo* (co-ordination TTT-Ohm pages)
(currently and formerly): Product manager, weekly magazine *Humo*
formerly:
Creative assistant, record company BMG

Gerrit Kerremans
General music co-ordinator, Flemish public radio network VRT (person-in-charge of music profile radio and television stations, music rights policy, VRT Publishing, structural and strategic deals with music sector, contact point music sector/pressure groups)
Deejay
formerly:
Music co-ordinator, radio station Studio Brussels
formerly:
Music producer, radio station Studio Brussels

Filip Saerens
General editor/editor-in-chief, magazine *RifRaf* Musiczine (general co-ordination)

Bart Steenhaut
Music editor with final responsibility for music, daily newspaper *De Morgen*
Frequent collaborator of radio stations Radio 1, Studio Brussel, Nostalgie
formerly:
Music journalist, daily newspaper *De Morgen*
formerly:
Music editor, magazine *Bonanza*

Luc Tirez
Music co-ordinator, radio station

Studio Brussels (person with final responsibility for music programming, including safeguarding and development of music policy, actions, compilations, Club69/Living Room/live events, etc.)
formerly:
Producer Music, radio station Studio Brussels
formerly:
Sales man, record shop Musicland (Louvain)

Peter Vantyghem
Chief editor of Culture and Media, daily newspaper *De Standaard* (person-in-charge of co-ordination and coverage of pop music)
formerly:
Music journalist, daily newspaper *De Standaard*

Evert Venema
Music co-ordinator/occasional presenter, radio station Radio 1 (person with final responsibility of music programming, including safeguarding and development of music policy, live events, actions, Radio 1 Sessions)
formerly:
'Channel watcher', VRT Music (co-ordinating function VRT Radio: screening of internal and external rival stations, general consultation)
formerly:
Music co-ordinator/occasional presenter, radio station Radio Donna

Bibliography

— Abts, K. (2005) 'De grammatica en dynamica van vertrouwen: Een sociologische verkenning'. In: *Ethiek & Maatschappij*, 8(2): 3-27.
— Adorno, T. W. (1972) 'Kultuurindustrie'. In: Hoefnagels H., *Sociologie en maatschappijkritiek*. Alphen a/d Rijn: Samson.
— Anderson, C. (2006) *The Long Tale: Why the Future of Business is Selling Less of More*. New York: Hyperion.
— Atton, C. (2009) 'Writing About Listening: Alternative Discourses in Rock Journalism'. In: *Popular Music*, 28(1): 53-67.
— Bannister, M. (2006) "Loaded': Indie Guitar Rock, Canonism, White Masculinities'. In: *Popular Music*, 25(1): 77-95.
— Bauman, Z. (1991) *Modernity and Ambivalence*. Cambridge: Polity Press.
— Bauman, Z. (2011) *Vloeibare tijden: Leven in een eeuw van onzekerheid*. Zoetermeer: Klement.
— Baumann, S. (2007) 'A General Theory of Artistic Legitimation: How Art Worlds Are Like Social Movements'. In: *Poetics*, 35: 47-65.
— Becker, H. S. (1982) *Art Worlds*. Berkeley: University of California Press.
— Becker, H. S. (2005) 'Making It Up As You Go Along: How I Wrote "Art Worlds"'. In: Mercure, D. (ed.), *L'analyse du social: Les modes d'explication*. Quebec: Les Presses de l'Université Laval: 57-73.
— Bénatouïl, T. (1999) 'A Tale of Two Sociologies: The Critical and the Pragmatic Stance in Contemporary French Sociology'. In: *European Journal Of Social Theory*, 2(3): 379-396.
— Bennett, A., Shank, B. & Toynbee, J. (eds.) (2006) *The Popular Music Studies Reader*. Oxon: Routledge.
— Berger, P. L. (1963) *Sociologisch denken*. Rotterdam: Universitaire Pers Rotterdam.
— Blokker, P. (2011) 'Pragmatic Sociology: Theoretical Evolvement and Emperical Application'. In: *European Journal of Social Theory*, 14(3): 251-261.
— Boltanski, L. & Chiapello, E. (2005) *The New Spirit of Capitalism (translated by G. Elliott)*. London: Verso (translation of: *Le nouvel esprit du capitalisme*. Parijs: Gallimard, 1999).

— Boltanski, L. & L. Thévenot, L. (2006) *On Justification: Economies of Worth* (translated by C. Porter). Princeton and Oxford: Princeton University Press (translation of *De La Justification: Les économies de la grandeur*. Paris: Gallimard, 1991).
— Bourdieu, P. (1984) *Distinction, A Social Critique of the Jugdment of Taste* (translated by R. Nice). Cambridge MA: Harvard University Press (translation of *La Distinction: Critique sociale du jugement*. Paris: Les editions de Minuit, 1979).
— Bourdieu, P. (1989) *Opstellen over smaak, habitus en het veldbegrip (chosen by D. Pels)*. Amsterdam: Van Gennep.
— Bourdieu, P. (1990) *The Logic of Practice* (translated by R. Nice). Cambridge: Polity Press (translation of *Le sens pratique*. Paris: Les Editions de Minuit, 1980).
— Bourdieu, P. (1993a) *The Field of Cultural Production*. Cambridge: Polity Press.
— Bourdieu, P. (1993b) *De regels van de kunst: Wording en structuur van het literaire veld* (translated by R. Hofstede). Amsterdam: Van Gennep (translation of *Les règles de l'art: Genèse et structure du champ literaire*. Paris: Editions du Seuil, 1992).
— Brennan, M. (2006) 'The Rough Guide to Critics: Musicians Discuss the Role of the Music Press'. In: *Popular Music*, 25(2): 221-234.
— Calinescu, M. (1977) *Faces of Modernity: Avant-garde, Decadence and Kitsch*. Bloomington & London: Indiana University Press.
— Chambers, I. (1985) *Urban Rhythms: Pop Music and Popular Culture*. New York: St. Martin's Press.
— Cutler, C. (1985) *File Under Popular: Theoretical and Critical Writings on Music*. London: RéR Megacorp.
— Debels, T. (2011) *De rinkelende kassa van de Vlaamse popmuziek: De top 100 van de rijkste Vlaamse zangers*. Antwerpen: Houtekiet.
— De Bruyne, P. & Gielen, P. (eds.) (2011) *Community Art: The Politics of Trespassing*. Amsterdam: Valiz.
— De Meyer, G. (1990) *Ontwikkeling, organisatie en werking van de communicatiemedia:*

Muziekindustrie. Leuven: Acco.
— De Meyer, G. (1994) *De zin van de onzin: De cultuur van de slechte smaak.* Antwerpen: Hadewijch.
— De Meyer, G. (1995) *Populaire cultuur.* Leuven: Garant.
— De Meyer, G. (2010) *Rock is dood.* Gent: Academia Press.
— De Meyer, G. & Trappeniers, A. (2007) *Lexicon van de muziekindustrie: Werking en vaktermen.* Leuven, Acco.
— Dobbelaere, K. (1987) *Sociologie.* Leuven: Acco.
— Dowd, T. J. (2004) 'Production Perspectives in the Sociology of Music'. In: *Poetics,* 32: 235-246.
— Drijkoningen, F. & Fontijn, J. (eds.) (1986) *Historische Avantgarde.* Amsterdam: Huis aan de drie Grachten.
— Elias, N. (1983) 'Kitschstijl en Kitschtijdperk (1939)'. In: Meijerink, G. (ed.), *Die Sammlung.* Amsterdam: Querido.
— Fonarow, W. (2006) *Empire of Dirt: The Aesthetics and Rituals of British Indie Music.* Middletown: Wesleyan University Press.
— Frith, S. (1981) 'The Magic That Can Set You Free: The Ideology of Folk and the Myth of the Rock Community'. In: *Popular Music, Vol. 1.* Cambridge: Cambridge University Press: 159-168.
— Frith, S. (1984) *Rock! Sociologie van een nieuwe muziekcultuur* (translation by B. van de Kamp). Amsterdam & Brussel: Elsevier (translation of *Sound Effects.* Londen: Constable, 1978).
— Frith, S. (1987) 'Towards an Aesthetic of Popular Music'. In: Leppert, R. & McClary, S., *Music and Society: The Politics of Composition, Performance and Reception.* Cambridge: Cambridge University Press: 133-50.
— Frith, S. (1988a) *Music for Pleasure,* Cambridge: Polity Press.
— Frith, S. (1988b) 'Video pop - Picking Up the Pieces'. In: Frith, S. (ed.), *Facing the Music: Pantheon Guide to Popular Culture.* New York: Pantheon: 88-130.
— Frith, S. (1996) *Performing Rites: On the Value of Popular Music.* Oxford: Oxford Univerity Press.
— Frith, S. (2001) 'Pop Music'. In: Frith, S., Straw, W. & Street, J. (eds.), *The Cambridge Companion to Pop and Rock.* Cambridge: Cambridge University Press: 26-47.
— Frith, S. & Horne, H. (1987) *Art into Pop.* London/ New York: Methuen.
— Gielen, P. (2003) *Kunst in netwerken. Artistieke selecties in de hedendaagse dans en de beeldende kunst.* Tielt: Lannoo.
— Gillet, C. (1983) *The Sound of the City.* London: Souvenir Press.
— Greenberg, C. (1986) *The Collected Essays and Criticism, vol 1: Perceptions and Judgments 1939-1944.* Chicago & London: The University of Chicago Press.
— Grossberg, L. (1992) *We Gotta Get Out of This Place: Popular Conservatism and Postmodern Culture.* New York: Routledge.
— Grossberg, L. (1997) 'Re-placing Popular Culture'. In: Redhead, S. (ed.), *The Clubcultures Reader: Readings in Popular Cultural Studies.* Oxford: Blackwell: 217-237.
— Hardt, M. en Negri, A. (2002) *Empire: De Nieuwe Wereldorde* (translated by J. Traats). Amsterdam: Van Gennep (translation of *Empire.* Cambridge & London: Harvard University Press, 2000).
— Hardt, M. & Negri, A. (2004) *De Menigte: Oorlog en democratie in de nieuwe wereldorde* (vertaald door G. Houtzager). Amsterdam: De Bezige Bij (translation of *Multitude: War and Democracy in the Age of Empire.* New York, Penguin Books, 2004).
— Harrington, A. (2004) *Art and Social Theory.* Cambridge: Polity Press.
— Harvey, D. (1990) *The Condition of Postmodernity.* Oxford: Basil Blackwell.
— Heesterbeek, T. (2002) *De spanning tussen underground en mainstream in de popmuziek* [university thesis]. Maastricht: Universiteit van Maastricht/ Faculteit der Cultuurwetenschappen.
— Heinich, N. (2003) *Het Van Gogh-effect en andere essays over kunst en sociologie.* Amsterdam: Boekmanstichting.
— Hennion, A. (1997) 'Baroque and Rock: Music, Mediators and Musical Taste'. In: *Poetics,* 24(6): 415-435.
— Hennion, A. (2001) 'Music Lovers: Taste as Performance'. In: *Theory, Culture & Society,* 18(5): 1-22.
— Hennion, A. (2002) 'Music and Mediation: Towards a New

Sociology of Music'. In: Clayton, M., Herbert, T. & Middleton, R. (eds.), *The Cultural Study of Music: A Critical Introduction*. London: Routledge.

— Hesmondhalgh, D. (1996) 'Flexibility, Post-Fordism and the Music Industry'. In: *Media, Culture and Society*, 18 (3): 496-88.

— Hesmondhalgh, D. (1999) 'Indie: the Institutional Politics and Aesthetics of a Popular Music Genre'. In *Cultural Studies*, 13 (1): 34-61.

— Hesmondhalgh, D. (2006) 'Bourdieu, the Media and Cultural Production'. In: *Media, Culture & Society*, 28(2): 211-231.

— Hibbett, R. (2005) 'What is Indie Rock?'. In: *Popular Music and Society*, 28 (1): 55-77.

— Hirsch, P. (1972) 'Processing Fads and Fashions: An Organization-Set Analysis of Cultural Industry Systems'. In: *American Journal of Sociology*, 77 (3): 639-659.

— Hirsch, P. (2000) 'Cultural Industries Revisited'. In: *Organization Science*, 11 (3): 356-361.

— Jameson, F. (1984) 'Postmodernism: Or The Cultural Logic of Late Capitalism'. In: *New Left Review*, 146 (jul/aug): 53-92.

— Jaspers, S. (ed) (2006) *Ultratop: 20.000 hits! 1995-2005*. Deurne: Book & Media Publishing.

— Jones, C. W. (2008) *The Rock Canon: Canonical Values in the Reception of Rock Albums*. Hampshire: Ashgate Publishing Limited.

— Jong, M.-J. de (1997) *Grootmeesters van de sociologie*. Amsterdam: Boom.

— Kärjä, A. (2006) 'A Prescribed Alternative Mainstream: Popular Music and Canon Formation'. In: *Popular Music*, 25/1: 3-19.

— Keunen, G. (1996) *Surfing on Pop Waves*. Brussel: Kritak/Meulenhoff.

— Keunen, G. (2002) *Pop! Een halve eeuw beweging*. Tielt: Lannoo.

— Keunen, G. (2009) *Business as Usual: De muziekindustrie in de analoge en digitale wereld* [students' course]. Tilburg: Fontys Hogeschool voor de Kunsten, and Hasselt: PHL Music.

— Keunen, B. & Keunen, G. (1996) 'Stadsnomaden in Downtown New York'. In: Boomkens, R. & Gabriëls, R. (eds.), *Een alledaagse passie*. Amsterdam: De Balie.

— Kreuzer, H. (1968) *Die Boheme. Beiträge zu ihrer Beschreibung*. Stuttgart: Metzerlersche Verlagsbuchhandlung.

— Kruse, H. (1993) 'Subcultural Identity in Alternative Music Culture'. In: *Popular Music*, 12(1): 33-41.

— Laermans, R. (1984) 'Bourdieu voor Beginners'. In: *Heibel*, 18(3): 21-48.

— Laermans, R. (1998) 'Moderne kunst en moderne maatschappij: Luhmanns kunsttheoretische observaties geobserveerd'. In: *De Witte Raaf*, 12(74): 20-24.

— Laermans, R. (2004) 'De draaglijke lichtheid van het kunstenaarsbestaan: Over de onzekerheden van artistieke carrieres'. In: *De Witte Raaf*, 112: 14-15.

— Laermans, R. (2008) 'Deconstructing Individual Authorship: Artworks as Collective Products of Art Worlds'. In: Demarsin, B., Schrage, E., Tilleman, B. & Verbeke, A. (eds.), *Art & Law*. Brugge & Oxford: die Keure/Hart Publishing: 50-61.

— Laermans, R. (2009) 'Artistic Autonomy as Value and Practice'. In: Gielen, P. & De Bruyne, P. (eds.), *Being an Artist in Post-Fordist Times*. Rotterdam: NAi Publishers.

— Laermans, R. (2010) *Sociologie*. Leuven: Acco.

— Laermans, R. (2011a) 'Het Aandachtsregime: Lees mij! Bekijk mij! Hoor mij!'. In: *609 Cultuur en Media*, 8(sept.): 12-14.

— Laermans, R. (2011b) 'The Attention Regime: On Mass Media and the Information Society'. In: Schinkel, W. & Noordegraaf-Eelens, L. (eds.), *In Medias Res: Peter Sloterdijk's Spherological Poetics of Being*. Amsterdam: Amsterdam Univerity Press: 115-132.

— Lahire, B. (2003) 'From the Habitus to an Individual Heritage of Dispositions: Towards a Sociology at the Level of the Individual'. In: *Poetics*, 31(sept.): 329-355.

— Latour, B. (1987) *Science in Action*. Cambridge & Massachusetts: Harvard University Press.

— Latour, B. (2005) *Reassembling the Social: An Introduction to Actor-Network-Theory*. Oxford: Clarendon Press.

— Law, J. (1992) *Notes on the Theory of the Actor Network: Ordering, Strategy and Heterogeneity*. Lancaster: Lancaster University/ Centre for Science Studies. www.comp.lancs.ac.uk/sociology/papers/Law-Notes-on-ANT.pdf

— Lee, S. (1995) 'Re-Examining the Concept of the 'Independent' Record Company: The Case of Wax Trax! Records'. In: *Popular Music*, 14(1): 13-31.

— Luhmann, N. (2000) *Art As a Social System (translated by E. M. Knodt)*. Stanford: Stanford University Press (translation of *Die Kunst der Gesellschaft*, Frankfurt am Main: Suhrkamp Verlag, 1995).

— Martin, P. (2003) 'Sociology'. In: Shepherd J. (ed), *'Continuum Encyclopedia of Popular Music of the World*, Volume 1*. London: Continuum: 126-139.

— Maso, I. & Smaling, A. (2004) *Kwalitatief onderzoek: Praktijk en theorie*. Amsterdam: Boom.

— Mauss, M. (1990) *The Gift* (translated by W.D. Halls). London: Routledge (translation of *Essai sur le Don*, 1950/1923).

— McLeese, D. (2010) 'Straddling the Cultural Chasm: The Great Divide Between Music Criticism and Popular Consumption'. In: *Popular Music and Society*, 33(4): 433-447.

— Meyer, H.-D. (2000) 'Taste Formation in Pluralistic Societies: The Role of Rhetorics and Institutions'. In: *International Sociology*, 15(1): 33-56.

— Negus, K. (1996) *Popular Music in Theory*. Cambridge: Policy Press.

— Negus, K. (2002) 'The Work of Cultural Intermediaries and the Enduring Distance Between Production and Consumption'. In: *Cultural Studies*, 16(4): 501-515.

— Nixon, S. & du Gay, P. (2002) 'Who Needs Cultural Intermediaries?'. In: *Cultural Studies*, 16(4): 495-500.

— Ollivier, M. (2006) 'Snobs and Quétaines: Prestige and Boundaries in Popular Music in Quebec'. In: *Popular Music*, 25(1): 97-116.

— OOR (ed.) (1982) *Oor's Eerste Nederlandse Popencyclopedie* - 1st edition. Amsterdam: Annoventura.

— OOR (ed.) (1984) *Oor's Eerste Nederlandse Popencyclopedie* - 2nd edition. Amsterdam: Annoventura.

— OOR (ed.) (1986) *Oor's Eerste Nederlandse Popencyclopedie* - 3rd edition. Amsterdam: Annoventura.

— Peterson, R. & Berger, D. (1975) 'Cycles In Symbol Production: The Case of Popular Music'. *In: American Sociological Review*, 40(April): 158-173.

— Peterson, R. & Kern, R. (1996) 'Changing Highbrow Taste: From Snob to Omnivore'. In: *American Sociological Review*, 61(5): 900-907.

— Peterson, R. A. (1997) *Creating Country Music: Fabricating Authenticity*. Chicago: The University Of Chicago Press.

— Peterson, R. A. & Anand, N. (2004) 'The Production of Culture Perspective'. In: *Annual Review Sociology*, 30: 311-334.

— Regev, M. (1994) 'Producing Artistic Value: the Case of Rock Music'. In: *Sociological Quarterly*, 35(1): 85-102.

— Regev, M. (1997) 'Rock Aesthetics and Musics of the World'. In: *Theory, Culture and Society*, 14 (3): 125-142.

— Regev, M. (2002) 'The "Pop-Rockization" of Popular Music'. In: Hesmondhalgh, D. & Negus K. (eds.), *Popular Music Studies*. London: Arnold: 251-264.

— Schaevers, M. (1981) 'Amateurfotografie: Tussen Kunst en Kiekjes'. In: *Heibel*, 15(4): 2-22.

— Shuker, R. (2008) *Understanding Popular Music Culture* – 3rd edition. Londen & New York: Routledge.

— Silber, I.F. (2003) 'Pragmatic Sociology as Cultural Sociology: Beyond Repertoire Theory?'. In: *European Journal of Social Theory*, 6(4): 427-449.

— Skinner, K. (2006) '"Must Be Born Again": Resurrecting the Anthology of American Folk Music'. In: *Popular Music*, 25(1): 57-75.

— Stratton, J. (1982) 'Between Two Worlds: Art and Commercialism in the Record Industry'. In: *Sociological Review*, 30(2): 267-285.

— Stratton, J. (1983a) 'What is Popular Music?'. In: *Sociological Review*, 31(2): 293-309.

— Stratton, J. (1983b) 'Capitalism and Romantic Ideology in the Record Business'. In: Middleton, R. & Horn, D. (eds.), *Popular Music Volume 3*. Cambridge: Cambridge

University Press: 143-156.
— Straw, W. (1991) 'Systems of Articulation, Logics of Change: Communities and Scenes in Popular Music'. In: *Cultural Studies*, 5(3): 368-88.
— Street, J. (1986) *Rebel Rock: The Politics of Popular Music*. Oxford: Basil Blackwell.
— Swanborn, P. G. (1996) *Case-study's: Wat, wanneer en hoe?* Amsterdam: Boom Onderwijs.
— Thornton, S. (1990) 'Strategies for Reconstructing the Popular Past'. In: *Popular Music*, 9(1): 87-95.
— Thornton, S. (1995) *Club Cultures: Music, Media and Subcultural Capital*. Cambridge: Polity Press.
— Toynbee, J. (2000) *Making Popular Music: Musicians, Creativity and Institutions*. Londen: Arnold.
— Valckenaers, H. (2009) *Een beleidsaanbeveling voor het subsidiëren van alternatieve managementbureaus: de noodzakelijkheid en wenselijkheid binnen het Vlaamse pop-rockcircuit* [PhD]. Brussel: Vrije Universiteit Brussel/ Agogische Wetenschappen.
— Van den Braembussche, A.A. (2007) *Denken over kunst: Een inleiding in de kunstfilosofie*. Bussum: Coutinho.
— Vanherwegen, D. (2008) *Alleen Elvis blijft bestaan?: Een beschrijvend onderzoek naar carrières van Vlaamse professionele popmuzikanten* [PhD]. Leuven: KUL/ Faculteit Sociale Wetenschappen/ Departement Sociologie.
— Van Venrooij, A. (2009) 'The Aesthetic Discourse Space of Popular Music: 1985-86 And 2004-05'. In: *Poetics*, 37: 315-332.
— Verduyn, L. (2003) *Showbizz in Vlaanderen: De 100 rijkste artiesten*. Leuven: Van Halewyck.
— Virno, P. (2004) *A Grammar of the Multitude*. Los Angeles: Semiotext(e).
— Von Appen, R. & Doehring, A. (2006) 'Nevermind The Beatles, Here's Exile 61 and Nico: "The Top 100 Records of all Time": A Canon of Pop and Rock Album from a Sociological and an Aesthetic Perspective'. In: *Popular Music*, 25(1): 21-39.
— Watson, M. R. & Anand, N. (2006) 'Award Ceremony as an Arbiter of Commerce and Canon in the Popular Music Industry'. In: *Popular Music*, 25(1): 41-56.
— White, H. & White, C. (1965) *Canvases and Careers: Institutional Change in the French Painting World*. Chicago: The University of Chicago Press.
— Wicke, P. (1987) *Rock Music: Culture, Aesthetics and Sociology*. Cambridge: Cambridge University Press.
— Williamson, J. & Cloonan, M. (2007 'Rethinking the Music Industry'. In: *Popular Music*, 26(2): 305-322.
— Wolff, J. (1987) 'The Ideology of Autonomous Art'. In: Leppert, R. & McClary, S., *Music and Society: The Politics of Composition, Performance and Reception*. Cambridge: Cambridge University Press: 1-12.
— Zwaan, K. (2009) *Working on a Dream: Careers of Pop Musicians in the Netherlands* [PhD]. Utrecht: Universiteit Utrecht.

Media: TV/ newspapers/ weeklies

— BBC (1996) *Dancing in the Street* [TV-broadcast]. BBC, Bristol, Part 2 (director unknown).
— Chipps, W. (21.08.2004) 'Hitching Brands to the Stars'. In: *Billboard*, 116 (34): 40.
— Christman, E. (04.03.2006) 'Grabbing Sales by the Long Tail'. In: *Billboard*, 118 (9): 22-23.
— Christman, E. (11.11.2006) 'Too Much is Never Enough'. In: *Billboard*, 118 (45): 35-37.
— De Standaard (16.12.2010) 'Studio Brussel schrapt "Hit 50"'. In: *De Standaard*: D3 (author unknown)
— Hirschberg, E. (30.09.2006) 'Music in Advertising: Once Selling Out, Now Buying In'. In: *Billboard*, 118 (39): 4.
— Hoefkens, K. (11.09.2012) 'Van achterbuurt naar raad van bestuur'. In: *De Standaard*: D4-D5.
— JIM (08.2008) *Regi's World* [TV-broadcast]. JIM, nov. 2008 (director unknown)
— Keunen, G. (23.09.1998) 'Mixmaster Morris op de barricaden'. In: *De Standaard* (no page).
— Mitchell, G., Crosley, H., Paoletta, M. (20.05.2006) 'Product Tie-ins Seem Endless for Snoop Dogg and Diddy'. In: *Billboard*, 118 (20): 26.
— Paoletta, M. (17.09.2005) 'The Music Upfront. Consumer Brands,

Music Biz Building Bridges with More Long-term Relationships'. In: *Billboard*, 117 (38): 32-33.

— Paoletta, M. (18.02.2006) 'The Name Game'. In: *Billboard*, 118 (7): 26-27.

— Paoletta, M. (14.01.2006) 'Brands Find a Perfect Fit with Destiny's Child'. In: *Billboard*, 118 (2): 40-41.

— Paoletta, M. (30.09.2006) 'Expanding Your Brand'. In: *Billboard*, 118 (39): 36-37.

— Petitjean, F. (28.03.2009) 'De NV Kristel, Karen en Kathleen'. In: *De Standaard*: E8-E9.

— Post, H.-M. (14.01.2010) 'Mia's gooien Ultratop door elkaar'. In: *De Standaard*: 37.

— Sioen, L. (11.01.2009) 'Helmut Lotti op een keerpunt'. In: *De Standaard*: 24-25.

— Sioen, L. (24.01.2009) 'Sterartiest, sterrenmaker'. In: *De Standaard Magazine*: 17-18.

— Steenhaut, B. (02.04.2011) 'Britney Spears - Femme Fatale' [Cd-recensie]. In: *De Morgen* (no page).

— Vantyghem, P. (25.04.2009) 'Pop is de nieuwe alternatieve muziek'. In: *De Standaard*: C13

— Vantyghem, P. (29.01.2011) 'De muziekindustrie wankelt, maar geeft zich niet over'. In: *De Standaard*: C10-C11.

— Vantyghem, P. (21.09.2012) 'Belgen downloaden liever illegaal'. In: *De Standaard*: D2-D3.

— Waddell, R., Peters, M., Herrera, M., Donahue, A., Ben-Yehuda, A., Nagy, E. (06.03.2010) '2010 Moneymakers'. In *Billboard*, 122 (9): 19-22.

— Wille, O. (regie), Vandenbussche, W. (research & interviews) & Slenders, J. (montage) (25.10.2010) *Belpop: Clouseau* [Tv-uitzending]. Canvas.

— Wolk, D. (04/05/2005) 'Thinking About Rockism'. In: *Seattle Weekly* (no page). www.seattleweekly. com/2005-05-04/music/ thinking-about-rockism

Reports & online data

— BEA (24.02.2011) *Marktcijfers van videogames, muziek en video in 2010.* [17.02.2012, Belgian Entertainment Association: www.belgianentertainment.be/ index.php/nl/bea_nieuws_detail/

marktcijfers_van_videogames_ muziek_en_video_in_2010/]

— BEA (09.02.2012) Belgen kochten vorig jaar bijna 20 miljoen muziekdragers. [17.02.2012, Belgian Entertainment Association: www.belgianentertainment.be/ index.php/nl/bea_nieuws_detail/ belgen_kochten_vorig_jaar_ bijna_20_miljoen_muziekdragers/]

— IFPI (2011) *Digital Music Report 2011.* [17.02.2012, IFPI: www.ifpi. org/content/library/dmr2011.pdf].

— IFPI (2012) *Digital Music Report 2012.* [17.02.2012, IFPI: www.ifpi. org/content/library/DMR2012. pdf].

— Kerremans, G., Hautekiet, J., Lardon, S. & Devroe, I. (2009) *VRT-muziekbeleid: Iedereen verdient muziek.* Brussel: VRT.

— Legrand, E. (26.01.2012) *Music Crossing Borders - Monitoring the Cross-Border Circulation of European Music Repertoire Within the European Union.* Report commissioned by European Music Office & Eurosonic Noordeslag. [17.02.2012, EMO: www.emo.org/onair_news.php].

— Maeterlinck, O. (olivier. maeterlinck@belgianentertainment. be) (13.02.2012) Marktcijfers. [E-mail aan G. Keunen (gert@ briskey.be)].

— Nielsen (2012) Nielsen Music 360 Report. [25.11.2012, The Nielsen Company: www.nielsen.com/us/en/ insights/press-room/2012/music-discovery-still-dominated-by-radio--says-nielsen-music-360.html].

— NVPI (2010) *Marktinfo Audio Nederland 2010.* [17.02.2012, NVPI: www.nvpi.nl/sites/default/files/ nvpi-marktinformatie-audio-2010. pdf].

— NVPI (23.01.2012) Wereldwijde digitale muziekmarkt in de lift. [17.02.2012, NVPI: www.nvpi.nl/nieuws/wereldwijde-digitale-muziekmarkt-de-lift].

— Vlaamse Regering (2011) Beheersovereenkomst 2012-2016 tussen de Vlaamse Gemeenschap en de VRT.

About the Author

Alternative Mainstream

400

Gert Keunen (1969) is a teacher, publicist and musician. He holds a PhD in Cultural Sociology and is an associate lector in Music at Fontys Academy for the Performing Arts in Tilburg, where he is responsible for research. He also teaches music history and music industry at said Fontys Academy/Rock Academy, at PHL Music in Hasselt, at the Erasmus Academy/Rits in Brussels and at the School of Arts/Music Academy in Ghent. Before, he has worked as a label manager at record company Zomba/Rough Trade, as a music programmer at the Vooruit Arts Centre in Ghent and as a freelance music journalist for *De Standaard* and *De Morgen* daily newspapers and *Gonzo Circus* magazine. He is the author of *Surfing on Pop Waves: Een kwart eeuw popmuziek* (Kritak, 1996) and of *Pop! Een Halve Eeuw Beweging* (Lannoo, 2002).

As a sample artist and composer, working under the pseudonym Briskey, he has released the CDs *Cucumber Lodge* (2003), *Scarlett Roadhouse* (2006), Briskey Big Band Live At *Ancienne Belgique* (2008) and *Before-during-after* (2009). With the Briskey Live Band and the Briskey Big Band he has since performed at various stages and festivals in both Belgium and abroad. www.briskey.be

Index

Colophon

Colophon

Alternative Mainstream
Making Choices in Pop Music

Author
Gert Keunen

Antennae Series n° 12
by Valiz, Amsterdam

Part of the Fontys Series
'Arts *in* Society'

Translation Dutch-English
Jo Smets — Writemen Unlimited

Copy editing
Wendy van Os-Thompson

Index and proof check
Elke Stevens

Production
Pia Pol

Design
Metahaven

Paper inside
Munken Print 100 gr 1.5,

Paper cover
Bioset 240 gr

Printing and binding
Ten Brink, Meppel

Publisher
Valiz, Amsterdam, 2014
www.valiz.nl

ISBN 978-90-78088-95-0

This publication was made possible
through the generous support of

Fontys School of Fine and Performing
Arts, Tilburg

Fontys Hogeschool voor de Kunsten

The authors and the publisher have made every effort to secure permission to reproduce the listed material, illustrations and photographs. We apologise for any inadvert errors or omissions. Parties who nevertheless believe they can claim specific legal rights are invited to contact the publisher.

Distribution:
USA /CAN/LA: D.A.P., www.artbook.com
GB/IE: Anagram Books, www.anagrambooks.com
NL/BE/LU: Coen Sligting, www.coensligtingbookimport.nl
Europe/Asia/Australia: Idea Books, www.ideabooks.nl
ISBN 978-90-78088-95-0
NUR 651

Printed and bound in the Netherlands

Antennae

Antennae Series

Antennae N° 1
The Fall of the Studio
Artists at Work
edited by Wouter Davidts
& Kim Paice
Amsterdam: Valiz, 2009
(2nd ed.: 2010),
ISBN 978-90-78088-29-5

Antennae N° 2
Take Place
*Photography and Place
from Multiple Perspectives*
edited by Helen Westgeest
Amsterdam: Valiz, 2009,
ISBN 978-90-78088-35-6

Antennae N° 3
**The Murmuring of the
Artistic Multitude**
*Global Art, Memory and
Post-Fordism*
Pascal Gielen (author)
Arts *in* Society
Amsterdam: Valiz, 2009
(2nd ed.: 2011),
ISBN 978-90-78088-34-9

Antennae N° 4
Locating the Producers
Durational Approaches to Public Art
edited by Paul O'Neill
& Claire Doherty
Amsterdam: Valiz, 2011,
ISBN 978-90-78088-51-6

Antennae N° 5
Community Art
The Politics of Trespassing
edited by Paul De Bruyne,
Pascal Gielen
Arts *in* Society
Amsterdam:
Valiz, 2011 (2nd ed.: 2013),
ISBN 978-90-78088-50-9

Antennae N° 6
See it Again, Say it Again
The Artist as Researcher
edited by Janneke Wesseling
Amsterdam: Valiz, 2011,
ISBN 978-90-78088-53-0

Antennae N° 7
Teaching Art in the Neoliberal Realm
Realism versus Cynicism
edited by Pascal Gielen,
Paul De Bruyne
Arts *in* Society
Amsterdam: Valiz, 2012
(2nd ed.: 2013),
ISBN 978-90-78088-57-8

Antennae N° 8
Institutional Attitudes
Instituting Art in a Flat World
edited by Pascal Gielen
Arts *in* Society
Amsterdam: Valiz, 2013,
ISBN 978-90-78088-68-4

Antennae N° 9
Dread
The Dizziness of Freedom
edited by Juha van 't Zelfde
Amsterdam: Valiz, 2013,
ISBN 978-90-78088-81-3

Antennae N° 10
Participation Is Risky
*Approaches to Joint
Creative Processes*
edited by Liesbeth Huybrechts
Amsterdam: Valiz, 2014,
ISBN 978-90-78088-77-6

Antennae N° 11
The Ethics of Art
*Ecological Turns in the
Performing Arts*
edited by Guy Cools & Pascal Gielen
Amsterdam: Valiz, 2014,
ISBN 978-90-78088-87-5

Alternative Mainstream